LIBRARY OF NEW TESTAMENT STUDIES

*formerly the Journal for the Study of the New Testament
Supplement Series*

301

Editor
Mark Goodacre

Editorial Board
John M.G. Barclay, Craig Blomberg, Kathleen E. Corley,
R. Alan Culpepper, James D.G. Dunn, Craig A. Evans,
Stephen Fowl, Robert Fowler, Simon J. Gathercole,
John S. Kloppenborg, Michael Labahn, Robert Wall,
Robert L. Webb, Catrin H. Williams

To Valerie of course.
Many women have done well, but you surpass them all (Proverbs 31.29)!

PAUL'S USE OF THE OLD TESTAMENT IN ROMANS 9.1–9

An Intertextual and Theological Exegesis

BRIAN J. ABASCIANO

t & t clark

Copyright © Brian J. Abasciano, 2005
A Continuum imprint

Published by T&T Clark International
The Tower Building, 11 York Road, London SE1 7NX
15 East 26th Street, Suite 1703, New York, NY 10010

www.tandtclark.com

British Library Cataloguing-in-Publication Data
A catalogue record for this book is available from the British Library

ISBN 0567030733   (hardback)

Typeset by Servis Filmsetting Ltd, Manchester
Printed on acid-free paper in Great Britain by
MPG Books Ltd, Bodmin, Cornwall

CONTENTS

Acknowledgments   vii
Abbreviations   ix

Chapter 1
INTRODUCTION   1

Chapter 2
INTRODUCTION TO ROMANS 9–11   27

Chapter 3
PAUL'S USE OF THE OLD TESTAMENT IN ROMANS 9.1–5   45

Chapter 4
PAUL'S USE OF THE OLD TESTAMENT IN ROMANS 9.6–9   147

Chapter 5
THE SIGNFICANCE OF PAUL'S USE OF THE OLD TESTAMENT IN
ROMANS 9.1–9 FOR THE EXEGESIS AND THEOLOGY OF ROMANS
AND PAULINE INTERTEXTUALITY   216

Bibliography   236
Index of References   249
Index of Modern Authors   262

ACKNOWLEDGMENTS

This investigation is a revision of my Ph.D. thesis accepted by the University of Aberdeen, Scotland in 2003. I wish to thank the many people who have, in one way or another, helped me to complete this research and monograph. Professor I. Howard Marshall originally offered me a place to study at Aberdeen and has served as an inspiration to me in his scholarship and humility. Dr. Brian Rosner served as my first supervisor, overseeing the initial phases of this project when I set the abiding vision for the entire thesis. Dr. Paul Ellingworth supervised most of my doctoral research. I am very grateful for his excellent supervision and guidance, as well as his interest in my family and me beyond the academic realm. I also wish to thank Dr. Peter J. Williams for his additional supervision in the final phase of my doctoral work, and my examiners, Dr. Andrew Clarke and Dr. Stephen Chester, who recommended my thesis be accepted and provided helpful advice. Becca Vaughan-Williams of T&T Clark has been wonderful to work with. I am also very thankful for various fellow students who were in the NT department at Aberdeen and helped me with advice and friendship during my stay, especially John Heglie and Steve Chang (and Lisa and family). But above all, Ray VanNeste (and Tammie and family) helped us in so many ways.

God blessed us immensely through Gilcomston South Church, where we worshiped during our time in Aberdeen and whose church life has been a great inspiration. We are tremendously thankful for all their hospitality and prayer on our behalf. We are especially thankful for Grant Gebbie, who was our landlord in Aberdeen, introduced us to the church, and helped us in so many ways during our stay.

The seeds of this project were sown in Dr. Greg K. Beale's class on the OT in the New at Gordon-Conwell Theological seminary, where my passion for the use of the OT in the NT as well as its significance for Romans 9 were birthed. I am thankful for my education at Gordon-Conwell, especially the teaching and examples of Dr. Beale, Dr. Scott J. Hafemann, Dr. Douglas Stuart, and Dr. Gordon P. Hugenberger. I have also been grateful for the privilege of using the Goddard Library at Gordon-Conwell (where Jim Darlack has been helpful) and Andover-Harvard Theological Library at Harvard University (where Laura Whitney has been helpful) as I have conducted research in the U.S.A.

I remain very thankful to J. Ross Wagner, Jr. for graciously sending me a hard copy of his doctoral thesis at his own expense. I am also thankful to Douglas C. Mohrmann for sending me his doctoral dissertation in an e-mail attachment.

I have been extremely blessed to pastor full time at Faith Community Church in Hampton, NH while I worked on my thesis part time, and now while I have prepared this book. It has been an ideal situation to enable me to pursue scholarship, provide for my family, and serve my Lord. The church is our family, caring for us and praying for us throughout the years. We are so thankful for all that they have done.

My mom has prayed for my studies regularly and given financial gifts to our family along the way, and my brothers and sisters have remained interested in me and my education. But more than anyone else on earth, I am thankful for my wife, Valerie, the best woman in the world! She means more to me than I can say, and has been my constant friend, help, and support throughout our life together and my doctoral studies. I dedicate this book to her. I am also tremendously thankful for my children, Noah, Jacynth, and Benaiah. Our family is wonderful and an enormous blessing that words cannot do justice.

Above all, I am thankful to God, who has given me all these things and made all of this possible. More importantly, he has given me every spiritual blessing in Christ. And I am eternally grateful. 'To him be the glory forever! Amen' (Rom. 11.36).

ABBREVIATIONS

AB	Anchor Bible
AGJU	Arbeiten zur Geschichte des antiken Judentums und des Urchristentums
AnBib	Analecta biblica
ANET	J.B. Pritchard (ed.), *Ancient Near Eastern Texts Relating to the Old Testament* (Princeton: Princeton University Press, 3rd edn., 1978)
ANRW	Hildegard Temporini and Wolfgang Haase (eds.), *Aufstieg und Niedergang der römischen Welt: Geschichte und Kultur Roms im Spiegel der neueren Forschung* (Berlin: W. de Gruyter, 1972–)
BBR	*Bulletin for Biblical Research*
BDAG	W. Bauer, F.W. Danker, W.F. Arndt, and F.W. Gingrich, *A Greek-English Lexicon of the New Testament and Other Early Christian Literature* (Chicago: University of Chicago Press, 3rd edn., 2000)
BDF	F. Blass, A. Debrunner and R.W. Funk, *A Greek Grammar of the New Testament and Other Early Christian Literature* (Cambridge: Cambridge University Press, 1961)
BECNT	Baker Exegetical Commentary on the New Testament
BEvT	Beiträge zur evangelischen Theologie
BHT	Beiträge zur historischen Theologie
Bib	*Biblica*
BibInt	*Biblical Interpretation: A Journal of Contemporary Approaches*
BJS	Brown Judaic Studies
BTB	*Biblical Theology Bulletin*
CBAA	Catholic Biblical Association of America
CBQ	*Catholic Biblical Quarterly*
CBQMS	*Catholic Biblical Quarterly*, Monograph Series
ConNT	*Coniectanea neotestamentica*
CRINT	Compendia rerum iudaicarum ad Novum Testamentum
DNTB	C.A. Evans and S.E. Porter (eds.), *Dictionary of New*

	Testament Background (Downers Grove: InterVarsity Press, 2000)
DPL	G. Hawthorne, R.P. Martin, and D.G. Reid (eds.), *Dictionary of Paul and His Letters* (Downers Grove: InterVarsity Press, 1993)
EDNT	H. Balz and G. Schneider (eds.), *Exegetical Dictionary of the New Testament* (3 vols.; Grand Rapids: Eerdmans, 1990–93)
EKKNT	Evangelisch-Katholischer Kommentar zum Neuen Testament
EvQ	*Evangelical Quarterly*
ETL	*Ephemerides theologicae lovanienses*
ExpTim	*Expository Times*
FOTL	The Forms of the Old Testament Literature
FRLANT	Forschungen zur Religion und Literatur des Alten und Neuen Testaments
FzB	Forschung zur Bibel
HALOT	L. Koehler and W. Baumgartner *et al.*, *The Hebrew and Aramaic Lexicon of the Old Testament Study Edition* (ed. and trans. M.E.J. Richardson; 2 vols.; Leiden: Brill, 2001)
HNTC	Harper's NT Commentaries
HR	E. Hatch and H.A. Redpath, *A Concordance to the Septuagint and the Other Greek Versions of the Old Testament (Including the Apocryphal Books)* (3 vols. in 2; repr., Grand Rapids: Baker Book House, 1987)
HTKNT	Herders theologischer Kommentar zum Neuen Testament
HTR	*Harvard Theological Review*
HUCA	*Hebrew Union College Annual*
IBC	Interpretation: A Bible Commentary for Teaching and Preaching
IBS	*Irish Biblical Studies*
ICC	International Critical Commentary
ISFCJ	International Studies in Formative Christianity and Judaism
JBL	*Journal of Biblical Literature*
JJS	*Journal of Jewish Studies*
JSJSup	*Journal for the Study of Judaism in the Persian, Hellenistic and Roman Period*, Supplement Series
JSNT	*Journal for the Study of the New Testament*
JSNTSup	*Journal for the Study of the New Testament*, Supplement Series
JSOT	*Journal for the Study of the Old Testament*
JSOTSup	*Journal for the Study of the Old Testament*, Supplement Series
JSPSup	*Journal for the Study of the Pseudepigrapha*, Supplement Series
LCL	Loeb Classical Library
LD	Lectio divina

MTZ	*Münchener theologische Zeitschrift*
NCB	New Century Bible
Neot	*Neotestamentica*
NICNT	New International Commentary on the New Testament
NIDNTT	Colin Brown (ed.), *The New International Dictionary of New Testament Theology* (3 vols.; Exeter: Paternoster Press, 1975)
NIGTC	The New International Greek Testament Commentary
NIVAC	The New International Version Application Commentary
NovT	*Novum Testamentum*
NovTSup	*Novum Testamentum*, Supplements
NT	New Testament
NTS	*New Testament Studies*
OT	Old Testament
OTL	Old Testament Library
RevExp	*Review and Expositor*
SBL	Society of Biblical Literature
SBLDS	SBL Dissertation Series
SBLSCS	SBL Septuagint and Cognate Studies
SIHC	Studies in the Intercultural History of Christianity
SJLA	Studies in Judaism in Late Antiquity
SNTSMS	Society for New Testament Studies Monograph Series
SNTW	Studies of the New Testament and Its World
SOTBT	Studies in Old Testament Biblical Theology
SSEJC	Studies in Scripture in Early Judaism and Christianity
ST	*Studia theologica*
SVTP	Studia in Veteris Testamenti pseudepigrapha
TAB	The Aramaic Bible
TDNT	Gerhard Kittel and Gerhard Friedrich (eds.), *Theological Dictionary of the New Testament* (trans. Geoffrey W. Bromiley; 10 vols.; Grand Rapids: Eerdmans, 1964–)
THKNT	Theologischer Handkommentar zum Neuen Testament
TNTC	Tyndale New Testament Commentaries
TOTC	Tyndale Old Testament Commentaries
TPINTC	TPI New Testament Commentaries
TSAJ	*Texte und Studien zum antiken Judentum*
TZ	*Theologische Zeitschrift*
UBSGNT	United Bible Societies' *Greek New Testament*
VTSup	*Vetus Testamentum*, Supplements
WBC	Word Biblical Commentary
WD	*Wort und Dienst*
WUNT	Wissenschaftliche Untersuchungen zum Neuen Testament
ZTK	*Zeitschrift für Theologie und Kirche*

Chapter 1

Introduction

1.1. *Orientation to the Investigation*

Romans 9 is in need of a fresh exegetical analysis sensitive to recent developments in the study of Paul's use of Scripture. These developments derive, in part, from literary criticism and center around the concepts of intertextuality, citation, allusion, and echo. Richard Hays' *Echoes of Scripture in the Letters of Paul* has been particularly influential in stimulating attention to the 'meaning-effects' that result from Paul's scriptural citations, allusions, and echoes.[1] His basic method involves investigating the broader literary and theological contexts of Paul's scriptural citations and allusions in order to determine their significance for the meaning of Paul's discourse. This focus on 'the metaphorical significations produced when a literary text echoes voices from earlier texts'[2] has opened up new opportunities for approaching Paul's writings.

Hays has drawn attention to the dearth of critical reflection on the actual meaning of Old Testament citations and allusions in Paul. He points out that the great majority of critical studies of Paul's use of the Old Testament have concentrated

> on essential technical tasks of scholarship. The Pauline quotations and allusions have been cataloged, their introductory formulas classified,

---

1. Hays' influence may be seen in C.A. Evans and J.A. Sanders (eds.), *Paul and the Scriptures of Israel* (JSNTSup, 83; SSEJC, 1; Sheffield: *JSOT*, 1993). For sources on intertextuality, see B.J. Abasciano, 'Paul's Use of the Old Testament in Romans 9.1-9: An Intertextual and Theological Exegesis' (Ph.D. thesis; University of Aberdeen, 2004), 1–2 n. 1.

2. R.B. Hays and J.B. Green, 'The Use of the Old Testament by New Testament Writers', in J.B. Green (ed.), *Hearing the New Testament: Strategies for Interpretation* (Grand Rapids: Paternoster Press/Carlisle, 1995), 222–38 (230).

their relation to various Old Testament text-traditions examined, their exegetical methods compared to the methods of other interpreters within ancient Christianity and Judaism. The achievements of such inquiries are by no means to be disparaged: they have, as it were, unpacked and laid out the pieces of the puzzle. But how are the pieces to be assembled? Most of the 'unpacking' of the Pauline citations was complete more than a generation ago, yet we still lack a satisfying account of Paul's letters as 'hermeneutical events,' discourse in which Paul is engaged in the act of reinterpreting Scripture to address the concerns of his communities.[3]

This situation has led Roy Ciampa to observe, 'It is remarkable that most of the methods usually applied in the study of Paul's use of the Old Testament are not equipped to deal with the question of the significance of any particular usage within its literary context or for the broader understanding of the document in which it was found.'[4] This lack of attention to questions of the semantic significance of Pauline (and other) scriptural usage also explains the present surge in explorations of the meaning-effects generated by New Testament use of the Old. Indeed, Hays has called for 'studies that will attend not just to exegetical techniques and backgrounds, but also to the meaning-effects produced by Paul's allusions and intertextual juxtapositions'.[5] It is just such a study that I am proposing for Romans 9.1–9.

This investigation began as a comprehensive analysis of Paul's use of Scripture in the whole of Romans 9 which at once attends to the meaning and function of Scripture within the chapter and incorporates the results of such analysis into a thorough exegesis of the passage. Romans 9 is an excellent candidate for such study for a number of reasons. First, it suffers from the same neglect of attention to Old Testament semantic and rhetorical significance as is generally true in Pauline studies.[6] Yet second,

---

3. Hays, *Echoes*, 9.

4. R.E. Ciampa, *The Presence and Function of Scripture in Galatians 1 and 2* (WUNT, 2.102; Tübingen: Mohr Siebeck, 1998), 3.

5. R.B. Hays, 'Crucified with Christ', in D.J. Lull (ed.), *Society of Biblical Literature 1988 Seminar Papers* (Atlanta: Scholars Press, 1988), 318–35 (335 n. 53).

6. See the review of literature on the use of the OT in Romans 9–11 in Abasciano, 'Paul's Use', 117–37. Hays, *Echoes*, 64–68, treats Rom. 9.1–29, but his treatment is necessarily brief and far from comprehensive, and no one since him has attempted a comprehensive analysis along similar lines. Hays' student, J.R. Wagner, *Heralds of the Good News: Isaiah and Paul 'in Concert' in the Letter to the Romans* (NovTSup, 101; Leiden: Brill, 2002), ch. 2, has also examined Rom. 9.1–29, but his focus is on Paul's use of Isaiah in a broader section of Romans.

it is well known for its concentration of scriptural citations and allu-sions,[7] rendering it particularly suitable for observing Paul's use of Scripture as it has been traditionally studied,[8] and providing ample opportunity for study of resultant meaning-effects from various Old Testament passages. Third, Romans 9 is a highly charged passage theo-logically, which stands at the center of several contentious debates[9] that deserve consideration from the perspective of a study of the semantic effects of Paul's use of Scripture as they impact exegesis. Fourth, there is disagreement over the theme and literary placement of Romans 9–11 within the epistle,[10] and an exegesis of Romans 9 informed by an inter-textual investigation can throw fresh light on these long-debated ques-tions. Finally, Romans 9 has not received much recent, detailed attention on its own despite its presence in one of the most important sections in all of Paul's writings.[11]

However, as my research progressed it became clear that a detailed study of every scriptural allusion in the whole of Romans 9, as is being proposed here for only vv. 1–9, would be unworkable for one volume. Hays himself has called for 'the detailed exegesis of particular texts' as the only way of testing intertextual research and methodology.[12] It is my con-viction that intensive research on Paul's use of Scripture in specific texts combined with rigorous exegesis of those texts is necessary to grasp fully the meaning of what he has written. Therefore we must limit the scope of the present investigation to the first nine verses of Romans 9 lest we short-change the exegetical insight to be gained from Paul's interpretive activity.

7. According to B.S. Rosner, *Paul, Scripture & Ethics: A Study of 1 Corinthians 5–7* (AGJU, 22; Leiden: Brill, 1994), 190–91, Romans 9–11 contains nearly a third of Paul's scriptural citations, while H. Hübner, *Gottes Ich und Israel: Zum Schriftgebrauch des Paulus in Römer 9–11* (Göttingen: Vandenhoeck & Ruprecht, 1984), 149–154, lists at least 45 citations and allusions in ch. 9 alone.

8. See Hays, *Echoes*, 9–10, for a concise and helpful overview of the traditional issues addressed by critical scholarship.

9. See J.W. Aageson, 'Paul's Use of Scripture: A Comparative Study of Biblical Interpretation in Early Palestinian Judaism and the New Testament with Special Reference to Romans 9–11' (unpublished D.Phil. thesis; University of Oxford, 1984), 265–66.

10. See Abasciano, 'Paul's Use', 71–87.

11. There has been only one scholarly monograph on Romans 9 written in a major research language in the past century: J. Piper, *The Justification of God: An Exegetical and Theological Study of Romans 9:1–23* (Grand Rapids: Baker, 2nd edn., 1993).

12. R.B. Hays, 'On the Rebound: A Response to Critiques of *Echoes of Scripture in the Letters of Paul*', in Evans and Sanders (eds.), *Paul*, 78–79.

Although Romans 9–11 is clearly one unit, it is equally as clear that there are subsections within that unity, as is true of any significant literary passage. By exegeting a part (Rom. 9.1–9) with sensitivity to the whole (both chs. 9 and 9–11), we should in turn be able more clearly to define the part's relation to the whole and vice versa, thus advancing our exegesis of both. Indeed, lack of concentrated focus on a part can prevent a full understanding of that part, thereby impoverishing our understanding of not only the part, but of the whole as well (precisely because of their unity!). As John Piper has said, 'would it not mean an end to all careful scholarship if it were not possible to focus on one tree *without* losing sight of the forest?'[13] Furthermore, neither Rom. 9.1–9 nor 9–11 can be separated from the epistle so that we must consider both in the broader context of the whole book.

Rom. 9.1–9 is especially fitting for the proposed analysis because its Old Testament background has received even less attention than that of some other parts of the chapter and because it holds special import for understanding the whole of Romans 9–11 as the introduction and beginning stage of Paul's discourse that sets the course of his argument. Indeed, the programmatic statement that stands over all of Romans 9–11 (i.e., 9.6a) is found in these verses, as is both a second similarly programmatic statement standing subordinately over much of the same material (i.e., 9.6b) and what is probably the most discussed verse in the New Testament (9.5). An investigation of Paul's use of Scripture in these verses sharply attuned to the resulting meaning-effects has potential to help move Pauline studies forward. For as Scott Hafemann concludes in his survey of modern research on the life and letters of Paul:

> [A]t the heart of the debate concerning the Law and the role of justification in Paul's thought is the question of Paul's understanding of redemptive history (cf. Gal 3–4; 2 Cor 3:7–18; Rom 3:21–16; 9–11), which itself can only be solved by a renewed study of Paul's use and understanding of the OT within the larger question of the relationship of Paul and his gospel to Israel as the old covenant people of God . . . . Such a study is only now beginning to be undertaken . . . . The future of Pauline studies at this juncture in its history is dependent on just these kinds of studies if we are to move forward in our understanding of Paul as he understood himself: the Jewish apostle to the Gentiles, whose message came from the history of his people, their Scriptures, and the history of Israel's Messiah.[14]

13. Piper, *Justification*, 16; emphasis original.
14. S.J. Hafemann, 'Paul and His Interpreters', *DPL*, 666–79 (678). Cf. R.B. Hays, 'Adam, Israel, Christ – The Question of Covenant in the Theology of Romans: A Response to Leander E. Keck and N. T. Wright', in D.M. Hay and E.E. Johnson

Thus, this study is part of a broader vision for what we would call an intertextual exegesis of Romans 9, and beyond that, of Romans 9–11 as a whole.[15] Indeed, if our method proves viable, then it may hold promise for exegesis of Paul's epistles in general and merit consideration for application to the rest of the New Testament. Our analysis of Rom. 9.1–9 will serve both to illustrate this method and to make headway into the intertextual exegesis of Romans 9. Such an investigation will necessarily have implications for the ongoing debate concerning Paul's use of the Old Testament. Hence, the goal of this study is to contribute to our understanding of three areas of investigation germane to New Testament studies: (1) the exegesis of Romans 9; (2) the theological issues associated with Romans 9; and (3) Paul's use of Scripture.

1.2. *Methodology*

1.2.a. *Introduction and Emphasis*
Scholars have often been remiss about examining the original contexts of Paul's scriptural citations and allusions. Not infrequently we find claims that Paul disregarded the original contexts of his citations or engaged in atomistic exegesis without an accompanying *detailed* analysis of the Old Testament text. To be sure, there may sometimes be general comments made about the Old Testament passage in its original context which aim to show Paul disregarded it. But these are often too general to be helpful.

An example of this phenomenon can be seen in J.W. Aageson's often cited and generally commendable study, 'Paul's Use of Scripture'. Although he allows for the functional, referential role of some of Paul's citations in certain blocks of material, outside of that material he claims 'that there appears to be little or no direct evidence that the larger scriptural contexts were thematically important for Paul'.[16] His prime

---

(eds.), *Pauline Theology III: Romans* (Minneapolis: Fortress, 1995), 68–86 (84); D.M. Smith, 'The Pauline Literature', in D.A. Carson and H.G.M. Williamson (eds.), *It is Written: Scripture Citing Scripture: Essays in Honour of Barnabas Lindars* (Cambridge: Cambridge University Press, 1988), 265–91 (285–87).

15.   T.W. Berkley, *From a Broken Covenant to Circumcision of the Heart: Pauline Intertextual Exegesis in Romans 2:17–29* (SBLDS, 175; Atlanta: SBL, 2000), also uses the term 'intertextual exegesis', but he uses it of *Paul's* exegesis of Scripture rather than exegesis of Paul based upon his exegesis of the OT as we do.

16.   Aageson, 'Paul's Use', 111.

example is Paul's citation of Psalm 18.50[17] in Romans 15.9. He explains that,

> There does not appear to be any thematic material in this psalm which would enhance Paul's discussion. Rather, the use of this scriptural passage by Paul hinges on the presence of the word ἔθνη (LXX) which serves as a linking term in Romans 15:9–12. Hence, the use of Psalm 18:50 has probably been suggested to Paul by the verbal and thematic connection and not by the larger scriptural context of the passage.[18]

It is interesting, then, to find that Hays' treatment of the same passage demonstrates that the context of the psalm does in fact play an important role for Paul and his argument.[19] Indeed, for Hays, Ps. 18.49 (Eng.; 17.50 LXX; 18.50 MT) is one of Paul's 'clinchers' that he has saved for his climactic concluding summary of the letter's themes. It embodies 'his vision for a church composed of Jews and Gentiles glorifying God together',[20] and on it (along with the other citations in Rom. 15.7–13) Paul rests his case for his gospel of God's righteousness as promised in Scripture. Hays correctly warns us,

> Even here, where the significance of the passages for Paul's case is evident, we will miss important intertextual echoes if we ignore the loci from which the quotations originate. Both of the psalm passages refer not only to Gentiles, but also God's mercy (*eleos;* Ps. 17:51 LXX, Ps. 116:2 LXX), the attribute for which the Gentiles are said in Rom. 15:9 to glorify God. In neither instance does Paul quote the part of the text that mentions mercy, but the appearance of the word in these passages is hardly a case of blind luck. Paul has presumably selected these passages precisely because they bring references to God's mercy into conjunction with references to praise of God among the Gentiles.[21]

But the significance of Psalm 18's slightly broader context has not yet been exhausted. Hays goes on to point out other themes voiced in Ps. 18.50 (Eng.) which are related to other themes in Romans, such as 'Christ' and 'seed', and which form 'a satisfying *inclusio* with the letter's opening proclamation about God's son, who was promised in holy texts, "who came from the seed [*spermatos*] of David . . . Jesus Messiah

---

17. Aageson apparently refers to the MT versification.
18. Aageson, 'Paul's Use', 111–12.
19. See Hays, *Echoes*, 70–72.
20. Hays, *Echoes*, 71.
21. Hays, *Echoes*, 71–72.

[*Christou*]", who commissioned Paul to preach the obedience of faith among all the Gentiles (Rom. 1:3–5)'.[22]

This example should serve as a warning against giving insufficient attention to the original contexts of Paul's citations and allusions. What we need are not general descriptions of Old Testament contexts, but detailed exegesis of the relevant Old Testament texts which can then serve as the basis for a judgment about their significance for Paul in any single instance. Only then will we be able to make sound appraisals of the importance of broad scriptural contexts for Paul, and go on to assess his use of Scripture and its importance for understanding his discourse. Only then can we begin to take Paul seriously as an interpreter of Scripture. Otherwise, we may miss important clues to the meaning of Paul's rhetoric. Moreover, only when our Old Testament exegesis is set forth in some significant way, rather than in a very general summary, can we expect our analysis of Paul's use of Scripture to be readily accessible to the scrutiny of others.

Therefore, this study will place great emphasis on analyzing the original Old Testament contexts of Paul's citations and allusions. In so doing, it follows the lead of such distinguished studies as those of Dodd and Hays. In his classic book, *According to the Scriptures*, C.H. Dodd forcefully argued that the New Testament authors employed a contextual method of exegesis which operated flexibly 'upon intelligible and consistent principles'.[23] Old Testament passages

> were understood as *wholes*, and particular verses or sentences were quoted from rather as pointers to the whole context than as constituting testimonies in and for themselves. At the same time, detached sentences could be adduced to illustrate or elucidate the meaning of the main section under consideration. But in the fundamental passages it is the *total context* that is in view, and is the basis of the argument.[24]

Dodd's formulation adumbrated developments in literary criticism concerning the concepts of 'quotation' and 'allusion' to transpire some twenty to thirty-plus years later in the wake of the intertextual fervor sparked by Julia Kristeva.[25]

---

22. Hays, *Echoes*, 72.

23. C.H. Dodd, *According to the Scriptures: The Sub-structure of New Testament Theology*, (London: Nisbet, 1952), 126.

24. Dodd, *According to the Scriptures*, 126; emphasis original.

25. For a helpful introduction to the concept of intertextuality and the accompanying developments in the areas of 'quotation' and 'allusion', which simultaneously sets the specifics in a historical literary setting, see U.J. Hebel's preface and introduction to his *Intertextuality, Allusion, and Quotation: An International*

Most literary scholars now emphasize a relational and genealogical understanding of quotation. Its distinctive quality is

> its very ability to refer the reader to other texts, to make him or her aware of the text's relations to points of reference outside itself . . . quotations open up a deeper dimension. . . . They do not only refer to their original contexts, but also represent them in the quoting text. . . . This quasi-metonymical presence of the quoted text in the quoting text is, however, not restricted to the words of the quotation, but goes beyond the limits of the quotation and attains suggestive power. . . . The quotational element evokes the quoted text as a whole and, possibly its author, the latter's *oeuvre*, or the literary period in which it was written.[26]

Similarly, a new perspective on allusion emerged in the 1970s and 1980s which equated allusion with direct, overt reference. Many scholars have come to regard allusions not 'as casual references without any major impact on the meaning of the text, but rather as particularly intentional elements within the text's artistic structure'.[27] Just as with quotation, the relational quality of allusion has been stressed. '[T]he crucial feature of an allusion, no matter whether a literary allusion in the conventional sense or any other allusion to a person or event, is its effect to denote a specific relation between a text and an identifiable point of reference and its potential to connote additional associations.'[28]

Enter Richard Hays with his influential study. Although Dodd has been heavily criticized,[29] Hays has confirmed some of his basic

---

Bibliography of Critical Studies (Bibliographies and Indexes in World Literature, 18; New York and London: Greenwood, 1989). My discussion of these issues is indebted to Hebel's treatment.

26.   Hebel, *Intertextuality*, 4.

27.   Hebel, *Intertextuality*, 7.

28.   Hebel, *Intertextuality*, 8.

29.   See especially A.C. Sundberg, Jr., 'On Testimonies', in G.K. Beale (ed.), *The Right Doctrine from the Wrong Texts? Essays on the Use of the Old Testament in the New* (Grand Rapids: Baker, 1994), 182–94, and more recently, D.-A. Koch, *Die Schrift als Zeuge des Evangeliums: Untersuchungen zur Verwendung und zum Verständnis der Schrift bei Paulus* (BHT, 69; Tübingen: Mohr Siebeck, 1986). But convincing defenses of Dodd have been brought forward by I.H. Marshall, 'An Assessment of Recent Developments', in Beale (ed.), *Right Doctrine*, 195–216 (197–203, especially against Sundberg), and R.H. Bell, *Provoked to Jealousy: The Origin and Purpose of the Jealousy Motif in Romans 9–11* (WUNT, 2.63; Tübingen: Mohr Siebeck, 1994), 205–209 (especially against Koch). Criticisms of Dodd's conception of traditional textual fields tend to falter on a misunderstanding of his position. Dodd's portrait of 'the Bible of the early Church' is not offered as exhaustive or restrictive (see Marshall, 201; Bell, 206; Dodd, *According to the Scriptures*, 108).

insights,[30] albeit in a nuanced manner which advances Dodd's outlook to a higher level of sophistication via an intertextual literary approach. Hays' approach is to read Paul's letters 'as literary texts shaped by complex intertextual relations with Scripture'.[31] Intertextuality, for Hays, is 'the imbedding of fragments of an earlier text within a later one'.[32] He takes his cue for analyzing Paul's intertextual activity from John Hollander, who accords a central place to the literary figure of transumption, or metalepsis. Hays explains:

> When a literary echo links the text in which it occurs to an earlier text, the figurative effect of the echo can lie in the unstated or suppressed (transumed) points of resonance between the two texts. . . . Hollander sums up in a compact formula the demand that this sort of effect places upon criticism: 'the interpretation of a metalepsis entails the recovery of the transumed material.' Allusive echo functions to suggest to the reader that text B should be understood in light of a broad interplay with text A, encompassing aspects of A beyond those explicitly echoed. . . . Metalepsis . . . places the reader within a field of whispered or unstated correspondences.[33]

It is this phenomenon of matalepsis which Hays finds consistently at work in Paul's writing, and which means that, 'We will have great difficulty understanding Paul, the pious first-century Jew, unless we seek to situate his discourse appropriately within what Hollander calls the "cave of resonant signification" that enveloped him: Scripture.'[34] There is also, then, a historical dimension to such interpretation. So historical knowledge is to inform and constrain the interpreter's reading, even as the interpreter's readings have historical implications.

1.2.b. *Procedure*

Hays offers no precise method for analyzing echoes, but beckons us to tune our ears to Paul's echoes of Scripture by examining their original contexts and assessing their significance for the meaning of Paul's epistles. Although we do not necessarily affirm all the specifics of either Dodd's or Hays' formulations, it is this basic insight, consonant with recent intertextual literary approaches to quotation and allusion, which

---

30. G.K. Beale, 'Did Jesus and His Followers Preach the Right Doctrine from the Wrong Texts?', in Beale (ed.), *Right Doctrine*, 387–404 (390–91 n. 10), follows Dodd, and lists a number of other scholars who support his thesis.

31. Hays, *Echoes*, xi.

32. Hays, *Echoes*, 14.

33. Hays, *Echoes*, 20.

34. Hays, *Echoes*, 21.

helps form the foundation for the method of this study.[35] The specifics of that method will now be delineated.

Rather than always use the awkward combination of 'quotations and allusions', etc., we will often simply use the term allusion. This anticipates some of our later discussion of definitions which will conclude that allusion is the broader term and encompasses quotation. Hopefully, this practice will make the discussion a little smoother. With a view toward exegeting the text of Romans, we will analyze Paul's use of the Old Testament under four headings:[36]

1.2.b.1. The Old Testament Context.   Here we will exegete the broad context of Paul's allusion in the Hebrew text.[37] Although Paul uses the LXX[38] far more often than the Hebrew, we choose the Hebrew text for our primary analysis because it stands at the genesis of the textual tradition. Familiarity with the Hebrew will put us in the best position to assess all that developed from it, and will give us the broadest possible view through which to understand Paul's scriptural interpretation. We will not restrict ourselves to just a few verses surrounding the specific allusion, but will concern ourselves with the passage in which it is found, and that passage in its own literary and theological context. We will attempt to render ourselves as fit as possible to analyze Paul's use of the Old Testament and to make judgments about its significance for the exegesis of Romans 9.

1.2.b.2. Textual Comparison.   Paul's citations and allusions will be compared to the known textual traditions of the Old Testament passage

---

35. For a valuable recent survey of the historical development of intertextual method from foundational works to the present, see Berkley, *Broken*, 17–47.

36. The following methodological approach has been especially derived and adapted from G.K. Beale and his course, 'Old Testament in the New' at Gordon-Conwell Theological Seminary (Fall, 1994); Hays and Green, 'The Use'; and K. Snodgrass, 'The Use of the Old Testament in the New', in Beale (ed.), *Right Doctrine*, 29–51.

37. By speaking of *the* Hebrew text, I do not mean to imply that there was a single Hebrew text in Paul's day. The phrase is a general one used out of convenience. As is customary, the starting point of our work will be the MT.

38. As with the Hebrew, I do not mean to imply that there was a fixed Greek translation in Paul's day. Following Stanley, Tov, and others, we will use the terms 'LXX' and 'Septuagint' to refer to the collection of Greek translations in all their textual diversity, and 'Old Greek' to refer specifically to the original LXX translation of each book.

such as the MT, LXX, Targums, and early Jewish translations to deter-mine what, if any, known text Paul used, and identify any implications to be drawn from the textual form of the allusion. Due to the instability of both the Hebrew text and the LXX in Paul's day, we will be cautious about concluding that Paul altered the text.[39] Nevertheless, in light of Christopher Stanley's findings that ancient authors commonly gave free renderings of their sources according to the accepted literary standards of the day,[40] we will not hesitate to consider this option. The very form of Paul's citations and allusions can suggest his understanding of the bibli-cal text and what he was trying to communicate to his audience.

The comparison of versions can help us in another way. Since every translation is also an interpretation, the various Old Testament transla-tions can alert us to various traditions of interpretation within ancient Judaism. This leads us to the next analytical heading.

1.2.b.3. *Interpretive Traditions.* Here we are seeking to understand how the Scripture alluded to was interpreted and used in Judaism. This can help tell us if and how Paul was adopting, refuting, ignoring, or oth-erwise interacting with related Jewish exegetical traditions. It will also set Paul's scriptural interpretation in its proper historical and cultural context. As a Jew, Paul's understanding and sense of Scripture was formed by Jewish training and instruction. He viewed Scripture through the lenses of his Jewish background. As Brian Rosner comments, 'He did not receive his Bible in a vacuum.'[41] Therefore, we must attend to

39. On the history of the Hebrew text, see M.J. Mulder, 'The Transmission of the Biblical Text', in M.J. Mulder (ed.), *Mikra: Text, Translation, Reading, and Interpretation of the Hebrew Bible in Ancient Judaism and Early Christianity* (CRINT, 2/1; Assen: Van Gorcum; Philadelphia: Fortress, 1988), 87–135. On the Septuagint, see E. Tov, 'The Septuagint', in Mulder (ed.), *Mikra*, 161–88. For an especially understandable account of these issues, see E.R. Brotzman, *Old Testament Textual Criticism: A Practical Introduction* (Grand Rapids: Baker, 1994), 37–62, for the Hebrew text, and 72–80 for the LXX. For a helpful summary of the issues with special concern for Paul, see C.D. Stanley, *Paul and the Language of Scripture: Citation Technique in the Pauline Epistles and Contemporary Literature* (SNTSMS, 69; Cambridge: Cambridge University Press, 1992), 37–51.

40. Stanley, *Paul*. For a concise summary of his work as it bears specifically on this issue, see C.D. Stanley, 'The Social Environment of "Free" Biblical Quotations in the New Testament', in C.A. Evans and J.A. Sanders (eds.), *Early Christian Interpretation of the Scriptures of Israel: Investigations and Proposals* (JSNTSup, 148; SSEJC, 5; Sheffield: Sheffield Academic Press, 1997), 18–27.

41. Rosner, *Paul*, 57; see further 56–58 for an expansion of this point, where Rosner draws attention to modern theories of hermeneutics.

interpretive traditions that could have influenced Paul. C.A. Evans makes a similar point in his criticism of Hays, arguing that 'it would be more accurate to speak of the echoes of interpreted Scripture in the letters of Paul'.[42]

At the same time, the lenses of Judaism were not the only lenses Paul wore. Hays' rejoinder to Evans is instructive. He acknowledges the importance of attending to Jewish interpretive traditions, but declares, 'I continue to insist, however, that the work of interpretation must include careful attention to the manner in which Paul puts his own distinctive spin on the inherited traditions.'[43] There is both continuity and discontinuity between Paul and Judaism. The Christ event ensured that much. While Paul is influenced heavily by his past, he is not restricted by it, and may (and does) interact with the biblical text from a distinctive perspective as well as a Jewish one. He is free to engage in a fresh encounter with the biblical text, and is not limited to an encounter with interpreted Scripture. Nevertheless, the fact that I need to argue for a degree of freedom for Paul from his Jewish milieu highlights the importance of paying attention to his Jewish context.

In addition to tracing the Jewish exegetical history of Paul's allusions, we will also examine their interpretation and use in early Christianity as reflected in the rest of the New Testament. Since Paul shared a common faith with his fellow Christians, our understanding of his use of Scripture can be enlightened by their use of the same Scripture. Just as there was an exegetical history of various passages in Judaism, there may also have been Christian traditions of interpretation that could have influenced Paul.

A final word should be addressed to the use of rabbinic materials that were codified after the New Testament era.[44] The problem of how useful these materials are in view of their chronological distance from the first

---

42.   C.A. Evans, 'Listening For Echoes of Interpreted Scripture', in Evans and Sanders (eds.), *Paul*, 47–51 (50). Cf. the similar criticism of Hays by J.A. Sanders, 'Paul and Theological History', in Evans and Sanders (eds.), *Paul*, 52–57. Such concerns also help distinguish Wagner's (*Heralds*, esp. 15) method.

43.   Hays, 'Rebound', 73.

44.   For this language, see M. Knowles, *Jeremiah in Matthew's Gospel: The Rejected Prophet Motif in Matthaean Redaction* (JSNTSup, 68; Sheffield: *JSOT*, 1993), 166. Knowles has a good discussion of this problem as it relates to Matthew (166–70) that is applicable generally. The method he proposes for evaluating rabbinic materials appears basically sound, though we do not share his commitment to focusing primarily on what is dissimilar.

century is well known.[45] But it is commonly pointed out that these writings may well reflect ancient traditions stretching back to New Testament times and earlier. Parallels with the New Testament may often reveal dependence on a common tradition rather than literary dependence, which is impossible in the case of Paul depending on the Talmud, for example, and highly unlikely in the case of rabbinic dependence on Paul when the fact of increasing hostility between Christianity and Judaism from Paul's day onward is taken into account. Therefore, we will exercise caution in appealing to late rabbinic sources, but remain open to their echoing of common tradition, especially in cases of striking parallels to Paul's scriptural use. Reference to rabbinic literature does not in itself suggest a direct connection to Paul.

1.2.b.4. *The New Testament Context.*   Finally, we will address the New Testament context of Paul's Old Testament allusions. This is where we will address how Paul has actually used the Old Testament. We will seek to integrate all we have discovered into our exegesis of Romans 9 even as we relate our exegesis of Romans 9 to Paul's scriptural use, observing the dynamic interaction between Paul and sacred text, old context and new. Here Paul's use of the same or similar passages elsewhere will enter in, as well as the broad literary and theological context of Romans. Four aspects of the New Testament context stand out for special mention. Although we identify them here, we will not necessarily distinguish them in our treatments of New Testament context throughout the study because of their close overlap and disproportionate space requirements.

We will address the question of Paul's *hermeneutical approach* to the Old Testament text, attempting to identify any presuppositions at work behind Paul's interpretation.[46] We will also want to ascertain just how

45. See the landmark essay of S. Sandmel, 'Parallelomania', *JBL* 81 (1962), 1–13. Berkley, *Broken*, 17–47, highlights this issue among others in his methodological history.

46. Descriptions of the New Testament authors' presuppositions have been given by scholars such as Beale, 'Right Doctrine', 391–98; E.E. Ellis, 'Biblical Interpretation in the New Testament Church', in Mulder (ed.), *Mikra*, 691–725 (710–24); idem, 'How the New Testament Uses the Old', in I.H. Marshall (ed.), *New Testament Interpretation: Essays on Principles and Methods* (Grand Rapids: Eerdmans, 1977), 199–219 (209–14); R. Longenecker, *Biblical Exegesis in the Apostolic Period* (Grand Rapids: Eerdmans, 1975), 93–95; Snodgrass, 'The Use', 36–41. Cf. Hays, *Echoes*, 154–73. Less helpful for understanding Paul as an interpreter of Scripture, but still important, are Jewish exegetical methods operative in

Paul uses the Old Testament text, whether analogically, as direct fulfillment of prophecy, or some other way or combination of ways.[47] A second emphasis under New Testament context is the analysis of the *rhetorical significance* of Paul's Old Testament usage. Although I regard this as standard procedure in New Testament exegesis, it has recently been claimed that many studies on the use of the Old Testament in the New have ignored this aspect of the topic.[48] If this is true, then our attention to rhetorical matters should help to correct this imbalance, and shed light on how Paul's biblical allusion furthers his persuasive strategy.[49] This is mainly an exegetical question that addresses how the Old Testament quotation formally functions in Paul's argument, its logic, and its persuasive power.

Intimately related is the central matter of the *semantic significance* of Paul's use of the Old Testament. I regard this too as an acutely exegetical question, one which has often been ignored in exegetical treatments of Paul's epistles. The focus will be on describing the meaning-effects generated by Paul's Scripture use, that is, the ramifications of Paul's interpretive activity for his message. How does Paul's allusion affect the meaning of his discourse? What difference does the connection of old context and new context make to exegesis?

The last aspect of New Testament context we must mention is the *theological significance* of Paul's use of the Old Testament text. This simply refers to the theological implications effected by Paul's scriptural interpretation and presentation. What theology is reflected in Paul's understanding of Scripture? How does that translate into his discourse? What theological significance do the meaning-effects of Paul's allusion yield?

1.2.c. *Definitions*

Having outlined the emphasis and methodological procedure of this investigation, it is now time to turn to the basic methodological issue of

the first century, most notably, the so-called seven rules of Hillel. For these, see the works listed above by Longenecker (34–35), Snodgrass (43), and Ellis, 'Biblical Interpretation', 700–702.

47.   For a description of seven uses of the OT in Revelation, which can give insight into the various ways Paul uses the OT, see G.K. Beale, *The Book of Revelation* (NIGTC; Grand Rapids: Eerdmans, 1999), 86–96.

48.   C.D. Stanley, 'The Rhetoric of Quotations: An Essay on Method', in Evans and Sanders (eds.), *Christian Interpretation*, 44–58, though the assertion is questionable and Stanley's approach unbalanced.

49.   See Stanley, 'Rhetoric', 58.

defining terms. Stanley Porter has recently charged that the vast majority of studies of the Old Testament in the New do not bother to define
their terms.[50] So we will try to avoid this methodological flaw. This is not
as easy as it sounds, however, as evidenced by the uncertainty in literary
studies over definitions of quotation and allusion,[51] the two terms Porter
regards as most in need of definition.[52]

The difficulty is exacerbated by the fact that we are dealing with
ancient literature, produced in 'a culture of high residual orality'[53] which
did not employ quotation marks or other modern means of indicating
borrowed material. Nor did the ancients have the same literary standards as modern authors and scholars living in the age of the footnote.[54]
They clearly did not have the same concept of citation that we do. So
how do we define 'quotation' and 'allusion' when working with such
materials while modern theorists cannot even agree, even with abundant
punctuation markers available?

Unfortunately, there are no absolute or thoroughly precise definitions
available. The issues are complicated and varied, and we cannot enter
into a full treatment of them here.[55] The best that investigators can do is
to clearly, even if not precisely, define their own usage of the terms. We
concur with Moisés Silva's judgment that 'there is little to be gained by
attempting to formulate a definitive criterion to decide this question',[56]
and with Stanley say, 'To attempt to establish any hard and fast guide-
lines would be to misrepresent the broad diversity that characterizes
Paul's repeated appeals to the biblical text.'[57]

As Stanley's comment suggests, our own definitions cannot be too
precise without distorting the issues. Unfortunately, this leaves room for
subjectivity. But it seems that the danger of distortion from too much

---

50. S.E. Porter, 'The Use of the Old Testament in the New Testament: A Brief
Comment on Method and Terminology', in Evans and Sanders (eds.), *Christian
Interpretation*, 79–96 (81).

51. Hebel, *Intertextuality*, x, 4.

52. Porter, 'The Use', 95.

53. P.J. Achtemeier, *'Omni Verbum Sonat:* The New Testament and the Oral
Environment of Late Western Antiquity', *JBL* 109 (1990), 3–27 (3).

54. See Stanley, *Paul*; idem, 'Social'. Cf. R. Nicole, 'The New Testament Use of
the Old Testament', in Beale (ed.), *Right Doctrine*, 13–28 (20–21).

55. See Hebel, *Intertextuality*, 3, for a convenient description of some of the
issues.

56. M. Silva, 'Old Testament in Paul', *DPL*, 630–42 (634).

57. Stanley, *Paul*, 36. Cf. E.E. Ellis, *Paul's Use of the Old Testament* (Grand
Rapids: Baker, 1957), 11.

precision is greater than the danger of distortion through ambiguity. We will take some of Porter's advice by defining quotation more broadly than in most monographs on New Testament use of the Old, as is typical of commentary discussion. This is a more author-oriented approach, since we are interested in Paul's use of the Old Testament. So 'quotation' or 'citation' will refer to the reproduction of an earlier text. The number of words cannot be specified since theoretically an author can quote just one word.[58] Each case will need to be examined individually and judged against its context and what we deem to be Paul's intention based on our exegesis of the text.[59] There is also merit to the reader-oriented approach,[60] for quotation is usually connected to an intention to communicate to the reader that one is quoting. So we may distinguish between 'formal quotations', which are those citations accompanied by a citation formula (e.g., καθὼς γέγραπται), and 'informal quotations', which have no direct indication that they are quotations. Yet another category of quotation (some categories may overlap) is 'exact' or 'direct quotation' which refers to citation that reproduces the wording of a prior text precisely. A 'loose quotation' would be one that substantially reproduces the wording of a prior text, but differs in some respect(s). The basic terms 'quotation' and 'citation' are general, and can refer to any of these more specific designations.

'Allusion' will be used in two main ways in this investigation, one broader and the other narrower. In its broad sense, 'allusion' will refer to any intentional reference to a text, person, event etc. On this definition, allusion encompasses quotation, and can refer to it.[61] To quote is to allude, but to allude is not necessarily to quote. In its narrower sense, 'allusion' will refer to informal, intentional reference to a text, person, event, etc. other than quotation.[62] On this definition, there has been no attempt by the author substantially to reproduce an earlier text, though a reference is intended. Although the dual meaning of 'allusion' could

58. Cf. C. Ruse and M. Hopton, *The Cassell Dictionary of Literary and Language Terms*, (London: Cassell, 1992), 243.

59. Cf. Ellis, *Paul's Use*, 11, who also takes into account 'the intention of the apostle as judged from the context' when determining quotations.

60. See Stanley, *Paul*, 34, for the language of author/reader-oriented as applied to quotation.

61. This is in line with the recent definitions of allusion discussed earlier (see also below), which regard allusion as the broader concept. For a description of this debate, see Hebel, *Intertextuality*, 4–7.

62. Cf. Porter, 'The Use', 95.

result in some ambiguity, the context of the study should make the sense of the word clear in any specific instance, especially when it is important for the discussion.

There is a danger in using the terms citation and allusion. The labels tend to have a heuristic value that shapes one's interpretation of Paul's use of the Old Testament.[63] Quotation is thought to be more significant than allusion, and therefore attracts more attention and interpretive significance. But given our definition of allusion, which recognizes its close affinity with citation, and our intertextual approach to these two concepts, which emphasizes their ability to invoke broad original contexts and suggest additional associations, it should be clear that the present investigation attaches no such a priori valuations on quotation over against allusion. It is true that formal citations do often have a greater rhetorical impact through an implicit invocation of divine authority, but this is not always the case. Moreover, although rhetorical form is related to the meaning of the text, it is not identical with it. As Silva has noted, 'it is possible that a particular quotation, though explicit and verbatim, may play only an illustrative role and thus will not tell us very much about Paul's fundamental conceptions. Conversely, some of the apostle's arguments that do not contain any apparent citations reflect a very deep insight into, and dependence upon, OT themes.'[64] Each specific case of quotation and allusion must be judged on its own merits as to its interpretive significance and its relevance for our understanding of Paul's use of the Old Testament.

Four other terms deserve definition. 'Echo' will denote allusion without reference to conscious intention.[65] The term itself is to be considered neutral with respect to conscious intention, and will neither affirm nor deny conscious intentionality in and of itself. 'Meaning-effects' refers simply to the intended effect that Paul's use of the Old

---

63. Porter, 'The Use', 92.

64. Silva, 'Old Testament', 630. Cf. S. Moyise, 'Intertextuality and the Study of the Old Testament in the New Testament', in S. Moyise (ed.), *The Old Testament in the New Testament: Essays in Honour of J. L. North* (JSNTSup, 189; Sheffield: Sheffield Academic Press, 2000), 14–41 (17); G.R. Osborne, *The Hermeneutical Spiral: A Comprehensive Introduction to Biblical Interpretation* (Downers Grove: InterVarsity Press, 1991), 135.

65. Cf. Hays, *Echoes*, 29; J. Hollander, *The Figure of Echo: A Mode of Allusion in Milton and After* (Berkeley: University of California Press, 1981), 64; M. Thompson, *Clothed with Christ: The Example and Teaching of Jesus in Romans 12.1–15.13* (JSNTSup, 59; Sheffield: *JSOT*, 1991), 30.

Testament has on the meaning of his discourse.[66] Like Richard Hays, we will be working with a minimal definition of 'intertextuality': 'the imbedding of fragments of an earlier text within a later one'.[67] And finally, the related term 'intertextual' will be used to mean 'of the relationship between texts'.

1.2.d. *The Place of Intertextuality in New Testament Studies and This Investigation*

The mention of intertextuality raises a larger issue that merits consideration, namely, the place of the literary concept of intertextuality in the study of the New Testament's use of the Old. Over the past decade and a half there has been a steady, if trickling, stream of voices raising concerns over the naive adoption of the term 'intertextuality' by biblical scholars.[68] Some would like to see the term dropped from biblical studies,[69] while others would prefer to see it used in a way consonant with its poststructuralist roots.[70] Perhaps the most forceful and focused statement has been made by Thomas Hatina, who argues that intertextuality is inimical to historical criticism due to its poststructuralist

66. This is not a socio-pragmatic literary definition of the term (on which see briefly, A.C. Thiselton, *New Horizons in Hermeneutics* [Grand Rapids: Zondervan, 1992], 11–13), but a decidedly author-oriented one.

67. Hays, *Echoes*, 14. The present investigation's appropriation of this definition does not limit the concept to verbal reproduction, but takes it in its broadest sense to include any invocation of an earlier text. For the characterization of Hays' definition as minimal, see W.S. Green, 'Doing the Text's Work for It: Richard Hays on Paul's Use of Scripture', in Evans and Sanders (eds.), *Paul*, 58–63. For Hays' defense of his definition, see 'Rebound', 79–81.

68. See E. van Wolde, 'Trendy Intertextuality?'; in S. Draisma (ed.), *Intertextuality in Biblical Writings: Essays in Honour of Bas van Iersel* (Kampen: J.H. Kok, 1989), 43–49; Green, 'Doing'; Porter, 'The Use', 84–85; T.R. Hatina, 'Intertextuality and Historical Criticism in New Testament Studies: Is There a Relationship?', *BibInt* 7, 1 (1999), 28–43. Cf. Moyise, 'Intertextuality', 16; D.C. Mohrmann, 'Semantic Collisions at the Intertextual Crossroads : A Diachronic and Synchronic Study of Romans 9:30–10:13' (unpublished Ph.D. thesis; University of Durham, 2001), 1–2; S.D. Moore, *Poststructuralism and the New Testament: Derrida and Foucault at the Foot of the Cross* (Minneapolis: Fortress, 1994), 123.

69. Seemingly, Porter, 'The Use', esp. 84 n. 17; and certainly Hatina, 'Intertextuality'. Cf. Berkley, *Broken*, 49; S.-L. Shum, *Paul's Use of Isaiah in Romans: A Comparative Study of Paul's Letter to the Romans and the Sybilline and Qumran Sectarian Texts* (WUNT, 2.156; Tübingen: Mohr Siebeck, 2002) 15–16.

70. Wolde, 'Trendy'; Green, 'Doing'.

ideological origin, its conception of text as infinite and inseparable from the reader, and its opposition to the notion of influence.[71]

Hatina sounds a sharp note of warning which should be heeded by every biblical scholar who studies the New Testament's use of Scripture. The term 'intertextuality' ought not to be used naively without thought for its conceptual background. There is a danger of investigators merely jumping on the bandwagon of what Ellen van Wolde has called 'trendy intertexuality' and using the term only 'as a modern literary theoretical coat of veneer over the old comparative approach'.[72] Hatina is surely correct to conclude that intertextuality, *as a poststructuralist concept*, is incompatible with New Testament historical criticism. He has correctly observed, as others before him, that most biblical scholars use the term in a way that is foreign to its poststructuralist formulation. Nevertheless, Hatina's implicit insistence on abandoning the term goes too far in my opinion, and underestimates the complexity of the literary landscape.

Although Hatina shows awareness of the fact that literary critics disagree among themselves over the theory and practice of intertextuality, he does not seem to grasp the probable implication that a non-poststructuralist theory of intertextuality has been mediated to some biblical scholars through literary criticism.[73] Poststructuralist intertextuality is not the only type of intertextuality practiced by literary critics.[74] Therefore, it seems entirely appropriate for biblical scholars to adopt non-poststructuralist notions of intertextuality which are better suited to their realm of inquiry. Furthermore, there is no reason why a concept borrowed from literary criticism needs to maintain its pure

71.   Hatina, 'Intertextuality'.

72.   Wolde, 'Trendy', 43.

73.   This seems to be the case with Hays, who Hatina makes an example of, but who has followed the non-poststructuralist, intertextual approach of literary scholar John Hollander.

74.   See J. Clayton and E. Rothstein, 'Figures in the Corpus: Theories of Influence and Intertextuality', in J. Clayton and E. Rothstein (eds.), *Influence and Intertextuality in Literary History* (Madison: University of Wisconsin Press, 1991), 3–36 (18, 29); S.S. Friedman, 'Weavings: Intertextuality and the (Re)Birth of the Author', in Clayton and Rothstein (eds.), *Influence and Intertextuality*, 146–80. Hebel, *Intertextuality*, 12, documents that certain approaches to intertextuality soon began to emphasize its importance for the meaning of individual texts, a development which attracted heavy criticism from poststructuralists. He concludes, 'it appears safe to contend from today's point of view that an interpretive approach to intertextuality will prove to be the more fruitful perspective for scholars of literature' (13).

literary critical associations anyway. New Testament scholars have a distinctive interest, and the Bible is a unique literary work. It only makes sense that biblical scholars should adapt literary critical concepts to their own specific context, discarding what is unhelpful, and employing what is useful. Of course, scholars should not simultaneously operate on mutually exclusive theories, but they can and should adapt helpful language and amenable aspects of even hostile theories, as long as they are clear about the issues and terminology. In my judgment, the main contribution of Hatina's article is to underscore the importance of biblical scholars understanding the theoretical issues at stake (and Hatina describes these well), and making their own stance on the issues clear, especially the issues of author, meaning, and text.

Even more to the point for our discussion than some of the above observations, is the relationship of intertextuality to recent developments in quotation and allusion discussed earlier. Intertextuality has become an umbrella term which incorporates these two concepts.[75] Hebel credits intertextuality with 'resuscitating an area of literary scholarship that had been paralyzed by basically well-intentioned, but ultimately inconsequential, searches for yet another biblical or classical allusion or quotation in yet another text'.[76] Many older studies on influence and allusion apparently focused on identifying these aspects without much consideration of their interpretive and semantic significance.[77] This would appear to be mirrored by the almost exclusive focus on technical aspects of Paul's Scripture use which Hays claims to have reigned in Pauline scholarship,[78] and the recent widespread interest in deeper questions of interpretive significance. The developments in quotation and allusion studies have occurred under the influence of intertextuality, so that we may speak of an intertextual approach to quotation and allusion, which is, however, not inherently dependent on poststructuralist ideology. Again, these developments emphasize the ability of citation and allusion to refer to broad original contexts and to suggest additional associations. This, along with an emphasis on allusive interpretive significance, I take to be the primary contribution of intertextuality to the study of Paul's use of the Old Testament.

75.   Hebel, *Intertextuality*, 1, 4, 13.
76.   Hebel, *Intertextuality*, 1.
77.   Hebel, *Intertextuality*, 1, 6; Clayton and Rothstein, 'Figures', 5–6.
78.   E.g. Hays, *Echoes*, 9.

Thus, the present study will retain the language of intertextuality. But it should be noted that, along with Richard Hays, we do not regard use of the *term* as necessary for our work.[79] Rather, it is the intertextual *approach* to allusion that is foundational to the methodology of this investigation.[80]

Before leaving the topic of intertextuality it remains for us to identify our position on some of the key issues it raises. This study is located in the tradition of historical biblical criticism.[81] I assume the traditional notions of text and authorship. I assume that an author can create stable meaning through language, that meaning can be expressed through established forms, that the author's intention determines meaning, and that the text can adequately mediate an author's intended meaning.[82]

---

79. Hays, 'Rebound', 81.

80. This does not mean that our methodology is solely dependent on intertextual definitions of quotation and allusion. As mentioned earlier, Dodd anticipated such an approach without any connection to intertextuality, and within the framework of traditional historical criticism. But we do participate in what can now be called an intertextual approach to these issues.

81. This type of approach is represented well by the guidebooks of D. Stuart, *Old Testament Exegesis: A Primer for Students and Pastors* (Philadelphia: Westminster, 2nd edn., rev. and enl., 1984); G. Fee, *New Testament Exegesis: A Handbook for Students and Pastors* (Louisville: Westminster/John Knox, rev. edn., 1993); and Osborne, *Spiral*. I am using the term 'historical criticism' loosely to designate a standard approach to exegesis that seeks to understand the text in its historical context and draws on a wide range of critical methodologies which aid this goal, whether they are historically oriented or not. For the more technical definition, see R.N. Soulen, *Handbook of Biblical Criticism* (Guilford/London: Lutterworth Press, 1977), 78.

82. The classic modern statement of what has been called 'hermeneutic realism', and the related concepts of validity in interpretation and unchanging, determinate textual meaning; have been put forward by E.D. Hirsch, Jr., *Validity in Interpretation* (New Haven: Yale University Press, 1967). For a compelling case in favor of these concepts in a more nuanced statement which seeks to avoid the criticisms leveled against Hirsch's theory, see K.J. Vanhoozer, *Is there a Meaning in this Text? The Bible, the Reader, and the Morality of Literary Knowledge* (Grand Rapids: Zondervan, 1998); cf. Osborne, *Spiral*, 366–415; Thiselton, *Hermeneutics*; F. Watson, *Text and Truth: Redefining Biblical Theology* (Edinburgh: T&T Clark, 1997), 95–126. For a lively exchange over these issues *vis-à-vis* NT use of the OT, see S. Moyise, 'The Old Testament in the New: A Reply to Greg Beale', *IBS* 21 (May, 1999), 54–58, and G.K. Beale, 'Questions of Authorial Intent, Epistemology, and Presuppositions and Their Bearing on the Study of the Old Testament in the New: A Rejoinder to Steve Moyise', *IBS* 21 (Nov., 1999), 151–80.

I also assume that we can usually arrive at adequate knowledge of the author's intention through historical critical inquiry.[83]

1.2.e. *Criteria for Detecting and Interpreting Scriptural Allusions*
If we want to gain knowledge of Paul's intended meaning in Romans 9 and in his use of the Old Testament, sound methodological criteria are necessary. The well-known pitfall of 'parallelomania',[84] which exaggerates parallels and facilely assumes dependence based on similarity, lies potentially on the path of any investigation of this sort. Hays has provided what has become an almost standard list of criteria 'for testing claims about the presence and meaning of scriptural echoes in Paul',[85] which we have adapted for use as the basic criteria of this investigation:[86]

(1)   *Availability* determines whether the proposed source of an echo was available to the author and/or original readers.[87]

(2)   *Volume* of an echo is determined primarily by the degree of similarity of words, syntactical patterns, structure, and number

---

83.   For a defense of this position, see esp. Vanhoozer, *Meaning*.

84.   See Sandmel, 'Parallelomania'.

85.   Hays, *Echoes*, 29. See also Ciampa, *Presence*, 24–25; Thompson, *Clothed*, 30–36; Knowles, *Jeremiah*, 163–64; Rosner, *Paul*, 18–19; S.C. Keesmaat, *Paul and His Story: (Re)interpreting the Exodus Tradition* (JSNTSup, 181; Sheffield: Sheffield Academic Press, 1999), 52; Berkley, *Broken*, 49–50, 60–66; Shum, *Paul's Use*, 5–11; Wagner, *Heralds*, 11–13; Mohrmann, 'Collisions', 25–26 (cf. 6–7). Ciampa and Knowles adopt Hays' list outright; Keesmaat and Mohrmann do so with minimal modification; others adopt certain of Hays' criteria, and all these studies acknowledge dependence on his discussion. Thompson is notable for the most thorough and rigorous discussion of the issues. Porter, 'The Use', 82–84, has recently criticized Hays' criteria, but he misunderstands and misrepresents them, and demands a level of precision impossible to attain. See Abasciano, 'Paul's Use', 28–30, for a detailed defense of Hays' criteria.

86.   See Hays, *Echoes*, 29–31. Unlike Hays (33), who does not restrict his study to Paul's intention, the present study does limit its interpretation of Paul's scriptural echoes either to what Paul intended by them or to what those echoes can tell us about Paul's intention.

87.   Astonishingly, Shum, *Paul's Use*, 7, actually suggests that Paul may not have been familiar with all of Scripture. As far as I know, he is the only scholar to criticize Hays' criterion of availability on this basis. His comments already manifest a deficient approach to the historical prolegomena to assessing Paul's use of the OT that is more fully evidenced in his discussion of how much prophetic literature first-century Jews knew (21–33) and taints much of his discussion of criteria for detecting allusions/echoes; see Abasciano, 'Paul's Use', 34–35 n. 115.

of elements.[88] It also includes verbal coherence between the broader contexts of the OT and NT texts in question,[89] though this can only serve to strengthen (and not lessen) the likelihood of a proposed allusion according to the degree to which it is present, as does '[t]he presence of vocabulary links with other OT passages which also meet the criteria of exegetical use'[90] by Paul. Finally, the volume of an echo is also affected by the precursor text's degree of distinctiveness or prominence in Scripture as well as the amount of rhetorical stress the echo receives in Paul's discourse.

(3)   *Recurrence* concerns how often Paul cites or alludes to the same scriptural passage elsewhere. 'Where such evidence exists that Paul considered a passage of particular importance, proposed echoes from the same context should be given additional credence.'[91] In addition, the degree to which Paul alludes to the Old Testament in a given epistolary context can contribute to the general, relative probability of whether he does so in any specific case. In the context of Romans 9, Paul is developing an argument from Scripture. Therefore, the tenor of the argument raises the general probability of specific proposals that Paul alludes to Scripture.

(4)   *Thematic Coherence* addresses the fit of the alleged echo with Paul's argument. Does its meaning-effect cohere with other quotations in Romans or elsewhere in the Pauline corpus? 'Do the images and ideas of the proposed precursor text illuminate Paul's argument?'[92]

(5)   *Historical Plausibility* assesses whether Paul could have intended the alleged meaning-effect and whether his readers could have understood it. However, we should remember 'that Paul might have written things that were not readily intelligible to his actual readers'.[93]

(6)   *History of Interpretation* alerts us to whether other readers have heard the same echoes. If so, it strengthens our proposals. But

---

88. On structure and number as criteria, see Thompson, *Clothed*, 32; cf. Berkley's (*Broken*, 64) 'common linear development'.
89. Derived from Berkley, *Broken*, 61–62.
90. Berkley, *Broken*, 62–63.
91. Hays, *Echoes*, 30.
92. Hays, *Echoes*, 30.
93. Hays, *Echoes*, 30.

'this criterion should rarely be used as a negative test to exclude proposed echoes that commend themselves on other grounds'.[94]

(7)   *Satisfaction* asks whether the proposed reading makes sense. Does it illuminate Paul's discourse? 'Does it produce for the reader a satisfying account of the effect of intertextual relations?'[95]

Hays' caveat with respect to these tests bears repeating: 'There are always only shades of certainty when these criteria are applied to particular texts.'[96] We should not regard them as scientifically precise laws that will guide us into all truth, but as rules of thumb whose 'value lies in assisting the judgment of relative probability'.[97] Neither should we regard the application of these criteria as an objective mechanical process which discretely runs through each test and determines its specific contribution to the whole. But keeping with the conviction that exegesis is more an art than a science, these criteria should be understood to work together dynamically in mutually illuminating harmony, yielding a sense of probability which serves as the basis of judgment.

This should not be taken to mean that these tests cannot be distinguished or that they are all of equal importance. Indeed, two in particular stand out as especially weighty. The most important tests for us are 'volume,' (especially its aspects of verbal, syntactical, and structural coherence) and 'thematic coherence'. These two tests will bear the bulk of methodological weight in identifying and interpreting allusions in our study. I will not necessarily use these criteria explicitly in my treatments of individual texts, but they are to be understood as implicitly undergirding my judgments.[98] Still, we might draw upon any of the criteria as they become relevant to the discussion. Upon applying these criteria to a proposed allusion we may then appraise it as clear, probable, possible, or improbable,[99] although we will not necessarily explicitly employ these designations.

---

94.   Hays, *Echoes*, 31.
95.   Hays, *Echoes*, 31.
96.   Hays, *Echoes*, 32.
97.   Thompson, *Clothed*, 36.
98.   Hays, *Echoes*, 29.
99.   This scale is largely adapted from Beale, *Revelation*, 78, who provides helpful definitions for the first three categories mentioned above and rightly adds that 'a reasonable explanation of authorial motive should be given if a proposed OT allusion is to be accepted as clear or probable', a requirement I would consider to be implicit in our criterion of thematic coherence. Cf. Thompson's (*Clothed*, 36) scale.

It is important to remember that it is only in the context of detailed exegesis that these tests can be applied with any real success. Indeed, the most important control for the interpretive activity of the researcher in relation to seeking to determine Paul's authorial intention is coherence with the text of Romans 9.1–9, first in its immediate context and then in its broad context. In order to avoid offering imaginative misreadings of Paul that amount to little more than ingenious eisegesis founded upon our own creativity, we must anchor our exegesis in the coherence of our proposals concerning Old Testament background to the text of Romans. However, as Ross Wagner has well said, 'There is, finally, no "scientific" method of interpretation that can guarantee that the coherence – or incoherence – we find is not at least partially constructed by the interpreter.'[100] The best that we can do is to try and take account of our own presuppositions and preunderstanding in order to give the text priority and attempt to understand it on its own terms.[101] Of course, the internal consistency of our argumentation also serves as a control, as does interaction with previous scholarship. Ultimately, submission of one's work to the scrutiny of other interpreters must stand as the final safeguard for intertextual exegesis.[102]

Finally, we should acknowledge that it is sometimes claimed that Paul's audiences would not have benefited from the original contexts of his biblical allusions because of an alleged lack of scriptural knowledge among them.[103] But the important thing for exegeting Paul is determining his intention, and scholars have typically taken Paul to assume that his audiences knew the Scriptures well based on his use of the Old Testament.[104] Indeed, it seems likely that Paul would have expected

100. Wagner, *Heralds*, 32–33 n. 113.

101. See Osborne, *Spiral*, 411–15, for a sketch of controls for both exegesis in general and also for specifically working with one's presuppositions in exegesis.

102. Cf. Wagner, *Heralds*, 33 n. 113.

103. See C.D. Stanley, '"Pearls Before Swine": Did Paul's Audiences Understand His Biblical Quotations?', *NovT* 41, 2 (1999), 124–44. For an extended defense of the possibility of Paul intending his allusions as pointers to their original contexts, see Abasciano, 'Paul's Use', 33–49 (n. 113 critiques Stanley).

104. According to Stanley, 'Pearls', 124–25. Specifically in relation to Romans, cf. Hays, *Echoes*, 29, 201 n. 92; Wagner, *Heralds*, 35; J.D.G. Dunn, *Romans* (WBC, 38; 2 vols.; Dallas: Word, 1988), 1542 (citing Wilckens). This perception of Paul's assumptions about his audience is so certain that Stanley (124–25, 142–44) is actually forced to suggest that Paul misjudged their reader competence in order to argue that they could not understand his biblical quotations. It is also possible that Paul was aware of differing levels of scriptural competence among his readers and

(1) many in his audience to be sufficiently learned in the Scriptures so as to consider his biblical allusions in light of their original contexts, and (2) that those without the requisite scriptural knowledge could gain it through communal processes that would come into play around Paul's letter.[105] Moreover, the best guide we have to Paul's assumptions about his audience is the text of Romans, which would lead us to posit scripturally astute readers based on the abundant scriptural allusions and argumentation. Surely Paul's own discourse is a more reliable guide to understanding him and his readers than hypothetical reconstructions about what was possible for him to intend or conjecture about supposed reader competencies.[106]

Therefore, the possibility of investigating Paul's allusions as pointers to their original contexts is not to be cast aside a priori based on an assumption about Paul's original readers as scripturally ignorant. It remains for the present study to investigate what Paul in fact did in each and every instance of allusion in Romans 9.1–9. This in the end will be the strongest evidence for how Paul meant his allusions to be taken. Our findings will confirm Hays' assumption that Romans

> is most fruitfully understood when it is read as an intertextual conversation between Paul and the voice of Scripture, that powerful ancestral presence with which Paul grapples. Scripture broods over this letter, calls Paul to account, speaks through him; Paul, groping to give voice to his gospel, finds in Scripture the language to say what must be said, labors to win the blessing of Moses and the prophets.[107]

---

structured his discourse accordingly; cf. R.T. France, 'The Formula-Quotations of Matthew 2 and the Problem of Communication', in Beale (ed.), *Right Doctrine*, 114–34; Hays, *Echoes*, 21–22; Wagner, *Heralds*, 34–36; Stanley, 'Pearls', 139–41.

105.   See Abasciano, 'Paul's Use', 33–49.
106.   Cf. Porter, 'The Use', 95.
107.   Hays, *Echoes*, 35.

Chapter 2

INTRODUCTION TO ROMANS 9–11

The purpose of this chapter is to prepare for a close reading of Rom. 9.1–9 through consideration of Romans 9–11 as its broader context. This brief look at introductory issues related to Romans 9–11 will keep our investigation from being impeded by its narrow focus and give us greater insight into Rom. 9.1–9.[1]

2.1. *The Church in Rome*[2]

In 49 C.E. the Emperer Claudius expelled the Jews from Rome because of synagogue riots,[3] probably instigated by Christian preaching.[4] This act against the Jews has been the focus of much debate, and is

---

1. For what is probably now the most extensive introduction to Romans 9–11, see Abasciano, 'Paul's Use', 50–137; cf. Bell, *Provoked*, 44–79. Mohrmann, 'Collisions', ch. 1, provides a recent survey of studies on Romans 10, while W. Sanday and A.C. Headlam, *A Critical and Exegetical Commentary on the Epistle to the Romans* (ICC; New York: Charles Scribner's Sons, 1895), 269–75, give a broad-ranging survey of interpretations of Romans 9 to around the turn of the last century. On patristic interpretation, see P. Gorday, *Principles of Patristic Exegesis: Romans 9–11 in Origen, John Chrysostom, and Augustine* (New York; Toronto: Mellen, 1983).

2. See J.A. Fitzmyer, *Romans: A New Translation with Introduction and Commentary* (AB, 33; New York: Doubleday, 1993), 25–39, for a helpful, orderly, and concise survey of Rome and Roman Christianity at the time of Paul's writing.

3. There is some debate over whether there was an expulsion in 49 C.E., but this is the standard view and almost certainly correct. See J.C. Walters, *Ethnic Issues in Paul's Letter to the Romans: Changing Self-Definitions in Earliest Roman Christianity* (Valley Forge, PA: Trinity Press International, 1993), 51–52; Fitzmyer, *Romans*, 32; Dunn, *Romans*, 1.xlix.

4. So the vast majority, e.g., W. Wiefel, 'The Jewish Community of Ancient Rome and the Origins of Roman Christianity', in K.P. Donfried (ed.), *The Romans Debate* (Peabody, MA: Hendrickson, rev. edn., 1991), 85–101. Fitzmyer, *Romans*,

considered by some to be the key to understanding the historical back-ground of Romans as well as Paul's purpose and occasion in writing because of the tensions allegedly created by the return of Jewish Christians to a thoroughly Gentile church after Claudius' death in 54 C.E.[5] But while it must have exercised considerable influence on the contours of the Christian community, there is no need to rely on the Claudian expulsion as the definitive influence on Roman Christianity, for it would only have exacerbated a situation which was bound to have developed. It seems highly probable that, just as in the rest of the Gentile world, the church was bound to see a Gentile majority and a Jewish minority,[6] as the address of the letter suggests was actually the case (Rom. 1.5–6, 13; 11.13; 16; cf. 15.15–19).[7] As elsewhere this would make for tension and conflict between Jews and Gentiles in the church, all the more so since there was probably a significant minority of Jews possess-ing power and influence far out of proportion to its size,[8] as suggested by the type of evidence that has led some scholars to argue for a Jewish majority in the church,[9] such as the heavy Scripture use and concentra-tion on 'Jewish issues' throughout the letter.

31, concisely states the case for the dominant view. Against it, see esp. M.D. Nanos, *The Mystery of Romans: The Jewish Context of Paul's Letter* (Minneapolis: Fortress, 1996), 378–80.

5. E.g., Wiefel, 'Jewish Community'; Walters, *Ethnic Issues*, esp. 56–66. See J.C. Miller, *The Obedience of Faith, the Eschatological People of God, and the Purpose of Romans* (SBLDS, 177; Atlanta: SBL, 2000), 110–11, for a full descrip-tion of the typical reconstruction and a bibliography of challenges against it. For a nuanced view of the Claudian expulsion, see Abasciano, 'Paul's Use', 52–56.

6. It is admittedly a generalization to depict the groups involved as Jewish vs. Gentile; see Abasciano, 'Paul's Use', 56–57.

7. Now the view of the great majority of scholars, at least in terms of the address of the epistle. See e.g., W.G. Kümmel, *Introduction to the New Testament* (Nashville: Abingdon, rev. edn., 1975), 309–11; Dunn, *Romans*, 1.xliv–liv; Bell, *Provoked*, 68–72, 76–78; Nanos, *Mystery*, 75–84. We should note that there can be a difference between the make-up of Paul's historical audience and his rhetorical addressees, also known as the implied audience. We should beware of being too hasty in conclusions from Paul's rhetorical address, which may seek to reach Gentiles by addressing Jews and vice versa.

8. On the considerable influence of the Jewish minority, see Abasciano, 'Paul's Use', 55–56.

9. Those who favor a predominantly Jewish audience (again, at least in terms of address) include F. Watson, *Paul, Judaism and the Gentiles: A Sociological Approach* (SNTSMS, 56; Cambridge: Cambridge University Press, 1986), 103–104 (cf. 162); A.J. Guerra, *Romans and the Apologetic Tradition: The Purpose, Genre and Audience of Paul's Letter* (SNTSMS, 81; Cambridge: Cambridge University Press, 1995);

There does appear to have been conflict in Rome over the observance of Jewish ceremonial Law such as Sabbath, holy days, and food regulations (ch. 14). How contentious the situation became is impossible to know, but Paul's letter seems to reflect a situation marked by tension and conflict, but not all-out war. That is, the church appears to have managed a degree of unity which allowed for coexistence, interaction, and even corporate worship.[10]

It is now a matter of scholarly consensus that Romans was addressed to a concrete historical situation.[11] Even if Paul's greater purpose lay in 'his own consciousness and ministry',[12] the content of Romans was largely determined by issues in Rome, which he surely knew about given his connection to people at this large, highly visible and (probably) premier Gentile church, located in the capital of the Empire.[13]

2.2. *The Purpose of Romans 9–11*

In harmony with the recent trend of regarding Romans 9–11 as the climax of the theological argument of the epistle, the purpose of Romans itself comes to its most urgent theological expression in these

H. Räisänen, 'Römer 9–11: Analyse eines geistigen Ringens', *ANRW* 2.25.4 (1987), 2891–939 (2898). Cf. Fitzmyer, *Romans*, 32–33.

10. See C.C. Caragounis, 'From Obscurity to Prominence: The Development of the Roman Church between Romans and *1 Clement*', in K.P. Donfried and P. Richardson (eds.), *Judaism and Christianity in First-Century Rome* (Grand Rapids: Eerdmans, 1998), 245–79 (252–60), for a provocative argument against the theory 'that Roman Christianity consisted entirely of separate house groups' (259). For a more moderate view, see L. Lung-kwong, *Paul's Purpose in Writing Romans: The Upbuilding of a Jewish and Gentile Christian Community in Rome* (Jian Dao Dissertation Series, 6; Bible and Literature, 4; Hong Kong: Alliance Bible Seminary, 1998). Cf. W.L. Lane, 'Social Perspectives on Roman Christianity during the Formative Years from Nero to Nerva: Romans, Hebrews, 1 Clement', in Donfried and Richardson (eds.), *Judaism*, 196–244, who emphasizes the importance of separate house churches for understanding Roman Christianity.

11. Donfried (ed.), *Romans*, lxix. The exact date of Romans is not important for us to determine. It is enough to recognize with most interpreters that Paul wrote from Corinth sometime in the mid to late 50s C.E.

12. R. Longenecker, 'Prolegomena to Paul's Use of Scripture in Romans', *BBR* 7 (1997), 145–68 (153).

13. On the largeness of the Roman church, see e.g., M. Black, *Romans* (NCB; London: Marshall, Morgan, and Scott, 1973), 22–23; Fitzmyer, *Romans*, 35.

chapters. Scholars have made a number of suggestions for Paul's purpose in writing Romans,[14] and even more for the purpose of Romans 9–11.[15] The variety of proposals advanced suggests that the very popular general view championed by Wedderburn that Paul had several reasons for writing Romans is correct,[16] an approach that should be applied to Romans 9–11 as well. This does not mean, however, that every real purpose that can be discerned was of equal importance. Once Paul had a compelling reason to write, then all sorts of aims would come to bear, many of which would work towards fulfilling that larger goal, but not all of which are necessarily closely connected to it.

Only Paul's upcoming mission to Spain can explain why he wrote to Rome. He wanted 'to use Rome as a base of operations in the Western Mediterranean, much as he had used Antioch (originally) as a base in the East'.[17] As a result, Paul must visit Rome, something he had wanted to do for some time anyway, especially for mutual fellowship and to strengthen the Roman Christians through his preaching of the gospel (Rom. 1.10–15; 15.22–24). But this desire to go to Rome was not enough to bring him there; it was only when he would go to Spain in pursuit of his missionary call that he would finally make the trip on his way to this church he had never visited (15.23–24). In preparation for his visit, Paul writes a letter of introduction crafted to help procure the Roman church's support for his mission to the West. But Paul's gospel is controversial, and there is disunity and tension among the Roman Christians.

Several of the purposes of Romans arise out of Paul's hope of enlisting the Roman Christians' support when he arrives. Romans is in fact a letter of introduction. Accordingly, it gives a somewhat systematic presentation of Paul's gospel, for the church must know what he

---

14. See Donfried (ed.), *Romans*; L. Morris, *The Epistle to the Romans* (Grand Rapids: Eerdmans, 1988), 7–18; A.J.M. Wedderburn, *The Reasons for Romans* (Minneapolis: Fortress, 1991); Lung-kwong, *Purpose*. Miller, *Obedience*, gives a recent description of the Romans Debate in his opening chapter.

15. There have been at least twenty suggestions; see Abasciano, 'Paul's Use', 67–70.

16. Wedderburn, *Reasons*. Miller, *Obedience*, 14–16, takes issue with Wedderburn's multiple reasons approach, arguing unsuccessfully for a single aim; see Abasciano, 'Paul's Use', 64 n. 37.

17. N.T. Wright, *The Climax of the Covenant: Christ and the Law in Pauline Theology* (Edinburgh: T&T Clark, 1992), 234.

preaches and approve. They must also be unified behind his gospel. Hence, the presentation of Paul's gospel with an emphasis on the unity of Jews and Gentiles to a church suffering from tension and conflict over Jew/Gentile relations. Paul had to reckon with these two basic positions (and everything in between) in his presentation of the gospel to the Romans.

Certainly Paul wrote to shape the Roman church pastorally according to the will of God and his own apostolate and gospel, but his overarching concern is that the Christians at Rome be unified behind his gospel for his mission to Spain.[18] Therefore, Paul's presentation of his gospel comes with an emphasis on his missionary practice – Ἰουδαίῳ τε πρῶτον καὶ Ἕλληνι (Rom. 1.16; cf. 2.10). He must lay out the rationale for this controversial and apparently paradoxical missionary practice, bringing correction of a sort to both basic theological camps in Rome. 'Against' the Gentile majority and their (potential) pride, Paul's gospel insists that God has not written off the Jews and demands that mission include outreach to Jews, and more than that, prioritizes them![19] 'Against' the Jewish minority Paul insists that the gospel is the power of God for salvation for all, whether Jew or Gentile without distinction, and this apart from observance of traditional Jewish identity markers. The converts Paul wins will not be required to live like Jews in order to be Christians. Paul pursues this purpose most directly in Romans 9–11, where he brings it to a theological climax.[20]

On a literary level Romans 9–11 completes the exposition of the theme of the epistle (1.16–17), a summary statement of the gospel, by explaining the priority of the Jew and by defending the gospel Paul has presented at length against its most compelling objection – how the Christian gospel can be the fulfillment of Judaism/the Old Testament and its promises to Israel when the vast majority of Jews had rejected Christ and were therefore excluded from God's salvation and promises to them. He defends the covenant faithfulness of God. This is at the same time a defense of the gospel, for the gospel is essentially equivalent to the righteousness/faithfulness of God, or more precisely, it is its

18. Cf. Miller, *Obedience*, 19.

19. Insightfully, Wright, *Climax*, 234, has seen that one of Paul's purposes in Romans was to argue for a mission to Gentiles which includes Jews. Here we add that Paul's mission actually prioritized Jews.

20. Cf. Wright, *Climax*, 234.

content or the way God has effected his righteousness/faithfulness. To borrow the title of N.T. Wright's influential study, the gospel of Jesus Christ is 'the climax of the covenant'.

2.3. *The Theme of Romans 9–11*

When we turn to the theme of Romans 9–11, we again find a multitude of suggestions.[21] Out of these, the solid consensus is that the theme of Romans 9–11 is the faithfulness of God to his word/promises to Israel.[22] Many would specify this theme textually as contained in 9.6a. We would concur on both counts.

Most suggestions for the theme of Romans 9–11 are legitimately present in the text, and a few may rightfully be called the theme in a general sense. Indeed, many scholars may be found advocating more than one suggestion. Romans 9–11 is so complex that it may be described in a variety of ways. But the most appropriate is God's faithfulness to his word to Israel (9.6a).

One theme surely present in the text is that of the unbelief of Israel/her rejection of Jesus Christ. Indeed, this factor is 'almost universally held by exegetes' to be the background of Romans 9–11, the cause of Paul's grief, and the cause of the problem he addresses.[23] The few objections to this presupposition notwithstanding,[24] this stance is justified and unassailable. Often, this fact is stated as part of the theme so that what calls God's faithfulness into question is Israel's unbelief or rejection of Christ. But it is this assumption which must be questioned rather than the fact itself.

Many assume that what causes Paul's grief is Israel's unbelief. This is undoubtedly true on some level, but it is not what Paul addresses and it is not what he laments in the text. The actual problem he addresses

21.   There have been at least twenty-five. For these, see Abasciano, 'Paul's Use', 71–75.

22.   See e.g., C.E.B. Cranfield, *A Critical and Exegtical Commentary on the Epistle to the Romans*, (ICC; 2 vols.; Edinburgh: T&T Clark, 1975–79), 473; U. Wilckens, *Der Brief an die Römer*, II: Röm 6–11 (EKKNT, 2; Zürich: Benziger/ Neukirchen: Neukirchener Verlag, 1980), 181; Räisänen, 'Römer 9–11', 2893; Dunn, *Romans*, 518, 539; T.R. Schreiner, *Romans* (BECNT, 6; Grand Rapids: Baker, 1998), 491.

23.   L. Gaston, 'Israel's Enemies in Pauline Theology', in L. Gaston, *Paul and the Torah* (Vancouver: University of British Columbia Press, 1987), 80–99 (92).

24.   Gaston, 'Enemies', 92; M.A. Getty, 'Paul and the Salvation of Israel: A Perspective on Romans 9–11', *CBQ* 50 (1988), 456–69 (459).

is God's rejection of Israel rather than their rejection of Christ; he addresses their exclusion from salvation (e.g., 9.3, 8, 22–10.1). This point is subtle, but its significance is great. Just as a slight mistake in the direction set at the beginning of a journey can result in landing far off the original mark, so in exegesis. And so is the case with identifying Israel's unbelief as the problem posed to God's faithfulness. Practically, if it is the unbelief of Israel which is the problem Paul addresses, then Romans 9–11 can tend to be read as seeking to explain Israel's unbelief and God's responsibility for it. On the other hand, if it is rather God's rejection of Israel that is the issue, then, with most interpreters,[25] Paul is defending God's response to Israel's unbelief.

The theme of the faithfulness of God's word obviously contributes to the argumentative/apologetic purpose of Romans 9–11 discussed above. The exclusion of Israel from salvation throws God's faithfulness into question. How could he reject and condemn those he promised to save, and at the same time save those he never made any such promise to? As Ziesler puts it, 'if historical Israel was the recipient of God's promises to Abraham (vv. 4–5), and if God has now rejected her in favour of a new and multi-racial people, does that not impugn the faithfulness and reliability of God?'[26]

But how does the theme of God's faithfulness pursue the practical purposes of obtaining both the unity of Jews and Gentiles in the Roman church and support for Paul's missionary procedure of going to Jews first yet including Gentiles? By completing the development of the letter's theme with this subject, Paul shows that the ethnic component of the former is *necessary* to maintain the integrity of God's character. This provides defense for Paul's missionary methodology and even *demands* support for it. Likewise, the theme of chs. 9–11 promotes the unity of the Roman Christians by linking the truth of God's faithfulness to both an honored position for Jews and the inclusion of Gentiles apart from ceremonial Law-observance. It is probably the ideal theme to accomplish Paul's goals, for it grounds Paul's gospel and missionary practice in God's faithfulness and represents them as part of its very outworking.

25. According to O. Hofius, 'Das Evangelium und Israel: Erwägungen zu Römer 9–11', *ZTK* 83 (1986), 297–324 (303–304).
26. J. Ziesler, *Paul's Letter to the Romans* (TPINTC; Philadelphia: Trinity Press International, 1989), 234.

2.4. The Literary Placement of Romans 9–11[27]

The vast majority of scholars today have rightly rejected the notion that Romans 9–11 is merely an appendix to Romans 1–8.[28] The inherent connection to the rest of the letter is simply too great to ignore.[29] Indeed, there is a strong consensus that it is an integral, necessary part of the letter.[30] But we should go further and join with the many who now consider Romans 9–11 to be the climax of the theological argument (chs. 1–11).[31] It is not that Romans 1–8 are merely preparatory for chs. 9–11. Nor is it that Romans 1–8 could not logically stand on their own with some sense of satisfaction. It is more that Romans 9–11 contain the height of what Paul wants to say. They contain the most

---

27. For significant treatments of the placement of Romans 9–11 see H.-M. Lübking, *Paulus und Israel im Römerbrief: Eine Untersuchung zu Römer 9–11* (Frankfurt: Lang, 1986), 21–50; C. Müller, *Gottes Gerechtigkeit und Gottes Volk: Eine Untersuchung zu Römer 9–11* (FRLANT, 86; Göttingen: Vandenhoeck & Ruprecht, 1964), 49–57; E.E. Johnson, *The Function of Apocalyptic and Wisdom Traditions in Romans 9–11* (SBLDS, 109; Atlanta: Scholars, 1989), 110–23; R. Scroggs, 'Paul as Rhetorician: Two Homilies in Romans 1–11', in R. Hamerton-Kelly and R. Scroggs (eds.), *Jews, Greeks, and Christians: Religious Cultures in Late Antiquity* (Festschrift W.D. Davies; trans. J. Smith; SJLA, 21; Leiden: Brill, 2nd edn., 1976), 271–98; J. Cottrell, *Romans*, II (The College Press NIV Commentary; Joplin, Missouri: College Press, 1998), 34–39; Abasciano, 'Paul's Use', 80–87.

28. See D.J.-S. Chae, *Paul as Apostle to the Gentiles: His Apostolic Self-Awareness and Its Influence on the Soteriological Argument in Romans* (Paternoster Biblical and Theological Monographs; Carlisle, U.K.: Paternoster Press, 1997), 221; Donfried (ed.), *Romans*, lxx.

29. See esp. Lübking, *Paulus*, 21–50, for demonstration of connections between Romans 9–11 and 1–8. Cf. more recently, A. Reichert, *Der Römerbrief als Gratwanderung: Eine Untersuchung zur Abfassungsproblematik* (FRLANT, 194; Göttingen: Vandenhoeck & Ruprecht, 2001), 149–66.

30. See e.g., Ziesler, *Romans*, 37–39; P. Stuhlmacher, *Paul's Letter to the Romans: A Commentary* (trans. S.J. Hafemann; Louisville, KY: Westminster/John Knox, 1994), 144; Cottrell, *Romans*, 35–37; U. Luz, *Das Geschichtsverständnis des Paulus* (BevT, 49. Munich: Kaiser, 1968), 19–21.

31. See e.g., Wright, *Climax*, 234; Dunn, *Romans*, 519–20; Hays, *Echoes*, 63; B. Noack, 'Current and Backwater in the Epistle to the Romans' *ST* 19 (1965), 155–66. Lübking's (*Paulus*, 12) assertion that few have viewed Romans 9–11 as the climax of the epistle is incorrect, as is the claim of Chae, *Paul*, 215, and S.R. Haynes, 'Recovering the Real Paul: Theology and Exegesis in Romans 9–11', *Ex Auditu* 4 (1988), 70–84 (71), that the majority or consensus views Romans 9–11 as the climax or center of the epistle. N. Richardson, *Paul's Language About God* (JSNTSup, 99; Sheffield: Sheffield Academic Press, 1994), 26, is right to speak of a scholarly consensus concerning the integral role of Romans 9–11 in the epistle.

relevant statement of his theology for his practical purposes with respect to the Roman Christians and his paraenesis to them.

There is a solid, immediate connection between Romans 8 and 9–11 which carries great rhetorical power in its dramatic change of mood and tone.[32] For Romans 8 brings Paul's explication of the gospel as the fulfillment of God's promises to Israel to glorious climax. Yet, the Jewish people as a whole remain separated from the promises and salvation of the gospel. The greater Paul's ecstasy, the greater the challenge to the veracity of God's word and the gospel.

We must remember that the Roman Christians would have heard Romans 9–11 just before Paul heads into practical exhortation to unity in chs. 12–16, an implicit appeal for support of his gospel and mission to Spain in ch. 15, and an explicit appeal for support of his trip to Jerusalem, symbolic of Jew/Gentile unity and the acceptance/rejection of his ministry by Jewish Christianity,[33] in 15.25–32. We would also do well to remember that Gentiles were the majority. Consequently, Paul saves the most objectionable aspect of his gospel and missionary theology till the end of his argument so that he can argue from a position of strength, having presented material which would be readily accepted by the Gentile majority.

All of this is why Romans 9–11 is more epistolary in character than most of chs. 1–8, as has been noticed by various scholars.[34] Paul is getting to the heart of his most immediate practical concern while he is still engaged in his theological argument, which provides the rationale

32. Indeed, the great display of emotion in 9.1–5 points to an added factor, often noted, which moved Paul to deal with the subject of God and Israel – his great love for his people. In contrast to the traditional difficulty felt by scholars in connecting Romans 8 and 9, A.A. Das, *Paul, the Law, and the Covenant* (Peabody, MA: Hendrickson, 2001), 96, can now state confidently, 'Romans 9–11 flow naturally from the closing thoughts of Rom 8'.

33. On the importance of the collection to Paul, see e.g., G. Bornkamm, 'The Letter to the Romans as Paul's Last Will and Testament', in Donfried (ed.), *Romans*, 16–28 (17–18).

34. N.A. Dahl, 'The Future of Israel', in N.A. Dahl, *Studies in Paul* (Minneapolis: Augsburg, 1977), 137–58 (140–42); R. Badenas, *Christ the End of the Law: Romans 10.4 in Pauline Perspective* (JSNTSup, 10; Sheffield: *JSOT*, 1985), 89, and in a somewhat different way by C.H. Dodd, *The Epistle of Paul to the Romans* (MNTC; New York: Harper and Bros., 1932), 148–50; Scroggs, 'Rhetorician', and others who see a sermon here, an unlikely suggestion because the passage bears all the marks of having been crafted specifically for the Roman Christians. See Dunn's (*Romans*, 520) balanced view.

for his ensuing paraenesis. Therefore his tone becomes more paraenetic as he transitions from a theological emphasis to an exhortatory one. In short, Paul places Romans 9–11 where he does because these chapters are the climax of his theological argument, and this because they are the most relevant theology for advancing his purposes.[35]

2.5. *The Structure and Literary Character of Romans 9–11*

Barrett describes the typical view of Romans 9–11 well: 'after a predestinarian account of the fall of Israel in 9. 1–29, 9. 30–10. 21 provides a complementary account of the same lapse in which the fault is laid squarely at Israel's door, and in turn leads to a synthesis in chapter 11 in which Paul states his hope for Israel's future'.[36] But I would argue that the logic of Paul's argument in Romans 9–11 runs like this: Paul expresses his concern for and commitment to Israel in light of the problem of Israel's rejection/Gentile inclusion, which calls God's faithfulness into question (9.1–5). This elicits Paul's denial of the implicit charge against the veracity of God's word: God's promises to Israel have not failed (9.6a). This statement functions as Paul's thesis/theme. Everything that follows, with the exception of the climactic ending doxology (11.33–36), supports this assertion. Paul argues chiastically[37] and midrashically[38] in three movements that ground 9.6a: God's word has not failed because:

(A)   the Israel God made promises to is not ethnic Israel, but the Israel of God's call, fulfilled now in the Church of Jews and Gentiles, the eschatological messianic community (9.6b–33).

---

35. Cf. N.A. Dahl, 'The Missionary Theology in the Epistle to the Romans', in Dahl, *Studies*, 70–94 (86); Dunn, *Romans*, 519.

36. C.K. Barrett, 'Romans 9.30–10.21: Fall and Responsibility of Israel', in L. de Lorenzi (ed.), *Die Israelfrage nach Röm 9–11* (Monographische Reihe von <<Benedictina>> Biblisch-ökumenische Abteilung, 3; Rome: Abtei von St Paul vor den Mauern, 1977), 99–121 (99–100).

37. On chiasm in Romans 9–11, see Abasciano, 'Paul's Use', 90–93.

38. See Abasciano, 'Paul's Use', 95–97, where it is argued that Paul structures each main section of his argument on citations from the Torah, which are then elucidated by quotations mainly from other sections of Scripture. We should note that the structure of Romans 9–11 is also broadly analogous to a lament psalm (Hays, *Echoes*, 64).

(B)   Israel has failed the promises while God has been faithful to
           bring them to fruition in the gospel, giving Israel every oppor-
           tunity to participate in the fulfilled promises (9.30–10.21).[39]

(A')   God has not rejected ethnic Israel *per se* from potential inclu-
           sion in the community of promise, but is at work to bring them
           to salvation as he works for the salvation of the true Israel of
           Jews and Gentiles (11.1–32).

The first and final members of the chiasm come together in the concept
of Israel, the first denying an ethnic definition and the last affirming
the salvation of true Israel in fulfillment of the promise. The whole
argument erupts into praise and glory to God, shifting the logical weight
of the whole onto his awesome wisdom, power, and majesty (11.33–36).
Each of the three main sections provides a separate but complementary
defense of God's faithfulness to his word. The central element (the
gospel and its proclamation) of this chiasm reveals the means by which
the outer elements (the call and salvation of the true Israel) are accom-
plished, giving a measure of logical priority to the latter. Yet 9.30–10.21
plays an important role by reflecting Paul's purpose of recommending
his gospel ministry in chs. 9–11 and revealing that the gospel he preaches
is in fact the fulfillment of God's promises to Israel rather than their
undoing.

   Given the focus of this investigation, the structure of Romans 9
demands closer scrutiny. There is quite a variety of scholarly opinion on
this question.[40] I submit that the most appropriate structure for Romans
9 is based on the rhetorical questions located in 9.14, 19 (together with
the resumption of the diatribe), and 30. At each juncture, the οὖν clearly
indicates an inference being taken up from what precedes. These rhetorical features advance Paul's argument to its next stage, yielding the
following logical structure:[41]

9.1–5   Introduction: The problem of God's rejection of Israel in
           light of his promises to her.

9.6–13   The Israel God made promises to is not ethnic Israel, but
           the Israel of God's call/faith.

---

   39.   The grouping of 9.30–33 with both chs. 9 and 10 is due to its complex
function.

   40.   See Abasciano, 'Paul's Use', 98.

   41.   Cf. J.W. Aageson, 'Scripture and Structure in the Development of the
Argument in Romans 9–11', *CBQ* 48 (1986), 265–89.

9.14–18   God is just in his call/election because, as God, he has the right to dispense mercy and judgment on whom he will (i.e. on those who believe and disbelieve respectively).

9.19–29   God is just in his bestowal of mercy and judgment (based on faith and unbelief respectively) because he is the Creator God who has acted in faithfulness to his word to bless the vessels of his mercy.

9.30–33   While Gentiles have attained righteousness by faith, Israel has been rejected because she has pursued righteousness by works rather than faith.

Logically, 9.6–13 is primary, and the following sections support it. More specifically, 9.14–18 supports it by defending God's justice in the election it describes. Then, 9.19–29 supports 9.14–18 by defending the principle it has enunciated to support 9.6–13. All of this is in the context of God's rejection of ethnic Israel and calling of the Church of Jews and Gentiles, especially (but not exclusively) revealed by 9.19–29. Then 9.30–33 provides a summarizing conclusion that points forward to the next stage of the argument in 10.1–21.

Just as Romans 9–11, ch. 9 also has both a chiastic and scripturally structured character in addition to the governing logical structure. Aletti has convincingly demonstrated a concentric structure for 9.6–29: [42]

A = 6–9   *Israel* v.6 (2^x)
              sperma v.7 (2^x).8
  B = 10–13   *agapan* v.13
    C = 14–18   *eleein* v.15 (2^x).16.18
                    thelein v.[16].18 (2^x)
                    dynamis v.17
                    endeiknysthai v.17
    C' = 19–24   *thelein* v.22
                     endeiknysthai v.22
                     to dynaton v.22
                     to eleos v.23
  B' = 25–26   *agapan* v.25 (2^x)
A' = 27–29   *Israel* v.27 (2^x)
                 sperma v.29

42.   J.-N. Aletti, 'L'argumentation paulinienne en Rm 9', *Bib* 68 (1987), 41–56 (42). Cf. Dunn, *Romans*, 537, whose proposal can be used to fill out Aletti's further. See J.D. Harvey, *Listening to the Text: Oral Patterning in Paul's Letters* (Grand Rapids: Baker, 1998), 150–51, for a different approach.

This places the Israel that is the seed of Abraham at the poles of the chiasm, with God's covenantal love closely associated as the next rung. Thus God's call of his true covenant people stands at the outer layer of the chiasm while the central section defends God's justice in the exercise of his will and power to embrace whom he will (on the basis of faith/promise rather than ancestry/works/Law) as his covenant people and to extend his mercy and fulfilled promises to them. The pervasive presence of καλέω (9.7, 12, 24, 25, 26), which encompasses most of the chiasm, underscores that the justice of God's call and election of the new community as his covenant people (and the concomitant rejection of ethnic Israel) is the issue at stake in Romans 9.[43]

But how does this chiastic structure relate to the logical structure we have identified? They are complementary. The logical structure is primary – content takes precedence over form – and states that God's word has not failed because only those who believe in Christ are enjoying the fulfillment of Israel's promises, for he has called/regarded only those who have faith in Christ as his true covenant people (i.e., Israel) and has always recognized true Israel on the basis of faith and promise. In terms of the chiasm, God has set his covenant love upon those he regards as true Israel, Abraham's seed. It is this call or reckoning that is defended in the central section. Thus, the central section in this case supports the ends. But it is central because the burden of Paul's argument is this defense. Moreover, the faithfulness of God's word is also his righteousness. So there is a sort of equivalence between 9.6a and the function of Aletti's central section (9.14–24).

Turning to the role of Scripture in the structure of Romans 9, we may identify it as a midrash.[44] Gen. 21.12 functions as the primary Torah text,

43. Aletti, 'L'argumentation,' 45, argues that καλέω is absent from the central section because the question of God's justice refers to those who are not called. But the pervasiveness of καλέω and cognates in the chapter must still be accounted for, and it is clearly God's call which calls God's justice into question in the logical development of Paul's argument.

44. See W.R. Stegner, 'Romans 9:6–29 – A Midrash', *JSNT* 22 (1984), 37–52; Ellis, 'How', 203–204; idem, *Prophecy and Hermeneutic in Early Christianity* (WUNT, 2.18; Tübingen: Mohr Siebeck, 1978), 155. For criticisms of Stegner, see Hübner, *Schriftgebrauch*, 35–36; Aletti, 'L'argumentation', 45 n. 14; Räisänen, 'Römer 9–11', 2897–98 n. 38; Dunn, *Romans*, 537; and in defense of Stegner, see Abasciano, 'Paul's Use', 101–102.

and Gen. 18.10, 14 as the secondary text in a fashion similar to the form of the later rabbinic proem midrash.[45] Every Scripture citation in 9.6–29 is linked to one of these passages by one of the key words found in them (καλέω, σπέρμα, or υἱός), whether in their cited wording or in the citation's immediate original context (LXX).[46] Stegner cites Mihaly's observation that 'often, the Rabbis will cite the first half of a verse when the "proof" is contained in the latter part of the text or even in the following or preceding verse'.[47] This midrashic structure gives a discrete form to 9.6–29,[48] and alerts us to the fact that Paul's Pentateuchal texts are primary, carrying the greater weight of his argument.

It should be clear by now that Paul's use of the Old Testament is determinative for the structure of his argument in both Romans 9 and 9–11.[49] Aageson has found that as Paul calls upon Scripture to approach the issues at hand and to substantiate his argument, it actually directs and molds the argument.[50] Rightly he concludes 'that Paul's use of Scripture and the literary structure of the discussion in Romans 9–11 are inseparable'.[51] It is our contention that the connection is even more profound than Aageson realizes.

As for the literary character and rhetorical features of Romans 9–11, Badenas has probably provided the best treatment.[52] He appears to identify oscillation, characterized by back and forth movement and restatement, as the most basic pattern of Pauline thought. This strikes us as a distinctively scriptural manner of expression, and I would suggest, witnesses to Paul's prophetic and apocalyptic orientation in the

---

45.   Stegner, 'Midrash', 38–41; Ellis, 'How', 203–204. More specifically, Ellis, *Prophecy*, 218, finds that the passage 'has affinities with the *yelammedenu*-type discourse in which a question or problem is posed and then answered by a biblical exposition'. Cf. C.K. Stockhausen, '2 Corinthians 3 and the Principles of Pauline Exegesis', in Evans and Sanders (eds.), *Paul*, 143–164; Chae, *Paul*, 228–29.

46.   Stegner, 'Midrash', 40–41.

47.   Stegner, 'Midrash', 41.

48.   Cf. Stegner, 'Midrash', 49.

49.   See Aageson, 'Structure', for a standard demonstration of this assertion.

50.   Aageson, 'Structure', 273, 280. However, I think it unlikely that Paul developed his theology on these matters in the process of dictating Romans 9–11 as Aageson and others would have it.

51.   Aageson, 'Structure', 288.

52.   Badenas, *Christ*, 87–90. For Badenas, the main significance of his analysis is that Paul's argument is cohesive. On the question of the consistency of Paul's argument in Romans 9–11, see Abasciano, 'Paul's Use', 112–17, where I defend Paul's argument as coherent.

composition of these chapters.[53] For recapitulation is a characteristic feature of prophetic and apocalyptic literature.[54]

Paul stands in the biblical tradition of the Old Testament prophets, bringing a word from God to those he addresses. As the Old Testament prophets were covenant messengers who proclaimed the blessings and curses of the covenant to God's people, and often spoke of the eschatological restoration of Israel,[55] so Paul writes in the time of the inaugurated eschatological restoration as the official representative (i.e., apostle) of Jesus the Messiah, the Lord and mediator of the New Covenant. He brings a word of God which defends the faithfulness of God's past word to Israel in his present word to both Jew and Gentile alike in the gospel.

2.6. *Individual and Corporate Perspectives in Romans 9–11*

The nature of Paul's social orientation toward reality is the type of issue that one carries convictions about based on a scholarly impression of first-century culture, the New Testament writings, and other sociohistorical data, and consequently brings this conviction in the form of presupposition to the task of exegesis, a presupposition which has often simply been carried over automatically from individualistic western culture. An individualistic reading of Paul has long been the overwhelmingly dominant approach, until only recently with the appearance of the work of E.P. Sanders and the ensuing 'New Perspective on Paul'.[56] Sanders' work helped to usher in a far greater appreciation of the concept of covenant in Paul's thought resulting in a far greater emphasis on

53. Both strands of orientation have been observed previously. For the prophetic orientation of Paul's stance, see C.A. Evans, 'Paul and the Hermeneutics of "True Prophecy": A Study of Rom 9–11', *Bib* 65 (1984), 560–70; Luz, *Geschichtsverständnis*, 108–09. Paul's apocalyptic stance has been demonstrated by Johnson, *Function*.

54. Beale, *Revelation*, 135–37.

55. On the role of Israel's prophets as covenant messengers, see e.g., D. Stuart, *Hosea-Jonah* (WBC, 31; Waco: Word, 1987), xxxi–xxxii; M.G. Kline, *The Structure of Biblical Authority* (Grand Rapids: Eerdmans, 2nd edn., 1975), 57–62.

56. See esp., E.P. Sanders, *Paul and Palestinian Judaism: A Comparison of Patterns of Religion* (Philadelphia: Fortress, 1977) and Dunn, *Romans*, esp. 1.lxiii–lxxii. While the new perspective has enjoyed a precarious consensus for over a decade, it is now under increasing attack for ironically misrepresenting first-century Judaism. See e.g., D.A. Carson, P.T. O'Brien, and M. Seifrid (eds.), *Justification and Variegated Nomism* (WUNT, 2.140, 181; 2 vols.; Grand Rapids: Baker, 2001–2004) and others listed in Abasciano, 'Paul's Use', 109 n. 213.

corporate over against individual concerns, particularly concerning the relationship of Jews and Gentiles in the Church of Christ.[57] Now, the corporate perspective is widely accepted, and may even be called the firm consensus among New Testament scholars.[58]

This corporate perspective is probably nowhere more in evidence than in Romans 9–11. Yet a few voices have risen up in protest against this tide of corporate appreciation in the interpretation of these chapters.[59] There is some justification for these protests in that many advocates of a corporate perspective seem to advance a vague conception of Paul's corporate concerns which does justice to the importance of group identity and the relationship between Jews and Gentiles, but ignores the implications for individuals that Paul's argument so obviously has.

What is needed is an appreciation of the collectivist character of Paul and his first-century socio-historical milieu that integrates and recognizes the role of the individual.[60] Given the scope of this topic we cannot pursue the question in detail here. We must be content to limit our comments to what we deem important for our present purposes. First, we must recognize that Paul's thought was thoroughly covenantal, focused on the fulfillment of the covenant purposes of God in Christ and their consequences for Jews and Gentiles. Second, for Paul and virtually all Jews (and non-Jews in Mediterranean and Hellenistic culture) of his time, the group was primary and the individual secondary. This is an essential point to grasp for interpretation of Paul and the New

57. G.W. Burnett, *Paul and the Salvation of the Individual* (Biblical Interpretation Series, 57; Leiden: Brill, 2001), 1–6, has documented the increasing emphasis on the group in NT studies. He identifies the other major contributing force in the prevalence of collective over individual concerns as the use of the social sciences in NT studies beginning around the same time as Sanders' study appeared. For a convenient discussion of the present state of the question of the relationship between individual and community in biblical studies, see S. Burkes, *God, Self, and Death: The Shape of Religious Transformation in the Second Temple Period* (JSJSup, 79; Leiden: Brill, 2003), 17–29.

58. See Burnett, *Paul*, 1–2. But S.-W.(A.) Son, *Corporate Elements in Pauline Anthropology: A Study of Selected Terms, Idioms, and Concepts in the Light of Paul's Usage and Background* (Rome: Editrice Pontificio Instituto Biblico, 2001) decries the extreme overemphasis in Pauline scholarship on individual concerns in Paul's thought.

59. See the excursus on election in ch. 4 below. Even Burnett, *Paul*, 18, who seeks to redress an overemphasis on corporate aspects in Paul, regards Rom. 9–12 as solidly collectivist.

60. See Ellis, 'How', 212–13, for the right balance.

Testament. Modern westerners tend to view social reality in the opposite way: the individual is primary and the group secondary. So the individual is viewed as standing on his own, and corporate concerns are subordinated to individual concerns. One's view of the group is conditioned by one's view of the individual so that the group both draws its identity from the individuals in the group and is seen as merely a collection of individuals. But I would contend that Paul's (and his culture's) perspective was essentially corporate. The individual was not viewed as standing on her own, but was seen as embedded in the group to which she belonged. Corporate concerns generally took precedence over individual concerns, and when it did not, this was judged as wrong. Such corporate interest can be seen in Paul's primary concern for love and unity dominant in all his letters. The Pauline corporate perspective found individual identity based in the group rather than vice versa.

None of this means that in first-century Mediterranean and Hellenistic perception the individual was non-existent or that individuals had no self-consciousness or individuality or selfishness. Quite the contrary, a balanced corporate perspective addresses these very individual characteristics in subordinating them to collective concerns. Nor does Paul's corporate perspective mean that he had no interest in individual salvation. He had no interest in the salvation of the individual *as an individual alone*. Rather he was concerned with the individual as embedded in the people of God. Individual concerns are seen as corporately embedded. Once this is seen, then much of what Paul says can and must be applied to the individual – the individual who lives in community and whose identity derives from the covenant people of God. Much of what Paul says – his calls to unity, his exhortations to loving attitudes and actions, and even his description of salvation history – must apply at the individual level. It is individuals who are saved, individuals who love, and individuals who unite. However, for Paul and others of his first-century context, it would not have been individuals considered in and of themselves who so acted and were so treated, but individuals who acted as members of a group and were treated based on their membership in the group. Moreover, as H.C. Kee has so aptly stated, 'Although an act of decision could align the individual with one or another of . . . [the] competing factions within Judaism in this period, the outcome of the decision was a mode of community identity.'[61]

61. H.C. Kee, *Knowing the Truth: A Sociological Approach to New Testament Interpretation* (Minneapolis: Fortress, 1989), 5.

I would argue that here, as with so much of Paul's thought, the Old Testament provides the most suitable background for understanding his perspective. Drawing on the latest research, Burnett has recently described the Old Testament view of social reality well:

> Kaminsky . . . suggests that it is always the case that the 'individual's very self-understanding was derived from his or her relationship to the community'. It is the individual as a member of the community where the emphasis lies, not the individual as an 'autonomous entity before God.' . . . Both [collective emphases and individual responsibility] are important, but individualism only in so far as it is closely related to community life.[62]

This is precisely Paul's view.

With this in mind, and having assessed the broader context of Rom. 9.1–9, we are now ready to conduct a comprehensive intertextual exegesis of these important verses.

---

62.   Burnett, *Paul*, 76, citing J.S. Kaminsky.

Chapter 3

PAUL'S USE OF THE OLD TESTAMENT IN ROMANS 9.1–5

While Romans 9.1–5 is steeped in the Old Testament, there is only one significant allusion to a specific biblical text in these verses. Most commentators recognize an allusion to Exod. 32.32 in Rom. 9.3 even though there is no verbal similarity between the two texts.[1] Indeed, Cranfield considers it highly likely that Paul had Exod. 32.31–32 in mind,[2] Munck was of the opinion that there could 'be no doubt' about the parallel,[3] and Wiles claims that Paul 'must have had' Moses' intercession in mind.[4] Yet the allusion has never been fully explored for the significance it might have for Paul's argument. In accordance with the methodological procedure laid out in chapter one, this chapter will delve into this important background by (1) a detailed exegesis of Exod. 32.32 and its context (chs. 32–34) followed by (2) a comparison of the text of Romans 9.3 with the textual tradition of Exod. 32.32 followed by (3) a survey of the relevant ancient interpretive traditions surrounding Exod. 32.32. Finally, we will (4) examine the New Testament context of Exod. 32.32, which amounts to an exegesis of Rom. 9.1–5 in light of our research into its Old Testament background and associated interpretive traditions. Our analysis will show more clearly than ever before that Paul did allude to Exod. 32.32 and its

1. See D.J. Moo, *The Epistle to the Romans* (NICNT; Grand Rapids: Eerdmans, 1996), 559 n. 21.
2. Cranfield, *Romans*, 454.
3. J. Munck, *Christ and Israel: An Interpretation of Romans 9–11* (Philadelphia: Fortress, 1967), 29.
4. G.P. Wiles, *Paul's Intercessory Prayers: The Significance of the Intercessory Prayer Passages in the Letters of St. Paul* (Cambridge: Cambridge University Press, 1974), 256. E. Käsemann, *Commentary on Romans* (trans. G.W. Bromiley; Grand Rapids: Eerdmans, 1980), 258, who finds the parallel tempting and admits that the majority of exegetes hold to it, is one of the few to actually argue against it.

context, and that this allusion is important for a full understanding of
Rom. 9.1–5 and its context.

3.1. *The Old Testament Context of Exodus 32.32*

Exod. 32.32 appears in one of the most foundational passages in all of
the Old Testament, Exodus 32–34. Indeed, it functions for Israel in the
scriptural history as Genesis 3 does for humankind.[5] It records 'the paradigm of apostasy',[6] more than that, the paradigm of fall and restoration canonically recapitulated in passages such as Deuteronomy 32 and
frequently in the prophets. Moreover, the importance of chs. 32–34 for
the book of Exodus can hardly be overstated. Durham's comments are
to the point: 'If a narrative paradigmatic of what Exodus is really about
were to be sought, Exod 32–34 would be the obvious first choice.'[7]

Though not uncontested,[8] the tendency among recent interpreters is
to take Exodus 32–34 as a unity in its final, canonical form. This is in
fact the only approach that makes sense if we want to understand
Paul's use of these chapters, for he was certainly not interested in their
tradition-historical prehistory, literary sources, or redactional stages,
nor did he question their historicity. We should 'join Paul in positing the
Mosaic authorship, historical accuracy, and above all, divine authority
of Exodus 32–34' and 'seek to read the text as a narrative with *direct*
theological import and relevance for his world-view. Such a synchronic
reading of Exodus 32–34, with a focus on its final narrative form and
explicit theological themes, is the necessary first step in approaching
Paul's reception of this text'[9] in Romans 9. Therefore, the parts of
Exodus 32–34 must be interpreted with reference to one another, and
similarly, the whole should be interpreted against the larger context of
the book, and indeed the whole Old Testament. Moreover, Exodus

---

5. See S.J. Hafemann, *Paul, Moses, and the History of Israel: The Letter/Spirit
Contrast and the Argument from Scripture in 2 Corinthians 3* (Peabody, MA:
Hendrickson, 1995), 228–31; cf. T.E. Fretheim, *Exodus* (IBC; Louisville: John Knox,
1991), 279; C. Houtman, *Exodus Volume 3: Chapters 20–40* (Historical
Commentary on the Old Testament; Leuven: Peeters, 2000), 608.

6. R.W.L. Moberly, *At the Mountain of God: Story and Theology in Exodus
32–34* (JSOTSup, 22; Sheffield: *JSOT*, 1983), 46.

7. J.I. Durham, *Exodus* (WBC, 3; Waco: Word, 1987), 418; cf. G.H. Davies,
Exodus: Introduction and Commentary (London: SCM, 1967), 48.

8. According to Houtman, *Exodus*, 605.

9. Hafemann, *Paul*, 194, of Paul's use of Exodus 32–34 in 2 Corinthians 3;
emphasis original.

32–34 is a narrative, and should be interpreted with sensitivity to its character as story.

When approaching Exodus 32–34, it is important to recognize that Israel had only just been constituted a nation through their covenant with the Lord at the time of their sin with the golden calf (Exod. 19–31).[10] Moses is still receiving additional covenant stipulations and the covenant documents/tablets of the Law when the people break the covenant at its very heart, transgressing the commandments YHWH deemed important to repeat after the initial revelation of the Law at Mount Sinai, the prohibition against other gods and the making of idols (Exod. 20.3ff., 23).[11] Moreover, Moberly has pointed out that 'after the covenant ratification ceremony in Ex. 24, the people were in principle ready to move off from Sinai to the land which Yahweh would give them where they would live as his people'.[12] Furthermore, the absolute holiness of YHWH has been emphasized in the narrative prior to Exodus 32–34. The people may not approach the mountain of his presence lest they die; they must consecrate themselves even to see him at a distance; they could not bear the awesome sound of his voice and tokens of his presence (Exod. 19.10–13; 20.18–21). If they could not bear his presence in blessing, what could be expected when they had transgressed his covenant in the most blatant way possible?

The narrative progresses forward from the occurrence of the most disastrous of problems, threatening the very existence of the nation, to its resolution through a series of intercessions by Moses on behalf of the people amidst a back-and-forth contrast of events on top of the mountain in the divine sphere and at the bottom of the mountain in the human sphere. The narrative as a whole abruptly interrupts the book's course of events. The next step in the story was to be the construction of the Tabernacle followed by the conquest of the Promised Land. But Israel sinned and called all into question. It is a situation that must be resolved. Its abruptness works to highlight these chapters in the broader narrative and complements their central role.

We may divide Exodus 32–34 into nine sections:[13]

---

10. Cf. Moberly, *Mountain*, 44–45. It is well recognized that עֵגֶל specifically denotes a bull-calf. But with Moberly, 196 n. 8, and Hafemann, *Paul*, 195 n. 22, we will retain the standard designation 'calf'.

11. For Exod. 20.23 as a variation of the first two commandments, see Durham, *Exodus*, 319.

12. Moberly, *Mountain*, 45.

13. Moberly, *Mountain*, 5–6, 44–115, and Hafemann, *Paul*, 196–225, offer relatively similar structures.

32.1–6   Israel sins with the golden calf.

32.7–14   The Lord threatens destruction and Moses intercedes.

32.15–29   Moses breaks the covenant and brings its judgment upon Israel.

32.30–33.6   Moses intercedes a second time and YHWH restores the promise of land but in merciful judgment withdraws his presence, bringing the people to penitent mourning.

33.7–11   Moses enjoys the presence of YHWH in acute intimacy, while the people are separated from his presence and worship him from afar.

33.12–23   Moses intercedes a third time, receiving the pledge of the restoration of YHWH's presence to the people and a (limited) revelation of his glory.

34.1–9   The revelation of YHWH's glory, preparation for covenant renewal, and Moses' fourth and final intercession.

34.10–28   Renewal of the covenant, including stipulations and tablets.

34.29–35   The renewed covenant and the glory of YHWH mediated through Moses.

Moses' intercessions, interspersed throughout the narrative and providing its basic structure,[14] unfalteringly seek to gain back all Israel lost through its sin, from its literal existence to the presence of YHWH in their midst along with the election that accompanied that presence. Both YHWH's mercy and Moses himself become the key to the resolution of the problem posed by Israel's sin.

3.1.a. *Exodus 32.1–6*

Exod. 32.1–6 records Israel's sin with the golden calf. Moses' long stay on the mountain gave rise to the people's desire for 'a god [אלהים] who will go before us' (32.1).[15] It is for this purpose that they gathered against (על) Aaron,[16] to secure the presence and image of YHWH to lead them

---

14. Cf. Hafemann, *Paul*, 225.

15. Unless otherwise noted, all translations of Scripture in this investigation are the author's.

16. Contra Houtman, *Exodus*, 631. על could mean 'to' in this context, but the derisive tone of the people and their wicked intent suggests hostility. Durham, *Exodus*, 415–16, and B.S. Childs, *The Book of Exodus: A Critical, Theological Commentary* (OTL; Philadelphia: Westminster, 1974), 564, support this rendering.

into the Promised Land. In offering the absence of Moses as the reason for their demand, they signal that they seek in part a substitute for Moses.[17] It is not that the people regarded Moses as a god or as YHWH. Rather, 'Moses is the one who uniquely mediates Yahweh's guidance and leadership to the people' and 'the calf is a challenge to Moses' leadership; it is a rival means of mediating Yahweh's presence to the people'.[18] Therefore, while the plural אלהים could indicate that the people sought gods to replace YHWH with, it is more likely that it refers to a physical image of YHWH meant to embody and mediate his presence.[19]

So Aaron collected the people's golden earrings and fashioned a molten calf (32.2–4).[20] 32.4b gives expression to the horror of what has happened in the people's attribution of deity and the glory of the Exodus to the idol with the fateful words: 'This is your god, Israel, who brought you up from the land of Egypt.' The echo of 20.2 in these words gives a further sickening twist to the idolatry – perhaps worse than forsaking YHWH for other gods, they have equated him with a manmade statue![21] The whole episode culminates in worship of the calf with a cultic feast-orgy,[22] the utter depths of perversity from a biblical perspective.

3.1.b. *Exodus 32.7–14*

If there was any doubt that Israel's behavior was a reprehensible violation of the covenant only recently established, it is completely removed by YHWH's response recorded in 32.7–10. He informs Moses of Israel's sin, revealing that they had acted corruptly and quickly turned aside from the way he commanded them, his covenant way. Even the way he refers to Israel as 'your people whom you brought up from the land of Egypt' (v. 7) implies that their election is in danger. It soon becomes

---

17.   So Moberly, *Mountain*, 46–48; Hafemann, *Paul*, 196–98; Houtman, *Exodus*, 640; G.W. Coats, 'The King's Loyal Opposition: Obedience and Authority in Exodus 32–34', in G.W. Coats and B.O. Long (eds.), *Canon and Authority: Essays in Old Testament Religion and Theology* (Philadelphia: Fortress, 1977), 91–109 (95).

18.   Moberly, *Mountain*, 46.

19.   See Abasciano, 'Paul's Use', 143 n. 21.

20.   The variety of difficult questions surrounding the construction of the calf need not concern us here. For a concise yet thorough description of the syntactical and exegetical problems in 32.4, see Childs, *Exodus*, 555–56.

21.   The actual function of the golden calf is disputed (for the options, see Hafemann, *Paul*, 198 n. 33), but this is the only view with solid evidence in the text (32.4–5, 8).

22.   Childs, *Exodus*, 555, 566, argues convincingly for a sexual connotation to לְצַחֵק; but see Houtman, *Exodus*, 642–43.

clear that Israel's idolatry threatens not only her election, but her very existence as well. YHWH observes that Israel is corrupt in its character, calling them a stiff-necked people (עַם־קְשֵׁה־עֹרֶף; v. 9), that is, obstinate and rebellious. Then he directs Moses to leave him *in order that* his anger might burn against them and therefore destroy them, and that he might make Moses into a great nation. So YHWH proposes exterminating Israel and starting the nation over with Moses.

It might seem that Moses himself exhibits a stiff neck in refusing YHWH's command to leave him alone. But the command is directly connected to a purpose clause. This is more of an offer to Moses that is contingent upon his response, and thus an invitation to respond, rather than a literal command.[23] Yet, even though YHWH invites Moses to intercede on behalf of Israel and awaken his mercy so as to overcome his judgment, his offer to Moses appears sincere. Moses' response will largely determine Israel's fate. Fortunately for Israel, Moses took up YHWH's invitation. He sought YHWH's favor for his people (32.11–13).

Through his opening question, Moses suggests that YHWH should not destroy his people, furnishing two of four supporting reasons: (1) Israel's identity as YHWH's people, an implicit argument which runs through Moses' entreaty and is raised by his manner of speaking of Israel (a) as 'your people' (עַמֶּךָ; 32.11–12) in contrast to YHWH's designation of them as Moses' people (32.7), and (b) as the descendants of the fathers; and (2) YHWH's deliverance of Israel from Egypt, i.e., the Exodus in which he had already bestowed grace and favor upon them (21.11).[24] Moses follows with a second question providing the third reason supporting his request: YHWH's glory/reputation, which could be mistakenly maligned by the appearance of evil intent towards Israel from the beginning (32.12a).[25] Only after these two loaded questions does Moses directly state his request (32.12b): 'Turn from your burning anger and relent (וְהִנָּחֵם) concerning the harm (הָרָעָה) to your people!'

---

23.   It is worth noting that Moses himself 'commands' YHWH with an imperative (שׁוּב) in v. 12, but in context this must be understood as a request. Moberly, *Mountain*, 50, notes the remarkable fact that YHWH 'makes his action in some way dependent on the agreement of Moses'. See too Hafemann, *Paul*, 199, who also understands the command as an invitation to intercede similar to the pattern found in prophetic discourse. Cf. Genesis 18, the context of which is alluded to by Paul in Rom. 9.9.

24.   Cf. Durham, *Exodus*, 429.

25.   Coats, 'Opposition', 97, curiously argues that Moses does not appeal to YHWH's reputation and collapses this Mosaic argument into the final one of promise. Cf. Hafemann, *Paul*, 199 n. 37.

Now, Moses culminates his petition by offering his strongest argument – YHWH's own word of promise to the fathers (32.13): 'Remember Abraham, Isaac, and Israel, your servants who you swore to by yourself, and promised to them, "I will multiply your seed as the stars of heaven, and all this land which I said, 'I will give to your seed and they will inherit forever'."' Moberly has noted insightfully that Moses 'uses the special name "Israel" instead of Jacob, thus claiming God's promise in all its fullness'.[26] Thus, Moses' 'clinching argument'[27] is YHWH's faithfulness to his word. While it lies beyond the scope of our discussion to examine the logical relationships between Moses' four arguments in detail, we may say that they all tie in to YHWH's faithfulness to his relationship with his covenant people, most fittingly summed up by reference to his covenant promise to the fathers. And so Moses' prayer proves successful. He convinces YHWH to turn from his stated intention of destroying Israel (32.14).

It is commonly assumed that Moses' arguments practically force YHWH to assent to his request. This assumption generally attaches to the appeal to YHWH's faithfulness since it is Moses' climactic argument. It is thought that Moses has shown YHWH that if he were to carry out his plan to destroy Israel, then he would violate his promise and become unfaithful.[28] But this is not borne out by the text. Moberly is correct to say, 'Yahweh's faithfulness to his promise, to which Moses appeals in v. 13, becomes the reason why Yahweh spares the people',[29] but it does not necessarily follow that it was an inescapably persuasive reason. That is, YHWH could have gone through with his proposed actions to exterminate Israel and start over with Moses and still remain true to his promise to the fathers.[30] Indeed, YHWH himself alludes to the promise to Abraham in his proposal to Moses (cf. Gen. 12.3 and Exod. 32.10).[31] He still would have fulfilled his promise of descendants and land to Abraham and his seed through Moses, though destroying the nation would not lie comfortably with the spirit of the promise. Nevertheless, the text in no way presents YHWH as proposing evil, only

26. Moberly, *Mountain*, 50.
27. D.E. Gowan, *Theology in Exodus: Biblical Theology in the Form of a Commentary* (Louisville: Westminster/John Knox, 1994), 224.
28. See e.g., Hafemann, *Paul*, 200; Coats, 'Opposition', 98.
29. Moberly, *Mountain*, 50.
30. Fretheim, *Exodus*, 286, and Gowan, *Theology*, 224–25, are among the few to recognize this point, as does *Exod. R.* 44.10.
31. Cf. Moberly, *Mountain*, 50; Fretheim, *Exodus*, 286.

to be restrained by Moses. Rather, his mercy is exalted and will find its most sublime expression later in the narrative (33.19; 34.6–7).

Thus, rather than obliged to spare, YHWH is free to destroy Israel. They deserve it. But he is gracious and compassionate, and this is why Moses' arguments prove persuasive with him. This in no way mitigates the importance of Moberly's point that YHWH's faithfulness serves as the basis of his mercy here.[32] But it is to recognize that in this instance YHWH's mercy also serves as the basis of his faithfulness. He could have chosen a different way to be faithful to his word. But it was his propensity to show mercy that led him to choose this way, which accords with the fact that virtually everyone agrees that YHWH's mercy is one of the dominant themes of Exodus 32–34.

Nevertheless, we should not lose sight of the important theme of YHWH's faithfulness to his promise found here. Indeed, as our discussion has shown, YHWH's faithfulness is intimately connected to his mercy in Exodus 32. It is this 'theme of Yahweh's faithfulness to his promise despite seemingly impossible obstacles . . . evident in other JE stories, most notably the Abraham cycle (Gen. 12–25)' that enables Moberly to suggest 'an interpretation of Exod. 32–34 also in terms of a challenge to Yahweh's promise and the vindication of his faithfulness. The challenge is particularly potent in that it arises not from external danger . . . but from the sinfulness of God's own people . . .'[33] Needless to say, YHWH rises to the challenge and proves faithful.

This merciful expression of YHWH's faithfulness highlights the significance of Moses' role as intercessor to an even greater extent than usually acknowledged. For Israel's fate does rely on his intercession. Thus, we find here the traditional theological tension between divine sovereignty and human will/action.[34] The passage at hand presents a dynamic interaction between divine and human roles as YHWH limits his determinations to some extent by granting Moses a decisive role. Yet YHWH remains in control. Every decision rests finally with him even as he makes himself open to Moses' influence.

---

32. Moberly, *Mountain*, 50.

33. Moberly, *Mountain*, 52.

34. Highlighted by Moberly, *Mountain*, 51–52; Gowan, *Theology*, 222–27; Fretheim, *Exodus*, 283–87; Coats, 'Opposition', who all come to relatively similar conclusions to ours below. Besides the obvious intercessory context, such reflections tend to revolve around YHWH's command to Moses to leave him alone, understood as some sort of invitation to help determine the outcome of the situation (32.10) and the statement that YHWH did relent (32.14).

At this point in the narrative it is unclear what exactly will become of Israel. On the one hand, they have sinned so grievously that YHWH was about to destroy them. On the other hand, Moses has convinced YHWH not to do so, at least for the time being. But YHWH has made no commitment concerning their fate, the comment of 32.14 being editorial and not part of the inner narrative (cf. 32.30), and in any case lacking the idea of permanent commitment. What is Israel's status now? It does not take long to see that all is not well with Israel as the narrative turns to find Israel's only advocate pronouncing judgment upon her.

3.1.c. *Exodus 32.15–29*

Moses descends from the divine sphere at the top of the mountain to the sin-soaked reality of the people at the bottom. The text emphasizes the divine origin and character of the two tablets of the testimony carried by Moses down the mountain (32.15–16). When Moses sees the idol and the idolatrous festivity, he becomes enraged as was YHWH, and smashes the tablets, indicating the breaking of the covenant between YHWH and Israel. The covenant is annulled by the covenant mediator.[35] Israel is no longer YHWH's people, their election nullified.

Moses goes on to destroy the calf completely and punish the people by forcing them to drink its remains. Then Moses turns to Aaron. Their exchange highlights the sinful character of the people and Aaron's culpability in leading the people astray. Moses then wastes no time in bringing further judgment on the people, assuming the role of prophet and calling for all who are faithful to YHWH to gather to him, and then charging those who gathered, the Levites, to kill the guilty among the people.[36] These Levites seem to represent a faithful remnant.[37] They are clearly approved and can hope to obtain the blessing of the Lord (32.29). While the story of the Levites' actions is shrouded in obscurity, 'The key to understanding the episode is to appreciate that its central concern is

---

35. This is the standard interpretation of Moses' smashing of the tablets. See Moberly, *Mountain*, 53; Hafemann, *Paul*, 202; Durham, *Exodus*, 430; Fretheim, *Exodus*, 287; Gowan, *Theology*, 227; Davies, *Exodus*, 233; R.A. Cole, *Exodus: An Introduction and Commentary* (TOTC, 2; Downers Grove: Intervarsity Press, 1973), 218; J. Plastaras, *The God of Exodus: The Theology of the Exodus Narratives* (Milwaukee: Bruce, 1966), 240.

36. It is not clear whether the Levites killed only other Levites or anyone they found involved in idolatry, but the latter seems far more likely. See Moberly, *Mountain*, 55, on the question. On Moses' prophetic role here, see Childs, *Exodus*, 571.

37. Moberly, *Mountain*, 55; Hafemann, *Paul*, 203.

a life-or-death faithfulness to Yahweh. . . . The primary significance of the story is to show that death is the penalty for unfaithfulness to Yahweh and the covenant, whereas blessing (v. 29b) is the reward for faithfulness.'[38] The necessity of slaying brothers and sons probably stresses 'the costliness of faithfulness to Yahweh'.[39]

The sharp contrast between the Levites and the people as a whole intensifies the problem that has resulted from the people's idolatry. As things stand, the covenant has been nullified and three thousand people have been slain. Israel's fate is still very uncertain. This becomes clear as a new section begins and Moses draws attention to the magnitude of the people's sin and expresses an uncertain hope of making atonement for them ('perhaps [אוּלַי] I can make atonement for your sin'; 32.30).

3.1.d. *Exodus 32.30–33.6*

We have now arrived at the section in which Paul's allusion in Rom. 9.3 lies, Moses' second intercession on behalf of Israel. The covenant remains broken due to the people's sin and there is no telling what further measures YHWH will take against Israel. The purpose of Moses' intercession is to make atonement (כפר; 32.30) for Israel's sin and thus restore Israel's relationship with YHWH and all that their covenant relationship with him promised.[40]

Moses begins his intercession with a confession of the immensity of Israel's sin with the golden calf (32.31). This confession lays greater stress on Moses' ensuing request and thus implicitly appeals to YHWH's mercy. Moses begins to ask YHWH to forgive the people's sin, but never completes the thought, because in an emotive appeal he places himself on the line for the people he represents. He breaks off his request in mid-sentence to present the most powerful reason he could personally offer – his own life: 'But now, if you will forgive their sin – and if not, blot me out please from your book which you have written' (32.32).[41]

---

38. Moberly, *Mountain*, 55.

39. Moberly, *Mountain*, 55.

40. The LXX may stress the break between YHWH and Israel, and the need for their relationship to be reestablished by using θεός instead of the usual translation for YHWH, κύριος; see J.W. Wevers, *Notes on the Greek Text of Exodus* (SBLSCS, 30; Atlanta: Scholars Press, 1990), 536.

41. The Samaritan Pentateuch, LXX, and *Targ. Ps.-J.* ease this anacoluthon – and therefore must be considered secondary – by supplying an extra entreating imperative: 'If you will forgive their sin, *forgive.*' Cf. Durham, *Exodus*, 426, 432, who surprisingly represents haplography as equally serious an option as stylistic expression here.

The effect is to ground Moses' request with the deterrent of his death, essentially saying, 'If you will not forgive Israel, then blot me out of your book.' Moses does not offer his life as a substitute for the people here, but throws his lot in with them. Moses requests to suffer the fate of the people with them if YHWH will not forgive them. Thus, he attempts to make his life the price YHWH must pay for releasing his wrath on Israel.

Moses' entreaty relies on his own favor with YHWH as well as his own innocence in the matter of the golden calf. He may also be alluding to his former conversation with YHWH in which YHWH offered to begin anew with Moses as the father of the chosen people and Moses refused this request.[42] We may note an escalation here. In his first intercession, Moses refused YHWH's offer and pleaded on behalf of Israel. Here in his second intercession, Moses builds on YHWH's favor towards him evidenced in the exclusive offer of the covenant blessing and asks to be numbered with the transgressors. There is great power in this request, for even though YHWH could righteously start over with Moses, he could not fulfill his promise to Abraham if Moses too perished.

We should also take note of the role of the remnant in Moses' petition. As Hafemann has pointed out, 'after the judgment against those most directly involved has been executed, Moses can appeal to the faithful "remnant", as embodied in himself, as the basis for God's subsequent mercy'. [43] Thus, Moses' intercessory and mediatorial identification of himself with the people of Israel carries an even greater depth and potency than usually perceived.

Interpreters generally take Moses' request to be blotted out of YHWH's book (32.32) to refer to the book of life/the living, which contains the record of those who are alive and may have its general background in ancient registers of citizens and the like. To be blotted out of it means death.[44] This interpretation is adequate for understanding the general thrust of Moses' request, but fails to grasp its specific import.

The context of Exodus and the Pentateuch as a whole suggests that YHWH's book (סֵפֶר) proper is the book of the Law/Covenant which he

42. Cf. Cole, *Exodus*, 221.

43. Hafemann, *Paul*, 205. But Hafemann's broader argument goes too far in claiming that this point obligates YHWH to grant Moses' request and that 'the people now remaining can be considered to be under the umbrella of those who, like Moses, remained faithful'.

44. See e.g., S.R. Driver, *The Book of Exodus* (Cambridge: Cambridge University Press, 1911), 356; Gowan, *Theology*, 227, 286 n. 19.

wrote through Moses.[45] This is the book of the covenant, which contained all the words of YHWH (Exod. 24.4), that Moses had only recently read to the people at the ratification of the covenant, when they accepted it and committed themselves to it (Exod. 24.7). The reference to the book of the covenant in Exod. 24.7 is especially relevant for understanding the reference to YHWH's book in 32.32 because it is the last prior mention of a book in Exodus and because the context of covenant ratification is directly related to the context of Exodus 32–34. Faithfulness to this book of the covenant would bring blessing/life while unfaithfulness to it would bring curse/death.[46]

Deut. 29.19–20 (Eng. 29.20–21) is especially revealing for understanding the meaning of Moses' request in Exod. 32.32. This passage associates YHWH's book with his blotting out of the idolater, an action that is equated with no forgiveness, wrath, and pouring out the curses of the covenant written in the book of the Law upon him. Elsewhere, the end result of this judgment is said to be destruction/extermination (Deut. 28.61).

Drawing all of this together with the context of Exodus 32, I would suggest that YHWH's book in Exod. 32.32 is the registry of the elect covenant people,[47] a sort of companion document to the book of the covenant. To be blotted out from this book would mean being cut off from the covenant and its people and to bear the curse of the covenant, the ultimate end of which is death, the blotting out of one's name from under heaven. Thus, in Exod. 32.32, Moses asks YHWH to cut him off from the covenant and pour out its curses upon him along with the rest of Israel if he refuses Moses' request to forgive them.

YHWH's response to Moses' prayer is somewhat unclear and has been interpreted alternatively as either a denial or concession to Moses' request.[48] But perhaps its significance lies somewhere between these two

---

45. For the book of the covenant, see Exod. 24.7; cf. Deut. 29.21; 31.26. For the book of the Law or some such similar phrase, see Deut. 28.58, 61; 29.21; 29.27; 30.10; 31.24, 26. Cf. *Targ. Neof. Exod.* 32.32. *Exod. R.* 47.9 takes God's book as the Book of the Law (M. McNamara and R. Hayward, *Targum Neofiti 1: Exodus* [TAB, 2; Collegeville, MN: Liturgical Press, 1994], 133).

46. See Exod. 20.5–7 and references in the previous note; cf. Exod. 17.14–16.

47. Fretheim, *Exodus*, 290, makes a similar suggestion, citing Ezek. 13.9; Mal. 3.16. Cf. Durham, *Exodus*, 432; R.H. Charles, *The Book of Enoch* (Oxford: Clarendon, 1893), 131–33. Note Ps. 69.29 (LXX 68.29; Eng. 69.28); Dan. 12.1; Neh. 9.38–10.27.

48. See Moberly, *Mountain*, 57–58, on the two alternatives. Most interpreters take the former view; Hafemann, *Paul*, 205–206, opts for the latter.

extremes. On the one hand, YHWH's response constitutes a formal denial of Moses' request. Even so, YHWH does not answer Moses' request directly. Rather, he focuses his comments on identifying who he will punish – the sinners (32.33–34). The implicit contrast with Moses' request that he forgive the people's sin is obvious enough: no, he will not forgive them, but will blot out from his book whoever sinned against him, cutting them off from the elect people and subjecting them to the deadly curse of the covenant.

On the other hand, Moses has obtained some favorable disposition from the Lord for the people. Even though he will punish the guilty, he charges Moses to lead the people to the Promised Land and promises that his angel will go before them, implying guidance and success in the conquest (cf. 23.20–31; 33.2). Moses has finally won a permanent existence for Israel along with the restoration of the vital land promise. But these concessions are not unrestricted. YHWH ends this portion of his response (32.33–34) as he began it, with a declaration that he will punish the guilty (32.34b), yielding a chiasm:

A: 32.33   YHWH will punish the one who has sinned

B: 32.34a   The command to Moses to lead the people to the Promised Land

B': 32.34b   The promise of the angel to lead/guide Israel to the Promised Land

A': 32.34c   YHWH will punish the people

The accent lies on the exterior members of the chiasm – punishment for the sinners. These stand in adversative relationship to the central members, which grant the promise of land back to the people as well as the necessary angelic guidance. Despite granting some of Israel's promises back, implying their continued existence and a measure of forgiveness, YHWH will punish the guilty. That the emphasis lies here with the denial may be seen in the following verse (32.35), which functions as part of the answer to Moses' plea, an action following upon the verbal response and interpreting it. YHWH struck the people in some way, probably with a plague.[49]

But YHWH is not finished with Moses or the people. After the notice of the stroke against the people (32.35), he resumes his dialogue with

---

49. On other options concerning the significance of 32.35, see Abasciano, 'Paul's Use', 154 n. 55.

Moses. He expands on both the instruction to Moses to lead the people to the Promised Land and the promise of the angel-guide. The ray of hope shining through the first part of YHWH's response (32.33–34) to Moses' second intercession is now substantially darkened. It might have seemed that YHWH was restoring the former promise of a guiding angel in whom YHWH's name would dwell (Exod. 23.20–23).[50] But his judgment continues to fall. While he will still grant the Promised Land to Israel and even send his angel before them, his presence will not go in their midst: 'but I will not go up in your midst, for you are a stiff-necked people, lest I destroy you on the way' (33.3).

This is a devastating blow, indeed, the worst possible judgment that could fall, apart from absolute annihilation. As Durham comments,

> In the place of his Presence, there was to be only Absence. It is a punishment . . . that negates every announcement, every expectation, every instruction except those now being given. There will be no special treasure, no kingdom of priests, no holy nation, no Yahweh being their God, no covenant, no Ark, no Tabernacle, no Altar, no cloud of Glory.[51]

The supreme blessing of the covenant people was YHWH's presence. It is what made them his people, the determination, sign, and seal of their election. Thus, in denying his presence to Israel, YHWH is essentially confirming the covenant as broken and the abrogation of Israel's election.[52]

It is certainly correct, with most interpreters, to see the denial of YHWH's presence as a judgment upon Israel. But Hafemann has correctly seen that this is also an expression 'of divine mercy which makes it possible for Israel to continue on as a people'.[53] Indeed, the logical structure of 33.3 reveals that the emphasis actually lies on the merciful character of YHWH's judgment, for its purpose is that the people would be spared destruction, since their sinful condition would elicit YHWH's judgment.

---

50. While the position that the angel now promised to Israel is different than the one previously promised is strongly opposed by some, such as Childs, *Exodus*, 588; Moberly, *Mountain*, 61; Gowan, *Exodus*, 228, it seems clear that the guiding angel now at least functions differently. See Abasciano, 'Paul's Use', 155 n. 58.

51. Durham, *Exodus*, 437.

52. See also Durham, *Exodus*, 417–18; Fretheim, *Exodus*, 294; Houtman, *Exodus*, 685–86, on YHWH's presence as the determiner of election. The text indicates this significance to YHWH's presence in 33.16 and 34.9.

53. Hafemann, *Paul*, 208; emphasis removed. Though seldom seen, Fretheim, *Exodus*, 294, also sees it and perceptively relates it to Israel's status of non-election here based on the principle annunciated in Amos 3.2.

Nevertheless, the devastating consequences of the withdrawal of YHWH's presence laid heavy on Israel and become the focus of the narrative (33.4–6). The news of this judgment plunged them into the darkest grief.[54] The people went into mourning upon hearing this grievous news (הַדָּבָר הָרָע הַזֶּה), expressing their great grief by not putting on their ornaments, symbols of festivity[55] and the type of material they used to make the golden calf. 33.5–6 give an explanation for the people's response of grief.[56] We are told, 'For Yahweh had said to Moses, "Say to the sons of Israel, 'You are a stiff-necked people. If I go up in your midst for one moment, I would destroy you! Now, take off your ornaments from upon you in order that I may know what I will do with you.' " So the sons of Israel stripped themselves of their ornaments from Mount Horeb.'

This expansive repetition clearly emphasizes its content, not only by repetition, but also by intensification. After stressing the hardened sinfulness of the people, the text adds the detail that YHWH could not be with the people *for even a moment* without destroying them. Moreover, the divestment of the people's ornaments is now described (33.6) with the same verb (נצל) used for the despoiling of the Egyptians (3.22; 12.36), suggesting that they have lost what they gained in the redemption of the Exodus and that their sin has left them in the same condition as divinely condemned Egypt.[57]

YHWH's command for the people to despoil themselves appears to be a call for repentance, for its stated purpose is to enable YHWH to make a (favorable) decision about Israel. Repentance is here laid down as a condition for any hope of a significant future for Israel.[58] In addition to expressing the pain of YHWH's judgment upon them, Israel's grief also indicates repentance,[59] accompanied as it is by obedience to YHWH's command, and followed by sincere faith displayed in the matter of the Tent of Meeting (33.7–11) and heartfelt obedience in the building of the Tabernacle (chs. 35–40).

54. See Durham, *Exodus*, 436–37.
55. Durham, *Exodus*, 434–35, 437, helpfully translates עֲדִי as 'festive dress'.
56. The Hebrew conjunction וֹ beginning 33.5 is best taken causally as in most translations.
57. See Moberly, *Mountain*, 61. Cf. Hafemann, *Paul*, 208.
58. So Houtman, *Exodus*, 680.
59. Moberly, *Mountain*, 60–61, argues that the people have not repented, but see Abasciano, 'Paul's Use', 157 n. 67. Childs, *Exodus*, 589, and Houtman, *Exodus*, 678ff., 691–92, take Israel's grief as repentance, and *Targ. Ps.-J.* interprets going to the Tent of Meeting as repentance.

The repetitive character of 33.4–6 brings the emphasis of the narrative to rest on Israel's great sorrow at the loss of their election/the presence of YHWH. Their act of self-spoiling testifies to the fact that they have brought this judgment upon themselves. Their election and future are still in grave danger. Yet YHWH has offered a ray of hope by inviting them to repent and declaring that he is still undecided concerning their fate. The door has been opened for Moses to intercede once again.

3.1.e. *Exodus 33.7–11*

This next section records the setting up of the temporary Tent of Meeting for the periodic mediation of YHWH's presence and guidance and for communion between Moses and YHWH. Its main significance is twofold in accordance with the dual themes of YHWH's judgment and mercy in the previous section, but now with an emphasis on God's mercy.[60] In judgment, YHWH withholds his presence from Israel. Therefore, Moses sets up the Tent in which he would meet with the Lord 'outside of the camp, far from the camp' (33.7). The contrast between Moses' special, intimate relationship with YHWH and the people's separation from the all-important presence stresses the provision of the tent as an act of judgment.

However, the provision of the Tent is even more so an act of mercy, for through it YHWH grants Israel a limited measure of access to his presence and guidance, mediated through Moses. Moreover, YHWH's periodic visits to the Tent provided the opportunity for the people to worship, albeit from afar. Perhaps most importantly for the broader development of the narrative, the Tent of Meeting provides the 'medium through which Moses can meet with God on the way to the promised land, so that continual access to God is now assured, while the intimate nature of Moses' contact with YHWH is the basis upon which Moses' final intercession can be made'.[61]

---

60. Both Moberly, *Mountain*, 63, and Hafemann, *Paul*, 209–11, see the dual significance of the Tent. It is remarkable that so many interpreters find 33.7–11 disruptive to the narrative when it plays such an important role to its development. By contrast, Moberly and Hafemann view it as the turning point in the narrative; cf. M.R. Hauge, *The Descent from the Mountain: Narrative Patterns in Exodus 19–40* (JSOTSup, 323; Sheffield: Sheffield Academic Press, 2001), 73.

61. Hafemann, *Paul*, 210. However, Moses' third intercession is not his last if one accepts 34.9 as another intercession.

3.1.f. *Exodus 33.12–23*

We have now come to Moses' third and climactic intercession, which also contains Paul's second allusion in Romans 9 to the context of Exodus 32–34 (cf. Exod. 33.19; Rom. 9.15, 18). He will finally secure the object of his relentless pursuit. Moses begins his petition by drawing attention both to YHWH's previous command to lead the people to the Promised Land (33.12; cf. 33.1) and to the opposing fact, demanding a response, that YHWH had not informed Moses who would accompany him. Determining the exact meaning of Moses' concern has been a notorious problem for interpreters. Moses' contention is typically understood as a request to know the identity of either an earthly guide or the angel who will lead them, whether he will mediate the divine presence or not.[62] Any approach to Moses' concern must relate to YHWH's presence, since YHWH's answer (33.14) addresses this very issue and all would agree that the essence of Moses' overall petition in 33.12–17 is for YHWH's presence with the people (and all that implies). Yet, YHWH *has* told Moses the identity of the angel; he will not mediate the divine presence (33.1–3).

Therefore, I would suggest that, in one sense, Moses is asking to know the status of the people YHWH is sending with him, whether they are his elect people or not.[63] For while YHWH has told Moses who will go with him as a guide, he has specifically stated that the people's fate, and therefore their identity, is uncertain (33.5). Thus Moses' statement does not make a false assertion, but contributes to his request that YHWH reverse his decision not to go with the people, and rather dwell in their midst. This is tantamount to requesting that he take Israel again as his elect covenant people, and thereby restore to them all the blessings of election, for his presence constitutes election.

Having stated the problem, Moses begins to present further considerations that will serve as additional bases of his petition, reminding YHWH that he himself had said – thus appealing to his faithfulness to his word – 'I have known you by name and you have indeed found favor in my sight' (33.12c). To know by name indicates a special, intimate

---

62. See the contrasting views of Plastaras, *Exodus*, 263; Davies, *Exodus*, 240, and against reference to a guide of any sort, Moberly, *Mountain*, 69.

63. Cf. P. Enns, *Exodus* (NIVAC; Grand Rapids: Zondervan, 2000), 580, though contra Enns, the issue is not 'who will be left after the purge of 33.5', but, what is Israel's identity; are they/will they be God's people. Our suggestion is supported by the end of 33.13 in the LXX (ἵνα γνῶ ὅτι λαός σου τὸ ἔθνος τοῦτο), on which see Wevers, *Exodus*, 548.

knowledge of favor and election. Moses is YHWH's chosen covenant mediator and confidant. It is this favor that Moses appeals to as the basis of his request, which he has made indirectly in describing the problem, but now, in 33.13, begins to make directly.

James Muilenburg has drawn attention to the prominence of the verb 'to know' (ידע) in 33.12–17 along with its covenantal connotations.[64] Moses continues to act as the covenant mediator,[65] and as Muilenburg says, 'It is a *covenantal* knowing, a knowing between Lord and servant, between King and subject, between Suzerain and vassal.'[66] There is a depth to the Hebrew ידע that defies any simple definition.[67] The word surely sounds a strong note of intimacy here. But the covenantal implications of the word have seldom been recognized in this passage, and merit special attention, as they tie in so well with the covenantal context of Exodus 32–34[68] and shed new light on the meaning of the exchange between Moses and YHWH.

In covenantal contexts, ידע can mean, 'to acknowledge as a covenant partner'.[69] Each of the six occurrences of ידע in 33.12–17 is related to this basic covenantal sense of the term. Thus I would suggest that Moses' exclamation in 33.12 is best understood as pointing out the discrepancy between YHWH's stated intention to fulfill the covenantal land promise without the provision of his covenant presence: 'Look, you are saying to me, "Bring up this people", but you yourself have not let me acknowledge as a covenant partner who you will send with me!' This alludes to Moses' role as the covenant mediator. Just as he broke/annulled the covenant as YHWH's representative, so he seeks to renew it.

When Moses speaks of YHWH knowing him by name (33.12c), he refers to more than just a special, intimate knowledge, but such knowledge within a covenant context. YHWH has chosen Moses as the covenant mediator, which is part of his favor towards him, but presently

---

64.   J. Muilenburg, 'The Intercession of the Covenant Mediator (Exodus 33:1a, 12–17)', in P.R. Ackroyd and B. Lindars (eds.), *Words and Meanings: Essays Presented to David Winton Thomas* (Cambridge: Cambridge University Press, 1968), 159–181.

65.   Muilenburg, 'Intercession', 179.

66.   Muilenburg, 'Intercession', 179; emphasis original.

67.   See Muilenburg, 'Intercession', 159.

68.   Muilenburg, 'Intercession', 160, points out that we are dealing with part of the *locus classicus* of the Sinaitic covenant.

69.   See *HALOT*, 390, and esp. G.P. Hugenberger, *Marriage as a Covenant: A Study of Biblical Law and Ethics Governing Marriage Developed from the Perspective of Malachi* (VTSup, 52; Leiden: Brill, 1994), 267–78.

there is no covenant to mediate. When Moses asks to know YHWH's ways, he is asking to know his covenant ways for the purpose of knowing YHWH covenantally, that is, in intimate covenant relationship, which necessarily confers YHWH's favor (i.e., the promises/blessings of the covenant), Moses' ultimate goal (33.13). We might translate 33.13 as follows: 'And now, if, please, I have found favor in your eyes, let me please know your covenant ways in order that I may acknowledge you as a covenant partner in order that I may find favor in your eyes.' Thus, Moses is requesting a restoration of the covenant that he mediated, but now modified so as to be principally a covenant between him and YHWH, and then through him, with the people. Based on his past reception of YHWH's favor consisting in his election as the covenant mediator, he now asks that YHWH renew the covenant with him so that he may have the covenant blessing. He appears to build on YHWH's previous offer to make him the father of the covenant people, essentially accepting the offer to be the primary covenant partner, but insisting that Israel be included.

Moses' final argument begs the point at issue a bit: 'Consider also that this nation is your people' (33.13). He appears to be offering up Israel's history for consideration. They have been YHWH's people and really have no other identity, even though he does not now acknowledge them. It is probably no coincidence that YHWH grants Moses' request based on the first two reasons he offered – (1) Moses' special election/his role as covenant mediator; (2) YHWH's favor towards Moses – and ignores this third and final ground for his petition (33.17). Israel is corrupt and has no standing with YHWH. Everything depends on Moses and his relationship with the Lord as well as the character of YHWH himself.

YHWH's initial response to Moses' request is ambiguous, amounting to a partial concession. He says simply, 'My presence will go and I will give rest to you' (33.14). This is in essence a promise on YHWH's part to go with Moses personally and give him rest,[70] for the second-person pronoun (‏לְךָ‎) is singular, and Moses' response in 33.15–16 shows that he has not yet obtained what he is after, YHWH's presence with Israel and all that means, viz., renewal of the covenant and its promises. Moses' counter-response presses for inclusion of the people. It is a masterful entreaty, beginning with equal ambiguity, and then identifying the people of Israel with Moses in increasing explicitness until the people are center

---

70.   For this type of approach, see Moberly, *Mountain*, 74–75; Hafemann, *Paul*, 213–14; Coats, 'Opposition', 102. See Houtman, *Exodus*, 698, against it.

stage and their fate and identity intertwined with Moses. 'And he said to him, "If your presence is not going, do not bring us up from here. For how then will it be known that I have found favor in your eyes, I and your people? Is it not in your going with us, so that we will be distinguished, I and your people, from all the people who are on the face of the earth?"' (33.15–16). It is now absolutely clear what Moses is after – the presence of God with Israel as the elect people of God. Verse 16 reveals that YHWH's presence signifies the divine favor and election.

Finally, YHWH grants Moses' request on the basis of Moses' favor and election before him (33.17). As Moberly has said, the concession

> not only confirms Moses' special status, but makes the favoured position of Israel both mediated through, and dependent upon, Moses. . . . [T]he restoration of Israel and the renewal of the covenant does not put Israel in a position identical to that before its sin. Henceforth it is dependent upon the mercy of God mediated through Moses as the primary recipient of that mercy.[71]

Yet, Moses has not finished his intercession. He now dares to ask, 'Show me, please, your glory!' (33.18).

In making this bold request, Moses is essentially asking that YHWH now fulfill his promise,[72] revealing his covenant ways to him in order to establish the covenant and its blessing (cf. 33.13), and bestowing his all-important presence (i.e., his glory). So on the one hand, this is a basic repetition of the request of 33.13 and the next logical step for Moses to take. But on the other hand, Moses' request goes beyond anything he has asked thus far. YHWH's glory (כבוד) refers to the very essence or presence of YHWH in all its fullness, something which may be called glory because of its supreme worth, beauty, and magnificence. The glory, goodness (טוב), name, face/presence (פנים), and being of YHWH are all used synonymously in 33.18–23, though the various words indicate various nuances of the one glorious reality they all seek to describe.[73]

---

71. Moberly, *Mountain*, 75.

72. Cf. Durham, *Exodus*, 452, Houtman, *Exodus*, 700–701; Piper, *Justification*, 79–81.

73. See Piper, *Justification*, 84–88, for the argument that the glory, goodness, and name of YHWH are basically synonymous. But טוב probably does not lose its aesthetic character altogether. It is precisely YHWH's moral character that is aesthetically beautiful. Sarna is probably correct to take טוב to bear 'a technical, legal meaning of covenantal friendship' found in ancient Near Eastern treaties and elsewhere in the OT (cited by Enns, *Exodus*, 582), but the context requires that it mean more than this.

The variety of terms helps us to understand what Moses is asking and what YHWH grants. Moses asks to see – as the token and context of the establishment of a renewed covenant with Moses and Israel – YHWH himself, the very essence of his being, which is good and glorious and beautiful, and to be understood primarily in the realm of moral character and covenant. The fact that YHWH uniquely and characteristically appeared in theophanic glory to initiate covenants confirms our approach to Exodus 32–34,[74] as does the fact that the renewal of the covenant (34.1–28) in answer to Moses' request takes place in connection with the theophany here envisioned (though qualified by YHWH's response to follow).

There is another profound reason for Moses' daring request to see the Lord's glory. While he has obtained the promise of YHWH's presence and covenant for Israel, he has not procured a solution to the problem that YHWH's presence poses for Israel as a sinful people.[75] As we have seen, the denial of YHWH's presence was a merciful judgment upon Israel, for his presence could only mean destruction for them in their corrupt state (33.3, 5). Perhaps more than any, Hafemann has seen this crucial concern of the narrative:

> The answer to the problem of YHWH's presence is . . . a request that Moses himself now experience the solution to the problem! As a consistent development of the central role of Moses as the mediator of the covenant, Moses sees the answer to be a *private* theophany of the glory of God (33.18). Moses alone will experience the glory of God and then bring it back with him into the midst of his people, since in their hardened state they can no longer encounter it themselves.[76]

YHWH's answer to Moses' request is again a partial concession and denial: 'And YHWH said, "I myself will cause all my goodness to pass by your face, and I will proclaim the name of YHWH before you. And I will be gracious to whom I will be gracious, and I will have mercy on whom I will have mercy." But he said, "You cannot see my face, for man will not see me and live" ' (33.19–20). YHWH then goes on to describe the manner in which he will manifest this theophany and the provision

---

74.   On this phenomenon unique to Israel's Scriptures in the ancient Near East, see J.J. Niehaus, *God at Sinai: Covenant and Theophany in the Bible and Ancient Near East* (SOTBT; Grand Rapids: Zondervan, 1995), 108–17, 142–229.

75.   Moberly, *Mountain*, 75–76; Hafemann, *Paul*, 215.

76.   Hafemann, *Paul*, 215. Hafemann's approach was already present basically in R.T. Forster and V.P. Marston, *God's Strategy in Human History: God's Sovereignty and Human Responsibility* (Crowborough, East Sussex: Highland, 1973), 51–52.

he will make for Moses to experience it without dying (33.21–23). The denial of Moses' petition is that the revelation will be only partial. Moses will not be able to see YHWH's face directly. No person can endure that and live. But Moses will get to see YHWH's 'back' (אֲחֹרָי). The language is obviously anthropomorphic here and impossible to comprehend completely. But the general sense is clear – YHWH's face (פָּנִים) represents his full, unmediated presence, while his back represents a partial, restricted revelation.

The text represents Moses as having a total theophanic experience, both visual and audible/verbal. 33.20–23 communicate the supreme and incomprehensible majesty of the glory of God and his infinite superiority over humanity. The verses also testify again to the mercy of YHWH, since he makes provision for Moses to experience as much of his glory as humanly possible. Relatedly, the passage bears witness once again to the status and glory of Moses, who has seen the glory of God. But as important as the visual manifestation granted to Moses is, the emphasis of the theophany contemplated here in 33.12–23 necessarily falls on what Moses hears as the interpretation of what he sees.

The concession Moses receives is even more important for the forward thematic movement of the narrative than the denial. YHWH will cause all his goodness, the fullness of the divine glory, to pass by Moses, who will be shielded by the hand of God until only his back may be seen. Accompanying this sensual experience will be the proclamation of YHWH's name, which is given a summary interpretation in 33.19, to be expanded during the actual theophany recorded in 34.5–28.[77] It is the summary explication of the divine name in Exod. 33.19 that Paul cites in Rom. 9.15.

The summary meaning of YHWH's name (33.19, 'I will be gracious to whom I will be gracious . . .') is given in a tautologous idiom known as the *idem per idem* formula. The significance of the idiom as used here is twofold. First, it emphasizes the verbal idea through repetition. ' "The second verb serves as a predicate, and thus, like a cognate accusative, emphasizes the verbal action." When, as here, the formula is repeated with two verbs of related meaning, then the statement of the verbal meaning – the mercy of God – is as emphatic as the Hebrew language

---

77.   On the two options for understanding the relationship between the first and second parts of 33.19, whether the latter part (grace and mercy) grounds or interprets the former (YHWH's name), see esp. Piper, *Justification*, 84, who argues convincingly for an interpretive significance.

can make it.'[78] Second, by leaving the action unspecified, the formula emphasizes the freedom of the subject to perform the action in whatever way he pleases.[79] However, the freedom envisioned is not arbitrary.[80] Arbitrariness, an action or choice based on nothing outside of the agent, is not inherent to the sense of the formula. Rather the idiom simply stresses the freedom of the subject without respect to the presence or absence of motivating factors or reasons. In principle, it could be used of either an arbitrary or conditioned choice. Any decision concerning the type of choice depicted must be determined from context.

Significantly, in every actual Old Testament example of the idiom the context or circumstances would suggest that the choice/action envisioned would be, at least in part, based on factors external to the subject.[81] So, for instance, when Moses asks YHWH to send someone else as his messenger in Exod. 4.13, such a request would normally assume that the choice would be made partly on certain characteristics of the chosen one. But Moses uses the *idem per idem* formula because he does not care particularly who YHWH sends, as long as it is not him. He does not address the issue of grounds for the choice he requests, though that there would be some ground(s) external to YHWH partly forming the basis of the decision would be taken for granted. When YHWH responds in 4.14 by choosing another to accompany Moses

78.   Moberly, *Mountain*, 77–78, partly citing D.N. Freedman, 'The Name of the God of Moses', *JBL* 79 (1960), 151–56 (153).

79.   I have here adapted Piper's (*Justification*, 82) description of the idiom, who completely misses its emphasizing force and focuses exclusively on its connotation of freedom, impoverishing his understanding of the formula and Exod. 33.19. Even his understanding of the freedom indicated by the idiom is faulty, for he appears to construe it as arbitrary. Piper's mishandling of the formula and Exod. 33.19 may well undo the very foundation of his study if G.K. Beale, Review of J. Piper, *The Justification of God: An Exegetical and Theological Study of Romans 9.1–23*, *WTJ* 46 (1984), 190–97 (191–92) is correct to find his chapter on the passage to be 'the theological cornerstone for the entire monograph' validating its main thesis.

80.   Moberly, *Mountain*, 78; Freedman, 'Name', 153–54; Driver, *Exodus*, 362–63; Cole, *Exodus*, 226. More technically, the freedom envisioned is not necessarily arbitrary; the idiom does not address motivating factors whatsoever.

81.   For examples of the *idem per idem* formula, see Gen. 43.14; Exod. 3.14; 4.13; 16.2; Est. 4.16; 1 Sam. 23.13; 2 Sam. 15.20; 2 Kgs 8.1; Ezek. 12.25; Jn 19.22; 1 Cor. 15.10; and possibly Deut. 9.25, 1 Sam. 1.24, Zech. 10.8 (culled from Piper, *Justification*, 82; Freedman, 'Name', 153 n. 11; J.R. Lundbom, 'God's Use of the *Idem per Idem* to Terminate Debate', *HTR* 71 (1978), 193–201 [194]). The idiom's occurrence in Exod. 3.14 is especially important since it is also connected to the divine name; see Moberly, *Mountain*, 78; Childs, *Exodus*, 596.

(not replace him), he does specify an external basis for his decision. Similarly, when one makes a choice about what to have for dinner as in Exodus 16.23, one typically makes the choice in part based on the character of the food chosen. The basis of YHWH's choice of whom he will be merciful to must be determined from the context of Exodus 32–34.[82]

It is crucial to understand that the request YHWH is responding to is essentially, as we have seen, a request to restore his presence and covenant to Israel as a people, granting them forgiveness for their sin. The grace and mercy mentioned has primary reference to a sinful nation that stands under the judgment of God, and to individuals secondarily as they are connected to the group. It is also important to recognize a close parallel with Moses' prior intercession in 32.30–33.6, where YHWH told Moses the grounds for punishment (32.33) and demanded repentance as a condition of forgiveness, which was followed by the people's repentance (33.4–6) and renewed commitment to the Lord (33.7–11). In 33.19, YHWH reminds Moses that he will be merciful to whom he chooses, recalling this earlier context with its word that the guilty would be punished (32.33) and pointing forward to the same basic point in part of the fuller explication of the name found in 34.7.[83]

34.6–7 stresses YHWH's mercy while revealing that he will certainly not clear the guilty,[84] another way of stating the principle of 32.33 and showing the basis on which YHWH dispenses mercy.[85] As implied by the covenantally charged context and terminology, those who maintain covenant relationship with YHWH will be able to find forgiveness. But

82.   Piper, *Justification*, 75–89, essentially isolates Exod. 33.19 in important ways from its broader context, and therefore fails to see important contextual factors for its interpretation.

83.   This is not to say that YHWH is merely agreeing to grant mercy to those who do not need it; rather, it is a typical expression of the OT principles of personal responsibility and the availability of forgiveness for those who maintain relationship with YHWH, even though they might sin (cf. Deut. 24.16; Jer. 18.1–10; Ezek. 18). The sin referred to in 32.33 is the sin of apostasy, which breaks covenant relationship.

84.   This reflects the standard translation and understanding of 34.7. Piper, *Justification*, 85, argues unconvincingly for an alternative translation that relates to the completeness rather than certainty of absolution, supporting the unconditional bestowal of YHWH's mercy and punishment; see Abasciano, 'Paul's Use', 169–70 (esp. nn. 96–99), for critique.

85.   Contra Piper, *Justification*, 85–86, the fact that the Hebrew text of 34.7 does not explicitly identify the character of those who receive either mercy or punishment should not be taken as an indication of unconditional choice on YHWH's part, for the context makes clear the character of the objects of YHWH's mercy and judgment; see Abasciano, 'Paul's Use', 169–70 nn. 97–98.

those who are punished are those who have practiced iniquity (as well as their posterity who presumably follow in their path). The close parallel of Exod. 20.5–6, surely alluded to here, provides important background for 34.6–7, establishing the textual presupposition that YHWH extends mercy to those who love him and generally keep his commandments, but punishes to the uttermost those who hate him and do not maintain covenant relationship with him.

The *idem per idem* formula of Exodus 33.19 expresses in the most emphatic terms that YHWH is above all gracious and merciful, and that he will decide who he will extend his mercy to. But his sovereign freedom in bestowing mercy is not arbitrary. The connotation of freedom communicated by the idiom of 33.19 leaves the grounds upon which YHWH bases his choice of who will receive his mercy unspecified. This, of course, does not mean that there are no considerations outside of his own will that condition his choice. The point is rather that he determines the conditions for the dispensing of his mercy (and punishment). He will show mercy to whom he will show mercy. The context of Exodus 33.19 discloses who it is that YHWH will have mercy upon – those who repent of their sin, maintain covenant relationship with him, and who are connected to his righteous and faithful covenant mediator. Yet, the absence of explicit conditions inherent in the *idem per idem* formula does imply that there is no merit in the objects of YHWH's mercy that *require* him to extend mercy to them. It is his free choice, based on whatever conditions he pleases to lay down. YHWH is both gracious and sovereign. This is the essence of YHWH's name, that is, his glory or goodness.

3.1.g. *Exodus 34.1–9*

This section begins the description of the renewal of the covenant procured by Moses' intercession and completes the account of Moses' third intercession by describing the fulfillment of YHWH's promise to pass by Moses in all his glory, proclaiming his name. 34.5–7 records the theophany proper, giving a fuller explication of YHWH's name:

> Then YHWH passed before him and proclaimed, 'YHWH, YHWH, a gracious and compassionate God, slow to anger, and abounding in covenant lovingkindness and faithfulness, keeping covenant lovingkindness for thousands, forgiving iniquity, rebellion, and sin. But he will certainly not leave unpunished, visiting the iniquity of the fathers on the children, even on the children's children and on the third and on the fourth generation.'

This definitive revelation of YHWH conveys again the two contrasting themes of his mercy and judgment found throughout Exodus 32–34.

Moses responded to this supreme revelation of YHWH also in a two-folded way, first in worship, but second, with a final intercession: 'If, please, I have found favor in your eyes, my Lord, let my Lord please go in our midst, even though[86] it is a stiff-necked people, and forgive our iniquity and our sin, and take us as a possession' (34.9). His prayer is again founded on YHWH's favor towards him (who now completely identifies himself with Israel). Indeed, since knowledge of YHWH brings his favor (33.13), and Moses has received an unprecedented revelation of his glory, he may now appeal to unprecedented favor for the consummation of all he has pursued. Moses' request shows again that YHWH's presence is determinative of election, and that he seeks both that presence and the election for Israel, as well as the forgiveness required for them. It furthermore exalts YHWH's mercy once again.

3.1.h. *Exodus 34.10–28*

YHWH responds affirmatively to Moses' request by renewing the covenant. He promises miracles and success in conquest, and calls for obedience to the covenant stipulations given in 34.12–26, which 'emphasize those particular aspects [of the covenant] which are relevant to the sinful tendencies which Israel has displayed'.[87] Although the covenant has been renewed, it is significantly different in that YHWH has not made the covenant directly with Israel, but *with Moses* and with Israel (34.27), 'that is, directly with Moses on the mountain, and *through* Moses with the people'.[88] 'So the position of Israel in the restored covenant is not identical to what it would have been had the people never sinned. Henceforth their life as a people depends not only upon the mercy of God but also upon the intercession of God's chosen mediator.'[89] The Lord's mercy toward Israel is now dependent on their identification with the faithful covenant mediator.

---

86. See Moberly, *Mountain*, 89–90, for the three main options for interpreting כִּי here in 34.9 – causal, concessive, and emphatic concessive. Piper, *Justification*, 81, curiously argues for a straightforward causal sense over against the usual concessive interpretation.

87. Moberly, *Mountain*, 96; emphasis removed. He correctly notes that the many covenant stipulations previously given in Exodus but not now specified are presupposed.

88. Hafemann, *Paul*, 220–21; emphasis original.

89. Moberly, *Mountain*, 106 (cf. 75, 105).

3.1.i. *Exodus 34.29–35*

This final section of the narrative brings the new state of affairs to a climax as it records Moses' return to the people and his continuing, though enhanced, function as the (now glorified) covenant mediator. After experiencing the glory of YHWH, Moses' face now radiates that same glory.[90] Thus, Moses brings both the new covenant inscribed on the stone tablets and the very glory of YHWH to the people. Moses' glorified countenance and escalated covenant-mediatorial role serves to substantiate his authority. But more than this, as Hafemann has argued, it presents the resolution to the problem of how YHWH can dwell in the midst of a sinful people.[91] Moses has become the mediator of both the covenant Law and YHWH's covenant presence.[92]

At the sight of Moses' shining face, Israel was terrified, presumably because of the divine glory (cf. 20.18–21) and especially because of YHWH's statements that his presence would destroy the people (33.3, 5). Therefore, Moses would put a veil over his face unless before YHWH speaking with him or speaking YHWH's word to the people as the covenant mediator. Hafemann has again captured the theological thrust of the narrative at this point:

> Against the backdrop of the explicit statements of Exod. 32:9, 22 and 33:3, 5 and the function of the tent of meeting in 33:7–11, Moses' veiling himself should be seen as an act of mercy to keep the people from being destroyed by the reflected presence of God. The veil of Moses makes it possible for the glory of God to be in the midst of the people, albeit now mediated through Moses, without destroying them. . . . In view of the people's 'stiff neck' and idolatry with the golden calf, Moses' veil is the final expression of YHWH's judgment and mercy, which runs throughout this narrative and ties it together theologically. The fact that the glory must be veiled is an expression of Israel's sinful state and God's consequent judgment; the fact that the glory is veiled is an expression of God's unexpected mercy.[93]

---

90. The Hebrew text literally says that Moses' face was horned (קָרַן), but most scholars agree that this must refer to shining light. Neither the OT text nor Jewish tradition understood the glory on Moses' face to be fading as it is commonly held that Paul asserted in 2 Cor. 3.7–18; it was conceived of as permanent. See Hafemann, *Paul*, esp. 286–313, 347–62, on this point and the argument that Paul did not posit a fading glory either.

91. Hafemann, *Paul*, 221–25.

92. Hafemann, *Paul*, 222.

93. Hafemann, *Paul*, 223–24; italics removed.

Thus, the narrative is brought to a conclusion. The problem of how YHWH can be in covenant with a sinful people and dwell in their midst has been resolved along with the fate of Israel and her election. YHWH's merciful character and the mediation of his covenant and glory through his faithful servant make it possible for Israel to participate in the covenant and its blessings through their connection and identification with Moses. The reason for the unusual use of the verb meaning 'to have horns' (קרן; 34.29, 30, 35) to describe the glory shining from Moses' face now becomes clear. It is a contrasting allusion to the calf, which the people designated for the mediation of YHWH's presence and blessing.[94] The allusion implies that rather than the people's choice, it is the man of YHWH's own choosing (Moses) who will mediate his presence and blessing. YHWH himself will fix the terms of his salvation. In the words of 33.19, he will be gracious to whom he will be gracious, and show mercy to whom he will show mercy.[95]

3.2. *Textual Comparison of Romans 9.3 and Exodus 32.32*

We must now turn to a comparison of the text of Rom. 9.3 and the textual tradition of Exod. 32.32.

Rom. 9.3	ηὐχόμην γὰρ ἀνάθεμα εἶναι αὐτὸς ἐγὼ ἀπὸ τοῦ Χριστοῦ ὑπὲρ τῶν ἀδελφῶν μου τῶν συγγενῶν μου κατὰ σάρκα
Exod. 32.32 LXX	Καὶ νῦν εἰ μὲν ἀφεῖς αὐτοῖς τὴν ἁμαρτίαν ἄφες εἰ δὲ μὴ ἐξάλειψόν με ἐκ τῆς βίβλου σου ἧς ἔγραψας
Exod. 32.32 MT	וְעַתָּה אִם־תִּשָּׂא חַטָּאתָם וְאִם־אַיִן מְחֵנִי נָא מִסִּפְרְךָ אֲשֶׁר כָּתָבְתָּ

The preceding comparison shows that there is no verbal similarity between Rom. 9.3 and Exod. 32.32.[96] Nevertheless, the thematic coherence, volume, and recurrence of this allusion are so strong that most commentators recognize the parallel, as mentioned earlier. While the

---

94. See Moberly, *Mountain*, 108–109.

95. On the use of Exodus 32–34, or parts of it, in the rest of the OT, see Gowan, *Theology*, 240–43; Hafemann, *Paul*, 232–42; Childs, *Exodus*.

96. There is also no verbal similarity between Rom. 9.3 and LXX Est. 4.17, which has little claim to being a true allusion despite the contention of P. Bratsiotis, 'Eine exegetische Notiz zu Röm. IX.3 and X.1', *NovT* (1962), 299–300. There simply is not enough similarity between the two passages. There is slightly more support for an allusion in Rom. 10.1 since there is some faint verbal coherence, but not enough to convince. It is more likely that LXX Est. 4.17 forms part of the general backdrop

thematic connection between the old and new context is obvious enough, the volume and recurrence of this allusion call for brief explanation.

The volume of the allusion is high, not for explicit repetition of words or structure, which are absent, but for its distinctive place among Old Testament instances of intercessory prayer on behalf of Israel. Moreover, it occurs in one of the most prominent passages in all of the Old Testament, central to the Book of Exodus, part of the *locus classicus* of the Sinaitic/Mosaic covenant, and the paradigmatic passage of apostasy and restoration. As for the recurrence of the allusion, we note that Rom. 9.15 quotes Exod. 33.19 from the same context of Exodus 32–34. Moreover, Paul's allusions to Exodus 32–34 elsewhere show that the passage was important to him and strengthens the likelihood of an allusion in 9.3 (see 1 Cor. 10.7; 2 Corinthians 3; cf. Rom. 1.23; Phil. 4.3). Thus, Exod. 32.32 meets every test for a scriptural allusion discussed in our introductory chapter. There is strong warrant for treating it as such, and as we shall see, as a pointer to the broader context of Exodus 32–34.

There is very little difference between the MT and LXX of Exod. 32.32.[97] The only change of any real substance is the addition of an apodosis (ἄφες) to fill the anacoluthon of the MT in the first half of the verse.[98] But this is of no interpretive or theological import, and therefore testifies to the faithfulness of the LXX to the Hebrew text represented by the MT in this verse, which is also representative of the LXX translation of Exodus 32–34 in general.[99] Indeed, Hafemann has concluded that the LXX emphasizes the themes of God's presence in the midst of his sinful people, the problem this poses, and Moses' indispensable mediatorial role even more dramatically than the Hebrew textual tradition.[100]

---

of Jewish tradition *vis-à-vis* the willingness to sacrifice in order to help the nation as seen in the references mentioned by Dunn, *Romans*, 525. F. Siegert, *Argumentation bei Paulus: gezeigt an Röm 9–11* (WUNT, 34; Tübingen: Mohr Siebeck, 1985), 121, points to Num. 11.15 as a parallel to Rom. 9.3, but it has little to commend it beyond an extremely superficial similarity.

97. See Wevers, *Exodus*, 517–73, for a full description of the differences between the Hebrew and LXX of Exodus 32–34, including Septuagintal variants and with a concern for the translator's interpretation of the text. For a significant treatment of variations between the same, conducted with theological depth and a concern for Paul's interpretation of Exodus 32–34, see Hafemann, *Paul*, 242–54. Wevers, 537, lists several other minor changes in the LXX textual tradition of 32.32 not mentioned below.

98. See note 41 above.

99. See Hafemann, *Paul*, 242.

100. Hafemann, *Paul*, 245–46.

3.3. *Interpretive Traditions Surrounding Exod. 32.32*

The next step in our investigation is to survey the interpretive traditions surrounding Exod. 32.32 prior to or roughly contemporaneous with Paul. There are not many specific references to Exod. 32.32 in the relevant Jewish and Christian literature apart from the concept of the book of life. But there are many references to its broader context of Exodus 32–34, so much so that we cannot explore all of them. We must content ourselves with exploring what we regard as the most relevant material to Paul's argument in Romans 9–11.

3.3.a. *Pseudo-Philo/Liber Antiquitatum Biblicarum*
Pseudo-Philo retells the story of Exodus 32–34 in *LAB* 12, written sometime around the first century.[101] *LAB* 12.4 confirms that the fulfillment of God's promises to Israel was threatened by Israel's sin with the golden calf. The Lord responded to the incident by asking Moses, 'Are the promises that I promised to your fathers when I said to them, "To your seed I will give the land in which you dwell" – are they at an end?'[102] We may also observe that Ps.-Philo took the land promise of Gen. 12.7 as representative of the Abrahamic promises found in Genesis 12.[103] Thus, for Ps.-Philo, Israel's apostasy in Exodus 32 threatens the fulfillment of the Abrahamic promises.

Ps.-Philo depicts Moses as far more certain about the fulfillment of God's word and the restoration of Israel than the biblical account (*LAB* 12.6). Thus, the issue of the faithfulness of God's word is stressed even more by his interpretation of Exodus 32–34. As for the people of Israel, he took there to be a divinely recognized distinction among them over the relative degree of guilt in the worship of the golden calf: 'if

---

101. On the date of *LAB*, see D.J. Harrington, 'Pseudo-Philo: A New Translation and Introduction', in J.H. Charlesworth (ed.), *The Old Testament Pseudepigrapha* (2 vols.; New York: Doubleday, 1983–85), 2.297–377 (299), whose translation we use; H. Jacobson, *A Commentary on Pseudo-Philo's Liber Antiquitatum Biblicarum with Latin Text and English Translation* (2 vols.; Leiden: Brill, 1996), 199–210; L.H. Feldman, 'Prolegomenon', in M.R. James, *The Biblical Antiquities of Philo* (The Library of Biblical Studies; New York: KTAV, 1971), vii–CLXIX (xxviii).

102. Italics removed. Cf. similarly James, *Philo*, 111. But on dubious grounds, Jacobson, *Pseudo-Philo*, 111, 487, claims that both Harrington and James seriously misunderstand the text.

103. Jacobson, *Pseudo-Philo*, 488, points out that this is actually a conflation of Gen. 12.7; 17.8; Exod. 32.13; 33.1.

anyone had it in his will and mind that the calf be made, his tongue was cut off; but if he had been forced by fear to consent, his face shown' (*LAB* 12.7b).[104] This is a logical expansion of the biblical account based on the expressed conviction that those who committed the sin of apostasy would be punished, while those who did not would not be (Exod. 32.30–35). Ps.-Philo appears to attempt to account for the fact that Exodus presents (1) the people as a whole as sinning with the calf; (2) God as committing to punish all who sinned (32.33–34); and (3) only a portion of the people actually suffering punishment. Exodus does not explicitly address this question, but some type of distinction with respect to the degree of guilt among the people in the worship of the calf is the logical implication of the text.[105] The fact that *LAB* does not speak of the death of anyone for the idolatry of the calf, but of the cutting off of the tongues of the guilty, puts the real focus of the question of punishment onto the question of whether Israel as a nation will be cast away and destroyed, taken up in Moses' intercession on behalf of Israel (*LAB* 12.8–9).

Rather than the several Mosaic intercessions found in Exodus 32–34, Ps.-Philo presents only one, at the place where Exodus has Moses' second intercession (Exod. 32.30–35). It appears to be an interpretive summary of the essence of Moses' several intercessions. It is striking that Moses begins by identifying Israel as the Lord's vine, since Paul speaks of Israel as an olive tree in Rom. 11.17–24. Israel needs God's favor because it has lost its fruit and has not recognized its cultivator (12.8).[106] Israel's loss of fruit probably refers to its corruption or loss of righteousness through her apostasy (cf. Mt. 3.7–11; Lk. 3.7–9; Eph. 5.9, 11). Her failure to acknowledge the Lord (i.e. the Cultivator) was the heart of her sin. Though he does not mention the covenant explicitly, Ps.-Philo's interpretation is consonant with our covenantal interpretation, which finds covenant recognition to be central to the problem of Exodus 32–34.

Moses' argument in *LAB* 12.8–9 is similar to that in Exod. 32.11–13, but there are significant differences relevant to Romans 9–11. First, Ps.-Philo addresses the possibility of a new people replacing Israel,

---

104.   Cf. *Targ. Song.* 1.5, cited by Jacobson, *Pseudo-Philo*, 496.

105.   See Hafemann, *Paul*, 205, on this question.

106.   Jacobson, *Pseudo-Philo*, 498, and James, *Philo*, 112, read *emisit* rather than *amisit*, and so understand the vine to have put forth fruit rather than to have lost it. This is quite possible. But Jacobson bases his judgment principally on the false supposition that the loss of fruit is inappropriate to this context.

raised by Exod. 32.10. The Moses of *LAB* insists that God will have no people to glorify him if he destroys Israel, because a new chosen people will not trust the Lord who destroyed the former people. Intriguingly, many have argued that a similar thought precipitated Paul's argument in Romans 9–11.[107] Ps.-Philo again raises the issue of the faithfulness of God to his word even more strongly than Exodus does.

Second, the consideration of the faithfulness of God *vis-à-vis* the replacement of Israel by a new people is all the more significant since Moses moves from the abandonment of Israel to the abandonment of the world. He seems to equate the one with the other in some way. The underlying thought appears to be that Israel is the key to the blessing and well-being of the world.[108] For God to forsake Israel is for him to forsake the world, though Ps.-Philo does not develop the thought. Nevertheless, he shows clearly that he associated Exodus 32–34 with the possibility of God forsaking Israel and electing a new people, and with God's faithfulness to his promises to Israel, which he finds necessary for the good of the world.

Third, as Moses draws near to the end of his intercession, he again asks that God fulfill the word he had spoken (i.e. the promises he already made to Israel) as well as the promises that still *must* be spoken, apparently referring to all of the Scriptures that follow Exodus 32–34. This is another instance of the unwavering confidence of *LAB*'s Moses in the faithfulness of God to his word to Israel. He would never cast them aside without remedy.

One further passage from *LAB* deserves our attention. In 19.7 God speaks to Moses of Israel's future defection from him in idolatry, resulting in his forsaking of them to the destruction of their enemies. He likens that day to the day of his smashing of the tablets of the covenant recorded in Exod. 32.19. Their sin resulted in the writing of the tablets flying away. While most commentators find the point of similarity to be the date of these occurrences,[109] there seems to be more than just this going on. In view of the context of abandonment, it would seem that the Lord is again indicating that he will forsake Israel, the significance of the breaking of the tablets of the covenant for Ps.-Philo. This coheres with God's initial response to the golden calf in *LAB* 12.4, to forsake Israel, though he would eventually reconcile with them.

---

107. See e.g., Hays, *Echoes*, 64; Ziesler, *Romans*, 234; Piper, *Justification*, 46.

108. Cf. Gen. 12.3; Isa. 2.2–4; 56.6–8; 60.1–22; Mic. 4.1–5; Zech. 2.8–13; 14.1–21; Tob. 13.3–14; *Sib. Or.* 3.702–23; *T. Zeb.* 9.5–9; Philo, *Sobr.* 66; *Spec. Leg.* 2.163; *Vit. Mos.* 1.149; 2.224–25.

109. Jacobson, *Pseudo-Philo*, 625.

3.3.b. *The Testament of Moses*

T. Mos. 3.9 may allude to Exod. 32.13 in its placement of Moses' appeal to God's covenant faithfulness to the patriarchs in the mouths of the tribes of Israel. But since *T. Mos.* is based squarely on Deuteronomy, and the former's use of the name Jacob accords with the latter's usage (Deut. 9.5, 27) instead of the use of the name Israel in Exod. 32.13, it is certain that the prime allusion here is to Deut. 9.5, 27. Nevertheless, Deuteronomy 9–10 presents itself as a first-person narrative description of the events recorded in Exodus 32–34, and is therefore directly related to that passage. Hence, Exod. 32.13 may be regarded as part of the background to *T. Mos.* 3.9. In this pseudepigraphal passage, we have an allusion to Moses' intercession on behalf of Israel in the golden calf episode singling out his argument for God's forgiveness and restoration of Israel based on his covenant faithfulness to the fathers.

T. Mos. 3.9 testifies to what was likely a dominant conviction among Jews of the first century when it was written,[110] viz., that God would not ultimately forsake Israel but would certainly fulfill his covenant and oath to the fathers Abraham, Isaac, and Jacob. The firmness of God's covenant promises to Israel is in fact a major theme of *T. Mos.* (1.8–9; 3.9; 4.2–6; 12.2–13).[111] That the author connected this theme with the events of Deuteronomy 9/Exodus 32–34 is probably evidence that he recognized in them the first and great threat to Israel's covenant relationship with the Lord. Moreover, it is striking that this theme is grounded in the Lord's foreknowledge, a matter not unrelated to Romans 9.

Some would characterize the theology of *T. Mos.* as deterministic,[112] and indeed, there is some measure of determinism in the book. But it is open to question whether *T. Mos.* really advocates a full determinism, not only because it advocates human responsibility and judgment, but also because it nowhere states this explicitly except in 1.13 with reference to the nations, a passage we must come back to. The only other place where it might state a clear determinism (12.4–5) is only conjecture

---

110. For a helpful and concise discussion of the date of *T. Mos.*, see J. Priest, 'Testament of Moses: A New Translation and Introduction' in Charlesworth (ed.), *Pseudepigrapha*, 1.919–34 (920–21); for a full-scale introduction to the book, see J. Tromp, *The Assumption of Moses: A Critical Edition with Commentary* (SVTP, 10; Leiden: Brill, 1993), 27–131.

111. See Priest, 'Moses', 922.

112. See Priest, 'Moses', 922.

because the text is in need of emendation and partially illegible.[113] Rather, God's foreknowledge is emphasized throughout the work, including at 12.4–5. As Charles has pointed out, 'in xii. 4, 5, 13, it is God's foreknowledge, and not his predetermining purpose that is dwelt upon'.[114] Indeed, for the author of *T. Mos.*, it seems to be Israel as an entity that will persevere and find God's blessing, while individuals will be included/blessed or excluded/destroyed based on whether they keep the commandments (12.10–13).

The emphasis on foreknowledge shows up in connection with the allusion to the intercession of Moses (Deuteronomy 9/Exodus 32) through his prophecy of divine judgment upon Israel (see 3.10ff.). This leads us to the primary feature of Moses in *T. Mos.*, that of mediator, intercessor, and prophet.[115] Interestingly, references to Moses as mediator/intercessor are all connected to statements of predetermination or foreknowledge (1.14; 3.9–13; 11.11, 14, 17 with 12.4–13).

Moreover, these themes are also linked to the role of the nations with Israel in 1.12–14 and 12.4–12. We find that God created the world for Israel and intended to hide his purpose from the nations so they would incur guilt and presumably be judged/destroyed. As Tromp has observed, there is a contrast between 1.13 and 1.14 of '[t]he primeval election of Israel (established in the covenant mediated by Moses) . . . and the condemnation of the nations'.[116] So there is no vision for the salvation of the Gentiles, but only of Israel, the guilty of which God will use the nations to punish (12.11). All of this is highly relevant for Paul's argument in Romans 9. It seems unlikely, though possible, that Paul had read or heard *T. Mos.*, but it surely illuminates the type of thought within first-century Judaism that Paul was interacting with and in which Exodus 32–34 figured.

Tiede has drawn attention to the prophetic/intercessory role of Moses *vis-à-vis* suffering.[117] In his advocacy on behalf of Israel, Moses suffered for their sake (3.11, immediately following the allusion to Exodus 32!).

---

113. Priest's ('Moses', 934) conjectural translation is deterministic, while Tromp's (*Moses*, 262–63) emphasizes foreknowledge.

114. R.H. Charles, *The Assumption of Moses* (London: Adam and Charles Black, 1897), 50 n. 8.

115. See D.L. Tiede, 'The Figure of Moses in *The Testament of Moses*', in G.W.E. Nickelsburg (ed.), *Studies on the Testament of Moses* (Septuagint and Cognate Studies, 4; Cambridge, MA: SBL, 1973), 86–92.

116. Tromp, *Moses*, 143.

117. Tiede, 'Moses', 88.

Since the golden calf episode is in the background, we can take this suffering intercessor motif to go back to there at least; and what point in that context is more dramatic in this regard than Exod. 32.32? Moreover, *T. Mos.* portrays Moses as a prophet who delivered eschatological secrets relating to Israel, the Gentiles, and the covenant faithfulness of God to his word.[118] This raises the possibility that in Romans 9 Paul tapped into this current interpretive tradition regarding Moses. Surely we have seen that issues of the faithfulness of God to his covenant promises to Israel, God's sovereignty and foreknowledge, and Moses' role as mediator/intercessor/prophet attached to the golden calf episode, the foundational account bringing together his mediatorial and intercessory roles.

3.3.c. *1 Enoch*
1 En. 89.32–35, probably written in the second century B.C.E.,[119] presents the story of the golden calf as a vision-allegory in which the people of Israel are sheep, Moses is the lead sheep (eventually turned into a man), and the Lord is called the Lord of the sheep. The author took Exodus 32 to indicate that the majority of Israel 'had been blinded in their eyes and gone astray' (89.33). That is, they committed idolatry with the golden calf. But by slaying (some of) the sheep who had gone astray with the help of other different sheep (i.e. the Levites), Moses 'caused those sheep which went astray to return, and brought them back into their folds' (89.35); that is, he led them to repentance and renewed relationship with the Lord. Thus, the author of *1 Enoch* interpreted Exodus 32 as reporting (or implying) the repentance of the Israelites, necessary for their restoration. Despite the fact that he fully credits Moses with bringing about their repentance and restoration, it is interesting that he says nothing about his intercession on their behalf. This lays greater stress on the need for repentance and action in the Israelites.

3.3.d. *The Martyrdom of Isaiah*
Mart. Isa. 3.8–9 alludes to Exod. 33.20. If Jonathan Knight is correct that these verses are actually an early Christian attack on Judaism/the

---

118. Tiede, 'Moses', 88.
119. See E. Isaac, '1 (Ethiopic Apocalypse of) Enoch: A New Translation and Introduction', in Charlesworth (ed.), *Pseudepigrapha*, 1.5–89 (7), whose translation is used below.

authority of Moses,[120] then we would have an example of Exod. 33.20 being used to repudiate Judaism not too long after Paul wrote Romans, evidencing the type of attitude he sought to correct in Romans 9–11. It would fit into the body of early extra-biblical Christian literature as one of the earlier denunciations of Judaism *per se*, and a rather extreme one at that for its implicit disparagement of Moses, which would be quite unusual for such literature.[121] But there is no reason to posit such an unusual attitude towards Moses, for Knight's interpretation is unwarranted on the level of exegesis, and perhaps even dating.

It is beyond the scope of this investigation to delve deeply into the details of dating *Mart. Isa.*, but we should note that scholars have traditionally held the work to be composite, and dated the section containing 3.8–9 no later than the first century C.E.[122] As for exegesis, Knight seems to read too much out of what *may* be a polemical thrust in the text. The evil Belkira accuses Isaiah of being a false prophet partly on the basis of Moses' statement that no one can see the Lord over against Isaiah's claim to have seen the Lord. Knight assumes that the author of *Mart. Isa.* sides with Isaiah against Moses, and does not even consider the much more likely possibility that the author might argue that Moses and/or Isaiah has been interpreted incorrectly. But it may be that Knight has detected a real polemical situation behind *Mart. Isa.* 3.8–9 in which the statement of Exod. 33.20 was used by Jews 'to deny the possibility of mystical vision and the value of Christian theology'.[123] If so, it probably has nothing to do with disparagement of the authority of Moses, but rather correct scriptural interpretation and the Jewish polemical use of

120.   J. Knight, *Disciples of the Beloved One: The Christology, Social Setting and Theological Context of the Ascension of Isaiah* (JSPSup, 18; Sheffield: Sheffield Academic Press, 1996), 43–44, 190–96.

121.   Knight, *Disciples*, 33–39, dates *Mart. Isa.* sometime in the period 112–38 C.E. For the patristic literature on the golden calf episode, see L. Smolar and M. Aberbach, 'The Golden Calf Episode in Postbiblical Literature', *HUCA* 39 (1968), 91–116 (95, 98–101).

122.   On the composition and date of the book, see J.H. Charlesworth, *The Pseudepigrapha and Modern Research* (SBLSCS, 7; Missoula, MT: Scholars Press, 1976), 125–30; M.A. Knibb, 'Martyrdom and Ascension of Isaiah: A New Translation and Introduction', in Charlesworth (ed.), *Pseudepigrapha*, 2.143–76 (147–50); Knight, *Disciples*, 28–32. Knibb and Charlesworth suggest a second-century-C.E. date for the section containing the allusion to Exod. 33.20, while Knight argues for one author who shaped his sources, and focuses on the final form of the text.

123.   J. Knight, *The Ascension of Isaiah* (Sheffield: Sheffield Academic Press, 1995), 53.

Exod. 33.20 and Isa. 6.1. In that case, it would be significant that early Christians clashed with Jews over the former verse, which appears in a context of threat to the elect status of Israel.

Even more relevant for our purposes is that the false prophet Belkira uses Isa. 1.10 – a direct continuation of Isa. 1.9, quoted by Paul in Rom. 9.29 – against Isaiah in the very next verse, *Mart. Isa.* 3.10. The fact that Isaiah called Jerusalem Sodom and its leaders Gomorrah is used as evidence against Isaiah to condemn him to death. The significance for us is that the placing of Israel/Judaism in the place of wicked Gentiles and God's judgment was treated with utter contempt. Now the text is obviously critical of this, which leads us to suspect that this was a popular attitude that the author of *Mart. Isa.* sought to correct, whether it be the insider criticism of a Jewish author according to the typical dating of the passage, or the polemical criticism of an early Christian author according to the latest trend in dating the book. *Mart. Isa.* 3.8–10 is notable for revealing part of the socio-religious background behind Paul's argument in Romans 9–11 in what was likely a popular Jewish attitude of contempt for the identification of Jews with Gentiles in sin and divine judgment, an attitude Paul had to take into account as he crafted an argument that made such identifications. It is likewise notable for connecting this attitude with Isa. 1.10 and Exod. 33.20.

3.3.e. *4 Ezra*

4 Ezra 7.106 alludes to Moses' intercession on behalf of Israel in Exodus 32–34.[124] For the character Ezra, Moses serves as an example of successful intercession on behalf of the ungodly, a precedent that should also obtain on the day of judgment. But the angel Uriel reveals to Ezra that this is not so (7.112–15). *4 Ezra* 6.35–9.25 (Ezra's third vision) has a number of salient similarities to Romans 9 and will be dealt with in even more detail in the next chapter. For now, we will restrict our comments to observations given little or no attention in our later discussion.

First, we may observe that, just as Romans 9, Ezra's discussion with the divine messenger, which delves deeply into theodicy, begins with an

---

124. M.E. Stone, *Fourth Ezra: A Commentary on the Book of Fourth Ezra* (Hermeneia; Minneapolis: Fortress, 1990), 251, considers the allusion to be to Exod. 32.11–14, but since the reference is to Moses' intercession in general for those who sinned in the desert, it is better to acknowledge this as an allusion to his intercessory activity throughout Exodus 32–34.

expression of Israel's privileged status and a challenge to the reliability of God's promises to his people:

> All this I have spoken before you, O Lord, because you have said that it was for us that you created this world. As for the other nations that have descended from Adam, you have said that they are nothing, and that they are like spittle, and you have compared their abundance to a drop from a bucket. And now, O Lord, these nations, which are reputed to be as nothing, domineer over us and devour us. But we your people, whom you have called your firstborn, only begotten, zealous for you, and most dear, have been given into their hands. If the world has indeed been created for us, why do we not possess our world as an inheritance? How long will this be so? (6.55–59; NRSV)

For both Paul and the author of *4 Ezra* there was at least an apparent discrepancy between the elect status of Israel and the fact that she was not experiencing what God had promised her. What is more, they both come to the conclusion that in some way the elect status of ethnic Israel does not guarantee fulfillment of God's promises to Jews based on ethnicity. Thus, we have an allusion to Exodus 32–34 again connected to the theme of the faithfulness of God's word to Israel, and in this instance also connected to the consideration of the meaning of Israel's election. It is striking that *4 Ezra* argues that the election of Israel ultimately holds no secure promise for Jews based on ethnicity, an unusual stance. This author's position cannot be said to determine Paul's position, but it gives us a clearer picture of the types of issues whirling about in his first-century context and an example of the extreme reactions elicited by his socio-historical milieu.

Second, flowing from his theology of individual merit, the author of *4 Ezra* teaches that the majority of Israel will be lost because of its unfaithfulness, the logical consequence of passages such as 7.46–48 and 9.14–16. The allusion to Exodus 32–34 appears in connection with the assertion that the arrival of the eschaton will render ineffective any intercession of the righteous for the wicked. This perception of the state of Israel provides a comparable viewpoint to Paul's concern in Rom. 9.1–5 that the vast majority of Israel was separated from Christ and his salvation by its unbelief.

Third, arising from this accursed state of Israel is an expression of great grief similar to Paul's lament in Rom. 9.1–5:

> About mankind you know best; but I will speak about your people, for whom I am grieved, and about your inheritance, for whom I lament, and about Israel, for whom I am sad, and about the seed of Jacob, for whom

> I am troubled. Therefore I will pray before you for myself and for them,
> for I see the failings of us who inhabit the land (8:15–17).[125]

Such anguished sorrow demonstrates the severity of Israel's plight. Indeed, the text speaks of eschatological damnation. This suggests that Paul's language in Rom. 9.1–5 also relates to a plight of the severest proportions. Israel's suffering at the hands of the Gentiles is probably a secondary source of Ezra's grief over his people, which leads us to our next observation.

As can be seen in 6.55–59 quoted above, Ezra's quandary concerning Israel's election and the apparent failure of God's word to her is tied up with a certain measure of God's blessing having been granted to the Gentiles so that they rule over Israel. The problem is not only that ethnic Israel has not obtained the fulfillment of God's promises, though that is bad enough, but it is also that God has granted some sort of favor to the Gentiles over against Israel. A similar tension between the role of Jew and Gentile in God's end-time plan also figures in Paul's argument in Romans 9–11. This brings us to a final brief observation, viz., that both *4 Ezra* 6.35–9.25 and Romans 9–11 are eschatological in character.

It would be going too far to suggest that in 7.106 the author of *4 Ezra* interpreted Exodus 32–34 as directly having to do with all the themes we have identified, but it is notable that in his discussion of these themes he appeals to this passage in Exodus. One might object that it is the mere occurrence of intercession that establishes the link. Maybe so, but it is surely significant that the same themes treated by *4 Ezra* swirl around Paul's argument in Romans 9 where he alludes to some of the same passages, such as Exodus 32–34. Indeed, it seems likely that the author of *4 Ezra* understood Exodus 32–34 in relation to the faithfulness of God's word to Israel and the fate of the chosen nation, themes that could naturally be related to the role and status of the Gentiles in God's eschatological plan.[126]

3.3.f. *Philo*

Philo treats the golden calf episode directly and at some length in *Spec. Leg.* 3.125–27, *Vit. Mos.* 2.161–72, 270–74, each of which has a specific

---

125.   B.M. Metzger's translation ('The Fourth Book of Ezra: A New Translation and Introduction', in Charlesworth (ed.), *Pseudepigrapha*, 1.517–59 [542]).

126.   For additional allusions to Exodus 32–34 in the OT Pseudepigrapha, see *Sib. Or.* 3.17–19 (Exod. 33.20); *2 En.* 25.1 (Exod. 33.11; improbable allusion); 37.2 (Exod. 34.29ff.); *Ques. Ezra* 39 (Exod. 33.11, etc.); *1 En.* 47.3 (Book of Life).

focus on the faithful response of the Levites and the consequent establishment of their special ministry. The fact that Philo was most impressed by this aspect of the story reveals that he found its primary significance in its demonstration of what makes one worthy in God's estimation. Indeed, elsewhere he considered Moses to be the model of the virtuous wise man *par excellence*.[127] He goes so far as to quote Exod. 33.17 to show that Moses pleased God above all, drawing the conclusion that Moses was worthy of God's grace (*Deus Imm.* 109)! This could be the very type of thought Paul sought to counter in Romans 9. Paul would undoubtedly agree with the modern commentators who find that Exodus in no way attributes YHWH's capitulation to Moses' righteousness.[128] However, Philo probably did not think of such worthiness as meritorious (see below), but rather as that which inclined God to be favorable toward a person.

Quite a number of passages in Philo that allude to Exodus 32–34 develop the allusions in the vein of separation from the fleshly and natural on the one hand, and pursuit of God/wisdom/virtue/spiritual things on the other.[129] These share a common theme of separation from the earthly and mortal for pursuit of God as making one worthy in some way before God. In *Det. Pot. Ins.* 160 (quoting Exod. 33.7), for example, it made Moses a worthy suppliant.

Philo's most important allusion along these lines for our purposes comes in *Rer. Div. Her.* 20, where he quotes Exod. 32.32, the most direct focus of our attention. The context argues that it is the wise/virtuous who have good confidence for freedom of speech to advance positive claims upon God. Indeed, 'all the wise are friends of God, and particularly so in the judgement of the most holy lawgiver'.[130] So again, Philo advocates a worthiness before God based on wisdom and virtue. But this is probably not to be thought of as meritorious works-righteousness, for Philo goes on to extol the need for humility before the Lord (*Rer. Div. Her.* 24–31), confessing the impossibility of worthiness before God and of deserving to inherit his works (*Rer. Div. Her.* 33).

---

127. In this section on Philo's interpretation of Exodus 32–34, references for allusions to Exodus are cited in parentheses and follow the Philonic passages. See *Deus Imm.* 109 (33.17); *Poster. C.* 136 (32.7); *Leg. All.* 3.142 (34.28).

128. See e.g., Piper, *Justification*, 81.

129. *Poster. C.* 158 (33.20); *Fug.* 90 (33.26); *Ebr.* 67 (32.27–29), 96 (32.17), 100 (33.7); *Rer. Div. Her.* 20 (32.32); *Leg. All.* 2.54 (33.7); 3.46 (33.7); 3.101 (33.13); 3.142 (34.28); *Det. Pot. Ins.* 160 (33.7); *Gig.* 54 (33.7); *Migr. Abr.* 8 (various passages).

130. Colson's translation in LCL.

So it would seem that Philo's interpretation of Exodus 32–34 in general, and 32.32 in particular, seeks to identify what finds favor with God in people. This is relevant for Paul's argument in Romans 9–11, which may be understood as addressing essentially the same issue to some extent.

It is therefore interesting that Philo's citation of Exod. 32.16 in *Rer. Div. Her.* 167 follows a related interpretation of Exod. 25.22 that finds God's most fundamental characteristics to be his goodness and judgment. This is the twofold theme we found running through Exodus 32–34, most profoundly expressed by Exod. 34.6–7. Both Philo and Paul (Rom. 9.4; 9.30–10.4), partly influenced by Exodus 32–34, associated the Law with both God's goodness/mercy and his judgment.[131]

3.3.g. *Targums and Other Rabbinic Literature*

We must now turn to Jewish tradition later than Paul in its written form. There we find that the Targums translate Exod. 33.3, 5 entirely opposite to the Hebrew: 'but I will not remove My presence from your midst' (33.3) and 'if for one moment I were to remove My Presence from your midst I would destroy you' (33.5).[132] This is an attempt to defend Israel and her elect status, trying to make the biblical text assert that the Lord never left Israel, and implying that he would never do so, not even temporarily. Such an interpretation of these verses is in harmony with the defensive and apologetic readings of the golden calf episode in rabbinic literature generally, and testifies to the conflict that arose between Jews and Christians in general, and around Exodus 32–34 in particular.

---

131.   Other allusions to Exodus 32–34 in Philo have to do with either (1) wisdom/virtue, whether of its greatness: *Migr. Abr.* 85 (32.16), or its pursuit: *Poster. C.* 136 (32.7); or (2) the ineffability of God: *Poster. C.* 16 (33.12); *Mut. Nom.* 8 (33.13); 9 (33.23); *Poster. C.* 169 (33.23); *Fug.* 165 (33.23); or (3) the need for God: *Migr. Abr.* 171 (33.5). We should note that Philo's quotation of Exod. 33.13 in *Leg. All.* 3.101 appears in a context that treats predestination and foreknowledge (*Leg. All.* 3.65–106). Moreover, in relation to the idea of predestination Philo cites the same passage (Gen. 25.23; *Leg. All.* 3.88) Paul will cite in Rom. 9.12; see briefly Abasciano, 'Paul's Use', 190 n. 151; cf. P. Borgen, *Philo of Alexandria: An Exegete for His Time* (NovTSup, 86; Leiden: Brill, 1997), 51–56, 216–17, 239–40.

132.   Translations from B. Grossfeld, *The Targum Onqelos to Exodus: Translated with Apparatus and Notes* (TAB, 7; Wilmington, DE: Michael Glazier, 1988). *Targs. Neof.* and *Ps.-J.* are similar. Grossfeld, 92–93 n. 3, unconvincingly defends the targumic translations.

Rabbinic treatment of the golden calf episode focused mainly on defending Israel from her detractors.[133] Intriguingly, *Exod. R.* links Exod. 33.12 with Jeremiah 18, and Exod. 34.1 with Isa. 64.7; Mal. 1.6; Jer. 18.6; and Hosea 2,[134] all Old Testament contexts Paul alludes to later in Romans 9! This suggests that Paul chose these texts at least partially for their common theme of Israel's sinful and desolate state before the Lord and the possibility of restoration. Perhaps just as significant in relation to the rabbinic interpretation of the golden calf episode *vis-à-vis* Romans 9 is the fact that the rabbis found it necessary to defend themselves against the early Church, which came to use the passage to claim that God had rejected Israel, voided his covenant with them, and replaced her with the Church as his elect people. These are the very issues Paul addresses in Romans 9–11. Indeed, it is commonly acknowledged that such a replacement theology was active in the early Church of the New Testament period as well, and it is a matter of some debate where Paul came down on this issue, Romans 9–11 being a key text for determining his position. Our study will attempt to determine Paul's perspective through an exegesis that is especially attuned to his use of the Old Testament. For now, we observe that Exodus 32–34 is an ideal portion of Scripture to address such issues from, evidenced by the historical clash between Jews and Christians over the passage.

3.3.h. *Acts*

This brings us to a consideration of the use of Exodus 32–34 in the New Testament, pride of place going to the speech of Stephen in Acts 7. Stephen's speech traces the history of Israel with a special focus toward the end on her stiff neck and practice of rejecting God's prophets. 'He implicitly denies that he has spoken against the law of Moses, and makes himself out to be a defender of the law.'[135] He also attacks

---

133.   See Smolar and Aberbach, 'Calf'. For additional guidance in the rabbinic literature, see Hafemann, *Paul*, 228–30 n. 130. For a convenient compendium of rabbinic tradition related to Exodus 32–34, see L. Ginzberg, *The Legends of the Jews* (7 vols.; Philadelphia: Jewish Publication Society, 1909–38), 3.119–48. More extensively, see *Exod. R.* 41.6–47.9.

134.   See *Exod. R.* 45.1–2; 46.4–5. It is also worth noting that one rabbinic tradition has Moses unsuccessfully pleading mercy for Israel based on their readiness to accept the Torah when the descendants of Esau (i.e., Gentiles) rejected it (see Ginzberg, *Legends*, 3.126).

135.   I.H. Marshall, *The Acts of the Apostles: An Introduction and Commentary* (TNTC, 5; Grand Rapids: Eerdmans, 1980), 132.

the Jews for their failure to obey the revelation given to them in the Old Testament and for their rejection of the Messiah and the new way of worship which he brought. . . . Consequently, the speech has its part in the total story of Acts in showing that the Jews, to whom the gospel was first preached, had rejected it, and thus clearing the way for the church to turn away from Jerusalem and the temple and to evangelize further afield, and ultimately among the Gentiles.[136]

When Stephen comes to the golden calf episode in 7.40–41, he quotes Exod. 32.1, 23, and comments, 'They made a calf in those days and they brought a sacrifice to the idol, and they rejoiced in the works of their hands. But God turned away and gave them over to serve the host of heaven' (Acts 7.41–42a).

Thus, Stephen describes God's response to Israel's sin with the golden calf as turning away from them and giving them over to idolatry. He does not explicitly state that God returned to Israel or restored them. This does not deny that some sort of restoration took place at the time of Ezra and Nehemiah, but does appear intentional, indeed suggestive for the state of Stephen's contemporaries. The implication of the omission is that it is as if the restoration never happened, for the wicked impulse formed at the time of the great sin never left them, and the rest of Israel's sinful history flowed from this, culminating in the exile and presumably her miserable state in subjection to the Romans in the present time. That is, Israel is still in exile.[137] Israel's stiff neck was cemented at the time of the golden calf, and has remained so to the present time of eschatological fulfillment in Jesus the Messiah.

Thus, Stephen uses Exodus 32 to articulate a judicial hardening of Israel strikingly similar to what Paul describes in Romans 9–11. For Luke, it is a result of Israel's sin. This hardness motif is not only found in Romans at chs. 9–11, but also at 1.23–24, where Paul alludes to the golden calf episode *vis-à-vis* Ps. 106.20 (LXX 105), which interprets Israel's idolatry with the calf as exchanging their glory for the image of an ox that eats grass.[138] We will consider Paul's use of Ps. 106.20 further when we look at the New Testament context of Exod. 32.32. Here we note only that in Rom. 1.23–32, Paul uses the language of Psalm 106's

136. Marshall, *Acts*, 132.

137. For the concept of Israel's continuing exile in the first century, see e.g., T.R. Hatina, 'Exile', *DNTB*, 348–51; J.M. Scott, 'Restoration of Israel', *DPL*, 796–805. Hafemann, *Paul*, 392, finds this concept in 2 Cor. 3.16 *vis-à-vis* Exodus 32–34.

138. See Hafemann, *Paul*, 208 n. 65, on the allusion to the golden calf via Psalm 106 as the background for Rom. 1.23–24.

interpretation of the golden calf to describe idolatry that receives the divine punishment of a type of hardening, the giving over of people to their sin so that their own sin becomes its own punishment.

Stephen alludes to Exodus 32–34 again (see Exod. 32.9; 33.3, 5; 34.9) in Acts 7.51, suggesting that the hardheartedness which began with the golden calf now expresses itself in continually resisting the Holy Spirit. Given the function of the Holy Spirit in the New Testament, this rejection of the Spirit is a rejection of God himself. And given the function of the Holy Spirit in Acts, this rejection is a rejection of the mark of the elect people of God. Therefore, Stephen can also call his Jewish accusers 'uncircumcised in heart and ears' (ἀπερίτμητοι καρδίαις καὶ τοῖς ὠσίν), ironically placing them in the place of the Gentiles.

If the traditional authorship of Acts be accepted, and therefore its close connection to Paul through his missionary traveling companion, then these observations are all the more significant.[139] They become more significant still when we consider Stephen's speech against the context of the whole book, which portrays Paul's mission to the Jew first, but constantly turning to the Gentiles because of Jewish hardheartedness and rejection of the gospel culminating in Paul's application of Isa. 6.9–10 to the leaders of the Jews of Rome (Acts 28.25–27), which speaks of a judicial hardening of Israel, followed by Paul's bold statement, 'Therefore, let it be known to you that this salvation of God has been sent to the Gentiles; they also will listen' (Acts 28.28). The significance of all of this is heightened yet again by the fact that Paul probably alludes to Isa. 6.9 in some way in Rom. 11.8 in his discussion of the hardening of Israel.[140] We have found a Christian tradition of the first century, conceivably accessed by Paul himself(!), that found in Exodus 32–34 a characterization of Israel as stiff-necked and estranged from God, resulting in the judgment of hardening, and applied to the contemporary Jewish people. It was used to indict Israel severely for rejecting the prophets culminating in the rejection of the Messiah and the true meaning of the Law of Moses.

---

139.   For a concise and convincing argument for the traditional authorship of Acts, see Marshall, *Acts*, 44–46.

140.   S. Kim, *Paul and the New Perspective: Second Thoughts on the Origin of Paul's Gospel* (Grand Rapids: Eerdmans, 2002), 123, claims that there is an increasing recognition that Paul alludes to Isa. 6.9–10 in Rom. 11.7–10. It is also not insignificant that Mohrmann, 'Collisions', 185–86, has observed that the speech of Acts 7 is one of the closest NT parallels to Rom. 9–11 and finds the main point of Stephen's speech in Acts 7.51–53 (191), where allusion is made to Exodus 32–34.

3.3.i. *John*

Finally, we should mention Jn 1.17–18, where we find allusion to Exod. 34.6 (probably) and 33.20 respectively.[141] Whereas God is characterized by grace and truth, and no one can see him, Jesus Christ, as the divine Son of God, indeed, the only begotten God (μονογενὴς θεός), has both brought God's truth and grace and most fully revealed God the Father. The allusion appears in a context that is concerned with the rejection of Christ by his own people: 'He came to his own, and his own did not receive him' (Jn 1.11). The contacts with Romans 9–11 are again impressive.

John's contrast of the Law-giving through Moses and Jesus Christ's bringing of grace and truth is akin to Paul's statement in Rom. 10.4 that Christ is the goal (or end) of the Law. Whereas the Law brought a measure of grace and truth – it may be counted as one of Israel's great-est privileges after all (Rom. 9.4) – it found its fulfillment only in Jesus the Messiah.[142] Similarly, not even Moses, the greatest of Old Testament personages, could see God. Moses and the Law are great and glorious. But Jesus Christ far surpasses them. He is God and reveals him more fully than even the Law of Moses! This is an obvious assertion both of the inadequacy of Judaism apart from Jesus the Messiah and his deity (cf. Rom. 9.5). It is another example of first-century Christian tradition, positive toward the Law itself and faced with the wholesale rejection of Christ by the Jewish people, associating Exodus 32–34 with the inad-equacy of the faith of Israel in the present eschatological age unless completed in Christ.[143]

3.4. *The New Testament Context of Exodus 32.32*

Now that we have examined the Old Testament and related background behind Paul's allusion in Rom. 9.3, it is time to exploit what we have learned to understand Paul's use of Exod. 32.32 and exegete Rom. 9.1–5.

---

141.   Snodgrass, 'The Use', 46, claims that there is no doubt that Jn 1.14–18 is based on Exod. 33.17–34.6, and that an appreciation of this background is essential for a full understanding of the Johannine passage.

142.   For John's positive view of the Law as grace in these verses, see D.A. Carson, *The Gospel According to John* (Grand Rapids: Eerdmans, 1991), 131–34.

143.   Possible references to Exod. 32.32 in the NT via the Book of Life are: Lk. 10.20; Phil. 4.3; Rev. 3.5; 13.8; 17.8; 20.12, 15; 21.27. Other possible allusions to Exodus 32–34 in the NT include (Exodus references follow parenthetically): Heb. 11.12 (32.13); 1 Tim. 6.16 (33.20); Jas. 5.11 (34.6); Mt. 4.2 (34.28).

Having soared to the heights of the blessing of God in Christ for the elect (Romans 8), Paul now plunges to the depths of despair over the plight of those to whom the election had historically belonged but who are para-doxically separated from the elect community and its blessings. It is in fact the good news of the gospel that presses the horrific condition of Paul's kinsmen so forcefully into view. The better the news is of what God has done in Christ, the worse it is for the Jewish people, who have rejected their Messiah. Paul wants the Roman Christians to know beyond a shadow of a doubt that he feels the sting of this tragedy to the full.

As we have seen in ch. 2 above, Paul was writing to a church embroiled in conflict between Jews and Gentiles. And his gospel and missionary the-ology were potentially offensive to both Jews and Gentiles for various reasons. In light of the potential double-edged opposition Paul faced in Rome, we can see his rhetorical strategy at work, seeking the unity of Jews and Gentiles in the church at Rome and the common acceptance of his gospel and missionary practice. To the Jewish minority, Paul assures them of his love for the Jewish people, his great concern for their well-being, and his recognition of their privileged status. To the Gentile majority, he acknowledges ethnic Israel's cursed state but models the correct attitude towards the Jewish people – love and respect – and implicitly condemns any arrogance or hardheartedness towards them. Moreover, he provides an implicit rationale for prioritizing Jews in his missionary strategy – the privileges and blessings of the gospel and the election that it bestows most properly belong to the Jews as the historic people of God.

3.4.a. *Paul's Sincere Grief (Romans 9.1–2)*

So Paul begins his discussion of the faithfulness of God to Israel by saying, 'I am speaking the truth in Christ, I am not lying, my conscience bearing witness to me in the Holy Spirit, that I have great sorrow and unceasing grief in my heart' (Rom. 9.1–2). Thus Paul approaches the subject of Israel and her state in the most solemn of tones. The language of 9.1–5 is highly emotional and exalted, testifying to the importance of the topic for both Paul and his argument in the epistle,[144] and supporting the contention that we have arrived at the climactic segment of the theological section of the letter. Through repetition Paul assures his readers of the truth of what he affirms in 9.2, namely, his profound grief (over the accursed state of ethnic Israel).[145] By stating the truth of

144.   Cf. Schreiner, *Romans*, 478–79.
145.   On the often-noted repetition of 9.1–3, see esp. Dunn, *Romans*, 522.

his words both positively and negatively, he not only repeats his thought, but through a sort of merismus, strengthens it even further, as does the placement of Ἀλήθειαν at the beginning of the whole sequence.

By saying that he speaks the truth ἐν Χριστῷ, Paul indicates that his words are governed by union with Christ, and even motivated by him. Therefore, he cannot but tell the truth.[146] The phrase functions much as ἐνώπιον τοῦ θεοῦ does in Gal. 1.20 in connection with the same denial of falsehood (οὐ ψεύδομαι) we have here in 9.1, as ὁ θεὸς καὶ πατὴρ τοῦ κυρίου Ἰησοῦ οἶδεν does in 2 Cor. 11.31, again with οὐ ψεύδομαι, and as ἐν πνεύματι ἁγίῳ does in the following participial phrase. To say that his conscience bears witness ἐν πνεύματι ἁγίῳ means that the testimony of his conscience in this matter is similarly controlled by the Holy Spirit of God, ensuring the veracity of his statement. Whether Paul speaks of his conscience bearing witness to him, or with him to the Romans, does not make much difference for his overall purpose, which is to strengthen even more the impression that the assertion of his great grief in v. 2 is true. Nevertheless, Paul most likely means that his conscience testifies to him of his honesty, for Paul's other two uses of συμμαρτυρέω in the epistle (2.15 and 8.16) carry the meaning of 'testify to'.[147] Yet the suggestion that Paul is offering himself and the testimony of his conscience as two agreeing witnesses according to the biblical law of evidence[148] is attractive (cf. 2 Cor. 13.1). So it may be that Paul is invoking this law (Num. 35.30; Deut. 17.6; 19.15), but to the effect that he is signaling to the Romans that his statement can be believed because it is based on the surety of the testimony of three witnesses that have testified to him (his own conscience, Christ, and the Holy Spirit), who in turn testifies to them.

The fact that Paul goes to such great lengths to assure his readers of is that he has great sorrow (λύπη . . . μεγάλη) and unceasing grief (ἀδιάλειπτος ὀδύνη) in his heart. Again, Paul labors to state his point as strongly as possible through repetition via the synonyms λύπη and

---

146. Cf. 1 Tim. 2.7 for the same emphatic combination of ἀλήθειαν λέγω and οὐ ψεύδομαι.

147. See Abasciano, 'Paul's Use', 197–98 n. 169. As for the grammatical relationship between 9.1 and 9.2, it seems best to go the simplest route and take the ὅτι clause of the latter as dependent upon συμμαρτυρούσης rather than λέγω or ψεύδομαι (contra Cranfield, *Romans*, 452, but with Reichert, *Römerbrief*, 178 n. 155).

148. See e.g., Cranfield, *Romans*, 452. But O. Michel, 'Opferbereitschaft für Israel', in W. Schmauch (ed.), *In Memoriam Ernst Lohmeyer* (Stuttgart: Evangelisches Verlagswerk, 1951), 94–100 (95), thinks it impossible.

ὀδύνη,[149] both modified by intensifying adjectives. Such an incredibly strong statement of Paul's grief and veracity in stating it is surely no accident of eloquence. Paul appears to be addressing the slanderous charges circulating against him that he was an enemy of his own people and a blasphemer (cf. Rom. 3.8); there were even multitudes of Jewish Christians who were suspicious of him (Acts 21.20–21). We can get a feel for the type of opposition Paul faced from the charges of Asian Jews who seized him in the Temple according to Acts 21.28: 'Men, Israelites, help! This is the man who teaches all everywhere against the people, and the Law, and this place; and what is more, he has even brought Gentiles ["Ελληνας] into the Temple and has defiled this holy place.'[150]

But Paul is doing more than defending himself. As mentioned earlier, he is already setting the stage for an argument that will address the concerns of Jews and Gentiles alike in the Roman congregation and encourage them to unity. He is modeling the proper Christian attitude towards the Jewish people to be adopted by the Roman Christians,[151] and genuinely concerned for his people, the only attitude consistent with true faith,[152] indeed, the only one that could confirm the integrity and authenticity of his apostleship.[153] And there is yet another reason for Paul's unusual display of grief, one which has escaped interpreters. It is a typological fulfillment of the immense grief occasioned by the loss of Israel's election and the annulment of their covenant with the Lord as a result of their apostasy and idolatry in the matter of the golden calf (Exod. 33.4–6).

149.   Dunn, *Romans*, 523–24, suggests a meaningful allusion to Isa. 35.10 and 51.11, a suggestion that is intriguing and quite possible, but not enough to warrant exploration here. See Abasciano, 'Paul's Use', 198 n. 171, for evaluation. J.L. de Villiers, 'The Salvation of Israel according to Romans 9–11', *Neot* 15 (1981), 199–221 (201), rightly observes a chiastic pattern in λύπη-μεγάλη-ἀδιάλειπτος-ὀδύνη, cf. W. Schmithals, *Der Römerbrief: Ein Kommentar* (Gütersloh: Gütersloher, 1988), 327.

150.   Most interpreters seem to acknowledge that Paul may well be countering charges; see e.g., Moo, *Romans*, 556; E. Brandenburger, 'Paulinische Schriftauslegung in der Kontroverse um das Verheissungswort Gottes (Röm 9)', *ZTK* 82 (1985), 1–47 (5–7); Schmithals, *Römerbrief*, 328–30. Against the idea, see Cranfield, *Romans*, 453, offering no support, and more substantially but no more persuasively, Reichert, *Römerbrief*, 179. Dunn, *Romans*, 523, insightfully points out that Paul uses the denial formula, οὐ ψεύδομαι, in response to actual criticisms elsewhere (2 Cor. 11.31; Gal. 1.20).

151.   So Cranfield, *Romans*, 454; Fitzmyer, *Romans*, 543–44.

152.   Cranfield, *Romans*, 454.

153.   Cranfield, *Romans*, 454. Schreiner, *Romans*, 479, suggests concern for God's honor and faithfulness as a reason for Paul's extreme expression of grief

It is common to point out that Paul's expression of grief in these verses is similar to laments over Israel found in the Old Testament prophets and other Jewish literature.[154] This suggests that Paul is operating in the prophetic and apocalyptic tradition of the Old Testament and Judaism, confirming our findings in ch. 2 above. This impression is solidified by Paul's explanation of this grief, which follows, for it alludes to the intercession on behalf of Israel by the prophet Moses.

3.4.b. *The Allusion: Paul's Willingness to Be Accursed for His Kinsmen (Romans 9.3)*

3.4.b.1. *Preliminary Observations*   The logical connection between Rom. 9.2 and 9.3 is indicated by γάρ. But the exact significance of the connection is still unclear, for γάρ could be causal,[155] explanatory,[156] or perhaps some combination of the two.[157] I would suggest that the logic is complex in this highly emotional outburst. First and foremost, γάρ should be taken as explanatory. A primary causal meaning would require connecting v. 3 more with the assertion that Paul speaks the truth about his grief (v. 1) rather than directly with the fact of his grief (v. 2).[158] This is entirely possible, especially since Paul avows his truthfulness so strongly, but it does not give due consideration to the fact that the emphasis of his declaration falls on the fact of his grief. The insistence on his honesty supports the reality of his misery.

Moreover, the report of such an agonizing desire in v. 3 surely elaborates on Paul's heartache. Indeed, it expands on it by even more clearly revealing its depth. Paul has exhausted the resources of mere

---

(cf. R. Schmitt, *Gottesgerechtigkeit-Heilsgeschichte-Israel in der Theologie des Paulus* [Frankfurt: Lang, 1984], 73), but this does not make sense as the primary factor, which Paul plainly identifies in 9.4–5.

154. So e.g., Dunn, *Romans*, 524 (with references).

155. So Piper, *Justification*, 45; Moo, *Romans*, 557.

156. So Cranfield, *Romans*, 454; Morris, *Romans*, 347.

157. Cf. Schreiner, *Romans*, 479–81; M. Cranford, 'Election and Ethnicity: Paul's View of Israel in Romans 9.1–13', *JSNT* 50 (1993), 27–41 (30). γάρ could even be inferential here, but this has rarely been suggested as its prime significance.

158. This is how Sanday and Headlam, *Romans*, 228, take it. Cf. G. Stählin, 'Zum Gebrauch von Beteurungsformeln im Neuen Testament', *NovT* 5 (1962), 115–43 (135). γάρ can also introduce proof for a statement, a function that is akin to a causal sense. Such a meaning here is probably even more likely than the strict causal option, but is nonetheless better subsumed under the explanatory meaning as described below.

propositional language to describe the intensity of his grief. Now he clarifies it with an expression of desire so shocking in its intensity that many have asked if Paul could possibly mean what he says, and most conclude that he does not (in that he is speaking hypothetically). Therefore, v. 3 is better taken as an explanation of Paul's anguish. But in the explanation of his grief, Paul implicitly furnishes the reason for his deep sorrow. His willingness to be separated from Christ gives demonstrative proof of his misery (and his truth in stating it). But this only becomes clear as one processes the explanation, as does the inferential function of v.3 that shows the lengths to which Paul's grief could drive him. Thus, v. 3 does serve a causal/substantiating function, and secondary to that, an inferential function, but these are secondary to the explanatory. It is only 9.3's character as explanation that can accommodate its complex logical function.

This point is important because it helps us to identify Paul's main point. If vv. 3–5 ground v. 2, then the weight of Paul's language lies in his expression of grief in 9.2. But if they explain, then 9.3 carries his main point because it is an interpretive clarification of 9.2 and because 9.4–5 ground 9.3.[159] This leaves us with Paul's allusion to Exod. 32.32 as the main point of 9.1–5! And this, more than anything, may be what accounts for the complex logical connection between 9.2 and 9.3. Indeed, Paul's allusion to Exodus 32–34 holds the key to a full understanding of 9.1–5. Although the point has not been recognized previously in any real substance or detail,[160] the similarity in theme and subject matter between Exodus 32–34 and Romans 9–11 is remarkable.

159. Piper, *Justification*, 45, goes to needless trouble to try and explain why Paul's expression of grief in 9.2 is not the main point when grounded by 9.3. He correctly notes that 9.4–5 ground 9.3. On the inner logic of 9.1–5, cf. J. Murray, *The Epistle to the Romans* (NICNT; 2 vols. in one; Grand Rapids: Eerdmans, 1959–65), 2.8–9; Schmithals, *Römerbrief*, 330; P.J. Achtemeier, *Romans* (IBC; Atlanta: John Knox, 1985), 156, who finds Paul's major concern in 9.4–5, as does P.-G. Klumbies, 'Israels Vorzüge und das Evangelium von der Gottesgerechtigkeit in Römer 9–11', *WD* 18 (1985), 135–57 (138) (against Klumbies, see Schmithals, 335); Brandenburger, 'Schriftauslegung', 6, who appears to take the unusual view of 9.1 as the controlling statement. Cf. also Reichert, *Römerbrief*, 178ff., who finds three kinds of speech-acts in 9.1–5.

160. The most significant treatments are probably those of Wagner, *Heralds*, 45, 106, 351, 353 n. 34; L.T. Johnson, *Reading Romans* (New York: Crossword, 1997), 144–45; Morris, *Romans*, 347; Schreiner, *Romans*, 480; Moo, *Romans*, 559; H.L. Ellison, *The Mystery of Israel: An Exposition of Romans 9–11* (Exeter: Paternoster, 3rd edn., rev. and enl, 1976), 30–31; Dunn, *Romans*, 532; and above all, Munck,

There is much here for us to explore in our attempt to understand Paul's argument in Romans 9–11. But first, we must clear away some basic matters of exegesis pertaining to what Paul actually says in alluding to this foundational Old Testament passage, though our exegesis will not be uninformed by the Old Testament context, important as it is to Paul's argument.

3.4.b.2. *The Basic Meaning of Romans 9.3 in Intertextual Perspective*
In 9.3, Paul states with agonizing pathos, 'For I would pray to be accursed – I myself – from Christ for the sake of my brothers, my kinsmen according to the flesh!' Here is Paul's allusion to Exod. 32.32. The meaning of the imperfect indicative ηὐχόμην has attracted a lot of attention from interpreters. First, there is a question over the meaning of the word εὔχομαι, whether it means 'to pray' or 'to wish'. It usually denotes prayer in the New Testament, and it is arguable that it does so in every New Testament instance; certainly Paul's two other uses of the word refer to prayer (2 Cor. 13.7, 9).[161] So despite the many scholars who think that Paul speaks of wishing in Rom. 9.3,[162] word usage points toward a reference to prayer.[163] Wiles strengthens the case by pointing to Rom. 10.1 as a parallel, where Paul definitely speaks of his prayer for Israel.[164] And when we recognize that Paul is alluding to the prayer of Moses in Exod. 32.32, it becomes almost certain that Paul is speaking of prayer.[165]

Second, the imperfect tense of the verb has attracted even more attention than the actual meaning of the word because it is open to a number of possible interpretations and its most natural meaning apart from considerations of content would be to indicate something that Paul had

Christ, 27–30, and D.L. Bartlett, *Romans* (Westminster Bible Companion; Louisville, Kentucky: Westminster/John Knox, 1995), 85–86.

161.   The other NT uses occur in Acts 26.29; 27.29; Jas. 5.16; 3 Jn 2. See esp. Moo, *Romans*, 558 n. 16.

162.   See e.g., Schreiner, *Romans*, 476, 480; Piper, *Justification*, 20; BDAG, 417; C.K. Barrett, *A Commentary on the Epistle to the Romans* (HNTC; New York: Harper & Row, 1957), 176.

163.   Scholars who understand a reference to prayer include Cranfield, *Romans*, 454; Moo, *Romans*, 558; Dunn, *Romans*, 524 (cautiously); Wiles, *Prayers*, 19, 256; Hays, *Echoes*, 62.

164.   Wiles, *Prayers*, 256. K. Haacker, *Der Briefe des Paulus an die Römer* (THKNT, 6; Leipzig: Evangelische Verlagsanstalt, 1999), 181, also points to the proximity of ἀνάθεμα because of its cultic associations.

165.   So Cranfield, *Romans*, 454; cf. Fitzmyer, *Romans*, 544.

done in some way in the past.[166] Most interpreters find it too incredible to think either that Paul would pray or wish to be cursed and separated from Christ, and/or that he would think that the sacrifice of himself could save the Jews, and rightly agree in essence with Cranfield that ηὐχόμην is here 'equivalent to the classical imperfect indicative with ἄν, used where the prayer or wish is recognized as unattainable or impermissible'.[167] Here again, the Old Testament background behind Paul's allusion is significant. Moses' request to be blotted out of the Lord's book for the sake of his people was rejected. The prayer Paul speaks of had already been shown definitively to be unattainable.[168]

It has sometimes been objected that a hypothetical nuance to ηὐχόμην does not do justice to the gravity of Paul's lamentation.[169] The argument is quite weak when faced with the simple rejoinder that a willingness to sacrifice oneself for one's people is hardly a weak sentiment![170] And we can add that recognition of the allusion to Exod. 32.32 thoroughly militates against this objection. For Paul does not only make this statement to show his profound grief, but also to point to the typologically significant example of Moses and Israel at the time of the golden calf incident, on which he will pattern his response to the present situation.

What Paul would pray if it could bring about the salvation of his people is that he would be anathema from Christ (ἀνάθεμα εἶναι . . . ἀπὸ τοῦ Χριστοῦ), that is, that he would be devoted to destruction under the divine wrath. As most interpreters recognize, this is nothing short of eternal condemnation, or in a word, hell.[171] The term ἀνάθεμα denotes

---

166. See Cranfield, *Romans*, 455–57, for a full discussion of the four basic interpretive options relating to this imperfect. J. Morison, *Exposition of the Ninth Chapter of the Epistle to the Romans: A New Edition, Re-written, to which is Added an Exposition of the Tenth Chapter* (London: Hodder & Stoughton, 1888), 30–33, 178–86, treats the question at even greater length.

167. Cranfield, *Romans*, 455 (unfairly criticized by Dunn, *Romans*, 524). Cf. BDF § 359; BDAG, 417. Michel, 'Opferbereitschaft', 97ff., and more recently Hays, *Echoes*, 62, 206 n. 206, are among the few to opt for a reference to actual past action, while W.H. Davis, 'Anathema – Romans 9:3', *RevExp* 31 (1934), 205–207, may be the only one to support a present significance. Cf. K. Gábris' ('Das Gewissen – normiert durch den Heiligen Geist: Bibelarbeit über Röm. 9,1–5', *Communio viatorum* 27 [1984], 19–32 [24–25]) dissatisfaction with a purely hypothetical interpretation.

168. Rightly, Schreiner, *Romans*, 480. But see Gábris, 'Gewissen', 25–26, though she misunderstands Moses' petition.

169. See e.g., Davis, 'Anathema', 207.

170. See e.g., Cranfield, *Romans*, 456.

171. Cottrell, *Romans*, 47, notes that most scholars agree that anathema means hell here.

that which is devoted to God, whether as a votive offering or for destruction. The former meaning occurs only at Lk. 21.5 in the New Testament, where it is based on the alternative spelling ἀνάθημα, the form more typically used in relation to a votive offering.[172] Every other occurrence in the New Testament, all of which are in Paul except one, bears the meaning of 'accursed' or the like (1 Cor. 12.3; 16.22; Gal. 1.8, 9; Acts 23.14).

The LXX provides the main background to New Testament usage, translating the Hebrew חֵרֶם.[173] The usage in LXX Joshua 7 is instructive because it shows that the curse can be a consequence for violating the covenant, i.e., it can bring the covenant curse upon the sinner.[174] This is the very judgment intended for the Israelites who sinned with the golden calf as indicated by Moses and the Lord in Exod. 32.32–33.

The phrase ἀπὸ τοῦ Χριστοῦ clarifies the sense of ἀνάθεμα, and brings out the full horror of what Paul contemplates, especially in light of Rom. 8.35–39 to be heard only seconds before 9.3.[175] ἀπό clearly indicates separation.[176] And for Paul, to be 'in Christ' was the sum of all spiritual life and blessing (Rom. 3.24; 6.11, 23; 8.1, 2, 39; cf. 2 Cor. 1.20; Eph. 1.3). To be separated from him is the worst imaginable fate. Moreover, we would suggest that the language of being 'in Christ' is not only incorporative, but covenantal, connoting covenant membership. Jesus the Messiah is the covenant mediator and representative, summing up the

172. See BDAG, 63. Davis, 'Anathema', has argued that the term means 'votive offering' in Rom. 9.3, but he does not offer much evidence, while word usage, context, and the OT background argue against it.

173. ἀνάθεμα means 'votive offering' in LXX 2 Macc. 2.13, while ἀνάθημα has this meaning in LXX Jdt. 16.19; 2 Macc. 9.16; 3 Macc. 3.17. And ἀνάθεμα means 'accursed' or the like in LXX Lev. 27.28; Deut. 13.16, 18; 20.17; Josh. 6.17, 18; 7.1, 11, 12, 13; 22.20; 1 Chron. 2.7; Zech. 14.11, while ἀνάθημα has this meaning in LXX Deut. 7.26. חֵרֶם came to be used in rabbinic Hebrew of excommunication from the synagogue, while ἀνάθεμα came to be used of ecclesiastical discipline in the Church (see e.g., Cranfield, *Romans*, 457–58), but these types of meanings are obviously inappropriate here, not to mention anachronistic.

174. Cf. H. Aust and D. Müller, 'ἀνάθεμα', *NIDNTT*, 1.413–15 (414), on Judg. 21.11.

175. See Piper, *Justification*, 45.

176. See BDAG, 105 (1e); BDF, §211. On the possibility of an instrumental meaning for ἀπό here, with a sound refutation, see Piper, *Justification*, 44–45. The replacement of ἀπό by ὑπό in D and G, and by ὑπέρ in Ψ, are clearly secondary on both external and internal grounds, and appear to be attempts to soften the shocking sentiment Paul expresses. As Michel, 'Opferbereitschaft', 98, has observed, the full contrast with ἐν Χριστῷ in 9.1 is brought out fully here in 9.3.

people of God in himself. Those who become united to him by faith become 'in him', and therefore in the covenant and the elect covenant community.[177] As Michael Cranford has seen, 'That covenant boundaries are in view here is emphasized by ἀπὸ τοῦ Χριστοῦ, which denotes a separation from a sphere of identity. In terms of boundaries, ἀνάθεμα ἀπὸ τοῦ Χριστοῦ amounts to a movement out of covenant membership into a status of condemnation and wrath . . .'[178] Indeed, the Old Testament background behind Paul's allusion helps us to see that Paul does not simply speak about the wrath of God, but of the curse of the covenant, which was essentially separation from the elect community and destruction under the wrath of God. It was to be blotted out of the Lord's book, his registry of the elect covenant people, who were the recipients of his covenant promises.

If it were possible, Paul would make this ultimate sacrifice for the sake of his fellow Jews who had rejected Christ and were therefore separated from him under the deadly curse of the covenant. That Paul speaks of the Jewish people is certain from the designation he gives to them of τῶν ἀδελφῶν μου τῶν συγγενῶν μου κατὰ σάρκα. But that by calling them his brothers he is implying that they are within the elect community[179] is open to serious question. While it is true that non-literal uses of the word 'brother' in the Bible nearly always refer to 'fellow-members of the elect community',[180] it is also true that every such occurrence of the term ἀδελφός in Paul refers to fellow Christians. τῶν συγγενῶν μου κατὰ σάρκα is obviously added to qualify the sense of ἀδελφῶν. Moreover, as we shall see, 9.3 reveals that the Jewish people, who do not believe in Christ, are anathema.

Nevertheless, the fact that Paul calls unbelieving Jews his brothers does appear to be based on the covenantal use of the term. It grants recognition to Israel's national election and Paul's own participation

---

177. It is beyond the scope of this investigation to argue the case for the covenantal-incorporative significance of Jesus as the Messiah. For the basic concept, without the covenantal emphasis (ironically), see Wright, *Climax*, 18–55. One significant fact to note is that the kingship of David referred to by Wright (46–47) as demonstrating the incorporative sense of the idiom, 'in x', was established by covenant (2 Sam. 5.1–3).

178. Cranford, 'Election', 30.

179. So Cranfield, *Romans*, 459; Fitzmyer, *Romans*, 545. Cf. Käsemann, *Romans*, 258; Dunn, *Romans*, 424–25. The omission of μου in P[46] is probably due to haplography, as is the omission of the phrase τῶν ἀδελφῶν μου in B*, though it is possible that such a positive sentiment relative to the Jews was found objectionable.

180. Cranfield, *Romans*, 459.

in it, thereby underscoring his close relationship to his kinsmen and his great love and concern for them *vis-à-vis* their accursed state. Paul will shortly explain in 9.6ff. that Israel's national election was not necessarily unto salvation – though it certainly was meant to issue in this ideally as a result of participation in the blessings of the covenant and its conditional promises – but that participation in the true Israel and its salvation was always a matter of faith/calling.[181] At this point, however, he is subtly drawing attention to ethnic Israel's continuing election (see below) and his close relationship to them based on physical descent (κατὰ σάρκα).

Paul's use of κατὰ σάρκα with regard to his kinsmen does not carry his typical negative nuance, but is essentially neutral here,[182] denoting ethnic relationship. Nevertheless, there is a hint of limitation in the phrase. They are his brothers and kinsmen *only* according to the flesh.[183] But at this point there is no aspersion cast upon this relationship. It is intended to indicate Paul's solidarity with his people. Yet it does prepare for his argument in 9.6ff. that God's call is not based on physical ancestry. More immediately, it prepares for the assertion of 9.5 that the Messiah comes from the Jews physically, where there is again no aspersion on the relationship, but an even stronger connotation of limitation and anticipation of something that transcends the mere flesh.

Most interpreters understand Paul to be saying that he would pray or wish to deliver Israel from God's wrath by actually sacrificing his own salvation. Many go even further and suggest that Paul speaks of delivering Israel by taking her place under the judgment of God.[184] They tend to take the preposition ὑπέρ to imply substitution, which it certainly can do,

181. Cf. Moo, *Romans*, 559 n. 24, who distinguishes between a national and salvific election in Paul's argument, but mistakenly assumes that this is essentially a distinction between corporate and individual election. It is probably better to speak of one election that believers in Christ possess fully, but that unbelieving Jews possess in one sense, but not fully or eschatologically, in accordance with unbelieving Israel's similar possession of the name and blessings of election.

182. Contra Dunn, *Romans*, 525.

183. Cf. Dunn, *Romans*, 525; B. Byrne, *'Sons of God' – 'Seed of Abraham': A Study of the Idea of Sonship of God of All Christians in Paul against the Jewish Background* (AnBib, 83; Rome: Pontifical Biblical Institute, 1979), 83.

184. See e.g., Munck, *Christ*, 12, 30; Morris, *Romans*, 347; Moo, *Romans*, 559; Cranford, 'Election', 30; Käsemann, *Romans*, 258; Stählin, 'Beteurungsformeln', 135. J.M. Gundry Volf, *Paul and Perseverance: Staying In and Falling Away* (WUNT, 2.37; Tübingen: Mohr Siebeck, 1990), 162–63 n. 10, notes that this is a common position. B. Klappert, 'Traktat für Israel (Römer 9–11)' in M. Stöhr (ed.),

but by no means must do.[185] The more usual meaning of the word is the more general sense of 'for the sake/benefit of, in behalf of'.[186]

In any case, the Old Testament background of Paul's allusion would suggest that neither of these positions that understands Paul to envisage rescuing his people by sacrificing himself is correct. Although most interpreters of Romans seem to assume that Moses' prayer is to this effect, this is not the case.[187] He asks that the Lord curse him *if* he refuses to forgive Israel. That is, he asks to suffer the fate of the people with them if the Lord will not forgive, as an inducement to the Lord to restore them. This is what Paul posits of himself. He casts himself in a salvation-historical role on a par with Moses,[188] and contemplates making his life, salvation, and service the price God must pay to release his wrath on Israel. Just as Moses' request threatened the Lord's covenant purposes (by insisting on the complete eradication of Abraham's seed), so does the prayer Paul contemplates, for he is the Apostle to the Gentiles who is primarily responsible for administering the decisive stage of the eschatological fulfillment of God's covenant promises to bless the whole world, calling Jews and Gentiles alike into the covenant seed of Abraham in a ministry to the Gentiles that Romans 11 reveals as central to God's plan to save Israel.

Several additional exegetical insights flow from this intertextual interpretation of Paul's prayer. First, far from weakening the strength of Paul's language, it strengthens it by presenting an even greater identification of Paul with the Jewish people. It still declares his willingness to sacrifice himself for his people, yet it also casts his lot in with them. Second, it demands the meaning 'for the sake/benefit of' for the preposition ὑπέρ. Third, it strongly suggests that Paul considers his people to be anathema, for it means that he speaks of joining them in their plight. While many

Jüdische Existenz und die Erneuerung der christlichen Theologie (Munich: Kaiser, 1981), 58–137 (72), emphasizes that Paul speaks of prophetic substitution.

185. See BDAG, 1030–31. Gundry Volf, *Perseverance*, 162–63 n. 10, argues against the idea of substitution in 9.3 and for the weaker sense of benefit.

186. M.J. Harris, *'hyper'*, *NIDNTT*, 3.1196–97 (1197), concludes that the emphasis of ὑπέρ is representation, while it sometimes implies substitution.

187. Morris, *Romans*, 347, and F.F. Bruce, *The Epistle of Paul to the Romans* (TNTC, 6; Grand Rapids: Eerdmans, 1963), 184–85, are among the few to recognize this, though Morris suggests that Exodus may envision atonement by self-sacrifice, an unlikely understanding of the Exodus context.

188. See Munck, *Christ*, 29–30, for a classic statement of Paul's presentation of himself as a figure of NT *Heilsgeschichte* in Rom 9.1ff.; cf. Michel, 'Opferbereitschaft', 97ff. Lung-kwong, *Purpose*, 383–98, 410, has uncovered the surprising fact that the first-person singular is the most common person in Romans 9–11.

interpreters believe Paul to imply that his kinsmen are anathema based on the purported substitutionary nuance of ὑπέρ, our interpretation strengthens the case by avoiding dependence on this disputed meaning of the preposition in 9.3. Moreover, for those who do not insist on a substitutionary meaning for ὑπὲρ yet still find Paul to depict the Jewish people as anathema on the force of logic which runs, 'Paul's willingness to be cut off from Christ ὑπὲρ τῶν ἀδελφῶν μου makes sense only if Paul believes his brothers are in a plight as serious as the one he is willing to enter for their sake'[189] – an entirely convincing argument – our observation adds an even stronger argument to the case. Finally, there are some who deny that Paul portrays Israel as anathema.[190] To them we must point out that Paul's Old Testament allusion argues the very opposite, a fact that is in harmony with the view Paul expressed in 1 Thess. 2.13–16.

3.4.b.3. *Intertextual Motifs of Idolatry, Grief, Loss of Election, Merciful Judgment, the Faithfulness of God, Divine Sovereignty, and Human Free Will*   Paul regarded Israel to be in a state of apostasy for rejecting Christ. So he turns to the scriptural paradigm of Israel's apostasy, Exodus 32–34. There he found Israel embroiled in idolatry with the golden calf. In one of the few treatments to pay anything more than superficial attention to the meaning-effects of Paul's allusion to Moses' intercession, David Bartlett has argued,

> In the first chapter of Romans, Paul explicitly says that the primary sin of the Gentiles has been idolatry. Now, by his recalling the story of the golden calf, it may be that he also claims that Israel has fallen into idolatry. Idolatry is worship of a god who is not God. The God who is God is the God who justifies, makes right, all people through faith. To worship a god who justifies only *some* people through the Torah is to worship a god who is not God. Israel's idolatry is now not to worship gods in the form of beasts (as it was in the wilderness; as it still is for the Gentiles). Israel's idolatry is to worship a local god, a national god, as if God were not the God of all people and of all creation. . . . [Paul] is the new Moses because he calls his people away from other gods to the one God, the God of Jesus Christ.[191]

But the similarity between the idolatry of ancient Israel and the Israel of Paul's day is closer than Bartlett realizes. For as we have seen, ancient

---

189. Piper, *Justification*, 45. Cf. Schreiner, *Romans*, 481; Räisänen, 'Römer 9–11', 2896; Hübner, *Schriftgebrauch*, 16; Siegert, *Argumentation*, 122; Wagner, *Heralds*, 106.

190. Gundry Volf, *Perseverance*, 162–63 n. 10; Dunn, *Romans*, 524–25; Cranfield, *Romans*, 458–59 (apparently).

191. Bartlett, *Romans*, 85; emphasis original. Cf. Wagner, *Heralds*, 353 n. 34.

Israel sought in the golden calf a replacement for Moses, the Covenant Mediator, and a rival means of mediating the all-important presence of YHWH to the people. In doing so they distorted the true nature of the Lord and worshiped a false image of him. It would seem that for Paul, his kinsmen had done essentially the same thing. They had rejected the mediator of the New Covenant, Jesus Christ, who simultaneously mediates God's presence perfectly, in a way Moses never could. And they were clinging to a rival means of mediating God's covenant, presence, and blessing, one that God had not ordained for the present time of eschatological fulfillment. Moreover, they were clinging to a false conception of God, not only marred by ethnocentrism, but also by the rejection of the perfect revelation of the Lord. They had rejected God himself by rejecting the Messiah, 'who is over all, God blessed forever' (9.5).

Bartlett's reference to Romans 1 is also more perceptive than he seems to realize. For in 1.23, Paul alludes to the golden calf episode via Ps. 106.20 (LXX 105), which interprets the event as Israel exchanging their glory (YHWH) for the image of an ox that eats grass. Intriguingly, Paul uses this allusion in his argument for the equality of Jews and Gentiles in sin (1.18–3.20)! And if the current trend to take 1.18–32 as referring to all people in some way is correct, as we would argue,[192] then Paul uses the imagery of Israel's idolatry with the golden calf to describe the sin of both Jews and Gentiles alike, placing them in the same position before God. In any case, Paul certainly proceeds to say as much in the development of his argument, contending that Jews are no better off than Gentiles because they are all under sin (summarized in 3.9). Moreover, Exod. 33.6 suggests that because of her sin, Israel lost the gains of the Exodus redemption and stood in the same place as divinely condemned Egypt. Thus, following the lead of Exod. 33.6, Paul appears to have interpreted Exodus 32 to place Israel in the same position as the Gentiles,[193] i.e., outside of the covenant under the judgment of God.

---

192. Moo, *Romans*, 96, observes that scholars have traditionally taken 1.18–32 of Gentiles, and that the trend of recent scholarship is to reject or qualify this view. For the traditional view, see e.g., Fitzmyer, *Romans*, 270ff.; Bartlett, *Romans*, 28–31. Cranfield, *Romans*, 105–106, takes the passage almost equally of Jews and Gentiles. Moo, 97, presents a more balanced perspective.

193. Cf. our treatment above of the interpretive traditions found in *T. Mos.* 1.12–14; 12.4–12; *Mart. Isa.* 3.8–10; *4 Ezra* 6.55–59; Acts 7.51, and Paul's evocation of Ishmael, Esau, and Pharaoh as types of Israel in the following argument of Romans 9 (see ch. 4 below).

Moreover, as we noted in our discussion of Exodus 32–34 in Acts 7 above, Rom. 1.23–32 uses the language of Psalm 106's interpretation of the golden calf to describe idolatry that receives the divine punishment of a type of hardening. This is significant because the hardening of Israel is a major subject of Romans 9–11. Normal exegetical method would find an invitation to compare Paul's concept of hardening in Romans 1 and 9–11 in the similarity of subject. And given the common background of the golden calf, the Christian tradition of positing judicial hardening as the result of such idolatry, the likelihood that Paul intended Romans 1.18–32 to apply to Jews in addition to Gentiles, and Paul's connecting of Exodus 32–34 with the hardening of Israel elsewhere (2 Corinthians 3; see below), we have every warrant to read the hardening of Romans 9–11 in light of the hardening of Romans 1.

What this suggests is that the hardening of Israel spoken of in Romans 9–11 is a divine judgment resulting from her stubbornness, sin, and rebellion. This is in harmony with consistent New Testament Christian tradition on this point, not only in relation to Exodus 32–34 (Acts 7.40–41, 51), but in general, such as in Jesus' use of parables (Mt. 13.10–17; Mk 4.10–12; Lk. 8.9–10), Jn 12.37–41 (not insignificantly connected to the salvation of Gentiles through faith in Jesus!), and Acts 28.25–27 (of Paul), all of which cite Isa. 6.9–10, to which Paul in turn probably alludes in some way in Romans 11.8. We do not have space to analyze this early Christian tradition in detail, but we should make some observations.

First, the hardening of this tradition, both in its original context (Isaiah 6) and in its New Testament appropriations is a divine judicial hardening that brings judgment upon Israel by, in the language of Romans 1, giving her over to her own sin and its consequences so that her sin becomes its own punishment in a continually increasing cycle of judgment. But second, the tradition does appear to use this concept of hardening as an explanation for the Jews' rejection of the gospel. Nevertheless, the hardening is not viewed as absolute, prohibiting all Jews from faith. Rather, it appears to be a general, corporate hardening that prevented the Jews as a whole from accepting the gospel, but barred no one in particular from believing so that many Jews did believe. It was an exacerbation of Israel's already sinful state that made it less likely that Jews would believe, but not impossible. Paul used this hardening of Israel as an explanation of her unbelief to defend himself against criticisms based on the failure of his mission among Jews in 2 Cor. 3.7–18, again in allusion to Exodus 32–34 (and again, see below).

This all touches upon the question of whether in Romans 9–11 Paul presents the hardening of Israel, and therefore God, as the cause of Israel's unbelief or as the result of it. The data we have been reviewing suggests that the answer is not simply one or the other, but a complex combination of both. First and foremost, Paul's use of Exodus 32 at this point would suggest that his emphasis is on the guilt of Israel for their own sin and unbelief, and consequent rejection from the covenant under its fatal curse. That is certainly the emphasis of Exodus 32–34, the context of which is all the more significant for Paul's viewpoint, since he returns to it again when he first addresses the concept of hardening in Rom. 9.14–18 (cf. Exod. 33.19).

But this self-hardening has brought the judgment of God upon Israel, contributing all the more to their sin and unbelief, and naturally leading them to the ultimate apostasy – the rejection of Christ – bringing upon them an even more severe hardening according to the cycle of judicial hardening, without absolutely preventing any from believing (cf. Rom. 1.18–32; 11.5, 7–10, 13–14, 23, 30–31). But to repeat, the resonant significations of Paul's intertextual lament in 9.1–5, which introduces his argument in chs. 9–11 and introduces the plight of Israel to which his argument is partly directed, emphasizes the blameworthy stiff neck of Israel for which they themselves are responsible. This sets an orientation for approaching the theme of hardening as we encounter it in Romans 9–11, though we must allow the various texts to make their own contribution to an understanding of Paul's viewpoint.

As we have seen, what primarily grieved Paul was that his kinsmen were anathema, excluded from the covenant and devoted to destruction under the wrath of God. This could mean nothing other than the annulment of their election. As Paul interpreted the state of Israel in his day through the lens of Exodus 32–34, he saw that they had lost their election, just as Israel had at the time of the golden calf. The prayer he contemplates would seek to restore that election along with obtaining forgiveness for his people. But the Lord's answer to Moses became his answer to Paul as well. No, he will not simply restore the people. But he will grant them existence and a measure of blessing. However, he will punish the guilty. The application to Paul's context would appear to be that while Israel as a nation (i.e., based on ethnicity alone) remains rejected from the covenant, they retain a measure of God's blessing. Such blessing would include their priority in the gospel. But those who continue in sin by rejecting Christ will remain anathema, ultimately falling prey to its eternal curse.[194]

It is significant that Paul alludes to Moses' second intercession, where there is both blessing and curse for Israel, with the emphasis lying on the curse. It is here that Israel is told that although God will grant them existence and limited blessing, he would withdraw his presence from them, and thus, their election. It is true that God will eventually restore Israel's election in Exodus 32–34, but it is crucial that we pay attention to just how this happens (see below). Be that as it may, Paul appears to allude to this section of Exodus 32–34 especially for its stress on God's judgment upon Israel, indeed, her loss of election.

And this brings us to yet another striking aspect of the context of Exod. 32.32 in relation to Rom. 9.1–5 – the theme of immense grief over the loss of Israel's election. It is all the more striking when we realize that this grief is the main point of both Exod. 32.30–33.6 and Rom. 9.1–5.[195] Thus, Paul's allusion helps us to understand his grief even more fully. And it confirms what has often been assumed of Romans 9–11 from what Paul had written previously in Romans and from his other writings, but is now very often disputed: that Paul did indeed regard Israel's election to be nullified (and transferred to the Church through Jesus Christ, the true Israel). Moreover, it reveals just how profound was Paul's engagement with Scripture over the condition of his people, and how potent its effect on his response to their situation, both emotionally and theologically.

This is not to say that Paul's grief was a wooden, artificial response to Israel's plight that he forced upon himself to fulfill Scripture. He surely mourned the plight of his countrymen from the depths of his heart. But it is to suggest that the totality of his response was typologically oriented and typologically presented. Distraught at the loss of his people's election because of their apostasy, Paul has turned to the Scriptures and found the type of Israel's rejection from the election, and the overwhelming anguish that resulted. And from there (in part) he has fashioned both his own understanding of the present crisis and his own response. And just like Moses, he will not simply leave Israel rejected from the covenant.

Looking to the context of Paul's allusion, we find that the great sorrow over Israel's loss of election is also associated with repentance in

---

194. On potential objection to this parallel, see Abasciano, 'Paul's Use', 214 n. 20.
195. Recognizing Rom. 9.3 as an expression of Paul's grief.

response to the Lord's call for repentance with a view toward forgiveness and restoration. The metalepsis issues forth a similar call to the Israel of Paul's day to repent in order that they might find forgiveness and enter into the restoration available to them in Christ. More directly, it signals to the Roman Christians that God has not written off Israel, but would call them to repentance through Paul's gospel. Moreover, it holds out the hope that they will yet heed the word of God in the gospel of Christ.

Furthermore, this intertextual juxtaposition gives us greater insight into the nature of the Lord's judgment on Paul's people by suggesting that it is in fact a merciful judgment. In our exegesis of Exodus 32–34 we saw that the twin themes of the Lord's judgment and mercy figured prominently in the narrative, and that it is the mercy of the Lord which is dominant. Indeed, the purpose of the withdrawal of the Lord's presence and the concomitant abrogation of Israel's election was to spare the people from destruction because their sinful condition could only provoke God's wrath (Exod. 33.3–5). God's covenantal presence would mean destruction for a stiff-necked people.

This all adumbrates the contours of Paul's argument in Romans 9–11, for as Cranfield has observed, the keyword of these chapters is 'mercy'.[196] Moreover, Paul argues throughout the passage that God's judgment and hardening of Israel was for the purpose of mercy to both the Gentiles and the Jews (see esp. 9.22–29; 11.11–32). It would appear that Paul draws this general idea from Exodus 32–34 as he interprets his own ministry through its narrative. This insight helps us to see how, for Paul, God's rejection of Israel is actually an expression of mercy towards them. If the Lord did not reject ethnic Israel, then he would have to destroy them as his sinful covenant people. To cast them out of the covenant actually preserves them as a people and therefore gives them the opportunity to come to repentance and enter the renewed covenant. Thus, Paul's emphasis on mercy in Romans 9–11 along with his emphasis on judgment with a view toward mercy derive (at least in part) from Exodus 32–34. The scripturally astute auditor would therefore be prepared for the direction Paul's argument will take, and be able to grasp its meaning more fully.

196. Cranfield, *Romans*, 448. Cf. Gaston, 'Enemies', 97; A.T. Hanson, 'The Oracle in Romans XI.4', *NTS* 19 (1973), 300–302, who makes the intriguing observation that Jewish tradition identified the cave where Elijah heard the oracle to which Paul alludes in Rom 11.4 with the cleft of the rock where Moses received the theophany of Exod. 33–34, finding the chief connection for Paul in the concept of mercy.

Even the main theme of Romans 9–11, the faithfulness of God to his covenant word, may be traced back in part to Exodus 32–34. As we observed earlier, Moses' primary argument for the Lord to spare Israel in his first intercession is God's promise to the fathers (Abraham, Isaac, and Jacob/Israel; Exod. 32.13). This looks to be the background behind Paul's appeal to the very same basis for God's blessing even upon unbelieving Israel, who are enemies in relation to the gospel, but beloved in relation to the election (11.28). Just as in the case of ancient Israel, God's mercy to Paul's contemporaries is not *demanded* by his promise to the fathers (Romans 9). He could start over with Jesus Christ and all who are in him without extending any continuing privilege to ethnic Israel, and still fulfill his covenantal promise to Abraham *et al*. But his propensity to show mercy drives him to express his faithfulness in granting priority to the Jew and working for their salvation. The Lord's faithfulness serves as the basis of his mercy in Romans 9–11, even as his mercy serves as the basis of his faithfulness. And it all serves to exalt God's mercy: 'For God has shut up all in disobedience in order that he might have mercy on all' (11.32).

It is striking that Moberly could identify the 'theme of Yahweh's faithfulness to his promise despite seemingly impossible obstacles' as prominent in Exodus 32–34, comparing the passage to the Abraham cycle of Genesis 12–25, and suggesting 'an interpretation of Ex. 32–34 also in terms of a challenge to Yahweh's promise and the vindication of his faithfulness'.[197] For this is the very theme Paul will turn to in 9.6, and it is just such a challenge to God's promise that he will take on, turning indeed to the Abraham cycle, focusing on Genesis 18, 21, and 25. And by scholarly consensus, we may aptly describe Romans 9–11 as a vindication of God's faithfulness.

It is also noteworthy that interpreters have found the traditional theological tension between divine sovereignty and human will/action in the interaction between God and his servant Moses in Exodus 32–34. For that is yet another prominent motif widely recognized in Romans 9–11. Paul's allusion to a context filled with dynamic interaction between divine and human roles in the plan of salvation would suggest a model for understanding his musings over these issues. Just as the Lord limited his own determinations to some extent by granting to Moses a decisive role in his plan, and to a lesser extent, to Israel herself *vis-à-vis* the opportunity for repentance, so does he now limit his sovereignty,

---

197. Moberly, *Mountain*, 52.

giving both Paul and Israel (and Gentiles for that matter) decisive roles in the outworking of his plan for the salvation of the world. While God remains in control of the overall direction of everything, he does not determine every minute detail, but responds to the wills and actions of his creatures in general, and Paul and Israel in particular. His sovereignty involves the prerogative to relent from judgment in response to intercession and repentance.

Thus, Paul's allusion highlights the significance of his role in salvation history (far more than typically recognized). His transumption intimates that Israel's fate relies significantly on his ministry in their behalf as it did on Moses' (cf. Romans 11). Therefore, it contributes to Paul's implicit appeal for support of his gospel and ministry, and prepares the Christians at Rome for his similar appeal for support of his mission to Spain in ch. 15 with a view toward his upcoming visit to Rome. For through Paul's ministry, they can also play an instrumental role in the salvation of Israel and the world. In the words of Romans 10.14, 'How will they believe in the one whom they have not heard of?' On the other hand, God will not determine the response of those to whom Paul will take his gospel; rather, through Paul, God invites repentance so that he might decide their fate favorably.

3.4.b.4. *Moses, Paul's Ministry, the Restoration of Israel, and the Remnant.*   This now brings us to a consideration of the implications of Exodus 32–34 for Paul's argument in Romans 9–11 as regards the restoration of Israel to the covenant and its election. In our exegesis of Exodus 32–34 we have seen that one of the main problems of the narrative is how the election-bestowing presence of God could dwell in the midst of a sinful people (Israel) without destroying them. Moses had obtained the promise of the Lord's presence and covenant for Israel by appealing to his own favor with the Lord and seeking a restoration of the covenant, modified so as to be principally a covenant between him and YHWH, and then through him, with Israel in its identification with him. But this still did not provide a solution to the certain, fatal danger the Lord's presence posed for Israel in its corrupt character. The resolution would come through the Lord's mercy and Moses himself, as he became the answer to his own prayer by experiencing the glory of God and then bringing it back with him into the midst of the people. Indeed, Moses brought both a new covenant and the presence of the Lord to Israel.

I would like to suggest that Paul finds his own ministry as an apostle of Christ prefigured in the ministry of Moses recorded in Exodus 32–34.

The New Moses, Jesus Christ (cf. Acts 3.22; 7.37), has established the New Covenant based on his own favor with the Lord. This New Covenant is also a covenant principally between the Lord and Christ the Covenant Mediator, and then through Christ, with all who are identified with him through faith, i.e., his people, the true Israel, even the Church. And just like Moses, Paul saw the very glory of God in Christ and now seeks to bring that election-bestowing glory back to Israel in his preaching of the gospel ᾽Ιουδαίῳ τε πρῶτον καὶ Ἕλληνι. Jews who identify with Christ in positive response to Paul's gospel enter back into the covenant and election, receiving the eschatological blessing of the Spirit, the very glory and presence of God. Thus, it is through Paul's gospel and ministry that the glory of God is revealed and the New Covenant is brought to Israel.

One might question this scheme because both Jesus and Paul occupy the place of Moses, though in different ways. But this is not a very serious objection precisely because Jesus and Paul each fulfill Moses' role differently and especially because of Paul's identity as an apostle of Christ, functioning as his official representative and covenant messenger.[198] On the other hand, the proposed typological vision of Paul's ministry *vis-à-vis* Exodus 32–34 is consistent with basic convictions held by Paul. For he undoubtedly believed that: (1) Christ is the mediator of the New Covenant (1 Cor. 11.25; 2 Cor. 3.6); (2) Jesus was the very embodiment of the glory of God, which shined in his gospel (2 Cor. 4.4, 6; cf. Phil. 2.6; Col. 1.15, 19); (3) he saw this same glorious Jesus (1 Cor. 9.1; 15.8; Gal. 1.12, 16; cf. Acts 9.3–9; 22.6–11; 26.12–18); (4) Christ gives the eschatological blessing of the Spirit/glory of God to those who believe the gospel (preached by Paul) (Rom. 5.2; 8; 9.23; Gal. 3.1–14; 4.4–7, 21–31).[199]

Moreover, Paul's use of Exodus 32–34 in 2 Corinthians 3 provides strong confirmation of the view we are advancing here, for he interprets the passage in essentially the same way there.[200] We have mentioned

198.   In favor of the idea that Paul considered Moses as a type of Christ, see J.M. Scott, *Adoption as Sons of God: An Exegetical Investigation into the Background of* ΥΙΟΘΕΣΙΑ *in the Pauline Corpus* (WUNT, 2.48; Tübingen: Mohr Siebeck, 1992), 166. Interestingly, Scott points to 1 Cor. 10.1–13, where we will see below that Paul alludes to Exodus 32. Against the idea, see L.L. Belleville, 'Moses', *DPL*, 620–21 (620).

199.   As Hafemann, *Paul*, 422, correctly states, 'Paul, together with early Christianity as a whole, understood the indwelling of the Holy Spirit as the concrete and real presence of God himself.'

200.   For an exegesis of the passage that is truly intertextual and thorough, see Hafemann, *Paul*; cf. Hays, *Echoes*, 122–53; Wright, *Climax*, 175–92; Stockhausen,

2 Corinthians 3 several times in the course of our analysis, but have deferred discussion of this important passage until now because the context of Exodus 32–34 suggests the type of formulation we have set forth with respect to Romans 9–11 on its own in light of Paul's epistles and theology. But when we realize that Paul interprets the same context along remarkably similar lines elsewhere, then the significance of Exodus 32–34 for Romans 9–11 that we are proposing becomes greatly strengthened, and we can also reasonably look to 2 Corinthians 3 to fill out our understanding.

In 2 Corinthians 3, Paul continues the defense of his ministry, partly against some sort of judaizing threat.[201] Already we have some contact with Romans 9–11 since we have seen that Paul's vehement asseveration about his concern for the welfare of his Jewish brethren in 9.1–2 was partly aimed at opposition from Jewish Christians. In response to such opposition in Corinth, Paul insists that he is a minister of the New Covenant of the Spirit (3.6), who gives life (the representative and supreme blessing of the covenant in the OT). This New Covenant far surpasses the Old, which is abolished with the advent of its eschatological fulfillment (3.7–11; cf. 3.14).[202] Therefore, we have confirmation from Paul's interpretation of Exodus 32–34 elsewhere of the very controversial position, assumed in former times, that Paul takes some type of supercessionist stance in Romans 9–11 (cf. Acts 7).

'Principles'; L.L. Belleville, *Reflections of Glory: Paul's Polemical Use of the Moses-Doxa Tradition in 2 Corinthians 3.1–18* (JSNTSup, 52; Sheffield: Sheffield Academic Press, 1991). It is noteworthy that through the course of Hafemann's exegesis he consistently draws parallels with Paul's argument in Romans 9–11, though without the important insight that the same OT passage lies in the background there as well. It strengthens our case that apart from any thought of allusion to Exodus 32–34 in Romans 9–11, Räisänen, 'Römer 9–11', 2900, and F. Dreyfus, 'Le passé et le présent d'Israël (Rom 9, 1–5; 11, 1–24)', in Lorenzi (ed.), *Israelfrage*, 140–51 (135–36), find parallels between Rom. 9.4 and 2 Corinthians 3; cf. also Gábris, 'Gewissen', 28. But Luz, *Geschichtsverständnis*, 272 n. 23, is against any substantive parallel. For the view that Paul's Damascus Road Christophany, in which he saw the risen Jesus Christ as the image and glory of God, is part of the fundamental background of 2 Cor. 3.1–4.6, see S. Kim, *The Origin of Paul's Gospel* (WUNT, 2.4; Tübingen: Mohr Siebeck, 2nd edn., rev. and enl., 1984), 137–268 (generally), and esp. 5–13, 229–39.

201.   See S.J. Hafemann, 'Corinthians, Letters to the', *DPL*, 164–79 (177).

202.   Even Hafemann, *Paul*, e.g., 321–33, whose interpretation of 2 Corinthians 3 has been identified as the least negative towards the Old Covenant (Das, *Paul*, 77 n. 21), understands the passage to speak of the abolishment of the Old Covenant and its replacement by the New.

Another apologetic concern for Paul in 2 Corinthians 3 that he almost certainly had in mind in Romans 9–11 is the charge against his gospel that the very people who should have accepted it (i.e., the Jewish people), being the fulfillment of their Scriptures and covenant, had in fact rejected it.[203] Paul conducted his ministry with great boldness/confidence (παρρησία 3.12). And as we noted earlier, Paul turns to the hardening of Israel in 2 Cor. 3.12–18 *vis-à-vis* Exodus 32–34 as a partial explanation for the rejection of his gospel by the Jews. But in harmony with the emphasis of Exodus on the self-hardening of Israel, that is, their stubborn and rebellious character which issued forth in their apostasy with the golden calf, Paul's language does not focus on God's hardening of Israel, but their own historic obstinate character. Even though Moses veiled the dangerous glory of God shining from his face, 'their minds were hardened' (ἐπωρώθη τὰ νοήματα αὐτῶν, 3.13–14). He then makes the point that this same hardness has continued to the present day at the reading of the Old Covenant, turning Moses' veil into a metonymy for Israel's obdurate condition in relation to God and his word (3.14–15).[204] If anything in addition to themselves, Paul later attributes their blindness to Satan (4.3–4).

While the divine hardening of Israel may lie in the background of 2 Cor. 3.12–18 to some extent given the Christian tradition we have observed and Paul's use of the motif in Romans 9–11, that is not his emphasis in his interpretation of Exodus 32–34 in the Corinthian context.[205] Rather, he emphasizes Israel's sinful character and guilt. In view of the common background of Exodus 32–34 and some similarity in apologetic intent, this only confirms the conclusion we drew earlier that Paul's allusion to Exod. 32.32 in the introduction to his argument in Romans 9–11 suggests an understanding of a judicial divine hardening in the passage.

But just as we saw in other early Christian tradition, the hardening of Israel in 2 Corinthians 3 is also not absolute. 3.15–18 speaks of the possibility of Jews (especially, but not exclusively) turning to the Lord in conversion, as Paul rewrites Exod. 34.34 in application to the individual Jew with Moses as the type of the one who turns to the Lord and finds

---

203. On this apologetic concern in 2 Corinthians 3, see Hafemann, *Paul*, 362; R.P. Martin, *2 Corinthians* (WBC, 40; Milton Keynes, England: Word, 1986), 66–67.

204. For Paul's use of Moses' veil as a metonymy for Israel's hardened condition, see Hafemann, *Paul*, 371–86.

205. Emphasis on the divine hardening of Israel is one of the drawbacks of Hafemann's (*Paul*) study; see Abasciano, 'Paul's Use', 221–22 n. 232.

his hardness of heart removed. Significantly, the hardening is removed when (ἡνίκα) a person turns to the Lord (3.16), that is, as a result of conversion, for it is only removed 'in Christ' (3.14).[206] Therefore it is not the removal of hardening that leads to conversion, but conversion that leads to the removal of hardening.[207] Jewish hardness of heart surely makes conversion more difficult, but does not completely prevent it. It is no argument against Paul's mission, which includes (and prioritizes) evangelism to Jews.

The Jew who believes in Christ receives the Spirit of the Lord and experiences his glory, thereby undergoing progressive transformation into his glorious image as he continually beholds his glory (3.17–18), which would have wrought his destruction apart from the New Covenant and its Spirit based on the work of Christ. Paul's identification of the Lord with the Spirit emphasizes the Spirit as the very presence of God given to those who enter into Christ and the New Covenant. 2 Cor. 4.1–6 goes on to present Paul's ministry of proclaiming Jesus Christ as Lord as a display of the glory of God in Christ, who is the glory and image of God. But the gospel is veiled among the unbelieving, who are perishing. Applicable to both Jews and Gentiles, this surely means that Paul regarded Jews who did not believe the gospel to be perishing. In light of the significance of the glory/presence of God in Exodus 32–34 as the conveyor of election, we may say that Paul's interpretation of the passage in 2 Corinthians 3 suggests a reading of Romans 9–11 in terms of the mediation of the election-bestowing glory of God through Paul's gospel and ministry.[208] Indeed, such a statement of the matter brings greater clarity to Paul's theology of the Spirit found in Romans 8 and elsewhere even as these references sharpen our understanding of the nature of the election bestowed by the Spirit (see below).

A Pauline typological understanding of Exodus 32–34 *vis-à-vis* Romans 9–11 is also supported by Paul's other undeniable allusion to the

---

206. ἡνίκα occurs only in 2 Cor. 3.15–16 in the NT. In the LXX, ἡνίκα with ἐάν and the subjunctive always presents the associated action as in some way determinative for a subordinate contingent action (Gen. 20.13 [without subjunctive]; 24.41; 27.40; Exod. 13.5; Lev. 5.23; Deut. 25.19; 27.3; Josh. 24.20; 24.27; Jdt. 14.2). Moreover, ἡνίκα is so used in every one of its five occurrences in Exodus 32–34 (32.19; 33.8, 22; 34.24, 34), with Exod. 34.34 providing the basis of Paul's use in 2 Cor. 3.16.

207. Hafemann, *Paul*, never comes to terms with this wording of the text, but consistently *assumes* that the removal of hardening by the Spirit effects conversion.

208. Cf. Hafemann, *Paul*, 376 n. 132, who takes 2 Cor. 3.14–16 to develop in short form the basic history and nature of Israel Paul relates in Rom. 9–11.

Old Testament context in 1 Cor. 10.7, where he quotes Exod. 32.6. Indeed, the Corinthian context is again instructive for the Roman context. First, we observe that Paul addresses his predominantly Gentile audience as brothers (ἀδελφοί) in recognition of their New Covenant bond in Christ (1 Cor. 10.1), just as he spoke of his Jewish brethren as brothers in recognition of their common Old Covenant bond (Rom. 9.3). Second, and more significantly, Paul calls Israel 'our fathers' (οἱ πατέρες ἡμῶν, 1 Cor. 10.1), identifying them as the Corinthians' fathers, and therefore attributing to this Gentile church inclusion in the true eschatological Israel, which stands in continuity with Israel of the past.[209] This is the very identity of the Church that calls God's word into question and occasions Paul's argument in Romans 9–11; not that Gentiles *per se* are now the true Israel, but that the Church in Christ is the Israel of God (cf. Gal. 6.16), made up of both Jews and (primarily) Gentiles.

Third, Paul ascribes privileges to Old Testament Israel as prefigurements of Christian privileges in order to make the point that, as was the case with Israel of old, Christians' eschatological privileges do not guarantee that they will not fall under the fatal judgment of God if they persist in idolatry.[210] Rom. 9.4–5 just so happens to make much of the privileges of Israel, which nevertheless do not guarantee either contemporary ethnic Israel or the Church that they are immune to the deadly curse of the covenant if they fall into unbelief. Moreover, Paul makes this same sort of argument in Romans 11, applicable to both Jews and Gentiles, who stand or fall not on their privileges, but on their faith, which is the means of their possession of those privileges. Fourth, Paul tells us that 'these things became types [τύποι] of us in order that we might not be desirers of evil, just as they desired' (1 Cor. 10.6). It is immediately after this that he warns the Corinthians against being idolaters based on a quotation of Exod. 32.6. Thus, Paul identifies the situation of Israel at the time of the golden calf as a biblical type written down for the instruction of the Church as the eschatological people of God, 'upon whom the end of the ages has come' (10.11).

209. See Fee, *The First Epistle to the Corinthians* (NICNT; Grand Rapids: Eerdmans, 1987), 444, on 1 Cor. 10.1, who notes that this idea 'is thoroughgoing in Paul' and that Paul's language is also sure evidence of the Gentile Corinthian church's familiarity with the OT.

210. See Fee, *Corinthians*, 442–62. If Paul's reference to the cloud (νεφέλη,1 Cor. 10.1–2) refers to the presence of God in the midst of Israel as a prefiguration of the role of the Spirit, as it probably does (contra Fee, 445), then the context is all the more relevant to Paul's argument in Romans.

Through his allusion to Exod. 32.32, Paul takes upon himself the mediatorial, intercessory, and prophetic aura of Moses. The transumption fits the apologetic context of Romans 9–11 well, for as we have seen, Exodus 32–34 functions to substantiate Moses' authority. Now it subtly serves to substantiate Paul's authority as well. Indeed, as Hafemann has shown, Moses' authority was regularly assumed and then used to legitimize a given author's own authority in post-biblical literature.[211] And as we have seen in *T. Mos.* 3.9's allusion to Moses' intercession on behalf of Israel, the mediatorial/intercessory/prophetic persona of Moses was related to his activity in the episode of the golden calf. There could be no greater figure for Paul to evoke in order to set the stage for reception of his authoritative apostolic/prophetic revelation of eschatological secrets relating to God's purpose, Israel, the Gentiles, the faithfulness of God to his covenant promises to Israel, and God's sovereignty and foreknowledge.

Keeping in mind that the prophetic, mediatorial, and intercessory roles of Moses are inextricably intertwined, we would venture to say that Paul joins Moses in pronouncing covenant judgment upon Israel and calling faithful Israelites to join him in recognizing their brothers' apostasy and divine rejection (cf. Exod. 32.25–29; *T. Mos.* 3.9–14). Like Moses, he proclaims the termination of Israel's covenant as well as its renewal (cf. Exod. 32.19; 33.3–5; 34.29–35). And like Moses, he prays for Israel's salvation, willing to sacrifice himself in the attempt to convince God to spare them from his wrath and restore them to his favor.

Even the modest remnant motif of Exodus 32–34 might have some implications for Paul's argument in Romans 9–11. It happens to first appear in the narrative of Exodus 32–34 in connection with Moses' *prophetic* call to the Levites, who represent a faithful remnant, to kill their apostate brethren. The motif's reverberations in the New Testament context support the contention that Paul's reference to the accursed state of unbelieving Israel envisaged the fatal covenant curse in store for those who are unfaithful to the covenant by rejecting the Messiah on the one hand, and the blessings of the covenant for those who are faithful to it by embracing its messianic Lord on the other hand. In light of Paul's immense grief at the plight of his Jewish brethren, the necessity of slaying covenant brethren in the Old Testament context underscores in the Pauline context the costliness of faithfulness to the Lord and his covenant and the inevitable pain and separation from unbelieving Israel necessitated by allegiance to Jesus Christ.

211. Hafemann, *Paul*, 63–69.

The remnant motif surfaces again in Moses' self-sacrificial interces-sion on behalf of Israel recorded in Exod. 32.31–32 and alluded to by Paul. There, Moses implicitly appealed to the faithful remnant repre-sented by himself as part of the basis of his request for mercy for the people, revealing a profound identification of himself with the people of Israel. Similarly, the self-sacrificial prayer Paul contemplates would also appeal to the faithful remnant embodied in himself. This only deepens Paul's identification of himself with the Jewish people[212] and also prepares for his development of the remnant motif in his argument (Rom. 9.27–29; 11.1–10).

3.4.c. *The Privileges of Israel in Intertextual Perspective (Romans 9.4–5)*

Having seen numerous substantive parallels between the contexts of Exodus 32–34 and Romans 9–11 (along with some tenuous ones that gain greater plausibility from the cumulative force of the many undeni-able correspondences), we would expect the context of Paul's allusion to enrich our understanding of 9.4–5 as well, along with their enumeration of the privileges of Israel.

3.4.c.1. *The First Privilege (Israelites) with an Orientation to the Entire Catalog*

The form and structure of Rom. 9.4–5 has drawn atten-tion from interpreters for its impressive artistry.[213] Ἰσραηλῖται leads the list of privileges and sums them up as the name given to members of God's covenant people. The name 'Israel' was the special covenant name of the people of God, first conferred upon the patriarch Jacob, and con-sequently applied to his descendants.

It is commonly recognized that the name, which emphasized special status before God, was the preferred self-designation over against that of 'Jew(s)', which emphasized national and political identity and was typically used both by Jews in dealings with Gentiles and by Gentiles of

---

212. M. Barth, *The People of God* (JSNTSup, 5; Sheffield: *JSOT*, 1983), 82 n. 3, makes the interesting observation that, in light of the tribe's role in the OT, Paul's descent from Benjamin probably meant to him that he was representative of all Israel.

213. For particularly helpful treatments of the form/structure of 9.4–5, see Piper, *Justification*, 21–23; Dunn, *Romans*, 522; Schreiner, *Romans*, 482–85. Cf. Byrne, *Sons*, 81–84. See also Siegert, *Argumentation*, 122, for some additional insights not often noted.

Jews.[214] Now significantly, Paul changes his terminology by speaking primarily of Israel rather than Jews.[215] The move strengthens Paul's identification with his people. It may be that Paul also found some inspiration for his use of the designation 'Israel' in Moses' use of the name instead of the more usual 'Jacob' in his first intercession on behalf of the people (Exod. 32.13). Just as there, use of the covenant name evokes God's covenant promises to Israel in all their fullness, sharpening the problem Paul raises. Given the context of intercession (cf. Rom. 10.1), invocation of this honorable name strengthens the implicit appeal for their salvation and looks forward to Paul's argument for God's faithfulness based on his promise to the fathers in ch. 11.

The rest of Israel's privileges are grammatically subordinate to Ἰσραηλῖται in three relative clauses (ὧν . . . ὧν . . . ἐξ ὧν) that unpack its meaning.[216] The six items in the first relative clause are delicately balanced with the six feminine nouns set in two groups of three and the endings of the first, second, and third members corresponding in assonance to the endings of the fourth, fifth, and sixth members respectively:

ἡ υἱοθεσία	ἡ νομοθεσία
ἡ δόξα	ἡ λατρεία
αἱ διαθῆκαι	αἱ ἐπαγγελίαι.

There is close association and overlap between every element of this list and not just between the rhyming pairs;[217] they are all of one piece and

214. See e.g., Cranfield, *Romans*, 460–61; H. Kuhli, "Ἰσραηλίτης', *EDNT*, 2.204–205. But see Kuhli's (205) complaint that the difference between the two terms is frequently exaggerated, and Moo's (*Romans*, 561 n. 30) helpful qualification. Cf. Luz, *Geschichtsverständnis*, 269 n. 9, who essentially denies the distinction between these terms in Paul. Kuhli's (205) point that Ἰσραηλίτης is most often an expression of conscious solemnity', helps us to see that Paul's use of the word adds to the solemnity of his expression in Rom 9.1–5.

215. The term 'Jew(s)' is used in Rom. 1.17; 2.9, 10, 17, 28, 29; 3.1, 9, 29, while the term 'Israel/Israelites' is not used until 9.4, but then frequently in the rest of chs. 9–11 (Rom. 9.6, 27, 31; 10.19, 21; 11.1, 2, 7, 25, 26), whereas 'Jew' is only used again in 9.24 and 10.12.

216. Cranfield, *Romans*, 460, takes the three ὧν clauses along with οἵτινες as dependent on τῶν συγγενῶν μου κατὰ σάρκα, but Piper, *Justification*, 21, is surely correct to state that Ἰσραηλῖται is the antecedent of the three relative clauses. But the difference is not great since τῶν ἀδελφῶν μου τῶν συγγενῶν μου κατὰ σάρκα are the Ἰσραηλῖται described by the relative clauses. Cf. Schreiner, *Romans*, 486 n. 15.

217. For the special connection between the rhyming pairs, see Schreiner, *Romans*, 483ff.; Piper, *Justification*, 21 n. 12; cf. Scott, *Adoption*, 148–49. On the question of whether Paul authored this list or made use of a traditional Jewish

testify elegantly to Israel's glorious historical heritage. It is this heritage that makes their present situation so grievous.

9.4–5 ground Paul's allusion to Exod. 32.32, itself an expression of his immense grief at his people's accursed state. They reveal an additional factor that intensifies the greatness of his heart's unceasing pain – the (Jewish) people who have been excluded from the covenant and its blessings are the very people to whom these most properly belong as the historic bearers of the divine election. The content of vv. 4–5 alone assure us of their causal function. But the relative pronoun οἵτινες confirms this judgment in its use 'to emphasize a characteristic quality, by which a preceding statement is to be confirmed'.[218] It is their identity as bearers of the name of God's covenant people, with all the prerogatives inherent in that name, that makes the situation all the more tragic, especially in light of the fact that many Gentiles are participating in the eschatological fulfillment of that name and its blessings.

οἵτινες is dependent on τῶν ἀδελφῶν μου τῶν συγγενῶν μου κατὰ σάρκα,[219] making it clear that the same kinsmen who stand anathema under the covenant wrath of God are the same ones who bear the historic covenant name and privileges; they are Israelites. For them Paul would pray to be anathema from Christ 'inasmuch as they are Israelites, of whom is the adoption, and the glory, and the covenants, and the giving of the Law, and the service, and the promises, of whom are the fathers, and from whom is the Christ according to the flesh, who is over all, God blessed forever. Amen.' But this raises a serious problem. How can Israel be both anathema and the elect people, recipients of the covenant promises? That is (at least apparently) a contradiction in terms. It would seem to mean that God's promises to Israel as represented by

catalog, see esp. Piper (21–23), who argues convincingly for Pauline authorship; cf. Scott, *Adoption*, 148–49 n. 96; Räisänen, 'Römer 9–11', 2896 n. 29. Contrast the less plausible suggestion that the list arose from Hellenistic Jewish tradition, strongly asserted e.g., by H.W. Bartsch, 'Röm. 9, 5 und Clem. 32, 4: Eine notwendige Konjektur im Römerbrief', *TZ* 21 (1965), 401–409 (404); Byrne, *Sons*, 81–84, 128; cf. more recently and cautiously B. Byrne, *Romans* (Sacra pagina, 6. Collegeville, MN: Liturgical Press, 1996), 285.

218.   BDAG, 729. Cf. Moo, *Romans*, 560 n. 27; Schreiner, *Romans*, 482; Dunn, *Romans*, 526; Hübner, *Schriftgebrauch*, 14.

219.   There is no reason to distinguish between τῶν ἀδελφῶν μου and τῶν συγγενῶν μου κατὰ σάρκα as antecedent like Cranfield, *Romans*, 460, does, since the two are in apposition. Chae, *Paul*, 225–26 n. 51, agrees that the whole clause τῶν ἀδελφῶν . . . σάρκα functions as the antecedent of οἵτινες, but his criticism of Piper's application of Israel's privileges to unbelieving Israelites is wholly unconvincing.

these magnificent privileges have failed. Indeed, this is the problem that Paul addresses in the rest of Romans 9–11, to which the verses before us are the introduction.

Many interpreters stress Paul's attribution of these privileges to ethnic Israel in the present,[220] and deny what Paul's argument in Romans 1–8 implies – which is why he must now address this problem at all – and what our exegesis of 9.1–3 has found, that Paul does regard Israel defined ethnically and apart from Christ to have forfeited their election and covenant prerogatives under the curse of God. Many such interpreters emphasize the fact that Paul uses the present tense – οἵτινές εἰσιν 'Ισραηλῖται – which must then be supplied for the following relative clauses. Therefore, one might argue, Paul explicitly ascribes to ethnic Israel both the covenant name, encompassing the covenant blessings, and possession of the covenant privileges; so he cannot mean that they have forfeited their election or that they are anathema. Recognizing that Paul does depict unbelieving Israel as anathema, some argue that the significance of the name and its privileges is either strictly a historical/ temporal matter[221] and/or that such privileges do not promise salvation to every individual ethnic Israelite, but to ethnic Israel as a whole.[222]

But these approaches read too much into Paul's language here and pay too little attention to the immediate context of his argument, not to mention the Old Testament background we have been exploring. According to our own exegesis above, we must grant that Paul does attribute the special covenant name presently to unbelieving ethnic Israel, that this name encompasses the following privileges, and that he likewise attributes some type of possession of these same privileges to them. But to insist against 9.1–3, the Old Testament background, the rest of chs. 9–11, and chs. 1–8, that contemporary ethnic Israel fully enjoys the privileges ascribed to them in 9.4–5 is both unjustified and unnecessary. Paul does not explain in what sense his kinsmen according to the flesh are Israelites except to enumerate their privileges. Even less

---

220. See e.g., Schreiner, *Romans*, 485; Gundry Volf, *Perseverance*, 163–64 n. 13; Fitzmyer, *Romans*, 545; Cranfield, *Romans*, 460; Moo, *Romans*, 561; Dunn, *Romans*, 526; cf. idem, 'Did Paul Have a Covenant Theology? Reflections on Romans 9.4 and 11.27', in S.E. Porter and J.C.R. de Roo (eds.), *The Concept of the Covenant in the Second Temple Period* (JSJSup, 71; Leiden: Brill, 2003), 287–307 (302–303).

221. See e.g., L. Cerfaux, 'Le privilège d'Israël selon Saint Paul', *ETL* 17 (1940), 5–26 (esp. 12, 26–27); Klumbies, 'Vorzüge'; Dreyfus, 'passé'; G.S. Worgul, Jr., 'Romans 9–11 and Ecclesiology', *BTB* 7 (1977), 99–109 (99).

222. Piper, *Justification*, 24; Schreiner, *Romans*, 485; Moo, *Romans*, 562.

does he explain just how they possess these blessings. Indeed, his language is rather limited.

Paul's use of the genitival relative pronoun ὧν is a fairly meager expression of their possession of the covenant prerogatives and susceptible to more than one interpretation.[223] Rather than a genitive of possession, it is possible that it is a genitive of reference (cf. Rom. 15.18; 1 Cor. 7.1) or advantage or source[224] or means. The point is not to argue for an alternative translation of the genitival relative pronoun over against the usual possessive interpretation, though we prefer a literal translation in an attempt to capture the ambiguity and what we gather to be the weak sense of possession intended by Paul ('of whom is the adoption' etc.). But we are quite happy to admit that a possessive genitive is the most natural interpretation. The point I am making is that it is an ambiguous expression of possession, and it is dubious to hang one's interpretation of Romans 9–11 on Paul's language at this point. His language here is lofty and poetic after all, and room must be made for a bit of poetic license.

The important question is, in what sense does ethnic Israel now possess the privileges of 9.4–5? In light of our exegesis so far and our exegesis of Romans 9–11 in general, I would suggest that the answer is that these privileges belong to Israel in the sense that they most properly belong to Israel as the historic bearers of these privileges, but they do not in fact do so apart from faith in Christ. In other words, unbelieving Israel bears the name outwardly, but not in substance, and the prerogatives are first and foremost meant for them, but are not in fact theirs based on ethnicity, nor apart from faith in Christ. Indeed, the gospel is 'the power of God for salvation to all who believe, to the Jew first and also to the Greek' (1.16). This approach is borne out by both the context of Romans and the Old Testament background.

First and foremost, Paul addresses this exact issue in the very next verse in response to the very problem we are discussing! The fact that ethnic Israel as a whole is anathema and therefore not receiving the fulfillment of divine promises to her suggests that God's word has failed. The primary reason that Paul gives to deny this accusation is that there

---

223. Cottrell, *Romans*, 51–52, who relegates Israel's privileges to the past, prefers to translate literally in this section. J.G. Lodge, *Romans 9–11: A Reader-Response Analysis* (ISFCJ, 6; Atlanta: Scholars Press, 1996), 45, recognizes the use of the relative pronoun here as understated. Mohrmann, 'Collisions', 194–95, argues that Rom. 9.4–5 'contain no temporal reference'.

224. L.T. Johnson, *Romans*, 145, offers this as a real option.

are two Israels, and by implication two kinds of Israelites – those who are merely part of ethnic Israel (οἱ ἐξ 'Ισραήλ), and those who are part of true, eschatological Israel by faith, whether Jew or Gentile (οὗτοι 'Ισραήλ).[225] So unbelieving Jews can be ἐξ 'Ισραήλ, i.e., they can possess the name and prerogatives of Israel outwardly, but they might not fully and truly possess them, i.e., they might not actually be true Israel. Hence, the paradoxical statement of 9.6b.[226]

Later in his argument, Paul speaks metaphorically of Israel as an olive tree, and individual, unbelieving Jews as natural branches that have been separated from the tree. The significant thing in Paul's use of language there for our purposes is that he speaks of Jews who are separated from true Israel as possessing Israel though cut off from her: 'How much more will these who are natural branches be grafted into *their own* olive tree?' (11.24). Even though unbelieving Jews are cut off from true Israel, they still possess its name and prerogatives in that these had historically belonged to them, and most properly belong to them now, if they will only believe. They are the natural branches even if cut off.

---

225.   It is amazing how often the argument of 9.6ff. is ignored or skirted in addressing these questions. E.g., Dunn, *Romans*, 526, simply begs the question. Piper, *Justification*, 24, 30, who wants to ascribe the privileges of 9.4–5 to unbelieving Israel, eventually has to admit in view of 9.6ff. that they only apply to the elect among unbelieving Israel. Piper unwittingly involves himself in a contradiction here, since he makes much of the fact that Paul's grief over his kinsmen is because they are under the eternal wrath of God and that Paul could only be willing to enter such a fate himself for them if he believed this to be their fate. But if Paul believed these privileges to apply only to the elect among unbelieving Israel, who would certainly never face this fate, then the ground is ripped out from under Piper's otherwise convincing interpretation of 9.1–3. Chae, *Paul*, 225–26, on the other hand, untenably believes Paul applies these privileges only to believing Jews. Cf. M. Rese, 'Die Vorzüge Israels in Röm. 9,4f. und Eph. 2,12: Exegetische Anmerkungen zum Thema Kirche und Israel', *TZ* 31 (1975), 211–22 (217–18), who rightly sees that the advantages and Paul's heartache must apply to empirical-historical/unbelieving Israel (cf. also Luz, *Geschichtsverständnis*, 273; J.M. Österreicher, 'Israel's Misstep and Her Rise: The Dialectic of God's Saving Design in Rom 9–11', in *Studiorum Paulinorum Congressus Internationalis Catholicus 1961*, I [AnBib, 17; Rome: Pontifical Biblical Institute, 1963], 317–27 [319]).

226.   This mirrors the paradoxical relationship between Rom. 9.1–3 and 9.4–5 stressed by W. Kraus, *Das Volk Gottes: Zur Grundlegung der Ekklesiologie bei Paulus* (Tübingen: Mohr Siebeck, 1996), 296–98; cf. Lübking, *Paulus*, 59; D. Zeller, *Juden und Heiden in der Mission des Paulus: Studien zum Römerbrief* (FzB, 1; Stuttgart: Katholisches Bibelwerk, 1973), 113; Österreicher, 'Misstep', 320.

Again, in Rom. 2.25–29, Paul asserts that the Jew's circumcision becomes uncircumcision (spiritually) if he is a transgressor of the Law, whereas the uncircumcision of the Gentile who keeps the Law becomes circumcision (spiritually). Indeed, true Jewishness is spiritual and true circumcision is of the heart by the Spirit (who according to our exegesis bestows the divine election!). Just as one can possess the divine privilege of circumcision yet not truly possess it, so can Israel possess the name and prerogatives of the elect people of God, but not truly possess them, to Paul's overwhelming sorrow.

One final example should suffice, this time from the Old Testament background. In Moses' third intercession, he presented Israel's identity as God's people to YHWH in order to convince him to restore them to his favor, covenant, and election (Exod. 33.13). But Israel was no longer YHWH's people at that point. Nonetheless, Moses could assert, 'this nation is your people', not because he was lying or trying to trick YHWH, but because even though they were not actually his people at that point, they were most properly his people because of their history as such. In the same spirit, Paul cries out concerning his ethnic kinsmen who have been rejected from the covenant and its blessings, 'They are Israelites to whom belong all the blessings of the covenant!' It is this fact that makes their situation so heart-rending. They are from Israel but not Israel; they possess the olive tree but are cut off from it; they are Jews outwardly but not inwardly, circumcised but uncircumcised, God's people but not his people.

As is generally acknowledged, with this list of Jewish privileges Paul picks up on the discussion he began in 3.1 when he asked, 'What then is the advantage of the Jew, or what is the benefit of circumcision?' The answer is, 'much in every way' (3.2). He then begins to list Jewish privileges, but only mentions τὰ λόγια τοῦ θεοῦ, which we may regard as a summary description of the catalog in 9.4–5.[227] As we have seen, the honorific title ᾽Ισραηλῖται is not only the first privilege of this impressive listing as continued here in 9.4–5, but it too is a summary description of the rest of the catalog. Now Paul begins to unpack its meaning as he moves to the next privilege of his Jewish kinsmen: ἡ υἰοθεσία.

227. The phrase is frequently taken as the first privilege of a list continued in 9.4–5 (e.g., Scroggs, 'Rhetorician', 277 n. 19).

3.4.c.2. *The Adoption*   The next privilege, ἡ υἱοθεσία, refers to the adoption[228] of Israel as God's son contained in the Old Testament.[229] That is, it is equivalent to the covenantal election of Israel as God's people.[230] Indeed, covenant relationship in the ancient Near East and the Old Testament extended family obligations and responsibilities to those outside of the family, and engendered familial language among covenant partners.[231] God's adoption of Israel as his son, i.e., his covenant partner, involved his commitment to be their father, bestowing love, care, protection, discipline, and blessing, and required his people to act as faithful 'sons', responding to their father with love, trust, and obedience. In short, it designates the establishment of covenant relationship between the Lord and Israel, with all that includes.

Thus, ἡ υἱοθεσία essentially encapsulates all the privileges of 9.4–5 as well. And it is the ideal blessing to follow the sacred title Ἰσραηλῖται, which was for all intents and purposes conferred with Israel's adoption. This ties into the concept of calling that Paul develops in Romans 9, beginning in 9.7, which we will argue in ch. 4 refers to the naming of God's people.[232] Election is the choice of a people as God's son/covenant partner, which entails the bestowal of the covenant name, Israel/Christ, that is, the calling of God's people as his elect. Therefore, Fitzmyer's surprise that Paul does not include election in the list of Israel's privileges[233] is unwarranted, but not because of Chae's contention that Paul merely presupposes the election of Israel.[234] Rather, he chooses to speak of Israel's election in terms of adoption in 9.4, probably because (1) he

228.   Scott, *Adoption*, 13–57, shows conclusively that υἱοθεσία means 'adoption as son' rather than the more general 'sonship' (but see Byrne's [*Romans*, 252] critique; cf. Haacker, *Römer*, 184).

229.   See Exod. 4.22–23; Deut. 1.31; 14.1; 32.6; Isa. 1.2; 63.16; 64.8; Jer. 3.19–22; 31.9; Hos. 11.1; Mal. 1.6; 2.10.

230.   Dunn, *Romans*, 526, and K.H. Schelkle, *The Epistle to the Romans: Theological Meditations* (New York: Herder and Herder, 1964), 150, are among the surprisingly few to relate adoption directly to election in Rom. 9.4.

231.   I owe this point to Gordon Hugenberger and his course 'Theology of the Pentateuch', taught at Gordon-Conwell Theological Seminary (Spring 1996).

232.   The tie is strengthened by Byrne's ('*Sons*', 120) observation that 'calling' and 'sonship' are frequently associated in Jewish tradition regarding the establishment or reconstitution of Israel.

233.   Fitzmyer, *Romans*, 543.

234.   Chae, *Paul*, 226. H.J. Schoeps, *Paul: The Theology of the Apostle in the Light of Jewish Religious History* (London: Lutterworth, 1961), 237, and W.S. Campbell, 'The Freedom and Faithfulness of God in Relation to Israel', in W.S. Campbell, *Paul's Gospel in an Intercultural Context: Jew and Gentile in the Letter to*

wants to invoke the preceding discussion of adoption and the Spirit in Romans 8; (2) artistic composition demanded a feminine noun ending with -ια; and (3) he wants to maintain connection to the context of the Exodus he has alluded to, and to which so many of the listed privileges are especially linked.

At the same time ἡ υἱοθεσία also refers to the adoption of the eschatological people of God spoken of by Paul in his writings (Rom. 8.15, 23; Gal. 4.5; Eph. 1.5). Indeed, the word υἱοθεσία does not occur in a religious sense prior to Paul, who is the only New Testament author to use this term that is absent from the LXX.[235] We do not need to posit a sharp division between the past orientation of the privileges of Israel Paul lists and an eschatological significance as some do.[236] The blessings Paul mentions stand in a salvation historical continuum. The adoption of Old Covenant Israel has been fulfilled in the adoption of the New Covenant people of God, who receive the realization of the promises inherent in the former dispensation, just as, according to Rom. 8.15, 23, Christians participate in the inauguration of the eschatological adoption that will only be consummated at the resurrection. So for Paul, this Old Testament privilege always looked forward to its eschatological completion, and there is a progressive fulfillment in salvation history in which all who remain in covenant relationship with the Lord may participate. All of this applies to every one of the prerogatives Paul mentions, though the items most directly relate to their Old Testament expression in light of Paul's allusion to the period of their fundamental establishment when ethnic Israel more truly possessed them and because of the more obvious past orientation of some of the list's items. Nevertheless, the real apex of Paul's concern relates precisely to Israel's failure truly to possess the inaugurated eschatological fulfillment of these blessings.

Our understanding of the nature of ethnic Israel's possession of the privileges of 9.4–5 frees us to appreciate that even though they are

---

the Romans (SIHC, 69; New York: Peter Lang, 1992), 43–59 (44), both correctly recognize that the list of 9.4–5 testifies to the election of Israel. But Dreyfus, 'passé', 132, shortsightedly refuses to speak of the election of Israel at all in Rom. 9.1–5, since the term is not mentioned.

235. See Scott, *Adoption*, 55; Piper, *Justification*, 22–23, 32.

236. See above all Piper, *Justification*, 23–44; Schreiner, *Romans*, 483–85. For an approach that does not pit the past and the eschatological against one another, see Dunn, *Romans*, 533; cf. Moo's (*Romans*, 562–63) approach to the adoption and glory.

anathema in Paul's estimation, and therefore rejected from the covenant and its blessings in the present time of eschatological fulfillment, the privileges of the eschatological people of God belong to them ideally. By the same token, Gentiles who believe in Christ are admitted to the true Israel, joining the remnant of Jews who believe in Christ. They thus participate in the privileges of Israel. And thus Paul's grief is severely intensified.

As for the Old Testament background behind the adoption of Israel, it is important to recognize that the phenomenon was especially tied to the Exodus and the events surrounding it, and just as importantly, that it ultimately stretched back to the election of Abraham and the divine covenant with him. Israel was already God's son at the very beginning of the Exodus events, as evidenced by the foundational expression of her adoption in Exod. 4.22–23. This can only mean that Israel was God's son by virtue of the Abrahamic covenant, which was subsequently developed in the Mosaic covenant. Nevertheless, her adoption was uniquely established through the ratification of the covenant on Sinai.

Now, it is to this context of the institution of the Sinaitic covenant that Exodus 32–34 is organically and vitally connected. Indeed, it completes the narration of the establishment of the covenant by recording the first and great threat to its continuation before it was even fully completed, and by explaining a fundamental change to its nature. It is no accident that interpreters typically recognize that the privileges Paul lists generally go back to the Exodus complex (and we would add, ultimately to the Abrahamic covenant, which found fulfillment at Sinai). Paul's allusion to this context draws our attention to this passage for the most relevant understanding of Israel's adoption/election to his argument in Romans 9–11. It was an adoption that was abrogated because of Israel's apostasy, and then restored through the mediation of God's glory through the covenant mediator in the midst of the people, who were now identified with and dependent on him for enjoyment of the covenant and its blessings.

3.4.c.3. *The Glory*   It is therefore significant that the next benefit Paul lists is ἡ δόξα,[237] which he also connects to adoption, the Spirit, and

---

237. Paul's unusual (and perhaps unparalleled in antiquity) absolute use of the articular construction ἡ δόξα without any type of modifier for the divine glory is probably due mostly to stylistic considerations of assonance and economy; cf. Dunn, *Romans*, 526; Moo, *Romans*, 563 n. 43.

heirship in the preceding chapter. Most interpreters agree that 'the glory' in 9.4 refers to the manifest presence of God with Israel spoken of in the Old Testament, whether speaking of it in terms of the (personal) presence of God,[238] manifestation of the divine presence,[239] the Shekinah,[240] theophany,[241] or the like. Some may identify a certain aspect of the divine glory as foremost,[242] but the presence of God in the midst of his people is fundamental to them all. It was God's magnificent presence that appeared in the pillar of cloud and pillar of fire in the Exodus and desert wanderings (Exod. 13.21; 16.10), at the establishment of the covenant on Mount Sinai (Exod. 19.9–25; 24.12–18), and in the Tent of Meeting (Exod. 33:7–11), the Tabernacle (Exod. 29.43; 40.34–35), and the Temple (1 Kgs 8.11).

Paul's allusion to Exodus 32–34 directs us to the most relevant connotation of ἡ δόξα for his discussion in Romans 9–11. We saw that the glory of the Lord was a main theme of Exodus 32–34 and that its chief significance was to denote God's covenant presence, which bestowed his covenant and election with all of the accompanying blessings. Hence, Paul's use of the term in the wake of his emotive appeal to the intercession of Moses and immediately following mention of the elective adoption also carries this significance. Paul speaks of the glory of God as his manifest presence, which simultaneously establishes his covenant, confers his election, effects his adoption, and bequeaths his blessings. We once again have a term that implies all of the other items of this exalted catalog.

The suggestion that Paul's understanding of ἡ δόξα in 9.4 is especially dependent on the context of Exodus 32–34 is confirmed by Paul's heavy emphasis on the word in the argument of 2 Cor. 3.7–18, where, as we have seen, he draws heavily from Exodus 32–34. Indeed, Exod. 34.29–35 is the source of his δόξα language in 2 Corinthians 3! Moreover, the specific meaning of the term suggested by the Old Testament context is also confirmed by Paul's discussion of glory, adoption, the Spirit, and heirship in Romans 8. There he makes it clear that the Spirit of God and of Christ, i.e., the glory/presence of God, imparts the blessings of Christ to believers. Intriguingly, it is possession of the Spirit that determines

---

238. E.g., Schreiner, *Romans*, 484.
239. E.g., Cranfield, *Romans*, 462.
240. E.g., Ziesler, *Romans*, 237.
241. E.g., Barrett, *Romans*, 177.
242. E.g., Dunn, *Romans*, 526. Indeed, interpreters often use more than one designation to describe this privilege.

whether one belongs to Christ (8.9), bestows adoption (8.14–16), and makes one an heir of God and his glory (8.17ff.; cf. 8.30), all with a view to the ultimate consummation of these blessings in the future against the present tension of the already and not yet. What we see in Romans 8 is the activity of the Spirit as the glory/presence of God bestowing covenant membership and election, that is, the adoption that makes God's people heirs of all his blessings, including freedom, life, peace, glory, and resurrection. This conforms perfectly to Paul's typological application of Exodus 32–34 lying behind his argument in Romans 9–11.

But the mention of Paul's conception of glory in Romans 8 brings us to consider the suggestion that Paul refers to the future, eschatological glory often mentioned in his epistles. Piper is the chief proponent of this view in modern scholarship, which has few supporters.[243] But Piper has made a good case for the eschatological view citing (1) Paul's regular absolute use of δόξα without a modifier; (2) the Pauline context embracing Rom. 8.18, 21, related to eschatological sonship, and 9.23, which assumes that vessels prepared for glory includes Jews; (3) the Old Testament and Jewish conception of glory as an eschatological hope;[244] and (4) Jewish apocalyptic expectation of the manifestation of God's glory to and for Israel. Nevertheless, all of this is not enough to overwhelm the immediate context of Paul's catalog and Old Testament allusion.[245]

The answer lies in recognizing that the Old Testament glory of God and the eschatological glory of Christian hope are not mutually exclusive,[246] or even fundamentally distinct. Indeed, for Paul, the Old Testament glory of God comes to eschatological fulfillment in Christ. Just as with adoption, there is only one privilege of glory, the experience

---

243. Piper, *Justification*, 33–34. Others who find at least some eschatological significance here include, Byrne, *Sons*, 140; Moo, *Romans*, 563; Dunn, *Romans*, 526–27, 533–34. Against it, see F. Godet, *Commentary on St. Paul's Epistle to the Romans*, II (Edinburgh: T&T Clark, 1892), 135. For an approach somewhat similar to that taken here, see E.J. Epp, 'Jewish-Gentile Continuity in Paul: Torah and/or Faith (Romans 9:1–5)', in G.W.E. Nickelsburg and G.W. MacRae (eds.), *Christians Among Jews and Gentiles: Essays in Honor of Krister Stendahl on His Sixty-fifth Birthday* (Philadelphia: Fortress, 1986), 80–90; cf. Dreyfus, 'passé', 135–36.

244. Cf. Dunn, *Romans*, 526.

245. See e.g., Schreiner's (*Romans*, 484 n. 9) criticism of Piper.

246. As Moo, *Romans*, 563, does. Unfortunately, he does not carry this observation through to the other privileges listed in 9.4–5.

of which differs for God's people according to the salvation historical epoch. This is evident in Paul's concept of glory and the Spirit in Romans 8, where he states that we presently only have the first fruits of the Spirit, and in 2 Corinthians 3, where he speaks of a progressive glorification of believers in the Lord's own glory by the Spirit (3.18).

So the glory that God's covenant people possess as an inheritance is God's own glory, which they are granted increasing participation in over the course of salvation history culminating in the final glorification of believers. Moreover, just as with adoption, Paul probably regarded the glory of the past to have always pointed toward the glory of the future. The fact that this greatest of all privileges most properly belongs to ethnic Israel renders their separation from it exceedingly grievous and provides one of the strongest possible arguments for taking 'the light of the gospel of the [election-bestowing] glory of Christ, who is the image of God' (2 Cor. 4.4), to the Jew first, even though 'a veil lies over their heart' (2 Cor. 3.15) and 'the god of this world has blinded [their unbelieving] minds' (2 Cor. 4.4).

3.4.c.4. *The Covenants*   The next privilege, αἱ διαθῆκαι,[247] follows naturally from the previous three, for they are all covenant realities, Ἰσραηλῖται being the covenant name, ἡ υἱοθεσία the establishment of the covenant and the resulting state of covenant partnership (i.e., adoptive sonship), and ἡ δόξα the covenantal presence of God. The unusual plural has drawn speculation from interpreters as to which covenants it may refer to. According to Calvin Roetzel, 'almost unanimously commentators have interpreted the plural noun, διαθῆκαι, as a reference to different covenants which Yahweh established with the patriarchs – Abraham, Isaac, Jacob, Moses, etc'.[248] But there is no unanimity in identifying just which covenants Paul has in mind.[249] Suggestions range from those named by Roetzel to exclusion of one or more of them and/or addition of other figures such as Noah[250] and David[251] to the simple

247.   We agree with the vast majority of interpreters that the reading ἡ διαθήκη attested by P[46], B, D, F, G, b, vg[cl], sa, bo[mss], and Cyp, is probably not original despite the strong external support. See Abasciano, 'Paul's Use', 240–41 n. 286.

248.   C.J. Roetzel, 'Διαθῆκαι in Romans 9,4', *Bib* 51 (1970), 377–90 (377). Roetzel's own suggestion that the term actually means ordinances, commandments, or oaths is unconvincing; see Abasciano 'Pauls Use', 241 n. 287.

249.   See Piper, *Justification*, 34–35; Schreiner, *Romans*, 484 n. 11.

250.   E.g., Morris, *Romans*, 348.

251.   E.g., Murray, *Romans*, 2.5.

possibility that the plural is a manner of referring to either the Abrahamic[252] or the Sinaitic[253] covenant with respective various renewals to the alternate possibility that it is an all-inclusive reference to all the covenants mentioned in the Old Testament.[254]

Piper insightfully observes that the great diversity among commentators on this question testifies to the fact that Paul's terminology is open-ended at this point.[255] I would add that the exalted nature and intent of the entire catalog lends to a more comprehensive designation as well. Nevertheless, it is a listing of *Israel's* privileges; so it would seem fitting to limit the referents to those covenants specifically related to Israel or her patriarchs, including the New Covenant.[256] Still, even though we accept such an identification for αἱ διαθῆκαι, it may be that we can find something more specific at the forefront of the general idea in light of Paul's allusion to Exodus 32–34 in the previous verse.

In Exod. 32.13 Moses pleads for Israel on the basis of the Lord's covenant oath to Abraham, Isaac, and Israel (i.e., Jacob). And he does so to save Israel and her covenant with the Lord just instituted at Sinai. Indeed, as we have mentioned, Exodus 32–34 is part of the *locus classicus* of the Sinaitic covenant. Moreover, one of the main issues of the passage is the abrogation and renewal of the covenant. Putting all of this together, I would suggest that in light of Paul's allusion to Exod. 32.32, αἱ διαθῆκαι of 9.4 especially refers not so much to distinct covenants, but to the Abrahamic covenant and its various renewals and stages, encompassing both the Sinaitic/Mosaic covenant with its renewals and the New Covenant promised in the prophets. For the Sinaitic covenant is surely seen in Moses' intercession on behalf of Israel as an extension of the Abrahamic covenant even as the New Covenant is surely seen by Paul as a fulfillment of the same. But given the undeniable focus on

---

252. See Dunn, *Romans*, 527. Gábris, 'Gewissen', 29, surprisingly questions inclusion of the Abrahamic covenant.

253. See Dunn, *Romans*, 527; Moo, *Romans*, 563; cf. Cranfield, *Romans*, 462; Barrett, *Romans*, 177–78.

254. Moo, *Romans*, 563; Morris, *Romans*, 348; but both of these exclude the New Covenant, whereas Ellison, *Mystery*, 36–37, includes it too, as do Bruce, *Romans*, 185; Schmithals, *Römerbrief*, 331, and Dunn, *Romans*, 527, 534. Cf. Epp, 'Continuity', 83; Dreyfus, 'passé', 136–37.

255. Piper, *Justification*, 35. But he wrongly contends that covenants and promises are basically synonymous in 9.4 as does Schreiner, *Romans*, 484. Rather, the covenants contained promises, and therefore the two concepts are complimentary rather than synonymous.

256. Cf. Cottrell, *Romans*, 54.

the Mosaic covenant in Exodus 32–34, perhaps it would be more precise to say that αἱ διαθῆκαι in 9.4 especially refers to the Sinaitic/ Mosaic covenant with its renewals, understood as an extension of the Abrahamic covenant and looking forward towards the New. Furthermore, mention of 'the covenants' echoes the motif of covenant renewal found in Exodus 32–34 along with the type of Israel's rejection and restoration discussed in detail above.

Paul's use of the word διαθήκη elsewhere is instructive for appreciating what lies behind his ascription of the covenants as the special prerogative of Israel in the context of a lament (Rom. 11.27; 1 Cor. 11.25; 2 Cor. 3.6, 14; Gal. 3.15, 17; 4.24; Eph. 2.12). First, we observe that Paul regularly refers to the New Covenant. Second, we find a contrast between the Old and New covenants, the former bringing death, i.e., the curse of the covenant (=anathema), to Israel, while the latter brings life to all included in it by faith, including Jews who turn to the Lord (2 Cor. 3.7–18, where again, Exodus 32–34 is in view). Third, we find that Paul viewed the Abrahamic covenant as primary and the Mosaic covenant as a subordinate addition to it (Gal. 3.15–17). Fourth, he saw Christ as the true Israel/seed of Abraham to whom the covenant promises were made. Therefore, all who are in him are the true Israel and inherit Israel's promises (Gal. 3.15–17). But those not in him have a veil over their heart, and are subject to death (2 Cor. 3.7–18).

Fifth, the talk of the covenant in Galatians 3 is directly related to the adoption as sons. Belonging to Christ, which both Romans 8 and Galatians 3 link to possession of the Spirit, makes one Abraham's seed and an heir of the promises. This all in turn is related to significant terminology used shortly hereafter in Romans 9 (see ch. 4 below). Sixth, Galatians 3 clearly views the Old Covenant, marked by the Law, as preparatory for its fulfillment in Christ, a concept that, seventh, appears again in Paul's famous allegory of two covenants in Gal. 4.21–31, again using material connected to his ensuing argument in Romans 9 (see again ch. 4 below). It is important to note that he does not disparage the Old Covenant in and of itself, but in comparison to the New. The Old had its purpose, to be fulfilled in Christ. But clinging to the Old in the time of eschatological fulfillment is slavery; those who do are to be cast out of the covenant and denied participation in the fulfillment of its promises in accordance with Gen. 21.10, 12, part of the latter verse being omitted in the quotation in Gal. 4.30 but quoted in Rom. 9.7. It is also worth noting that Gal. 4.27 is one of two other uses of the plural, διαθῆκαι, by Paul outside of Rom. 9.4.

That leads us to the only other use of the plural by Paul, if Ephesians be accepted as authentically Pauline – Eph. 2.12. The context is once again significant, addressing Jew/Gentile relations. The author draws attention to the names by which Jews and Gentiles were called, at least by some – the Circumcision (τῆς . . . περιτομῆς) and the Uncircumcision (οἱ . . . ἀκροβυστία) respectively (2.11; cf. Phil. 3.3). Before they were in Christ, the now Gentile Christians were 'apart from Christ [χωρὶς Χριστοῦ; cf. Rom 9.3's ἀνάθεμα . . . ἀπὸ τοῦ Χριστοῦ], separated from the commonwealth of Israel and foreigners to the covenants of promise [τῶν διαθηκῶν τῆς ἐπαγγελίας], having no hope and without God in the world' (2.12). But now, in Christ, Gentile believers are made to share in Israel and her covenants of promise, which are only available to Jews who are in Christ as well, for it is in Christ that God makes Jews and Gentiles one, effects reconciliation with himself, grants access to himself through the Spirit (!), etc. (2.12–21). And it is in Christ and the Spirit that the Church of Jews and Gentiles is the temple of God, a thought that is not unrelated to Rom. 9.4, as Paul will very soon mention Israel's privilege of the Temple service. It is almost as if Ephesians 2 is a commentary on the privileges of Rom. 9.4–5. If it is accepted as Pauline, then the ramifications for interpretation of Rom. 9.4–5 are immense. If not, it would still be significant as a first-century Christian interpretation of Paul written most likely by one of his disciples in his name.[257]

We should add that it is important to remember just what the covenant meant to Israel and her Scriptures. It was not simply some formal arrangement or commandment, but it was actually her relationship with the Lord. In it was contained everything pertaining to him in relation to them; as Exodus 32–34 testifies, it was inextricably intertwined with the election, and the glory, and every possible expectation of good associated with knowing the Lord God (cf. Eph. 2.12). Thus, yet again, Paul includes a privilege of Israel that essentially sums up all of the others. The fact that the Jewish people stand cursed outside of the covenant and its fulfillment when it most naturally belongs to them is grievous beyond words.

257. For a comparison of Rom. 9.4–5 and Eph. 2.12, see Rese, 'Vorzüge' (cf. more generally, Barth, *People*, 45–48). Rese's conclusion that the two texts contain different concepts of Israel is formally correct, but ultimately misleading. The concept of eschatological Israel is present implicitly already in 9.4–5, which laments ethnic Israel's empty possession of the name and blessings of the elect people, and Paul quickly qualifies the reference to ethnic Israel with the concept of eschatological/true Israel in 9.6ff.

3.4.c.5. *The Law-giving*   The next privilege Paul lists, ἡ νομοθεσία, arises directly out of αἱ διαθῆκαι, for it is the giving of the covenant Law that he refers to. There is debate over whether νομοθεσία here denotes the actual giving of the Law,[258] or its result, the Law itself,[259] either of which meanings it can bear. It is true that either meaning implies the other.[260] Therefore, whichever meaning we adopt we must remember that the other is also present. Reference to the act of law-giving is supported by the rarity of the word, appearing in Old Testament canonical literature only in LXX 2 Macc. 6.23 (cf. 4 Macc. 5.35; 17.16), together with the fact that this is the word's most literal meaning.[261] On the other hand, its occurrence in both 2 and 4 Maccabees to refer to the Law argues to the contrary, as does the supreme importance of the Law in the Old Testament and Judaism.[262] Moreover, the use of such an unusual word can be accounted for by the unusual structure of the catalog in which it appears, necessitating a rhyming parallel to the similarly unusual υἱοθεσία.[263] Nevertheless, it is not true that it is impossible 'to argue persuasively that Paul intended to stress the *event* at Sinai rather than the possession and content of the law' as Piper contends.[264]

For the context of Exodus 32–34 stresses exactly this. Israel's apostasy occurred at the very time the Lord was completing the giving of the Law to Moses. The text goes out of its way to stress the divine origin of the Law on the tablets given to Moses (32.15–16; cf. 31.18). And it portrays the nullification of the covenant by Moses' breaking of the tablets. Then, the giving of the Law is stressed again as part of the renewal of the covenant both in the Lord's oral communication to Moses (34.10–28) and on the new tablets of the Law (34.1, 4, 27–29).

Once again, the original context of Paul's allusion is highly relevant to the privilege at hand, and points the way to its proper interpretation. It suggests that Paul did indeed intend νομοθεσία as a reference to the giving of the Law. The metalepsis evokes the context of Law-giving found in Exodus 32–34 with its significance of establishment of the

---

258.   So the majority, as e.g., Moo, *Romans*, 563–64; Käsemann, *Romans*, 259; Epp, 'Continuity', 85–90.

259.   So e.g., Cranfield, *Romans*, 462–63; Piper, *Justification*, 36.

260.   See Piper, *Justification*, 36; Dunn, *Romans*, 527, who is also representative of those who simply affirm that it therefore refers to both.

261.   Cf. BDAG, 676; Moo, *Romans*, 564.

262.   See Piper, *Justification*, 36; Dunn, *Romans*, 527.

263.   See Piper, *Justification*, 36; Dunn, *Romans*, 527; Moo, *Romans*, 564 n. 48.

264.   Piper, *Justification*, 36; emphasis original.

covenant and bestowal of the divine favor and election. It goes hand in hand with the concepts of adoption, glory, and covenant embedded in the narrative, and like the other privileges Paul has mentioned to this point, essentially sums up the whole list. Moreover, it recalls the fact that the breaking of the covenant Law brought about both the annulment of the covenant and the covenant curse. Yet it also recalls that this glorious privilege was granted anew in the renewal of the covenant, dependent on God's faithfulness and mercy through the Covenant Mediator. Through this one word, latent with intertextual significance, Paul manages effectively to encapsulate the story of Israel's rejection and restoration.

There can be no question of whether ἡ νομοθεσία is primarily oriented toward the past. It obviously is. But just as with the previous blessings Paul has enumerated, it also has an eschatological significance. Indeed, just as the giving of the Law recorded in Exodus 32–34 was tied up with Israel's adoption, the divine glory, and the covenant, so is the 'giving of the Law' to their respective eschatological fulfillments as it is fulfilled in Christ. For in the previous chapters of Romans (especially ch. 8), in which Paul has attributed Israel's privileges to Christ, and through him to the Church, he has not neglected the Law. But now, in its eschatological fulfillment, it is the Law of the Spirit of life in Christ Jesus (Rom. 8.2). Thus, we might say that, for Paul, the eschatological giving of the Law is not so much a completely new Law, though some aspects of it have been rendered obsolete, but the giving of the Law in the heart in fulfillment of the Old Testament promise of the New Covenant (cf. Jer. 31.31–34; Ezek. 36.27; 2 Cor. 3.3–6). This is equivalent to the giving of the Spirit, who enables believers to obey the Law from the heart, fulfilling its requirement (Rom. 8.4; 6.17–18; 2 Corinthians 3).

Thus, with the eschatological adoption, gift of the Spirit/divine glory, and New Covenant comes a new possession of the Law in freedom and power to which the original giving of the Law always pointed. Just as the event at Sinai, the New Covenant νομοθεσία signifies the divine favor and election. How tragic that the original recipients now do not truly possess their own Law – they are in slavery and condemned to death (Rom. 8.1–17; Galatians 3–4) – and have missed its fulfillment!

3.4.c.6. *The Service/Worship*   ἡ λατρεία follows nicely upon νομο-θεσία, since the latter contained the former. Virtually all interpreters agree that ἡ λατρεία refers primarily to the cultic service that reached its apex in the worship of the Lord in the Temple, though some extend the meaning of the term beyond this to include non-sacrificial worship of God such as Scripture reading, prayer, and the religious observance of the home and synagogue.[265] Not surprisingly, Paul's allusion to Exod. 32.32 can shed light on this privilege as well. For Exodus 32–34 is closely related to Israel's cultic worship.

First, it interrupts the flow of Exodus' narrative, bringing an abrupt halt to its natural progression, which was to proceed to the construction of the Tabernacle followed by conquest of the Promised Land. Israel's sin brought an end to this blessing along with all the rest of their prerogatives inherent in their adoption and covenant with the Lord. It was the Lord's glory that was to fill the Tabernacle. The withdrawal of his presence from Israel denied them the worship. Thus, this prerogative is part and parcel of the other ones that we have examined. It was part of the covenant administration to maintain Israel's relationship with the Lord.[266] Its possession implies the other items in this catalog, as has each term we have examined. Just as the sin of Exodus 32–34 elicits the negation of the promised Tabernacle, so does the resolution of the problem result in the construction of the Tabernacle (Exodus 35–40). Hence, against the backdrop of Paul's allusion to this context, ἡ λατρεία invokes the same type of Israel's fall-rejection-restoration, this time in the guise of the cultic service that was denied to Israel along with its adoption, divine glory, covenant, and Law, and restored with the same through the mediation of God's glory – the key to all the rest – via the Covenant Mediator. The focus on the Tabernacle in the Exodus context suggests that Paul's reference certainly included this mode of Israel's worship in addition to its fulfillment in the more permanent Temple located in Jerusalem.

Second, the cultic worship was stressed in the covenant stipulations repeated in the second *giving of the Law* (Exod. 34.10–28). It was precisely in this area of sacrificial worship that Israel fell, giving their hearts to an idol rather than the living God. Therefore, while the entire Law God had given is presupposed, Exodus 34 emphasizes this very aspect represented by λατρεία. Now, Israel has again fallen into idolatry, this time by clinging to cultic sacrifices that cannot avail before God and rejecting the once-for-all sacrifice that he has provided in his own son for

265. So Cranfield, *Romans*, 463; Morris, *Romans*, 349; Dreyfus, 'passé', 137–38. Opposed by Moo, *Romans*, 564; Schreiner, *Romans*, 484. Epp, 'Continuity', 83, somewhat uniquely appears to take this broader meaning as primary. On LXX usage, see Piper, *Justification*, 37.

266. See Piper's (*Justification*, 38) helpful sketch of the supreme importance of this benefit.

forgiveness and life. This points all the more strongly towards the eschatological fulfillment of this privilege in what Paul would have considered to be the ultimate covenant renewal, the New Covenant, in which believers in Christ are the true Circumcision and worship in the Spirit of God (Phil. 3.3; cf. Eph. 2.11–21 discussed above), and indeed, are themselves the Temple of God/the Holy Spirit (1 Cor. 3.16–17; 6.19; 2 Cor. 6.16; Eph 2.21–22), all based upon the ultimate sacrifice of Christ.

Similar to what we have seen in each of the privileges Paul has enumerated, he refers to the one privilege of service understood most directly in its past Old Testament expression, most keenly revealed in Exodus 32–34 and its broader context, but understood as pointing toward its eschatological fulfillment, so that at base he refers to the one prerogative filled with past, present, and future import. In fact, Paul uses the word and its cognate verb (λατρεύω) elsewhere only in a spiritual sense, except for the latter's use in Rom. 1.25, where, interestingly enough, it describes idolatrous cultic worship in the context of allusion to the golden calf episode.[267] His only other use of λατρεία appears in Rom. 12.1, where he uses it to call the Roman Christians to worship that is a total life response to what God has done in Christ (i.e., his mercies as described in Romans 1–11) amounting to a living sacrifice. This is equivalent to the Christian life of sanctification that Paul described in Romans 6, which leads to eternal life. It is this sacrificial worship that is man's duty and great privilege in Christ, but that Paul's kinsmen fail to participate in because of their unbelief.

3.4.c.7 *The Promises* αἱ ἐπαγγελίαι[268] is the last privilege belonging to the first relative clause describing Ἰσραηλῖται. Three basic referents

267. λατρεία occurs in Rom. 9.4; 12.1; λατρεύω occurs in Rom. 1.9, 25; Phil. 3.3; 2 Tim. 1.3. Even in Rom. 1.25, a broader reference for λατρεύω is not excluded in light of a possible parallel to 1.21 (cf. Dunn, *Romans*, 63) and its previous occurrence in 1.9. H. Strathmann, 'λατρεύω, λατρεία', *TDNT*, 4.58–65 (62–65), notes that the NT writings tend to spiritualize this verb. H. Balz's ('λατρεύω, λατρεία', *EDNT*, 2.344–452 [344]) comment is especially interesting in light of our argument relating to its idolatrous intertextual connotations in this context: 'Λατρεύω always alludes to worship, often where the place of God is occupied by other entities, thus where true worship is perverted and misguided.'

268. The singular, ἐπαγγελία, is read by P[46], D, F, G, a, bo[mss], but this has less external support than the parallel singular variant for διαθῆκαι earlier in 9.4 that we rejected. The singular here probably resulted from the earlier change to the singular in many cases (cf. Dunn, *Romans*, 521–22), and it is easy to see how homoioteleuton could easily occur in others.

have been suggested with a good deal of overlap between them: (1) the promises to Abraham/the fathers (most usually to Abraham, and then repeated to Isaac and to Jacob);[269] (2) the messianic promises;[270] (3) the many promises of God to his people.[271] The Abrahamic promises are favored by Paul's emphasis on them in Romans 4 (albeit in the singular; see esp. vv. 13, 14, 16, 20), a chapter particularly related to Romans 9 (see our next ch.), his reference to the fathers in the words that immediately follow (9.5), his discussion of Abraham and the divine promise to him in the following verses (9.7–9), his articulation of Christ's work as confirmation of God's promises to the fathers (15.8) in what is often taken as a summary of his concern in Romans (15.7–13), and his focus on the promises to Abraham in Galatians 3–4, also significantly related to the subject matter of Romans 9. The messianic promises are supported by the reference to the Messiah in 9.5 as well as their singular importance in early Christianity. As with its plural counterpart in the first triad of privileges (αἱ διαθῆκαι), we would argue that αἱ ἐπαγγελίαι should be given as broad a meaning as possible within the limits of its present context. That would mean option three mentioned above, that αἱ ἐπαγγελίαι refers to all of God's promises to Israel. But just as with the previous plural, there is no reason to deny a special focus within the general reference.[272]

Therefore, in light of the evidence reviewed above, it seems most likely that Paul speaks especially of the promises to the fathers. And we can add a further piece of supporting evidence from the Old Testament background suggested by Paul's allusion to Exod. 32.32. Moses specifically appeals to the promise to the fathers Abraham, Isaac, and Israel/Jacob in his first intercession on behalf of Israel in Exod. 32.13. It is again significant that the Old Testament context understands all of the blessings bestowed upon Israel in its covenant with the Lord established at Sinai – of which Paul's list is a fair summary – to be a fulfillment of God's promises to Abraham, Isaac, and Jacob. For it suggests that this may also be Paul's view, and that he therefore understood God's work in Christ as a fulfillment of both the fundamental promises to Abraham and their development in the Mosaic covenant, as confirmed

269. See e.g., Epp, 'Continuity', 83–84. Fitzmyer, *Romans*, 547, adds the promises to Moses and David, while J.C. O'Neill, *Paul's Letter to the Romans* (Harmondsworth: Penguin, 1975), 152, speaks of the patriarchs and the prophets.

270. See e.g., Barrett, *Romans*, 178; Cranfield, *Romans*, 464.

271. See e.g., Piper, *Justification*, 39; Morris, *Romans*, 349.

272. Cf. Cranfield, *Romans*, 464.

by all we have seen in relation to this list of Israel's privileges. But to say this automatically brings the messianic character of the promises into view, since Paul finds their fulfillment only through the Messiah. Nevertheless, it is the Abrahamic genesis of the promises that stands out most conspicuously against the general context of Romans, the specific context of Romans 9, and Paul's allusion to Exodus 32. The point at issue is the fact that the promises that believers in Christ have become heirs of are the very promises that were first given to Abraham, and then through him to Israel.

The mention of αἱ ἐπαγγελίαι is an excellent example of the eschatological tension that has characterized the entire list of Israel's privileges. The promises were given incipiently to Abraham and found increasing fulfillment over the course of salvation history. Now, in the time of inaugurated eschatological fulfillment, the very people whose heritage contains these promises do not participate in their fulfillment while many who had no such heritage do. This is because, as Paul has made clear in Romans 4 and elsewhere (esp. Galatians 3–4), faith has always been the means of inheriting the Abrahamic promises, and now, it is faith in Christ; indeed, he is the seed to whom the promises were ultimately made along with all who are covenantally united to him by faith.[273] As much as any member of the sixfold list expounding the privileges of ᾽Ισραηλῖται, αἱ ἐπαγγελίαι sums up the entire catalog. Piper rightly comments 'that for Paul the promises of God flow together into a summation of all the good that God can possibly offer his people'.[274] The accursed state of Israel that has resulted from their rejection of Christ is what incites Paul's grief, calls God's word into question, and elicits the argument of Romans 9–11 in defense of God's faithfulness.

3.4.c.8. *The Fathers*   The fact that among the many promises of God to Israel, those to the fathers are first and foremost in view leads directly into the second relative clause explicating the meaning of ᾽Ισραηλῖται: 'of whom are the fathers' (9.5a). Interpreters have offered various suggestions for the identity of the fathers Paul invokes. Piper and Schreiner claim that most interpreters take οἱ πατέρες to mean Abraham, Isaac, and Jacob.[275]

---

273. For an excellent treatment of Gal. 3.10–20, see Wright, *Climax*, 137–74. A. Sand, 'ἐπαγγελία, κτλ', *EDNT*, 2.13–16 (15), recognizes the paradoxical possession of the promises by Israel and equates it with the mystery of Israel.
274. Piper, *Justification*, 39.
275. Piper, *Justification*, 40 n. 46; Schreiner, *Romans*, 486.

But quite a few add other designations to these three patriarchs such as the twelve sons of Jacob,[276] the wilderness generation,[277] David,[278] or generally 'the fathers of distinction in redemptive history from Abraham onwards'.[279] Such broadening additions miss Paul's specific concern for the fulfillment of the Abrahamic promises as expressed in Romans 4, and more importantly, 9.6–13, where he specifically names Abraham, Isaac, and Jacob.[280] Moreover, we may now add that Paul's allusion to Exodus 32 also suggests that the fathers he has in mind are Abraham, Isaac, and Jacob, for as we have seen, these are precisely the fathers Moses mentions in his intercession for Israel, to whom YHWH owes covenant faithfulness. Furthermore, this is not just a superficial parallel, but a theme directly linked to a major concern of both passages – the faithfulness of God to his word.

Most interpreters rightly reject any reference to a concept of the 'merits of the fathers' here and/or in 11.28.[281] Rather, Paul speaks of οἱ πατέρες as one of Israel's great benefits in the fashion of Exodus 32, which pleads for the Lord's mercy and forgiveness to Israel based on the Lord's covenant promise to the fathers. The parallel strengthens the already obvious connection to αἱ διαθῆκαι and αἱ ἐπαγγελίαι. Israel's election and privileges derive from God's covenants with and promises to Abraham, Isaac, and Jacob. Thus, οἱ πατέρες also encompasses the whole of Israel's prerogatives like the others we have analyzed. The problem Paul wrestles with is that by and large the patriarchs' physical descendants are not experiencing the realization of the covenant promises made to the fathers in the time of their eschatological fulfillment. The answer he will present is that the true descendants of the patriarchs are only those who believe in Christ, whether Jew or Gentile, and that God grants priority to the Jew and works specially for her salvation in merciful faithfulness to his covenant promises to the fathers. Indeed, the patriarchs have eschatological significance in the New Covenant. They are the fathers of all who believe in Christ, in whom the Abrahamic promises have come to fulfillment.

---

276. E.g., Bruce, *Romans*, 185.
277. E.g., Dunn, *Romans*, 528.
278. E.g., Stuhlmacher, *Romans*, 145–46.
279. Murray, *Romans*, 2.6.
280. Cf. Piper, *Justification*, 40, and treatment of αἱ διαθῆκαι and αἱ ἐπαγγελίαι above.
281. In relation to 9.4, see e.g., Piper, *Justification*, 41; Schreiner, *Romans*, 486.

3.4.c.9. *The Christ*   The mention of fulfillment in Christ brings us to the final privilege Paul lists: 'and from whom is the Christ according to the flesh, who is over all, God blessed forever. Amen' (9.5b). This is now the third and final relative clause explaining the significance of 9.4's Ἰσραηλῖται. But Paul changes his wording slightly from the simple ὧν of the last two clauses to ἐξ ὧν, signaling both a shift in perspective and that he has come to the climactic and greatest privilege of Israel. To say that the Messiah comes *from* Israelites is to state his ethnic identity as an Israelite,[282] and to state therefore the supreme honor of the Jewish people, and their supreme advantage of having the Savior of the world come to them first, and act first and foremost for their sake (Ἰουδαίῳ τε πρῶτον!). But in contrast to saying that he is *of* Israel or *belongs to* Israel, it is also to draw attention to the fact that ethnic Israel does not now truly 'possess' their own Messiah; they have rejected him in unbelief.[283] This is especially confirmed by the limiting phrase τὸ κατὰ σάρκα, which conveys that the Messiah comes from Israel only with respect to the flesh/physical ancestry.[284]

It is not as if Paul could not have used the same grammatical construction of Israel's relationship to the Messiah as he did of the other privileges he has listed.[285] As we have argued concerning Paul's rhetoric, ethnic Israel both possesses and does not possess each of the prerogatives Paul names, in different senses respectively. But now, at the climax of this glorious catalog, Paul chooses to give expression to ethnic Israel's superficial possession of these blessings. Why would he do so?

First, it is an exquisite rhetorical move. Paul has allowed the accursed state of Israel to recede ever so slightly and briefly to the background of his rhetoric as he has listed the people's great prerogatives. But at the very point that Paul arrives at the climactically pivotal privilege, he rips the bulk of its benefit away, and with it, that of all the rest of Israel's benefits. And it all goes to support Paul's grief at his kinsmen's accursed

---

282.   Piper, *Justification*, 42. This use of the ἐκ-construction here suggests a similar meaning for the construction in 9.6b (οἱ ἐξ Ἰσραήλ), confirming that what is at issue in Romans 9–11 is ethnic false possession vs. faith-based true possession of the election and blessings of God.

283.   Cf. Moo, *Romans*, 565; Schreiner, *Romans*, 486.

284.   BDF § 266.2, states that the article here 'strongly emphasizes the limitation ('insofar as the physical is concerned')'; cf. BDAG, 688 (2f). Piper, *Justification*, 43, astutely adds that the neuter article makes κατὰ σάρκα adverbial rather than adjectival in relation to the masculine Χριστός.

285.   Rightly, Piper, *Justification*, 42–43.

state as expressed in his contemplated prayer of self-malediction (9.3). That is, after all, the purpose of this exalted catalog – to communicate the privileged position of Israel as powerfully as possible in order to lament the grievous fact of their exclusion from it and to raise the challenge to God's word that this poses.

Secondly, it is precisely because Christ is the climactic privilege of Israel that Paul would choose to indicate his people's separation from him. For more than any other privilege, Christ sums up all the rest; indeed he encompasses them uniquely. One's relationship to Christ determines one's possession of the rest of the privileges. Thus, through this one turn of phrase Paul is able to sum up the problem of Israel, which he must now address.

But Paul's rhetorical strategy has not yet finished its climb to the heights of Israel's privilege. For in the final clause he reveals the supreme dignity of Israel's Messiah in contrast to his strictly earthly origin (τὸ κατὰ σάρκα) – he is Lord over all, God blessed forever! 9.5b (ὁ ὢν ἐπὶ πάντων θεὸς εὐλογητὸς εἰς τοὺς αἰῶνας, ἀμήν) has probably been discussed more than any other verse in the New Testament.[286] To state the matter as simply as possible, the fundamental issue is whether the clause in whole or in part refers to ὁ Χριστός or to God the Father, and most importantly, whether Paul applies θεός to Christ.[287] The issues are detailed and complex, and have been clearly delineated in the voluminous literature.[288] Consequently, we need not cover the same ground here. Suffice it to say that we find the traditional interpretation most convincing, as represented by our translation

---

286.   See Sanday and Headlam, *Romans*, 233; B.M. Metzger, 'The Punctuation of Rom. 9:5', in B. Lindars and S.S. Smalley (eds.), *Christ and Spirit in the New Testament* (Festschrift C.F.D. Moule; Cambridge: Cambridge University Press, 1973), 95–112 (95); cf. Lodge, *Romans 9–11*, 47.

287.   Metzger, 'Punctuation', 95–96, lists eight possible punctuations with supporters; cf. Moo, *Romans*, 565. Additionally, a few have supported the textual emendation ὧν ὁ (in place of ὁ ὢν); so Ziesler, *Romans*, 239; Haacker, *Römer*, 179, 187; Bartsch, 'Konjektur'; W.L. Lorimer, 'Romans ix. 3–5', *ExpTim* 35 (1923–24), 42–43 (who further inserts ὁ ὢν after θεός), first mentioned but rejected by the seventeenth-century Socinian Jonasz Schlichting (on whom see esp. Cranfield, *Romans*, 465). But with no manuscript evidence it is certainly to be rejected as pure conjecture. Against it, see esp. Metzger, 99–100.

288.   For full discussions, see Metzger, 'Punctuation'; Cranfield, *Romans*, 464–70; Sanday and Headlam, *Romans*, 233–38; Godet, *Romans*, 136–43; Morison, *Exposition*, 43–51; O. Kuss, *Der Römerbrief*, III, (Regensburg: Pustet, 1978), 677ff.; idem, 'Zu Römer 9,5', in J. Friedrich, W. Pöhlmann, and P. Stuhlmacher (eds.),

above.[289] Before moving on to our primary concern of the significance of Paul's allusion to Exodus 32 for this controversial question, we will content ourselves with two observations that have perhaps not received as much attention as they deserve, one of a hermeneutical nature, and the other, broadly exegetical.

First, I would like to point out that the more objective data, such as Greek grammar/style, Pauline doxological style, standard doxological form,[290] etc., favor a reference to Christ. The main argument against the Christological interpretation is that Paul does not incontestably call Christ θεός anywhere else. But almost everyone acknowledges that Paul viewed Christ as divine, and that he all but calls him God elsewhere.[291] So many scholars find it quite conceivable that he would also apply the title to him even if this was not his custom. The hermeneutical point I wish to add to this is that it is methodologically suspect to insist that Paul could not have spoken in this manner when it is at least plausible that he did so, evidenced by the many interpreters who so understand him, and it is the most natural way to take his grammar. In such a theologically charged arena, it is best to let more objective criteria determine exegesis rather than a priori convictions of what we think Paul could or could not say.[292]

Second, the Christological interpretation of Rom. 9.5b accords best with the purpose of the catalog of Israel's privileges in which it is found, to support Paul's lament of Israel's accursed state as embodied in his consequent willingness to sacrifice himself for them. While it is true that such a list of Israel's blessings might naturally lead to a doxology, to say that the context favors praise to the God of Israel over against reference to

Rechtfertigung: Festschrift für Ernst Käsemann zum 70. Geburstag (Tübingen: Mohr Siebeck; Göttingen: Vandenhoeck & Ruprecht, 1976), 291–303.

289. Of the two main options that take 9.5b as a relative clause modifying Χριστός, I have taken the one that separates θεός from ἐπὶ πάντων, primarily because of the participle following the article ὁ, which is by no means a conclusive consideration in and of itself, but in the absence of any other objective factors tips the scales in the direction I have taken; see further Abasciano 'Paul's Use', 255 n. 328, where one will also find an extensive listing of those who favor a reference to Christ on the one hand and God the Father on the other.

290. Despite the recent attempt of Reichert, *Römerbrief*, 184–85, to neutralize the doxological evidence; see Abasciano, 'Paul's Use', 256 n. 329, for critique.

291. For the case, see e.g., Cranfield, *Romans*, 468; Metzger, 'Punctuation', 109–10.

292. See Metzger, 'Punctuation', 110–11, for an extended development of this essentially hermeneutical point.

the divine nature of Christ[293] ironically severs the list from its context and treats it in isolation from its purpose in that context. To say, as Käsemann does, 'The main point here is that of Israel's blessings',[294] is true only very narrowly. The point of a list of blessings is, of course, blessing. But the point of listing the blessings at all in this context is to grieve their forfeiture and to raise the challenge to God's faithfulness that must therefore be addressed. Thus, while it is conceivable that Paul launches into a doxology at the climax of his agonizing lament out of a sort of theological reflex, this does not seem very likely given the careful artistry employed throughout the whole passage, especially vv. 4–5. It seems far more likely that Paul draws attention to the incredibly exalted nature of Israel's Messiah, and thus paradoxically brings us to Israel's greatest privilege and their greatest woe – their Messiah who has come to them is none other than God himself, but they have rejected him and thereby all the aforementioned blessings, which are wrapped up in him.

This leads us to consideration of the ramifications of Paul's allusion to Exodus 32–34 for the meaning of Rom. 9.5b. For as we have seen, the allusion suggests that by rejecting Christ Paul's unbelieving kinsmen have fallen into an idolatry that surpasses even that of the golden calf. Hence, the intertextual idolatry motif argues for a reference to Christ as God. One could argue that because Christ fulfills the role of Moses in Paul's typology, the allusion need not argue for a reference to his deity in Rom. 9.5b. But this is to miss the typical escalatory character of antitypes, Paul's view of Christ as divine by almost any reckoning, and additional considerations based on Exodus 32–34 which also argue for a Christological interpretation.

The phrase ὁ ὢν ἐπὶ πάντων indicates that the referent is Lord over all things. πάντων is ambiguous, and could refer to all people, or all (impersonal) things, or all things bar none. Keeping in line again with the exalted nature and purpose of the list before us, we take the phrase to indicate sovereignty over absolutely everything. But we again think that there is a more specific reference that comes to the fore of the multitude encompassed by πάντων – the connotation of all people, suggested by Paul's emphasis in Romans on God as the God of all people, and Christ as the Lord of all, both Jew and Gentile.[295] This then ties in

---

293. So Dunn, *Romans*, 529; Käsemann, *Romans*, 260; L.T. Johnson, *Romans*, 147. Bartsch's ('Konjektur', 403) claim that a doxology to Christ would be meaningless in this context is nothing short of astonishing.

294. Käsemann, *Romans*, 260.

295. The form appears in Rom. 1.8; 4.11, 16; 8.32; 9.5; 10.12; 12.17; 12.18; 15.33.

to part of contemporary Israel's idolatry, which has been suggested by Paul's allusion to Exodus 32. Ethnic Israel worships a false, ethnocentric conception of God that conceives of him as 'the God of Jews only' (Rom. 3.29), who only justifies the circumcised, those who are of the Law rather than anyone who has faith in Christ. Thus, the special connotation of πάντων in Romans as referring to all people and the intertextual idolatry motif rooted in Exodus 32–34 are mutually supporting – the former helping to establish the validity of the latter, and the latter underscoring the presence of the former in the present context.

The chief intertextual observation relating to the meaning of Rom. 9.5b is the glory motif of Exodus 32–34. Recalling our exegesis of the Old Testament context and our discussion of ἡ δόξα above, we have seen that God's glory denotes his personal covenantal presence, indeed, his very self manifest in all its magnificence and moral beauty. It is a presence that bestows election and all its benefits. We have also seen that Paul's defense of his ministry in 2 Corinthians 3 based on Exodus 32–34 was dominated by the concept of glory, and that this glory was ultimately the very glory of God embodied in and revealed through Christ, himself the glory and image of God, and mediated through the Spirit.[296] At the same time, we saw that in Romans 8 Paul directly related his concept of glory to the Holy Spirit of God, who is also the Spirit of Christ (8.9) and the glory/presence of God. The upshot of all of this is that Paul conceives of Christ as the personal presence of God which conveys election, covenant membership, and all related blessings. That is, Paul believed Christ to be God and his allusion to Exodus 32 thus supports a Christological interpretation of Rom. 9.5b. Indeed, in light of the significance of the glory of God in Exodus 32–34 as adopted by Paul, the common function of Christ and the Spirit as the glory/presence of God carries Trinitarian implications.

3.5. *Summary/Conclusion*

While most interpreters recognize Paul's allusion to Exod. 32.32 in Rom. 9.3, the echo has never before been fully explored for its relevance to

---

296.   The present argument is strengthened if Kim, *Origin*, 205–52, is correct to link Paul's conception of Christ as the εἰκὼν τοῦ θεοῦ to the Damascus Christophany and 2 Cor. 3.1–4.6 on the one hand and to OT/Jewish descriptions of epiphanies/theophanies on the other. Cf. the theophanic connotations of Jn 1.17–18's use of Exod. 33.20 and 34.6 in relation to the divine Christ discussed earlier.

Paul's argument in Romans 9–11. Our investigation has found that Paul's use of Exodus 32–34 is of enormous weight for his argument, holding significance for a number of exegetical details as well as broader themes and rhetorical movements. The similarity in theme and subject matter between the old and new contexts is striking. Both are concerned with the apostasy and hardheartedness of Israel, the resulting divine judgment and loss of election along with all its promises, the ensuing tremendous grief, the faithfulness of God to his covenant word and his great mercy, and the restoration of Israel to election and blessing in a 'new' covenant established primarily with the Covenant Mediator and mediated to the people only through connection with him and the glory of God shining through him. Indeed, it appears that Paul has gone to the scriptural paradigm of the fall and restoration of Israel, Exodus 32–34, to understand and express the present stage of salvation history and the outworking of the eschatological fulfillment of the covenant promises of God.

James Scott has argued persuasively that Romans 9–11 fits into the Deuteronomic view of Israel's history, which basically articulated the sin-judgment-restoration pattern running through the Scriptures of Israel, and perhaps best represented by the Song of Moses in Deuteronomy 32 and taken up in subsequent Jewish tradition.[297] But what seems to have escaped Scott and others is that the story of this Deuteronomic tradition is first the story of Exodus 32–34. Indeed, it appears that much of Paul's argument can be traced back *in part* here in seed form. Just as it has been claimed that Deuteronomy 32 contains Romans *in nuce*,[298] we may say that Exodus 32–34 contains Romans 9–11 *in nuce*. Paul has taken upon himself the mediatorial, intercessory, and prophetic aura of Moses in a typologically conditioned response that conceives of his own ministry as the vehicle through which the election-bestowing 'glory of God in the face of Christ' is brought back to Israel in 'the gospel of the glory of Christ, who is the image of God' (2 Cor. 4.4, 6). Paul's grief is a typological fulfillment of Israel's sorrow at their loss of election resulting from their idolatrous apostasy. Even his utilization of the remnant motif later in his argument may be fore-shadowed in Exodus 32's remnant motif, the first glimpse of which could be the self-sacrificial prayer contemplated in Rom. 9.3. God's judgment upon Israel in Paul's day is an escalated fulfillment of his merciful

---

297. Scott, 'Restoration', 802–805. Cf. Bell, *Provoked*; Hays, *Echoes*, 163–64.
298. Hays, *Echoes*, 163–64.

judgment upon Israel of old, placing them in the same hardened position as the Gentiles under his wrath, yet granting them opportunity for repentance and forgiveness *vis-à-vis* Christ and the New Covenant as God once again limits his sovereignty in giving Paul, Israel, and the Gentiles pivotal roles in his plan of salvation for the whole world.

None of this is to suggest that Exodus 32–34 was the determinative influence on Paul's argument in Romans 9–11 or its primary background. But it is to suggest that Exodus 32–34 supplies important background informing Paul's rhetoric, and that his allusion in Rom. 9.3 functions as a pointer to this context, providing a foundational orientation in the introductory section for approaching the argument of Romans 9–11. As for more specific exegetical insights relative to Rom. 9.1–5 generated by attention to Paul's use of Exod. 32.32 in Rom. 9.3 that remain to be mentioned, we have suggested that the allusion supports:[299] (1) ηὐχόμην as a reference to prayer rather than a wish; (2) a hypothetical meaning for the imperfect tense of ηὐχόμην; (3) ἀνάθεμα as a reference to the curse of the covenant, which was essentially separation from the elect community and destruction under the wrath of God; (4) the contention that, for Paul, unbelieving Israel is anathema; (5) the idea that Paul contemplates a prayer that would offer to join his people in their accursed state as an inducement to the Lord to spare them rather than the standard view of Paul's prayer/wish to refer to some sort of substitution; (6) the contention that Paul casts himself in a salvation-historical role on a par with Moses; (7) a stronger sense of Paul's identification with the Jewish people; (8) the meaning 'for the sake/benefit of' apart from any nuance of substitution for the preposition ὑπέρ in Rom. 9.3.

Concerning the exalted catalog of Israel's privileges in Rom. 9.4–5, we have found that in light of Paul's allusion to Exod. 32.32, Exodus 32–34 and its broader context provides the most appropriate place to begin analysis of the background of this impressive list. Indeed, it appears as a fair summary of the blessings given to Israel in her covenant and election distinctively established at Sinai. Immediately following Paul's allusion, many of the items in the catalog effectively evoke the fall-rejection-restoration pattern of Exodus 32–34 in which these very privileges were rescinded from Israel and ultimately restored to them. Continuing our list of more specific exegetical insights, we have suggested

---

299. Since the intertextual matrix of Paul's allusion is thoroughly integrated into our exegesis, the following list is not necessarily exhaustive.

that Paul's allusion supports: (9) use of the covenant name Ἰσραηλῖται as invoking God's covenant promises to Israel in all their fullness; (10) the possibility that Paul found some inspiration for his use of the designation Ἰσραηλῖται in Moses' use of the root name in Exod. 32.13; (11) an understanding of ethnic Israel's possession of the blessings of election as ideal rather than actual, partial and outward rather than fully and in truth; (12) ἡ δόξα as the covenant-and-election-bestowing glory of God; (13) αἱ διαθῆκαι as a reference to the Sinaitic/Mosaic covenant with its renewals, understood as an extension of the Abrahamic covenant and looking forward towards the New; (14) ἡ νομοθεσία as a reference to the giving of the Law rather than the Law itself; (15) Paul's mention of ἡ λατρεία as including the Old Testament Tabernacle; (16) αἱ ἐπαγγελίαι as referring especially to the promises to the fathers Abraham, Isaac, and Israel/Jacob; (17) the suggestion that Paul understood God's work in Christ as a fulfillment of both the fundamental promises to Abraham and their development in the Mosaic covenant; (18) οἱ πατέρες of 9.5a as Abraham, Isaac, and Jacob/Israel; (19) the Christological interpretation of 9.5b, which applies θεός to ὁ Χριστός.

We have also discovered that Jewish interpretive traditions surrounding Exod. 32.32 and its broader context treat themes that are highly relevant to Paul's argument in Romans 9–11. Ancient interpreters of Exodus 32–34 engaged issues of the faithfulness of God to his word to Israel, the restoration of Israel, the question of whether Israel as a nation could be cast away and destroyed, the possibility of a new people replacing Israel, Israel's role in relation to the world/Gentiles, divine foreknowledge, divine predetermination, Moses' prophetic/mediatorial/intercessory role, eschatological secrets relating to Israel and the Gentiles, the necessity of repentance for restoration, an attitude of contempt for the identification of Jews with Gentiles in sin and divine judgment, Israel's privileged elect status, identification of that which finds favor with God in people, and the fate of Israel. Later rabbinic tradition sought to defend Israel against the early Church, which came to use the golden calf episode to claim that God had rejected Israel, voided his covenant with them, and replaced her with the Church as his elect people. This position *vis-à-vis* Exodus 32–34 was anticipated already in the New Testament, where the passage was used to characterize contemporary Israel as stiff-necked and estranged from God under the divine judgment of hardening (Acts 7), and to express the inadequacy of the faith of Israel in the present eschatological age unless completed in the divine Christ (Jn 1.17–18).

Paul's prophetically and apocalyptically charged lament of Rom. 9.1–5 serves a complex literary and rhetorical purpose. Its grave tone signals the climactic character of the argument to which he now turns even as its discreet and tactful expression presents the grievous and controversial rejection of ethnic Israel that creates the fundamental problem Paul must address. From the beginning of his discourse in Romans 9–11 Paul pursues the practical purpose of Romans in general and chapters 9–11 in particular of procuring the unity of Jews and Gentiles in the Roman church behind his gospel and missionary praxis, giving assurance of his sincere love and respect for the Jewish people, which he models as the proper Christian attitude towards them. All of this comes to pointed expression in Paul's allusion to Exod. 32.32 in Rom. 9.3, which the logic of the passage reveals to be the main point of 9.1–5, an intensely dramatic expression of grief over the accursed state of ethnic Israel/the Jewish people that intimates with respect to Paul a prophetic authority and salvation historical role of the highest order among mortal men. Thus, Paul's allusion to Exod. 32.32 is central to his introduction to the argument of Romans 9–11. Indeed, its echo of the grief over the loss of Israel's election and vision of its restoration provide an orientation for approaching the whole of Romans 9–11 and suggests that Paul's use of the Old Testament may well provide the keys to a full understanding of what Paul has written here.

Chapter 4

PAUL'S USE OF THE OLD TESTAMENT IN ROMANS 9.6–9

Paul makes two Old Testament quotations from Genesis in Rom. 9.6–9 (Gen. 21.12 and 18.10, 14). These passages are directly connected to one another within the original broader narrative of which they are a part, the story of Abraham and the fulfillment of God's promise to give him seed/descendants. In order to prepare for an exegesis of Rom. 9.6–9 and Paul's use of these biblical texts, this chapter will look at these texts and associated material in the order of their appearance in their original narrative context. First, there will be an exegesis of Gen. 18.10, 14 and its context, followed by a textual comparison with the text of Romans, and then a survey of relevant interpretive traditions. Then, this same procedure will be followed for Gen. 21.12. Finally, we will seek to draw on what we discover to elucidate what Paul has written in Rom. 9.6–9.

4.1. *The Old Testament Context of Genesis 18.10, 14*

Gen. 18.10, 14 are part of a much larger passage encompassing all of chapters 18 and 19.[1] We may divide this larger passage into four sections:[2]

| 18.1–15 | The Lord's promise of Isaac's birth against the backdrop of doubt |
| 18.16–33 | The Lord reveals his plan for Sodom and Abraham intercedes on its behalf |

---

1. See G.J. Wenham, *Genesis* (WBC, 1–2; 2 vols.; Dallas: Word, 1987), 2.40–45; S.R. Driver, *The Book of Genesis* (Westminster Commentaries; London: Methuen & Co., 11th edn., 1920), 191; and perhaps more importantly, Josephus, *Ant.* 1.196–206; Philo, *Abr.* 167.
2. See Wenham, *Genesis*, 2.40. This is a typical construal of the passage's structure, though some commentators divide the sections into smaller units.

19.1–29   The Lord rescues Lot and his family from Sodom
19.30–38   Lot's daughters commit incest with him and bear his
            children.

That Genesis 18–19 form a single, unified narrative in the text as it now
stands is shown by the continuity of characters, the similarity between
the two chapters, and the time references in 18.1 and 19.1.[3] The
announcement of Isaac's birth (18.1–15) is directly connected with the
following narrative (18.16–33) as Abraham's heavenly guests get up to
leave and are escorted by Abraham, who ends up in dialogue with the
Lord over the fate of Sodom and Gomorrah. 18.1–15 is the necessary
introduction to 18.16–19.29.[4]

Gen. 18.1 is an editorial comment which summarizes the events of
ch. 18 in theocentric terms. We are told that Abraham experienced a
YHWH theophany, the end of which is clearly indicated in 18.33 when
YHWH leaves Abraham. 18.1–15 has two sections, vv. 1–8 and vv. 9–15.
The first half of the passage (vv. 1–8) sets the scene for the promise of a
son to Abraham and Sarah. Abraham sees three 'men', who he pleads
with to visit with him for dinner and refreshment. The reader will eventually realize that one of these 'men' is actually YHWH himself, and that
the other two are angels.[5] This first half of the passage chiefly consists of
a description of Abraham's lavish hospitality towards these 'men', the
true identity of whom he presumably does not know until later on when
they begin to display supernatural powers (see 18.9ff.). The point is to
demonstrate Abraham's piety through a depiction of his hospitality. This
sets the stage for the main concern: the promise of a son to Abraham and
Sarah. Abraham is a righteous and faithful man before the Lord, and will
therefore receive the fulfillment of his promise. The emphasis of the
passage (18.1–15) clearly rests on vv. 9–15 and the promise of a son.

But the emphasis of 18.9–15 is even more specific than the Lord's
promise of a son to Abraham and Sarah. The narrative comes to focus
on the reliability of YHWH's promise, a theme brought to the fore by
Sarah's doubt expressed through her laughter and highlighted by the
Lord's rebuke. 18.9 is the first indication since the summary statement

---

3.   Wenham, *Genesis*, 2.40, 43–44.
4.   Cf. Wenham, *Genesis*, 2.43.
5.   So most commentators. G. von Rad, *Genesis: A Commentary* (OTL;
Philadelphia: Westminster, rev. edn., 1972), 204, takes the three men together as a
manifestation of YHWH, but 18.1, 22, and 19.1 are decisive in favor of the consensus.

of v. 1 that Abraham's visitors are out of the ordinary. Their supernatural knowledge of Sarah's name is revealing. The fact that they use Sarah's new name is significant, for the recent change of Abraham's wife's name from שָׂרַי to שָׂרָה (17.15) reflects God's promise that Abraham would have a son by her. The fact that the visitors ask about Sarah's whereabouts indicates their specific concern for her, and suggests that the following message is as much for her as for her husband. Indeed, in light of the broader narrative in which God's promise to Abraham of a son by Sarah is at issue, it appears that the message is meant even more for Sarah's ears than Abraham's, since Abraham has already received this promise (17.15–21), and Sarah's response and interaction with the Lord becomes the main emphasis of the passage.

Upon hearing that Sarah was nearby, the Lord[6] utters the astounding promise: 'I will surely return to you at this time next year; and behold, Sarah your wife will have a son' (18.10). Now the text makes it a point to let us know that Sarah is physically behind the Lord/visitor.[7] The significance of this fact will become clear when the Lord communicates his awareness of Sarah's reaction to his promise (v. 13). Sarah laughs to herself and is behind the speaker; so there is no natural way he could have known her response. Thus the Lord's omniscience is portrayed. This contributes to the main point of the passage by buttressing the presentation of the Lord's greatness and power so that his ability to fulfill his promise is manifested.

Verse 11 presents the difficulties inherent in this striking word of promise. Abraham and Sarah were very old. More specifically, the crux of the matter is that Sarah was past childbearing. Thus the reason for Sarah's laughter (v. 12) is given. The immensity of this obstacle of old age is so great that it is mentioned three times in as many verses (vv. 11–13). Sarah simply cannot believe that such a thing could happen. It seems ridiculous that she could bear a child when so old and past childbearing. In natural experience, it is impossible. So she laughs in unbelief. She doubts YHWH's promise. The Lord's response to Sarah's laughter confirms that it was indeed a laughter of unbelief. His strong rebuke in vv. 13–14 asserts his omnipotence ('Is anything too difficult for

6.   Though the text does not explicitly identify the speaker.

7.   Following the Samaritan Pentateuch and the LXX, which read הוא, since the point of the narrative is to alert us to the relative positions of the speaker and Sarah. Nevertheless, the MT's היא, which refers to the entrance of the tent as behind the speaker, still brings out the same point, even if less directly; cf. Wenham, *Genesis*, 2.48.

the Lord?') and reiterates the promise. Verse 14 contains the thrust of the passage: Sarah will have a son within the year because nothing is too difficult for the Lord. Sarah's futile denial of her laughter before an omnipotent and omniscient God along with the Lord's straightforward rejoinder – 'No, but you did laugh' – reinforce the main point of v. 14 by drawing attention again to Sarah's unbelieving laughter. Verse 15 is odd given Sarah's denial and the Lord's flat-out contradiction of that denial without further qualification or explanation. The scene leaves us with the reassurance of the fact that Sarah did indeed laugh. But it is the very oddness of v. 15 which serves to highlight Sarah's doubt of God's word and so lays greater stress on the crucial v. 14 – the Lord declares his dependability in keeping his promise based on his omnipotence in the face of Sarah's unbelief.

The reasons for the emphasis on Sarah's laughter in this passage go beyond the connection to vv. 12–14. The present story presupposes and relies on the similar account of Abraham's response when God first made the same promise to him (17.15–21). Like Sarah, Abraham also laughed in unbelief, citing the same basic reason – he and Sarah were too old. That Abraham's laughter originated from unbelief is shown by his subsequent request that Ishmael would live before God. He essentially ignores God's promise except to laugh at it, and proceeds to request God's blessing on Ishmael. As with Sarah, God rebukes Abraham and reiterates the promise. It is here that God designates that the son's name is to be Isaac (Hebrew יִצְחָק; 'he laughs'), an obvious reference to Abraham's unbelieving laughter. Thus Isaac's name itself is a reminder of the infallibility of God's word in accomplishing the seemingly impossible. The name will at the same time become the symbol of God's power to turn the blameworthy laughter of unbelief into the God-glorifying laughter of joy resulting from the fulfillment of his promise (see 21.6).

18.16–33 is the second major section of chs. 18–19. It also falls into two segments, vv. 16–21 and vv. 22–33. The former segment records both the Lord's deliberation over whether to reveal his mind concerning Sodom to Abraham and his initiation of Abraham's intercession on behalf of the city. The text portrays the entire interaction between YHWH and Abraham as YHWH's doing, initiated and directed by him. This is simply a natural outgrowth of the omnipotent, omniscient picture of the Lord painted by vv. 1–15. The elaborateness of YHWH's deliberation in vv. 17–19 contributes to the impression that his statement of intention towards Sodom (vv. 20–21) is meant to elicit the ensuing intercession from Abraham (who is portrayed as a prophet privy to the divine counsel).[8] Verse 33 then confirms this impression by stressing the Lord's initiative: 'Then YHWH left when he finished speaking with Abraham.' From beginning to end the conversation between YHWH and Abraham is presented as YHWH's will and design. The significance of this fact lies in the implication that the point made by the conversation is to be understood as the point the reader is to embrace. It is not as though the text is presenting YHWH as a temperamental deity whom Abraham must plead with to do right. Rather, YHWH is presented as wanting to display his own righteousness, justice, and mercy.

The point of the conversation recorded in 18.23–32 is to demonstrate YHWH's justice in his treatment of human beings.[9] The Lord's justice is the basis of Abraham's intercession (v. 25) and is demonstrated by his granting of Abraham's requests so that he will spare all of Sodom if he finds even ten righteous people (צדיקם) there. In the words of Abraham, YHWH is revealed as 'doing justice' (יעשה משפט, v. 25). This justice consists in distinguishing between the righteous and the wicked, treating them as they deserve and not the same (vv. 23, 25). The Lord's positive response to Abraham's drastic plea shows that such injustice as treating the righteous and wicked alike is truly far from him (חללה, v. 25). Indeed, the Lord's willingness to grant the entire city's preservation for the sake of a mere ten righteous not only shows his commitment to justice, but pushes this narrative toward a concomitant demonstration of mercy.[10]

The following description of Sodom's wickedness and destruction and Lot's rescue (19.1–29) then concretely demonstrates YHWH's justice. There is found to be only one righteous person in Sodom – Lot.[11] The fact that the Lord rescues Lot and his family before he destroys the city takes the demonstration of his righteousness to a higher level, revealing that he will not even allow one righteous man to perish with the wicked. Scholars have often puzzled over why Abraham stops his intercession at ten rather than taking it to the logical conclusion of one. While noting various suggestions for an answer to this question, Blenkinsopp comments that 'historical-critical reading of the text has

8.   On the portrayal of Abraham as a prophet in Genesis 18, see Wenham, *Genesis*, 2.44, 50, 53.

9.   For a layout of various positions and issues surrounding this passage, see E. Ben Zvi, 'The Dialogue between Abraham and YHWH in Gen 18:23–32: A Historical-Critical Analysis', *JSOT* 53 (1992), 27–46.

10.   Cf. Driver, *Genesis*, 196, and V.P. Hamilton, *The Book of Genesis: Chapters 18–50* (NICOT; Grand Rapids: Eerdmans, 1995), 25.

11.   Even Lot's wife and daughters turn out to be wicked (19.26, 30–38).

not produced a satisfactory explanation of this feature of the text'.[12] This is probably due to a lack of attention to the literary character of the text. When this is understood, the function of Abraham's petition ending at ten can be readily discerned. We have already argued that it is the Lord (not Abraham) who directs this intercession.[13] As it stands, 18.22–33 reveals the Lord as more than just, for he is willing to spare a whole city of wicked people for a mere ten righteous. By leaving unstated the Lord's willingness to rescue even one righteous from the just destruction of a wicked city, *inter alia*, the text intensifies the demonstration of the Lord's justice in 19.1–29 when the Lord goes above and beyond established expectations in his actual judgment. Indeed, the narrative depicts the Lord's dealings as compassionate (or merciful; חמלה, 19.16) and gracious (חסד, 19.19).

19.29 clearly ties Lot's salvation to Abraham's intercession in 18.23–32. True to his word, God acted justly, demonstrating his righteousness. 19.30–38 fills out the story by recording the origin of the Moabites and Ammonites through the incestuous conduct of Lot's daughters. The existence of these peoples is therefore shown to be due to Abraham's intercession (and consequently the Lord's justice and mercy). Abraham has become a blessing to the nations by his intercession and the resulting birth of Moab and Ben-ammi, the progenitors of the Moabite and Ammonite nations respectively.

We must now delve deeper into the connections between the major sections of Genesis 18–19. One of our primary concerns is the connection between the fulfillment/dependability of the promise (18.1–15) and theodicy (18.16–33),[14] since these two motifs appear strikingly in Romans 9. A careful examination will reveal that the connections are deep and varied.

---

12.   J. Blenkinsopp, 'The Judge of All the Earth: Theodicy in the Midrash on Gen 18:22–33', *JJS* 41 (1990), 1–12 (9–10). We should note that there is merit to the suggestion that the corporate perception of reality among the ancients plays a role. Ten was probably considered the lowest number of a significant grouping. While part of the answer, see below for an even more pressing consideration.

13.   Wenham, *Genesis*, 2.53, makes this point in relation to the ending of Abraham's prayer at ten people, rightly dismissing the common suggestion that Abraham was too afraid to continue. But he does not go on to consider why the Lord ends the discussion at this point.

14.   T.W. Willett, *Eschatology in the Theodicies of 2 Baruch and 4 Ezra* (JSPSup, 4; Sheffield: *JSOT*, 1989), 32 (cf. 11–12), defines theodicy broadly as 'any attempt to explain evil and death in religious terms'. He acknowledges that this definition encompasses many more specific types of theodicy, and provides a survey of Old Testament and early Jewish theodicy (12–32). For a much more thorough treatment

On one level, the justice of God serves as a ground for the dependability of his word. God's word is dependable because he is ethically just. The one who would never treat the righteous and wicked alike, and who will do only that which is right as the Judge of all the earth, can be trusted to fulfill his word. This makes two main grounds for the infallibility of the Lord's word: (1) his omnipotence (18.14); and (2) his justice/righteousness (18.16–33).

On another level, the Lord's fulfillment of his promise to Abraham (18.19c) itself functions as a ground for the justification of God provided in 18.22–32. The fulfillment of the promise demonstrates the righteousness of God. We might even say that the righteousness of God consists in the fulfillment of his promise. Since YHWH's decision to reveal his mind concerning Sodom to Abraham initiates Abraham's intercession, and since the entire God-justifying dialogue is to be understood as orchestrated by YHWH, we may consider YHWH's decision to represent the results of that decision, namely, Abraham's intercession and its justification of YHWH. If this be granted, then the fact that vv. 18–19, which highlight the fulfillment of the Lord's promises to Abraham, stand in causal relationship to v. 17, which states YHWH's intention to reveal his mind in the form of a question expecting a negative answer, means that the fulfillment of his promise is the ultimate ground of the Lord's decision to demonstrate his justice through dialogue with Abraham.[15] In short, the Lord is righteous because he fulfills his word.

Relatedly, the Lord's decision to manifest his justice through conversation with Abraham is based on Abraham's role as a blessing to the nations (18.18). We have just seen that 18.18 supports 18.17 causally. Now we must consider the specific promise referred to in 18.18b.

---

of the sources, see A.L. Thompson, *Responsibility for Evil in the Theodicy of IV Ezra* (SBLDS, 29; Missoula, MT: Scholars Press, 1977), 5–64. When we speak of theodicy in Genesis 18 or Romans 9, we have a narrower definition in mind: justifying the ways of God to human beings.

15.   The precise logical relationships in 18.17–19 are as follows: V. 17 states YHWH's intention to reveal his mind concerning Sodom to Abraham. V. 18 states fulfillment of specific divine promises to Abraham connected to the seed promise, functioning as a ground for v. 17. Verse 19 then actually functions as a ground to v. 18, signaled by כִּי. The logical stress of v. 19 falls on the fulfillment of the Lord's promises to Abraham as this is presented as the ultimate purpose (לְמַעַן) of the Lord's election of Abraham. So then the general statement of the Lord's intention to bring about what he promised becomes the basis of the specific promises of v. 18, and together they form the basis of v. 17.

The Lord decides to reveal his mind to Abraham because 'in him all the nations of the earth will be blessed'.[16] Indeed, Abraham's intercession may be seen as a beginning fulfillment of this promise since Abraham intercedes on behalf of 'the nations' here, and through that intercession helps to establish the nations of Ammon and Moab.[17] So the very conversation which the Lord enacted to manifest his justice, at the same time effects the fulfillment of his promise, albeit it proleptically.

At this point we might ask whether the specific child-promise implies a distinction among Abraham's descendants so that its fulfillment raises the issue of God's justice in dealing with men. This may be part of the rationale for connecting the theodicy of 18.16–33 with the child-promise of 18.1–15. The text does not draw attention to the distinguishing nature of the promise here. Yet the point is made earlier (ch. 17) and later (ch. 21) in the Abraham narrative of Genesis. In light of this broader narrative, it is plausible that the distinguishing nature of the promise can be taken as one of the connections between theodicy and promise-fulfillment in Genesis 18.

We may regard 18.16–33 to be the center of chs. 18–19, declaring the justice of God and providing the *leitmotif* which unifies the sections. Yet we should not lose sight of the major theme of the dependability of God's word. It is a dominant theme throughout the Abraham narrative of Genesis, especially in chs. 17–21. Indeed, ch. 20 will immediately pick up this theme again as the fulfillment of YHWH's promise is threatened by Abimelech taking Sarah as his wife. And as we have seen, the two themes of theodicy and the infallibility of God's word are closely connected in these chapters. Together they constitute the main thrust of the broader context of 18.10, 14 quoted by Paul.

4.2. *Textual Comparison of Romans 9.9 and Genesis 18.10, 14*

It is now time to turn to a textual comparison of Rom. 9.9 and Gen. 18.10, 14. The following underline codes have been used to classify the

16.   The translation of this phrase, the basic form of which also occurs in Gen. 12.3; 22.18; 26.4; 28.14, has been greatly debated by Old Testament scholars. The basic issue is how the niphal of ברך is to be taken, whether as a passive, middle, or reflexive. Fortunately, we know Paul took this verb passively (Gal. 3.8), whether through his reading of the Hebrew or mediated through the LXX. For a good, concise discussion of the options see Wenham, *Genesis*, 1.277–78.

17.   W. Brueggemann, *Genesis* (IBC; Atlanta: John Knox, 1982), 169, also links the nations of 18.18 with Moab and Ammon of 19.30–38.

relationship between Rom. 9.9, Gen. 18.10, 14 LXX, and the MT, which is listed without reference to the other passages.

None	All agree
Single	NT differs from all others
<u>Double</u>	NT and Gen. 18.10 LXX agree against 18.14 LXX
D̤o̤t̤t̤e̤d̤	NT and Gen. 18.14 LXX agree against 18.10 LXX
D̲a̲s̲h̲e̲d̲	Gen. 18.14 LXX differs from NT and 18.10 LXX
Squiggle	Gen. 18.10 LXX differs from NT and 18.14 LXX
<u>Bold Underline</u>	Present in all but NT

Rom. 9.9:   <u>κατὰ</u> τὸν καιρὸν τοῦτον <u>ἐλεύσομαι</u> καὶ ἔσται τῇ Σάρρα υἱός

Gen. 18.10 LXX: ἐπαναστρέφων ἥξω   πρὸς σὲ   <u>κατὰ</u> τὸν καιρὸν τοῦτον εἰς ὥρας, καὶ ἕξει υἱὸν Σαρρα ἡ γυνή σου.

Gen. 18.10 MT: שׁוֹב אָשׁוּב אֵלֶיךָ כָּעֵת חַיָּה וְהִנֵּה־בֵן לְשָׂרָה אִשְׁתֶּךָ

Gen. 18.14 LXX: εἰς τὸν καιρὸν τοῦτον <u>ἀναστρέψω</u>   πρὸς σὲ εἰς ὥρας, καὶ ἔσται τῇ Σάρρα υἱός

Gen. 18.14 MT: לַמּוֹעֵד אָשׁוּב אֵלֶיךָ כָּעֵת חַיָּה וּלְשָׂרָה בֵן

Although most scholars regard Rom. 9.9 as a conflation of LXX Gen. 18.10 and 18.14, Stanley has challenged this view contending that it 'founders on the observation that the Pauline quotation contains only one word found in v. 10 and not in v. 14, the preposition κατά'.[18] He contends that Paul is quoting only from Gen. 18.14. Yet, by his own admission he is unable to give any clear exegetical motive for such a change. The alternative possible explanations he does mention are less than convincing, viz., that κατά is a more specific temporal designation than εἰς and accords with Paul's dehistoricized treatment of Genesis here, or an unattested manuscript variant, or a memory slip. First, it is not at all clear that κατά is any more specific than εἰς in temporal

18.   Stanley, *Paul*, 104. However, Stanley fails to note that ἐλεύσομαι is much closer in meaning to 18.10's ἥξω than to 18.14's ἀναστρέψω. This observation is all the more significant when we recognize that ἥξω is a unique translation of אשוב in the LXX of Genesis; see J.W. Wevers, *Notes on the Greek Text of Genesis* (SBLSCS, 35; Atlanta: Scholars Press, 1993), 250. In fact, it is the only occurrence in the LXX of ἥκειν as a translation of שוב. As for ἔρχομαι, it translates שוב in the LXX only in Judg. 11.8 and 2 Chron. 10.5. See HR, 548–53, 605–606.

phrases.[19] But even if so, it is also unclear how a more specific temporal reference would lend itself any better to a dehistoricizing discourse. Furthermore, even if this suggestion were still deemed valid, it could very easily be subsumed under a conflation theory, since it could be regarded as one of Paul's reasons for conflating Gen. 18.10 and 18.14. The latter two possibilities (unattested ms. variant and memory slip) are speculative[20] and therefore inferior to the conflation theory which has evidence to support it in the text, namely, the presence of κατά in LXX Gen. 18.10, and its absence in 18.14, both of which Paul was certainly aware.

Therefore, it appears that the common view of Paul's allusion to Genesis 18 is also the correct one – Paul has conflated LXX Gen. 18.10 and 18.14.[21] Why he did so is not as clear. But I would suggest Paul has taken κατά from Gen. 18.10, knowing full well that τὸν καιρὸν τοῦτον . . . καί is present in both verses, and combined it with ἔσται τῇ Σαρρα υἱός from v. 14, in order to quote from both. In so doing Paul captures the essence of Gen. 18.1–15 most vividly. Both verses state God's word of promise and would do nicely to encapsulate the heart of the passage. But it is v. 14 which most sharply sets forth the concern of the narrative – the infallibility of the Lord's promise over against a challenge to his faithfulness. Therefore, Paul's citation does lay greater stress on v. 14. Yet, by including κατά from v. 10 he manages to allude specifically to both the original statement of the promise, which is subsequently doubted, and the response to that doubt, which affirms the reliability of the Lord's word. Thus, by the conflation of these two verses Paul forms a sort of allusive inclusio which encompasses the pivotal moments of the narrative and evokes the promise-doubt-affirmation

19.   Stanley's citation of BAGD, s.v. κατά, II.2a, is unwarranted, since the entry makes no comparison with εἰς. κατά may also be indefinite in temporal phrases (see BDAG, 512 [2b]) while εἰς can be used definitely as in Gen. 18.14 LXX and Acts 13.42.

20.   Indeed, Stanley, *Paul*, has himself argued persuasively that memory failure is generally an unlikely explanation for differences between Paul and his presumed *Vorlagen*. But Stanley's questionable assumption that Paul often engaged in non-contextual proof-texting keeps him from seeing some good explanations for Pauline alterations which originate from the original broader contexts of OT passages; see B.S. Rosner, Review of Christopher D. Stanley, *Paul and the Language of Scripture: Citation Technique in the Pauline Epistles and Contemporary Literature*, *EvQ* 68:4 (1996), 360–62 (361).

21.   Of course it is possible that Paul may simply have made his own translation *en toto* or used a manuscript that is no longer extant. But the limited evidence we have seems to support best Paul's quotation as a conflation, as the consensus has concluded.

sequence, elegantly and effectively supporting his point in Rom. 9.6 that
the word of God has not failed, also against a doubting objection.

Paul's use of ἐλεύσομαι appears to be motivated by the desire to present
the promise in an eschatologically friendly manner.[22] By leaving out the
specific time references of Gen. 18.10, 14, Paul frames the quotation so
that it is even more applicable to his present circumstances.[23] Since Paul
can assume his audience's familiarity with the outcome of the story,[24] he
is free to eliminate the notion of return found in the Old Testament verses
without losing the force of the specific context, thereby broadening the
application of the promise from the child-promise to all the promises of
God to Israel mentioned in Rom. 9.4, God's faithfulness to which Paul
begins to defend in 9.6.

4.3. *Interpretive Traditions Surrounding Genesis 18.10, 14*

We now turn to a survey of the interpretive traditions surrounding
Gen. 18.10, 14 that might be relevant for Paul's use of these verses.
Given the mass of material available from ancient sources, we must
select only what we deem to be the most relevant. Many of the issues that
interested ancient interpreters concerned specific details of the text such
as Sarah's laughter, Lot's character, the identity of the three 'men',
whether the angels really ate or not, the nature of Sodom's sin, and the
nature of God's knowledge concerning Sodom.[25] However, these are not
Paul's specific concerns in Romans 9, though his use of Genesis 18
undoubtedly reflects exegetical decisions concerning some of them. As
we will argue below, Paul appears to be interested in broader themes
found in Genesis 18–19, namely, the steadfastness of God's word and
theodicy. As we might expect, these two themes do appear in the literature of ancient Judaism in connection with Genesis 18.

22. Dunn, *Romans*, 541–42.

23. Stanley, *Paul*, 104–105. These time references include εἰς ὥρας and the
notion of return represented by ἐπαναστρέφων and ἀναστρέψω. It is interesting to
note that Philo, *Abr.* 126, regarded the language of Gen. 18.10 itself as inherently
suggestive of timeless reality (cf. *Mut. Nom.* 267).

24. Even a scholar as skeptical of Paul's first-century audience's scriptural knowledge as Stanley (*Paul*, 104) admits that Paul expects his readers to know this story.

25. See J.L. Kugel, *A Guide to the Bible as It Was at the Start of the Common
Era* (Cambridge, MA; London: Harvard University Press, 1998), 328–50, for a
demonstration of these issues from a sampling of ancient texts. Richardson,
Language, 34–44, is notable for his treatment of Jewish sources related to Paul's OT
allusions in Rom. 9.6–13.

4.3.a. *4 Ezra*

The late first-century book of *4 Ezra* alludes to Abraham's intercession on behalf of Sodom in 7.106.[26] This passage rings with similarities to Paul's musings in Romans 9.[27] During Ezra's third vision (6.35ff.) he dialogues with the Lord through an angel mediator. As we saw in the previous chapter, this theodicy discussion begins like Romans 9 with a challenge to the reliability of God's promises to his people (6.55–59). The Lord's answer raises for Ezra the terrible fate of the wicked, and with a question he moves the conversation to that topic.

Ezra's sensitive question elicits a strong rebuke similar to Paul's response to his interlocutor in Rom. 9.20–21: 'You are not a better judge than the Lord, or wiser than the Most High!' (7.19).[28] But Ezra remains undaunted. Later in the conversation his concern resurfaces in the form of distress over the small number who will be saved and the consequent large number who will face eschatological torment (7.45ff.). After hearing of what takes place after death to the souls of the wicked and righteous respectively, Ezra asks whether the righteous will be able to intercede for the ungodly on the day of judgment. The answer is negative, 'for then all shall bear their own righteousness and unrighteousness' (7.105). It is here, in Ezra's response, that we encounter the allusion to Gen. 18.22–32: 'How then do we find that first Abraham prayed for the people of Sodom, and Moses for our ancestors who sinned in the desert' (7.106) and so on in vv. 107–10 with references to the intercession of other figures. His point is, 'So if now, when corruption has increased and unrighteousness has multiplied, the righteous have prayed for the ungodly, why will it not be so then as well?' (7.111). Again, the decisive nature of the world to come stands against the possibility of intercession at that time. This brings Ezra to lament the miserable fate of the vast majority of humankind (7.116–126).

The divine response emphasizes human free will, and then connects it to what is one of Paul's chief concerns in Romans 9–11, the concept

---

26.   For a concise introduction to *4 Ezra*, including dating and bibliography, see Metzger, *Ezra*, 517–24; Charlesworth, *Research*, 111–16. For a fuller introduction, see Stone, *Ezra*, 1–47.

27.   Indeed, the similarity of *4 Ezra* to Romans generally has given rise to an entire monograph on the subject: B.W. Longenecker, *Eschatology and the Covenant: A Comparison of 4 Ezra and Romans 1–11* (JSNTSup, 57; Sheffield: *JSOT*, 1991).

28.   Translations of *4 Ezra* are from the NRSV unless otherwise noted. The next verse, *4 Ezra* 7.20, calls to mind Rom. 3.4, which is directly related to Romans 9.

of faith: 'But they did not believe him [Moses] or the prophets after him, or even myself who have spoken to them' (7.130; cf. 9.7–12). Ezra then begins to extol God's mercy; he is gracious toward those who repent (7.133). He maintains an extended focus on God's mercy until he turns to the timing of eschatological signs in 8.63. In his prayer Ezra shows deep concern for all people, but then, in a manner reminiscent of Paul's lament for Israel in Rom. 9.1–5, narrows his deepest concern to his own people (Israel) as he seeks the Lord's grace and mercy for them (8.15–17).

As Ezra continues, his passionate plea for mercy points up a positive result of human sinfulness – it gives opportunity for the expression of God's mercy, which is equated to the declaration of his righteousness and goodness: 'For in this, O Lord, your righteousness and goodness will be declared, when you are merciful to those who have no store of good works' (8.36; cf. also 8.31–32). Paul appears to make a similar point in Rom. 9.14–18 where he too connects the mercy of God and the demon-stration of his righteousness (cf. Rom. 3.3–5). But unlike the thought of Romans 9, the Lord tells Ezra that he will not concern himself with the unrighteous, but only with the righteous (8.37–38). He then compares human beings to seeds and plants (8.41; cf. 9.21–22; Rom. 9.20–21; 11.16–24). Also unlike Paul, Ezra takes exception to such a comparison. Man is not like seed, but has been created in the image of God. Ezra is rebuked however. He cannot love God's creation more than God does. The ultimate answer lies in the free will of the creature:

> For they also received freedom, but they despised the Most High, and were contemptuous of his law, and forsook his ways . . . though knowing full well that they must die . . . For the Most High did not intend that men should be destroyed; but they themselves who were created have defiled the name of him who made them, and have been ungrateful to him who prepared life for them (8.56, 58–60; Metzger's translation).

Several aspects of *4 Ezra* 6.35–9.25 stand out for special mention because of their relevance to Romans 9. First, there is the pervasive element of theodicy initially raised by a question over the faithfulness of God's word. Second, there is a persistent refrain of human free will as the justification of God's dealings with men (7.10–16, 21–22, 72–74, 127–31; 8.56–58; 9.7–12). Third, this free will is connected to the concept of faith in 7.127–31 and 9.7–12. The reason so many do not choose life is that they do not believe Moses, the prophets, nor the Lord himself. For both Paul and the author of *4 Ezra*, the ultimate reason for separa-tion from God is unbelief, though the precise content of that faith is different.[29] Interestingly, the concepts of faith and works are used interchangeably throughout the book.[30] Fourth, there is the heavy emphasis on God's mercy from 7.132 on, and a connection to the righteousness of God made in 8.36. The typical Jewish assumption that God forgives those who repent is stated explicitly.

Fifth, there appears to be an allusion to Isa. 45.11 in 8.7. The significance of this allusion is that it follows on the heels of Isa. 45.9, which Paul alludes to in Rom. 9.20–21. In *4 Ezra* the allusion is used in a context which deals with God's mercy, and more importantly, expresses concern for Gentiles. God's mercy is unquestionably one of Paul's concerns in Romans 9, and though there is debate over the extent to which the relation of Jew and Gentile is at issue, it is certainly related in some way to the argument (e.g. Rom. 9.24, 30). Here we find the author of *4 Ezra* alluding to the same context in Isaiah as Paul over similar themes. Sixth, and relatedly, there is the remarkable concern of Ezra for Gentiles as well as Jews (e.g. 7.116–31; 8.4–14).[31] That *4 Ezra* deals with Gentiles sympathetically amidst so many other parallels with Romans 9 merits attention. Seventh, there is the comparison of humanity to seeds/plants. Although the immediate purpose of the comparison and the materials involved are quite different than Paul's potter and clay metaphor, Ezra's response to the comparison highlights one of Paul's main emphases in his metaphor – God as creator and man as creature. Human beings are not like seed whose fate depends on God's bestowal of rain. The creator/creature relationship calls for God's mercy. While Paul does not explicitly qualify his potter/clay metaphor with recognition of man's dignity like Ezra, he does, like Ezra, carry the metaphor forward to a cynosure of God's mercy. Finally, there are some incidental similarities in the manner of presentation such as Ezra's lament for Israel and expression of their privileged status (8.15–17 and 6.58–59 respectively; cf. Rom. 9.1–5).

None of this is meant to suggest dependency on the part of Paul or the author of *4 Ezra*. That is highly unlikely. The importance of *4 Ezra* 6–8 for Romans 9 is that it gives us another first-century Jew's perspective on similar issues. It helps us to define more clearly the types of concerns and ideas surrounding Genesis 18 and its related themes in Paul's day. More specifically, *4 Ezra* 6–8 provides us with an example of

29. Cf. Stegner, 'Midrash', 46, on Gen. 21.12.
30. See Stone, *Ezra*, 296.
31. Metzger, *Ezra*, 521, refers to this as 'his universalism'.

how Genesis 18 (as well as Exodus 32 and Isa. 45.11) was used elsewhere in Judaism contemporaneous with Paul. We have found not that Paul was necessarily following a specific exegetical tradition, but that he seems to have tapped into a general traditional approach to Genesis 18 which links it with theodicy, the dependability of God's word to Israel, God's mercy, and a concern for the salvation of the Gentiles. The specifics of *4 Ezra*'s treatment, like the persistent free will solution to the problem of theodicy, cannot be thought of as determining Paul's argument, but they must be considered when interpreting Paul's stance.

4.3.b. *Philo*

We now turn to another first-century Jewish author, who gives far more attention to Genesis 18–19, Philo of Alexandria. For him, Abraham's hospitality is a dominating theme of the passage.[32] The three 'men' of the section are indeed God accompanied by two angels; yet at the same time they represent three different human dispositions. In his exposition Philo touches on issues relevant to theodicy and universalism. He explains that 'God, inasmuch as he is not liable to any injury, gladly invites all men who choose, in any way whatever to honour him, to come unto him, not choosing altogether to reject any person whatever' (*Abr.* 127).[33] Unlike *4 Ezra*, Philo's assertions of human free will and God's concern for all humankind actually emerge from an exposition of Genesis 18–19, albeit a not so straightforward one. Later in his discussion, Philo touches on theodicy more directly. He reveals that much of his discussion of the destruction of Sodom has aimed to show God's goodness and separation from evil (*Abr.* 142–43). This is why only the two angels went to Sodom; God would not directly involve himself in the destruction 'so that he might be looked upon as the cause of good only, and of no evil whatever antecedently' (*Abr.* 143). Elsewhere, Philo even connects Sarah's laughter to the absolute goodness of God (*Spec. Leg.* 2.53–55).

In *Leg. All.* 3.9–10 Philo includes a treatment of Gen. 18.23 in his discussion of the principle that the wicked are inclined to run away from

---

32. See Philo, *Abr.* 107; 167. For a comparison of Paul's thought in Romans 9–11 with the thought of Philo *vis-à-vis* scriptural interpretation, see K. Haacker, 'Die Geschichtstheologie von Röm 9–11 im Lichte philonischer Schriftauslegung', *NTS* 43 (1997), 209–22.

33. All translations of Philo are from C.D. Yonge (trans.), *The Works of Philo: New Updated Edition Complete and Unabridged in One Volume* (Peabody, MA: Hendrickson, 1993).

God. His understanding of the passage is relevant to Romans 9 for its view of what characterizes the righteous and wicked respectively. Abraham is an example of the righteous who are manifest to the Lord and well known by him, and who stand before him and do not flee. But the wicked flee from the Lord and seek to escape his notice. For Philo, there was no possibility of worthiness before God. Yet one could be righteous and just. In fact, in *Congr.* 106–109 Philo discusses the ten righteous of Gen. 18.32 in connection to humility as the key to acceptance with God. Of course, what makes a person righteous is a chief concern of Romans generally, not least the ninth chapter (e.g., Rom. 9.30–33). So there is some similarity in Paul's and Philo's conceptions of what makes someone righteous. There is no legalistic standard of perfect adherence to the Law, but a standard of approaching the Lord in humble faith. The main difference appears to be the nature and content of that faith – trust in Jesus Christ as the Messiah. With Philo we again see the issues of theodicy, free will, universalism, and faith emerging from engagement with Genesis 18–19.

4.3.c. *4Q180*

It is no surprise that 4Q180, a work known for its interest in angels and destiny, is interested in the angels of Genesis 18–19. Ages of Creation 3 is concerned to explain why God says he will go down to see the situation of Sodom (Gen. 18.21). The author was apparently afraid that Gen. 18.21 could be misconstrued to mean that God was not omniscient and did not already know the condition of Sodom. We are assured that, 'Before He created them, He knew [their] designs.'[34] The point seems to be that God really did know about Sodom's condition, and only went to confirm what he already knew via his foreknowledge. Unfortunately, the text is not very extensive or well-preserved, but it does show that Gen. 18.20–21 raised the issue of God's sovereignty and foreknowledge for the author.

4.3.d. *Targums and Other Rabbinic Literature*

Moving beyond Paul's time, the most striking addition to Genesis 18 by the Targums is the mention of opportunity for repentance for the people of Sodom and the consequent opportunity to be spared.[35] Apparently

---

34. Translation from T.H. Gaster, *The Dead Sea Scriptures with Introduction and Notes* (New York: Anchor/Doubleday, 3rd edn., rev. and enl., 1976), 524.

35. *Ps.-J.*, *Neof.*, and some versions of *Onq.*

the targumists felt the need to paint God's justice even larger and more sharply than the biblical text by making explicit what much biblical tradition assumes – that God will mercifully forgive those who repent (cf. Jer. 18.1–10; Ezekiel 18; Jon. 4.2). The possibility of repentance and forgiveness for Sodom is held out in other rabbinic literature as well.[36] *Genesis Rabbah* even claims that God tried to bring Sodom to repentance for many years prior to the destruction through earthquakes and various afflictions.

This concern to justify God's judgment against the ungodly by pointing to his willingness to forgive the penitent takes its lead from Genesis itself, not in the specific portrayal of God's willingness to forgive, but in the presentation of his mercy and the accentuation of the guilt and responsibility of the Sodomites. Such stress on human guilt is, as Balentine has argued, a fundamental characteristic common to virtually all Old Testament theodicies.[37] This should alert us to the possibility that Paul may draw on this idea in his theodicy.

Stegner has observed that *Gen R.* 53.4 juxtaposes Gen. 18.10, Num. 23.18 (which proclaims the steadfastness of God's word), and Gen. 21.1 (which also testifies to the steadfastness of God's word).[38] He probably stretches the connection of Sarah with the theme of the steadfastness of God's word too far, trying to find significance in her prophetic status in Jewish tradition.[39] Nevertheless, he has made a valuable contribution in drawing attention to the fact that 'Paul and Genesis Rabbah agree in juxtaposing the theme of God's faithfulness to His word and God's promise to Sarah'.[40] However, his conclusion that Paul appears to be following exegetical traditions may be too strongly stated.[41] We need not conceive of Paul as following a specific exegetical tradition also witnessed to by later rabbinic material, though that is possible; rather he is probably following a traditional approach to the text. But this is to be expected since the theme of dependability is so prominent in the Old Testament passage.

36. See Blenkinsopp, 'Judge', 3.
37. S.E. Balentine, 'Prayers for Justice in the OT: Theodicy and Theology', *CBQ* 51 (1989), 597–616. Cf. Thompson, *Responsibility*, 64.
38. Stegner, 'Midrash', 47.
39. Stegner, 'Midrash', 47.
40. Stegner, 'Midrash', 48.
41. Yet Stegner has been criticized wrongly for relying too much on later material; see note 44 in ch. 2 above. Nevertheless, the lateness of the material should caution us against too quickly concluding that Paul followed specific exegetical traditions.

4.3.e. *Luke*

When we turn to the non-Pauline writings of the New Testament we do not find Genesis 18–19 directly connected to theodicy. We do, however, find allusion to the classic statement of the omnipotence of God in the face of doubt found in Gen. 18.14. Lk. 1.37 puts the question of Gen. 18.14 in positive form when the angel Gabriel assures Mary of God's ability to give a child to a virgin.[42] The similarity between the Lucan and Genesis contexts is noteworthy. Both contain the promise of a miraculous birth cast into some doubt by the sheer physical impossibility standing in the way of the fulfillment of the promise. Luke may attest to a Christian tradition that drew on Gen. 18.14 as a statement of the faithfulness of God's word. Of course, dependence by Paul is unlikely, but it is probable that he shared in a typical Christian approach to Gen. 18.14.

4.3.f. *Hebrews*

We also find allusion to Genesis 18 in connection to the concept of faith in Heb. 11.11. But the allusion is rather general and more to the miraculous conception and birth recorded in Genesis 17–21 than to any specific verse in those chapters.[43] This does not mean that there is no allusion to Genesis 18, but that it is a more abstract and diffuse allusion than Paul makes in Rom. 9.9. It still strengthens the mounting impression that Genesis 18 was interpreted as dealing with faith in early Judaism and Christianity, especially when we recognize that many ancient interpreters did not practice non-contextual, atomistic exegesis, but were interested in the stories of their Scripture as wholes. The context of Hebrews 11 makes the point that God-pleasing faith has to do with trusting God's promises even when those promises have not yet been realized. This is similar to the issue Paul is dealing with in Romans 9–11 – an apparent failure of God's word, and the proper attitude of faith in response.

---

42.   Cf. Mt. 19.26; Mk 10.27; it is not clear that these are actual allusions.

43.   If one takes Sarah as the subject of Heb. 11.11 as the nominative case would suggest, then the probable reference would narrow to Genesis 18 and 21. But it is better to understand Abraham as the subject and αὐτὴ Σάρρα στεῖρα as either a Hebraic circumstantial clause or as a dative of accompaniment; see B.M. Metzger, *A Textual Commentary on the Greek New Testament* (Stuttgart: UBS, 2nd edn., 1994), 602.

4.4. *The Old Testament Context of Genesis 21.12*

Having completed our exploration of Gen. 18.10, 14, we will now take up an analysis of Gen. 21.12 and related material. Gen. 21.12 appears in the account of the birth and weaning of Isaac recorded in 21.1–21.[44] This passage may be divided into two sections: (1) vv. 1–7 (the birth of Isaac); and (2) vv. 8–21 (the weaning of Isaac and expulsion of Hagar and Ishmael). The fact that v. 8 clearly presupposes the birth of Isaac recorded in vv. 1–7 connects the two sections. The next natural milestone in Isaac's life after his birth, naming, and circumcision (all recorded in vv. 1–7), i.e., his weaning (v. 8), provides the context for the expulsion of Hagar and Ishmael. The birth leads to the weaning, and the birth and weaning together lead to the expulsion.

Gen. 21.1, although written in prose like the surrounding narrative,[45] employs the common Hebrew poetic device of synonymous parallelism to emphasize the fact that God fulfilled the promise which was called into question by the impossibly old age of Abraham and Sarah, doubted and laughed at by them, and threatened by Abimelech. Here, 'we arrive finally at the birth of the awaited child . . . we have the central fulfillment within the Abraham tradition. The birth of the child is the fulfillment of all of the promises, the resolution of all of the anguish.'[46] Verse 2 then repeats the fact of fulfillment a third time, noting that it came about at the appointed time God had promised to Abraham. Verses 1–2 clearly recall the earlier narrative of Genesis 17 and 18 in which God promised to Abraham the birth of a son by Sarah within a year's time. In fact, the use of the word לַמּוֹעֵד ('at the appointed time') in v. 2 specifically recalls the use of the word in Gen. 17.21 and 18.14 where the Lord speaks the promise to Abraham.

Verse 3 continues the report of the fulfillment of the earlier narrative. Abraham names Isaac (i.e., 'he laughs') as God had directed (17.19), recalling the skeptical laughter of Abraham and Sarah, now transformed into a testimony both to God's faithfulness to his word and to

---

44. Those who view 21.1–21 as a unit include Wenham, *Genesis*, 2.76ff.; G.W. Coats, *Genesis with an Introduction to Narrative Literature* (FOTL, 1; Grand Rapids: Eerdmans, 1983), 152ff.; and von Rad, *Genesis*, 230ff. Those who do not take it as a single unit generally separate the passage into two units comprised of vv. 1–7 and vv. 8–21, which are obviously related to one another, the latter presupposing the former.

45. Hamilton, *Genesis*, 73, even claims that the whole verse is poetry. In any case, the verse displays poetic characteristics.

46. Brueggemann, *Genesis*, 180.

the joy that his fulfilled word brought the formerly barren couple. The fact that it was Sarah who bore Isaac to Abraham is also repeated, calling attention yet again to the fulfillment of the promise, since Sarah's maternity was the crucial and problematic issue. The naming of Isaac also depicts Abraham's obedience to God's command, though the emphasis here in v. 3 remains on the fulfillment of God's promise. The naming of the boy sets the seal of consummation on his miraculous birth and testifies to God's faithfulness.

The note of Abraham's obedience is struck even louder in v. 4, which tells us that Abraham circumcised Isaac in accordance with God's command. God's faithfulness to his word inspired faithfulness to his commands in Abraham. The circumcision of Isaac symbolizes the faithfulness of Abraham in commanding his children to keep the way of the Lord (cf. 18.19). Moreover, just as the naming of Isaac underscored his miraculous birth as the fulfillment of promise, so his circumcision concretizes it even more.

Verse 5 resumes the emphasis on the fulfillment of the promise by reporting that Abraham was one hundred years old at Isaac's birth. His great age (along with Sarah's) was the chief obstacle to the fulfillment of the promise. Mentioning this factor in the context of the promise's fulfillment magnifies the fact of fulfillment over against seemingly impossible obstacles, thus magnifying God's faithfulness to his promise as well as his ability to be faithful. Verse 5, along with vv. 1–4, naturally functions as the basis of Sarah's celebration of the birth in vv. 6–7. Indeed, the content of v. 5 is repeated more generally in the latter part of Sarah's song (v. 7b). Verse 5 seems to have been introduced primarily in preparation of Sarah's celebratory words.

The narrative climaxes in Sarah's poem of vv. 6–7. She celebrates God's faithfulness to his word with a song of praise. What God has done – made joy for Sarah and for all who hear of his remarkable faithfulness – wells up into a poetic expression of joy. The poem itself makes its primary statement in v. 6, playing on the name of Isaac, which, as we have already noted, means 'he laughs' (צחק): 'God has made laughter for me; everyone who hears will laugh [צחק] because of me.'[47] Verse 7

---

47. Some have argued that while v. 6a speaks of Sarah's joyous laughter, v. 6b speaks of the laughter of ridicule (*at* Sarah). Hamilton, *Genesis*, 72, 74, argues for the laughter of ridicule throughout the verse. But ridicule is too out of harmony with the context of fulfillment and joy to be the primary significance of any of its laughter, and most commentators rightly hear primarily the laughter of joy here.

accomplishes the same purpose of celebrating the fulfilled promise, but plays a supporting role as a ground for v. 6. No one could have imagined Sarah nursing children, yet she bore a child to Abraham in his old age. This state of affairs is amazing, and glorifies the greatness of God's act in fulfilling his promise. Here is the reason for the joy of Sarah and everyone who hears of her experience. Thus, the great play on Isaac's name in v. 6 constitutes the main essence of the passage. Westermann is correct to say that Gen. 21.1–7 is intended to bring chs. 17 and 18 to a conclusion.[48]

The second section, vv. 8–21, moves to the next significant occasion of Isaac's life – his weaning. The summary statement that Isaac grew is connected to the statement of his weaning (v. 8), since his weaning is also a mark of his survival in a time of high infant mortality. As such, it holds promise for his permanent place as Abraham's heir. So Abraham threw a great feast to celebrate. At this celebration of Isaac (יִצְחָק), Sarah saw Ishmael mocking (מְצַחֵק) him (v. 9).[49] The precise nature of this mockery is uncertain, but probably has to do with Isaac's status as heir or the circumstances of his birth.[50] Coats sums up the situation well:

> The threat of Ishmael throughout the narrative is that he would replace Sarah's son, or Sarah's lack of a son, as the heir of Abraham. Now the wordplay, so crucial for the whole story, sets out the weight of the conflict . . . It suggests . . . that Sarah saw Ishmael . . . playing the role of Isaac. Indeed, the act implies some disdain on Ishmael's part, perhaps an equivalent to the curse of Hagar in 16.4.[51]

This mockery on the part of Ishmael incites Sarah's maternal rage. The sight of the seventeen year-old-son of her husband's slave-woman acting with disdain towards her son, who was to be Abraham's heir, drives her to demand the expulsion of Hagar and Ishmael (v. 10). Her reason is that Ishmael should not inherit with Isaac.[52]

---

48. C. Westermann, *Genesis 12–36: A Commentary* (Minneapolis: Augsburg, 1985), 331ff.

49. On the lack of an explicitly identified object for Ishmael's action in the Hebrew text and the problem of determining the meaning of the piel participle מְצַחֵק here, see Abasciano, 'Paul's Use', 281 n. 61. Fortunately, we know that Paul took Isaac as the object of Ishmael's mockery, described as persecution (ἐδίωκεν) of Isaac (Gal. 4.29).

50. Wenham, *Genesis*, 2.82.

51. Coats, *Genesis*, 153.

52. The background to Sarah's request is to be found in the second-millennium B.C.E. Lipit-Ishtar Lawcode, which denied the right of inheritance to children by a slave if mother and children were freed; see *ANET*, 160.

Quite understandably, Sarah's request greatly distressed Abraham. Ishmael was Abraham's son, and he loved him. The thought of casting him out of his house into a cold, cruel world with no protection was too much for him to bear. Wenham describes Abraham's reaction as explosive, and informs us that, 'Elsewhere, men explode in anger when they are merely "displeased" (e.g., Num 11:10; 1 Sam 18:8). When God is "displeased" with someone, death often follows (e.g., Gen 38:10; 2 Sam 11:7). Only here is anyone said to be *"very* displeased." '[53] Therefore, God himself intervenes, addressing Abraham: 'Do not let it be displeasing in your eyes concerning the lad and concerning your slave-woman. Everything Sarah says to you, listen to her voice, for in Isaac your seed will be called. And I will also make the son of the slave-woman into a nation, for he is your seed' (vv. 12–13).

God's directive to Abraham not to be distressed over Sarah's demand, but to heed it, is based on two considerations: (1) Abraham's descendants will be named/identified/appointed through Isaac; and (2) God will make Ishmael into a nation. Thus God comforts and assures Abraham in his deep distress so that he will do as Sarah asks. Paul quotes the first of these assurances in Rom. 9.7. The meaning of this statement is that only Isaac's descendants will be called (or regarded as) Abraham's covenant descendants (cf. Gen. 17.15–21).

With the second assurance, fears of Ishmael suffering and dying as a result of expulsion from the safety and provision of Abraham's household can be abandoned. The reason given for making Ishmael into a nation is that he also is Abraham's seed/descendant, just not the covenantal seed. Therefore, he will receive special blessing from God, but not Abrahamic-covenantal blessings.

In response to God's word of comfort, Abraham acts in faith, promptly sending Hagar and Ishmael away (v. 14). The rest of the narrative details Hagar's and Ishmael's ordeal in the wilderness as a result of their expulsion (vv. 14b–19), and summarizes their fate more generally, particularly Ishmael's (vv. 20–21). Hagar and Ishmael run out of water as they wander in the wilderness, and Hagar gives her son and herself up for dead (vv. 15–16). But God miraculously intervenes, reassuring Hagar of his care for the lad, and providing life-sustaining water for them (vv. 17–19).

Verses 14–21 function as a demonstration of God's faithfulness to his promise to Abraham (v. 13; 17.20) and to Hagar (16.10–12) to bless

---

53. Wenham, *Genesis*, 2.83; emphasis original. The Hebrew term for displeasure here is רעע.

Ishmael. Verses 14–19 demonstrate God's faithfulness with respect to Ishmael concretely, in a specific situation in which death threatened to take the lad. Verse 20 then completes this specific demonstration with a general description of God's care for him: 'And God was with the lad, and he grew.' The rest of vv. 20–21 give sparse details which mark Ishmael's growth and indicate his well-being. Thus, vv. 14–21 fit into the overall theme of the passage – God's faithfulness to his word.

The main themes of this narrative, namely, the dependability of God's word, the calling of Isaac and his descendants, and the exclusion of Ishmael, are directly related to one another. The first seven verses of ch. 21 declare God's faithfulness to his word of promise, culminating in Sarah's poetic celebration in vv. 6–7. It is then the fulfillment of this promise that leads to the rejection and expulsion of Ishmael. On the most superficial level, the realization of Isaac's birth gives Sarah cause to be concerned for his future inheritance, and to desire the elimination of his rival. On a deeper level, the context of the Abraham narrative, particularly Genesis 17, shows that the promise itself included the notion that Sarah's son, and he alone, would be the one through whom God's covenant people would be identified. At the first annunciation of the promise in which Sarah is specified as the mother (17.15–21), God makes a distinction between Isaac and Ishmael. Now, 21.12 recalls the distinguishing nature of the promise. The fulfillment of the promise implies the rejection of Ishmael.

But then, ironically, the rejection of Ishmael elicits reiteration of the promise to bless him (v. 13; cf. 17.20) and also puts the fulfillment of that promise in jeopardy by exposing him to the terrors of the wilderness, separated from Abraham's loving protection. This situation leads to the demonstration of God's faithfulness to his promise of care for Ishmael, a promise which goes hand in hand with the more prominent promise of a son by Sarah. So the promise of a son to Abraham and its fulfillment implies both the rejection of Ishmael and the further demonstration of God's faithfulness.

We have seen that the main theme of Gen. 21.1–21 is God's faithfulness to his word. The theme of theodicy which we discerned in Genesis 18–20 may now be related to Gen. 21.1–21 in a way we have already seen within Genesis 18 – God's righteousness consists in his faithfulness to his word. 'Within the overall plan of Genesis, this account of Isaac's birth and Ishmael's expulsion is of decisive importance in the unfolding of the patriarchal promises.'[54]

54. Wenham, *Genesis*, 2.88.

4.5. *Textual Comparison of Romans 9.7 and Genesis 21.12*

We now turn to a textual comparison of Rom. 9.7 and Gen. 21.12, which reveals that Rom. 9.7 fully agrees with the LXX of Gen. 21.12, itself a close translation of the Hebrew.

Rom. 9.7   ἐν ᾿Ισαὰκ κληθήσεταί σοι σπέρμα.
Gen. 21.12 LXX   ἐν ᾿Ισαὰκ κληθήσεταί σοι σπέρμα.
Gen. 21.12 MT   בְּיִצְחָק יִקָּרֵא לְךָ זָרַע

4.6. *Interpretive Traditions Surrounding Genesis 21.12*

The final step in our investigation of Paul's use of the Old Testament in Rom. 9.6–9 before moving to an exegesis of this text is to survey the relevant interpretive traditions surrounding Gen. 21.12.

4.6.a. *Jubilees*

The second-century-B.C.E. *Jubilees* cites Gen. 21.12 twice. The first instance comes in *Jub.* 16.16 in the context of the report of Isaac's birth. Though not to the same extent as Genesis, *Jubilees* 16 emphasizes the fulfillment of God's word to Abraham and Sarah. The author reports that six years after Isaac's birth Abraham experienced a theophany in which the divine blessing was imparted to him in the declaration of both the extension of his life until he would have six more sons and the blessed destiny of his descendants. Here, as part of this divine blessing, we encounter a loose quotation of Gen. 21.12 followed by an intriguing interpretive expansion:

> And through Isaac a name and seed would be named for him. And all of the seed of his sons would become nations. And they would be counted with the nations. But from the sons of Isaac one would become a holy seed and he would not be counted among the nations because he would become the portion of the Most High and all his seed would fall (by lot) into that which God will rule so that he might become a people (belonging) to the Lord, a (special) possession from all people, and so that he might become a kingdom of priests and a holy people (16.16b–18).[55]

First, we may note that *Jub.* 16.16 adds the establishment of a name to the blessing of seed for Abraham. Rather than the addition of a new thought, this should be understood as an interpretive expansion of the

---

55. All quotations from *Jubilees* are taken from O.S. Wintermute, 'Jubilees: A New Translation and Introduction', in Charlesworth (ed.), *Pseudepigrapha*, 2.35–142.

naming of seed. *Jubilees* has created a hendiadys from Gen. 21.12 meaning that Abraham would obtain glory (i.e. a name) through his seed/offspring. This may well represent the author of *Jubilees*' interpretation of the Gen. 21.12 phrase against the broader narrative context of the Abraham story (Genesis 12–25). This small alteration is probably an allusion to the foundational promise given to Abraham in Gen. 12.1–3 and *Jub.* 12.22–24, economically drawing on the language of one of the several enumerated blessings – 'and I shall make your name great' – as an evocation of the entire sequence. In so doing, the author of *Jubilees* implies that the fundamental blessings promised to Abraham were to be fulfilled through Isaac and his descendants. The fact that, 'The promise of fruitfulness for Abraham in Gen. xvii, 6 has been altered to a promise of greatness (*Jub.* xv, 8)'[56] shows that the author equated greatness with fruitfulness, and perhaps saw greatness as a general description of the promises to Abraham. If this be so, then we have a precedent, accessible to Paul, of connecting the promises to Abraham to Gen. 21.12. This then might shed light on Rom. 9.1–5 and Paul's enumeration of the blessings and privileges of Israel. The fact that he almost immediately moves to a quotation of Gen. 21.12 may indicate that he was conceiving of those blessings and privileges as emanating from the Abrahamic promises, especially the seed promise.

Next, we find that the promise to make Ishmael a nation recorded in Gen. 21.13 (cf. Gen. 21.18; 16.10–12; 17.20) is transferred to all of the seed of Abraham's sons. This expansion probably represents a logical extension of the reason given in Gen. 21.13b for the promise: 'he is your seed'. Nevertheless, we can see a heightening of the promise here in almost eschatological style. The statement that all of the seed of Abraham's sons would be counted with the nations appears to indicate that they would be identified with them in their exclusion from the covenant and their wickedness as Gentiles. This is in line with *Jubilees*' concern for separation from the impure nations/Gentiles.[57] Already in the second century B.C.E., Ishmael was viewed as representative of all of the seed of Abraham who were not included in the Abrahamic covenant

---

56. G.L. Davenport, *The Eschatology of the Book of Jubilees* (Leiden: Brill, 1971), 51 n. 1. Davenport also notes that the promise of fruitfulness is again altered to one of greatness in 15.20, but with respect to Ishmael. This strengthens the likelihood that the author equated the two concepts.

57. For the exclusive nationalism of *Jubilees*, see e.g. J.C. Endres, *Biblical Interpretation in the Book of Jubilees* (CBQMS, 18; Washington, DC: CBAA, 1987), 228–31; Wintermute, 'Jubilees', 48.

yet were recipients of the blessing of God in a lesser but still significant sense. Even in the Old Testament itself, Ishmael came to be associated with the enemies of Israel (Genesis 37; Ps. 83.7 [Eng. 83.6]).

It is striking how the author of *Jubilees* now draws out similar implications as Paul from Gen. 21.12, viz., the same principle of distinction evident in the election of Isaac and rejection of Ishmael remains operative beyond that specific case. It is not physical descent from Abraham or Isaac that determines covenant election and blessing, but God's sovereign choice. The author of *Jubilees* applies the principle in a more concrete and limited way than Paul. There would be a distinction made among the sons of Isaac as there was between Isaac and Ishmael. One of his sons would become the covenant seed, separate from the nations and special to God. All those descended from this one holy seed would be God's chosen people, part of his kingdom, participating in the blessings of his rule, and fulfilling the great promise of Exod. 19.5–6 to be a kingdom of priests and a holy people. The allusion to Exod. 19.5–6 suggests that this one holy seed will become a holy nation because of his obedience to God's covenant, the condition laid down in that passage. It is through identification with the one holy seed, Jacob, that God's people are chosen. Jacob becomes the covenant identifier.[58] Thus there is a clear expression of corporate representation in *Jub.* 16.18 evidenced by the identification of the one singular seed with his plural seed.

Paul applies the principle of distinction in a more general and abstract way. *Jubilees* applies the principle to the next generation, but stopped there. All of Jacob's seed would be chosen by God. But Paul abstracts a general principle of the way God works in salvation history from Gen. 21.12 and applies it to identifying true Israel in the present, just as in Rom. 9.10–13 he goes on to find the principle operative in the specific case of Jacob and Esau. Paul proposes a different covenant identifier – faith – and a different covenant representative – Jesus Christ. But despite these differences, we appear to have identified an interpretive tradition stretching back to at least *Jub.* 16.16–18 which took Gen. 21.12 to imply a further distinction among Isaac's seed, a tradition Paul probably knew from at least *Jubilees*.[59] We will see below that later rabbinic tradition corroborates our findings.

---

58. On Jacob's central role in the covenant in *Jubilees*, see Endres, *Jubilees*, 228–31.

59. Wintermute, 'Jubilees', 49, claims that Paul was clearly familiar with expressions and ideas which appear in *Jubilees*.

Yet there is more to learn from *Jubilees*. *Jub.* 15.30–32 sheds further light on 16.16–18, revealing further connection to themes relevant to Romans 9.

> For the Lord did not draw Ishmael and his sons and his brothers and Esau near to himself, and he did not elect them because they are the sons of Abraham, for he knew them. But he chose Israel that they might be a people for himself. And he sanctified them and gathered them from all of the sons of man because (there are) many nations and many people, and they all belong to him, but over all of them he caused spirits to rule so that they might lead them astray from following him. But over Israel he did not cause any angel or spirit to rule because he alone is their ruler and he will protect them and he will seek for them at the hand of his angels and at the hand of his spirits and at the hand of all of his authorities so that he might guard them and bless them and they might be his and he might be theirs henceforth and forever (15.30–32).

Here Ishmael and Esau are directly related to one another as being non-elect, despite their descent from Abraham, apparently because the Lord knew their character to be wicked. This suggests a conditional election/rejection. Ishmael and Esau are 'counted with the nations' (cf. 16.17). Furthermore, God is said to have caused spirits to lead the nations astray from following him, while Israel is free of any such hindrance and enjoys God's protection and blessing. Thus we appear to have a case of determinism associated with the rejection of Ishmael and Esau as they are associated with the nations. On some readings, Paul's argument in Romans 9 also has a strong deterministic edge. In *Jubilees*, it is the Gentiles who are chosen to go astray and Israel who is chosen as God's people. For Paul, the reverse is true – and that is what presents the problem that takes Paul three whole chapters to deal with – Gentiles are chosen as God's people and the majority of Israel is hardened.

Given that there is at least an apparent determinism in both *Jubilees'* and Paul's treatment of Ishmael, we may note that in *Jubilees* this 'determinism' is neither absolute nor unconditional according to 10.8, where Mastema's (i.e. Satan's) request for demons to remain at his disposal for leading the nations astray is based on the evil nature of humanity. Conversely, the election of Israel, which includes protection from spiritual harm unto blessing and relationship with God, will not keep them from falling away from God's covenant, resulting in separation from him like the Gentiles (15.33–34). So Israel's election also appears as conditional in *Jubilees*, at least with respect to its members remaining in covenant relationship with God.

The second citation of Gen. 21.12 appears in a straightforward retelling of the weaning of Isaac and expulsion of Hagar and Ishmael (*Jub.* 17.6).[60] Like *Jub.* 16.16, 17.6 adds the establishment of a name to the blessing of seed for Abraham. We can see that Paul did not strictly follow *Jubilees*' interpretation of Genesis since 17.4 interprets Ishmael's action which provoked Sarah's ire to be playing and dancing and bluntly asserts that Sarah was jealous (cf. Gal. 4.29). But 17.17 does view the expulsion of Hagar and Ishmael as a test of Abraham's faith. The concept of faith, here embodied in the faithfulness of Abraham, again comes up in connection with Jewish exegesis of a passage alluded to by Paul in Romans 9.

4.6.b. *Philo*

Faith also plays a role in Philo's understanding of Genesis 21. In *Mut. Nom.* 138 he tells us that very few can hear and so receive the sound of God-inspired laughter emanating from divine truth.[61] This is due to the evil of superstition in the souls of many. In other words, false faith renders most people unable to hear and receive God. This is relevant to Paul's argument in Romans 9–11 *vis-à-vis* the hardness motif. For Philo, in view of Genesis 21, it is sinful, false faith that renders one incapable of hearing and receiving God. It is difficult to see just how Philo could take Gen. 21.6 in this direction, but it is significant that he does given its tie to the context of Gen. 21.12.

Philo emphasizes Isaac's supernatural birth as one begotten of God (*Leg. All.* 3.219; *Mut. Nom.* 137; *Det. Pot. Ins.* 124). In line with his name, Isaac represents joy and laughter. Caused by God directly, he is God's special work (*Det. Pot. Ins.* 124). Yet Philo does not emphasize the corresponding natural birth of Ishmael as Paul does in Gal. 4.21–31. What he does emphasize is Ishmael's inferiority to Isaac (*Sobr.* 8ff; *Cher.* 3–10; cf. *Poster. C.* 130–31). Isaac was joy and the possessor of wisdom, while Ishmael is associated with elementary instruction and sophistry, immaturity, and even wickedness. For Philo, Hagar and Ishmael represent the necessary but basic knowledge and instruction

---

60.   Josephus, *Ant.* 1.213–19, also retells the story in a rather straightforward way, requiring no detailed treatment.

61.   Philo misquotes Gen. 21.6 transforming it into the very opposite: 'For whoever hears this will not rejoice with me', though he quotes Gen. 21.6 correctly in *Det. Pot. Ins.* 123; *Leg. All.* 82.

who give way to Sarah and Isaac of the new dispensation of perfect virtue, wisdom, and joy.

Though the connection is not great, there is some similarity in the way Philo sees Hagar and Ishmael as a necessary stage leading to a more complete stage (i.e., Sarah and Isaac) to the way Paul sees a development in the people of God, the necessary and truly chosen physical Israel giving way to the fulfillment of the Church. Paul identifies true Israel with Isaac (Gal. 4.21–31), whether this be understood as the Church (most likely), or as believing physical Israel. The similarity is too general to indicate a common exegetical tradition. It is probably due to the potential inherent in the story. But Philo's use of Genesis 21 gives evidence of another first-century Jew's finding in the story of Isaac's birth and Ishmael's expulsion the elementary and necessary giving way to the full and complete.

4.6.c. *Targums and Other Rabbinic Literature*

Turning to the targums, *Onqelos*, *Pseudo-Jonathan*, and *Neofiti* all agree in emphasizing God's faithfulness to his promise in Gen. 21.1–7.[62] *Pseudo-Jonathan*, whose translation of Gen. 21.9 identifies Ishmael's idolatry as the reason for Sarah's anger, also implicitly includes the idea in its translation of Gen. 21.12, identifying him as one 'who has abandoned the training you have given him'.[63] Thus, Ishmael's wickedness is given as a reason to Abraham for his rejection. Though much later than Paul, this ancient interpretation reminds us that Paul understood Ishmael's behavior as evil (Gal. 4.29) and so could have influenced his understanding of Gen. 21.12 as well.

Stegner draws attention to the resemblance between rabbinic and Pauline treatment of Gen. 21.12. He points out that, 'The rabbis frequently quoted Genesis 21.12 to show who belonged to Israel.'[64] He correctly observes that it is significant 'that both Paul and later Rabbinic literature use the same text to show who belonged to Israel' and associate Esau with Gen. 21.12.[65] He further calls attention to *Gen R.* 53.12

---

62. *Neof.* does so in a marginal gloss on 21.7. B. Grossfeld, *The Targum Onqelos to Genesis: Translated with a Critical Introduction, Apparatus and Notes* (TAB, 6; Wilmington, Delaware: Michael Glazier, 1988), 85, comments that the addition of Onqelos in 21.7 accentuates God's character of fulfilling what he promises.

63. Translation from M. Maher, *Targum Pseudo-Jonathan: Genesis. Translated, with Introduction and Notes* (Collegeville, MN: The Liturgical Press, 1992).

64. Stegner, 'Midrash', 44.

65. Stegner, 'Midrash', 45.

(and *Ned* 2.10), which interprets Gen. 21.12 to mean that those who believe in two worlds will be called the seed of Abraham, and those who reject such faith will not be so called. Stegner makes the significant point that both *Genesis Rabbah* and Paul maintain 'it is not physical descent alone, but those who have a certain type of faith or belief who are regarded as children of Abraham'.[66] I would add that both *Genesis Rabbah* and Paul specifically interpret the phrase 'in Isaac' to refer to those who have faith. Stegner's suggestion that Paul, *Genesis Rabbah*, and *Ned* 2.10 preserve a Palestinian exegetical tradition, is hard to weigh. The correspondence is general, though striking. It may be that Paul held this interpretation as a Pharisee and then modified it in relation to Christ. In any case, it is noteworthy that both Paul and the rabbis would find the determining factor in belonging to God's people to be faith rather than ancestry and interpret the phrase, 'in Isaac', to indicate this.

It is also significant that all these sources agree in restricting the seed of Abraham to some of Isaac's descendants and not all.[67] To Stegner's references we would add *Ned* 31a, which contains the same interpretation, but even more explicitly identifies those not regarded as seed with the Gentiles/heathen, mentioning Ishmael and Esau. Given the same interpretation in *Jubilees*, we probably do have an exegetical tradition here, one which associated Gen. 21.12 with the faithfulness of God to his word, linked Ishmael and Esau with the Gentiles, and found a source for defining true Israel in Gen. 21.12.

4.6.d. *Hebrews*

Finally, we must consider the citation of Gen. 21.12 in Heb. 11.18, its only other citation in the New Testament. We have already seen that Heb. 11.11 alludes to Genesis 18 and connects it to the concept of faith. Now we see that the same author in the same chapter connects Gen. 21.12 to faith in an even more direct way. In this case, Gen. 21.12 explains the sticking point of Abraham's testing in the call to sacrifice Isaac. The fact that Isaac was the one through whom the covenant promises would be realized made sacrificing him inexplicable, for it would prevent the fulfillment of God's promise. The author of Hebrews, however, goes on to argue that the faith of Abraham by

---

66. Stegner, 'Midrash', 46.

67. Though I disagree with Stegner's ('Midrash', 45) claim that *Gen R.* 53.12 and Paul take ב as a partitive preposition.

which he offered up Isaac was of such a character so as to rely on the consideration that God could raise the dead. The author of Hebrews does not use Gen. 21.12 to identify the true heirs of God's promise as Paul does, but it is significant that his larger argument concerns both heirship (esp. 11.7–9) and faith, more specifically, heirship of righteousness and promise through faith.[68] In Romans 9 Paul uses Gen. 21.12 to prove that the true heirs of God's promises and righteousness are precisely those who believe God and his promises in Christ. Furthermore, both Hebrews 11 and Romans 9 appeal to Gen. 21.12 in connection with an affirmation of God's faithfulness to his word, reflecting the tenor of the Genesis context, Hebrews 11 drawing out even more clearly the emphasis on God's omnipotence found in Genesis. This all suggests that a significant portion of early Christianity understood Gen. 21.12 as related to faith, promise, and God's faithfulness to his word.[69]

4.7. *The New Testament Context of Genesis 21.12 and 18.10, 14*

We have finally come to the point at which we can examine Rom. 9.6–9 in light of its Old Testament and related background. Many scholars now rightly regard Rom. 9.6a as the theme of the whole of chs. 9–11: 'But it is not that the word of God has failed.'[70] Paul is defending the faithfulness of God to his promises to Israel. As Wright and others have argued, Paul 'has systematically transferred the privileges and attributes

---

68. It is perhaps not insignificant that the language of reckoning (λογισάμενος, Heb. 11.19) appears immediately after the citation of Gen. 21.12 (cf. Rom. 9.8). While the word is not used in the same way as in Rom. 9.8, it is interesting that similar language pops up in connection with Gen. 21.12.

69. Although he does not consider the nature of the tradition, Luz, *Geschichtsverständnis*, 101, judges that Rom. 9.7 and Heb. 11.18 probably reflect a community tradition on Gen. 21.12 (incorrectly citing Gen 11.12).

70. See ch. 2 above. Some regard 9.6a as governing only some of Paul's argument, e.g., Kraus, *Volk*, 298; Moo, *Romans*, 553–54; Haacker, *Römer*, 190; Brandenburger, 'Schriftauslegung', 10, 16ff. F. Wilk, *Die Bedeutung des Jesajabuches für Paulus* (FRLANT, 179; Göttingen: Vandenhoeck & Ruprecht, 1998), 311–14, makes an appealing case for finding an allusion to Isa. 40.7–8 in Rom. 9.6a (cf. Haacker, 190–91; idem, 'Geschichtstheologie', 211 n. 15), but fails to convince for a lack of verbal agreement. It is more likely that Paul makes general allusion to a number of texts which speak of the infallibility of God's word (see Dunn, *Romans*, 538–39, for references), though Wilk's case is strong enough for us to conclude that Isa. 40.7–8 is foremost among them.

of "Israel" to the Messiah and his people'.[71] This raises an obvious problem for Paul's argument. If God's promises to Israel have been transferred to the Church (or at least fulfilled in the Church), and the vast majority of Israel remain outside of the Church because of their rejection of Jesus the Messiah, then Israel has not received the fulfillment of the promises made to her and is cut off from God and his salvation. This calls into question God's faithfulness to his promises. If he did not remain true to his word to Israel, then how could he be trusted to fulfill those same promises to the Church or be regarded as faithful or righteous?

4.7.a. *The Faithful Word of God and the True Israel (Romans 9.6)*

So Paul vehemently denies that any such conclusion can be drawn from what he has said. The word of God has not failed. Scholars have offered various opinions on the precise meaning of ὁ λόγος τοῦ θεοῦ here such as the purpose,[72] election,[73] promise(s),[74] gospel,[75] or Scriptures[76] of God. But Byrne is surely correct to say, 'Paul means the whole complex of God's address to Israel, recorded in the scriptures and grounding the

---

71. Wright, *Climax*, 250 (cf. 237). Cf. Byrne, *Romans*, 282; idem, *Sons*, 127ff.; G.K. Beale, 'The Old Testament Background of Reconciliation in 2 Corinthians 5–7 and Its Bearing on the Literary Problem of 2 Corinthians 6:14–7:1', in Beale (ed.), *Right Doctrine*, 217–47 (230–31); Haacker, *Römer*, 180. Nanos, *Mystery*, 112, catalogs an impressive list of terminology applied by Paul to both Christians and non-Christian Jews.

72. E.g., Cranfield, *Romans*, 472–73; Piper, *Justification*, 49–50.

73. B. Mayer, *Unter Gottes Heilsratschluss: Prädestinationsaussagen bei Paulus* (Würzburg: Echter, 1974), 170.

74. E.g., Dunn, *Romans*, 539; the majority view. While S.K. Williams, 'The "Righteousness of God" in Romans', *JBL* (1980), 241–90 (281), is wrong to limit the phrase to 'the pledge to Abraham that through him *all* peoples of the earth would become the children of God through faith' (emphasis original; see Abasciano, 'Paul's Use', 303 n. 90), insightfully citing 9.9's reference to the promise of a son by Sarah, his intriguing suggestion is right to recognize the Abrahamic character of the promise in view, as does Hofius, 'Evangelium', 300 n. 13.

75. E. Güttgemanns 'Heilsgeschichte bei Paulus oder Dynamik des Evangeliums: Zur strukturellen Relevanz von Röm 9–11 für die Theologie des Römerbriefes', in E. Güttgemanns, *Studia Linguistica Neotestamentica* (Munich: Kaiser, 1971), 34–58 (40–42); R.D. Kotansky, 'A Note on Romans 9:6: *Ho Logos Tou Theou* as the Proclamation of the Gospel', *Studia Biblica et Theologica* 7 (1977), 24–30; more recently, Reichert, *Römerbrief*, 189–90.

76. Moo, *Romans*, 572–73, combines this option with the idea of promise. Cf. H. Schlier, *Der Römerbrief* (HTKNT; Freiburg: Herder, 1977), 290.

privileges just listed.'[77] Yet certain aspects of this broad concept probably come to the fore. First, this word has been written in the Old Testament, the foundational characteristic on which the others are built. That is partly why Paul goes on to argue his case from Scripture. Any interpretation of the phrase must be able to relate it to Paul's lament in 9.1–5, since the denial of 9.6a arises out of that lament and the accompanying list of Jewish privileges. The apparent failure of these privileges to effect the salvation which is their corollary presents the problem Paul must address. And it is precisely through the Scriptures of Israel that these promised privileges were 'spoken'. Indeed, in light of the benefits and privileges of Israel, which all emanate from the Abrahamic covenant and promises, this word is one of promise (9.9, ἐπαγγελίας γὰρ ὁ λόγος οὗτος). Therefore, ὁ λόγος τοῦ θεοῦ has its greatest referent in the promises of God to Israel recorded in Scripture.[78] This judgment is confirmed by the parallel phrase, τὰ λόγια τοῦ θεοῦ, found in the related 3.2 and also referring to the Scriptures of Israel with special reference to the promises of God.[79] Yet God's scriptural promises cannot finally be separated from his purpose or his election or his word or his gospel.

This understanding of ὁ λόγος τοῦ θεοῦ underscores the current scholarly emphasis on the Jewishness of Paul and the orientation of the present study, which finds Paul's Jewish heritage to be the most helpful background for understanding his thought. It also reminds us that 'it is a mistake to make a hard distinction between the significance the phrase has here and its significance elsewhere in the NT',[80] for although the phrase may often refer to the proclamation of the gospel of Jesus Christ, Paul's usage should alert us to the fact that such proclamation was conceived of as based on and originating in the Scriptures of Israel and as a fulfillment of God's promises to Israel.

---

77. Byrne, *Romans*, 293.

78. This is essentially Moo's (*Romans*, 572–73) position. Piper, *Justification*, 49–50, makes a good case for the purpose of God by pointing to the 'remaining purpose' of 9.11 as parallel. Purpose is surely an aspect of ὁ λόγος τοῦ θεοῦ here, but 9.1–5, 8–9 should be recognized as the more immediate context. For a synonymous phrase (τὸ ῥῆμα τοῦ θεοῦ) in a context with some striking parallels, see *Pss. Sol.* 9.2; G. Maier, *Mensch und freier Wille nach den jüdischen Religionspartien zwischen Ben Sira und Paulus* (WUNT, 12; Tübingen: Mohr Siebeck, 1971), 342, 400, even suggests that Paul may be countering the psalm's advocacy of free will.

79. Piper, *Justification*, 125, admits this meaning of the phrase in 3.2, while Kraus, *Volk*, 298 n. 174, also finds the phrase of 3.2 synonymous to the one in 9.6.

80. Cranfield, *Romans*, 473.

To defend his main assertion that God's word has not failed, Paul states, 'for not all who are from Israel are Israel'. That is, not all who belong to ethnic/physical Israel are true, spiritual Israel, which is heir to the promises.[81] It is almost universally acknowledged that Paul uses the term ᾽Ισραήλ in two different senses in 9.6b.[82] But there is debate over the meaning of the second occurrence of ᾽Ισραήλ. The first occurrence obviously refers to ethnic Israel. But the latter occurrence could refer to either (a) the Church composed of both Jews and Gentiles who believe in Jesus Christ,[83] or (b) Jews who believe in Jesus Christ (i.e. Jewish Christians).[84] Another interpretation has recently emerged which regards this second occurrence of ᾽Ισραήλ as ambiguous or indeterminate.[85] Byrne's version of this view has most to commend it: 'Paul has not yet defined this "Israel"; it is better to see him as stating simply

81. Reading a genitive of derivation indicating ancestral descent like the similar constructions of 9.5; 11.1, though an adjectival genitive or one of possession or relationship are all quite possible. All are really in view. In any case, οἱ ἐξ ᾽Ισραήλ are equivalent to the ᾽Ισραηλῖται of 9.4. This interpretation of the phrase does not demand that the first 'Israel' of 9.6 refer to the patriarch Jacob/Israel; it can just as easily refer to the people and the phrase to descent from, or relationship to, the people (cf. Piper, *Justification*, 42), despite the contention of Haacker, 'Geschichtstheologie', 212 n. 16. For texts attesting to some sort of belief in salvation based on ethnicity, see Mt. 3.9/Lk. 3.8; *m. Sanh.*10. 1; cf. Jn 8.37–39; Dunn, *Romans*, 539.

82. Gaston, 'Enemies', 94, has offered the strange view that οἱ ἐξ ᾽Ισραήλ refers to those outside Israel, i.e. Gentiles and apostate Jews. But this completely misunderstands Paul's argument and has been soundly refuted on contextual and grammatical grounds by Johnson, *Function*, 139 n. 103, 193–95.

83. See e.g., Schmithals, *Römerbrief*, 339–42; Wright, *Climax*, 238, 250; for an extensive list see Abasciano 'Paul's Use', 305 n. 98. Chae, *Paul*, 228 n. 64, denies this designation, but it is difficult to see how his formulation (230), is any different.

84. The majority view; held by e.g., Cranfield, *Romans*, 473–74; Piper, *Justification*, 65–71; G. Harvey, *The True Israel: Uses of the Names Jew, Hebrew and Israel in Ancient Jewish and Early Christian Literature* (AGJU, 35; Leiden: Brill, 1996), 228–32; for an extensive list see Abasciano 'Paul's Use', 305–306 n. 99.

85. Lodge, *Romans 9–11*, 50–60, 64–67, argues this from a dubious reader-response perspective that believes meaning to be an activity of readers rather than a property of the text. C.H. Cosgrove, *Elusive Israel: The Puzzle of Election in Romans* (Louisville: Westminster/John Knox, 1997), argues this more plausibly from a less radical perspective that still accords some role for the reader in constructing meaning and via the ancient rhetorical device of co-deliberation. For criticism of Cosgrove's approach from a rhetorical perspective, see J.D. Kim, *God, Israel, and the Gentiles: Rhetoric and Situation in Romans 9–11* (SBLDS, 176; Atlanta: SBL, 2000), 118–19 n. 10.

that the two "Israels" are not coextensive. This leaves open the possibility that the '(true, called) Israel' can include Gentile believers – a possibility which Paul depicts as a reality in vv. 24–29.[86] This amounts to a cautious affirmation of option (a) (Israel = the Church).

Byrne's point that Paul has not yet defined true Israel must be admitted. So any definition must be derived from the context of Paul's argument, Romans generally, and Paul's other writings. It is important to recognize from the outset that whoever this true Israel is, it is a recipient of both the call of God referred to throughout the chapter and the promised blessings of God described in 9.4–5. Those who support option (b) (Jewish Christians) rely on the fact that Paul's examples from the Old Testament are of distinction within Abraham's physical descendants. But this cannot count for much since almost any example from the Old Testament would deal with ethnic Israel. In fact, Paul's use of Abraham actually supports a reference to believers in general since Abraham the believer (τῷ πιστῷ Gal. 3.9) was really pre-Israel and associated with faith and universalism in Paul, the New Testament, and early Judaism[87] (cf. Rom. 4.10). Moreover, Paul has already used Abraham significantly in Romans (ch. 4), and this should incline us to interpret what Paul says now as building on what he has already said. He has said that Abraham's seed/descendants are those who believe in Jesus Christ whether Jew or Gentile (the burden of Romans 4).[88] Since this point is central to the epistle to this point, it should weigh heavily in consideration of 9.6.

9.1–5 has also been heralded as supporting a Jewish referent for the second occurrence of Ἰσραήλ in 9.6.[89] Paul has clearly spoken of ethnic Israel in 9.1–5 and related her to the covenantal blessings of Abraham. Therefore, it is claimed that the ecclesial interpretation of Israel would

86.   Byrne, *Romans*, 293, a view he basically articulated earlier, in *Sons*, 130. Cf. Wagner, *Heralds*, 49–50; Klumbies, 'Vorzüge', 142–44.

87.   For a survey of early Jewish uses of Abraham, see J.S. Siker, *Disinheriting the Jews: Abraham in Early Christian Controversy* (Louisville: Westminster/John Knox, 1991), 17–27. Our own treatment of Jewish exegetical traditions surrounding Genesis 18 and 21 has found the concepts of faith and universalism associated with Abraham. For treatment of Abraham in Romans 9–11, see K. Berger, 'Abraham in den paulinischen Hauptbriefen', *MTZ* 17 (1966), 47–89 (77–83); N.L. Calvert, 'Abraham', *DPL*, 1–9 (8).

88.   Cf. Wagner, *Heralds*, 49 nn. 16, 18.

89.   See e.g. Moo, 574; S. Westerholm, 'Paul and the Law in Romans 9–11', in J.D.G. Dunn (ed.), *Paul and the Mosaic Law* (WUNT, 89; Tübingen: Mohr Siebeck, 1996), 215–37 (222).

contradict this. But Paul's declaration in 9.6b is purposely expressed in a self-contradictory way in acknowledgment of the apparent contradiction.[90] It appears that God's word of promise to Israel has failed precisely because ethnic Israel as a whole has excluded itself from the elect people of God by rejecting the Messiah, the covenant identifier and the representative of the covenant people, thereby forfeiting the covenant promises and blessings. In short, they are not receiving the promised blessings which nevertheless are being realized in the Church as Paul has argued throughout Romans even from the beginning (cf. 1.1–2).[91] That is the problem that Paul deals with in Romans 9–11, and that is why he must demonstrate God's faithfulness to his word, that is, his righteousness. The answer Paul gives is that the promises were not made to ethnic Israel but to the covenant people of God, the seed of Abraham and true spiritual Israel.[92] These considerations render hollow the claim that an ecclesial understanding of the second Israel in 9.6 contradicts 9.1–5.

Returning to a point we already began to make, when we take into account that Paul has: (1) explicitly argued that the seed of Abraham are those who have faith in Jesus Christ, whether Jew or Gentile (Romans 4); and (2) explicitly argued that ethnic Jewishness is not true Jewishness, but that inward Jewishness – or circumcision of the heart, or the obedience of faith – makes one truly Jewish whether ethnic Jew or Gentile (Rom. 2.17–29);[93] and (3) applied the blessings and privileges of Old Testament Israel to the Church composed of both Jew and Gentile, then we would expect the second occurrence of Ἰσραήλ in 9.6 to be just what Paul has argued about the Church – the elect people of God identified by faith and recipient of the covenantal promises of God to Israel. We may add to this a fact which many advocates of position (b) admit, that Paul's thought in Romans and elsewhere conceives of the Church as true

90. Cf. Dunn, *Romans*, 587.

91. Cf. Hays, *Echoes*, 34.

92. Thus Watson's (*Paul*, 227 n. 9) criticized statement (by e.g., Dunn, *Romans*, 540) is on target in that the Jewish people were never elected for salvation based on ethnicity; cf. Cranford, 'Election', 35, who supports Watson; and similarly Räisänen, 'Römer 9–11', 2900–901; Hübner, *Schriftgebrauch*, 20–22.

93. For an intriguing intertextual study of Rom. 2.17–29, see Berkley, *Broken*. He finds that Paul has redefined Jewish identity spiritually as circumcision of the heart needed by and available to both ethnic Jews and Gentiles, though allowing for a special place to ethnic Israel in God's plan. Indeed, he finds that 2.17–29 lays 'the groundwork for redefining who is true Israel, the children of Abraham' in chs. 4 and 9 (152).

Israel.[94] Schreiner, who advocates position (b), nevertheless states the case well:

> Paul almost certainly labels the church 'the Israel of God' in Gal. 6:16, and this follows from the fact that the church is the true circumcision (Rom. 2:28–29; Phil. 3:3) and the true family of Abraham (Rom. 4:9–25; Gal. 3:7, 14, 29). Moreover, Gentiles are grafted onto the olive tree of Israel (Rom. 11:17–24), and OT texts that refer to Israel are applied to Gentiles who believe in Christ (9:24–26).[95]

Furthermore, the fact that in 9.24–29 Paul represents the called of God to be from both Jews and Gentiles suggests that this is precisely his definition of the true Israel.[96] Finally, redefinition of 'Israel' as a group based not on ethnicity but on faith and existential experience of God may be found elsewhere in early Jewish literature.[97]

Excursus: The Translation of Romans 9.6b and the Corporate Nature of Election

John Piper seems to base his understanding of the second occurrence of Ἰσραήλ in Rom. 9.6 as referring to the elect within ethnic Israel upon the grammar of the verse.[98] He argues that οὐ γὰρ πάντες οἱ ἐξ Ἰσραὴλ οὗτοι Ἰσραήλ should be translated as 'for all those from Israel, these are not Israel'. Although this translation might seem peculiar at first, it has been followed by several scholars.[99] One reason why some more recent commentators might follow Piper or give this translation more credence than one might expect is that Piper gives concrete reasons for his construal of

---

94. See Fitzmyer, *Romans*, 560; Moo, *Romans*, 573–74.

95. Schreiner, *Romans*, 494.

96. This invalidates Moo's (*Romans*, 574) use of 9.27–29 to limit Israel to Jewish Christians. The whole of 9.24–29 clearly explicates Paul's understanding of the called, which according to 9.6–7 must be equivalent to true Israel, a 'remnant' from both Jews and Gentiles.

97. See e.g. E. Birnbaum, *The Place of Judaism in Philo's Thought: Israel, Jews, and Proselytes* (BJS, 290; Studia Philonica Monographs, 2; Atlanta: Scholars Press, 1996); Longenecker, *Eschatology*, 152–53, 274ff. Cf. P. Spilsbury, *The Image of the Jew in Flavius Josephus' Paraphrase of the Bible* (TSAJ, 69; Tübingen: Mohr Siebeck, 1998), 145; the Qumran community's concept of true Israel as reflected in texts such as CD 3.13–14 (cited by J.W. Aageson, *Written Also for Our Sake: Paul and the Art of Biblical Interpretation* [Louisville: Westminster/John Knox, 1993], 92).

98. See esp. Piper, *Justification*, 65–67.

99. Dunn, *Romans*, 539; Moo, *Romans*, 573; Schreiner, *Romans*, 493; Wilk, *Jesajabuches*, 313.

the sentence, whereas virtually no other commentators justify their constructions, as Piper complains. Despite Piper's complaint, the reason for this is probably that the typical construction of the passage is the most natural way to take the Greek. οὐ would generally modify what immediately follows it rather than a more distant phrase. Therefore, there must be some good reasons to follow Piper's awkward rendering. He gives two reasons for taking οὐ to modify the clause οὗτοι 'Ισραήλ rather than as typically understood, πάντες: (1) οὗτοι refers to a definite group while οὐ πάντες is indefinite; (2) he also points to Rom. 7.15 (οὐ γὰρ ὃθέλω τοῦτο πράσσω, ἀλλ᾽ ὃ μισῶ τοῦτο ποιῶ.) as a grammatical parallel, in which οὐ must modify the verb πράσσω at the end of the phrase rather than the closer verb θέλω due to the contrastive nature of the following phrase. But the arguments do not stand up under scrutiny.

First, while it may be true that the negation οὐ πάντες is indefinite, it is not necessary to press for a definite referent for οὗτοι, for it functions as a copula[100] in this verbless clause, highlighting the contrast between οἱ ἐξ 'Ισραήλ and the second occurrence of 'Ισραήλ. This seems to be the assumption that lies behind the vast majority of translations. So there is no compelling reason to take οὐ as modifying a phrase so distant on the grounds of definiteness.

As for Rom. 7.15, I must question whether οὐ modifies the second clause. Piper is correct to say that οὐ cannot modify θέλω since the next clause would repeat rather than contrast what Paul has just said, as ἀλλ᾽ demands. But this does not mean that οὐ must then modify the next verb five words away in the next clause. Piper appears to assume that οὐ must modify a verb. But that is not the case. οὐ can modify any word, verb or not, and even clauses.[101] I would suggest that the most natural way to take the Greek would be to construe οὐ as modifying the relative clause ὃ θέλω: 'for not that which I wish, this I do, but that which I hate, this I do'.[102] Of course, this might be awkward in English. But we must be careful not to let English translation determine our understanding of the Greek text. The accusative relative clause is thrust forward to the beginning of the

100.   Cf. Mk 6.2/Mt. 13.56 where τούτῳ differs in number from the subject and is used as a copula. Cf. also the use of הוא in biblical Hebrew and Aramaic as a copula.

101.   See BDAG, 733, where Rom. 9.6 is also listed as an example of the negation of πάντες. Another option would be to take οὐ to negate the whole sentence.

102.   Cf. Dunn, *Romans*, 375, 389, who takes οὐ to modify an implied verb 'to be', tantamount to modifying ὃ θέλω. We could translate Rom. 9.6 similarly. This would find support from 9.7a where οὐδ᾽ arguably (see below) negates the whole subordinate clause introduced by ὅτι.

sentence for emphasis, while the demonstrative pronoun is also used for emphasis.[103] Perhaps the best translation of Rom. 9.6b would recognize the copulative function of οὗτοι and yet capture its simultaneous emphasizing function: 'For not all who are of Israel are actually Israel.'

The larger concern of Piper's construction of 9.6b is his estimation that it establishes Paul's argument as concerned with individual election unto salvation. Although many modern scholars are convinced that Paul implies nothing about the salvation of individuals in Romans 9,[104] there remains a persistent strain who think that he does. Piper is probably the most detailed and forceful modern proponent of this view *vis-à-vis* Romans 9, and is followed by the recent commentaries of Moo and Schreiner.[105] Although the general trend in recent years has been to reject this view, there has been little significant interaction with Piper's arguments on these points, despite the fact that his work is generally regarded as a standard exegesis of Rom. 9.1–23. Often phrased as a single issue, there are actually two main issues here which are separate but related: (1) whether Paul speaks of an individual or corporate election; (2) whether he speaks of an election unto eternal destiny or historical role.

Piper argues convincingly that Paul is speaking of eschatological salvation based on his grief-filled lament in 9.1–5.[106] Our exegesis of 9.1–5

103. Rom. 7.16 furnishes another clear example of the relative accusative placed at the beginning of a sentence for emphasis: εἰ δὲ ὃ οὐ θέλω τοῦτο ποιῶ. Here also, the demonstrative pronoun refers to the relative clause. We should not think that if a relative clause or word is negated that the demonstrative pronoun for that reason could not be used, especially since its purpose is to give emphasis.

104. Moo, *Romans*, 571, calls this group 'an increasingly large number'. Indeed, several recent treatments of Romans 9 have found that Paul is not discussing the eternal fate of individuals: e.g. Wright, *Climax*, 238–39; Fitzmyer, *Romans*, 563; Byrne, *Romans*, 299.

105. See also T.S. Schreiner, 'Does Romans 9 Teach Individual Election unto Salvation? Some Exegetical and Theological Reflections', *JETS* 36/1 (March 1993), 25–40 (cf. my forthcoming response to Schreiner in *JETS*: 'Corporate Election in Romans 9: A Reply to Thomas Schreiner'); D.J. Moo, 'The Theology of Romans 9–11: A Response to E. Elizabeth Johnson', in Hay and Johnson (eds.), *Pauline*, 240–58 (252); Kuss, *Römerbrief*, 928–29.

106. Piper, *Justification*, 17–46, 64–65. Piper argues just as convincingly from the vocabulary and structure of 9.6b–8 and analogous Pauline texts (67–71). For a recent, detailed treatment which argues that Paul does not speak of final division or condemnation in Romans 9–11, see S. Hillert, *Limited and Universal Salvation: A Text-Oriented and Hermeneutical Study of Two Perspectives in Paul* (*ConNT*, 31; Stockholm: Almqvist & Wiksell International, 1999), 126–51, and Abasciano, 'Paul's Use', 312–13 n. 123 for critique.

has confirmed this insight. Moreover, 10.1, which is parallel to 9.1–3,[107] shows that Paul's concern is for the salvation of his kinsmen: 'Brothers, the desire of my heart and my prayer to God for them is for their salvation.' As Paul moves to a new stage in the argument of Romans 9–11 he restates his concern for his fellow Jews' need for salvation. This arises directly out of the preceding promise of salvation for those who believe found in 9.33.

Though not often considered, I would like to suggest that while Paul is speaking of eternal destiny, he does so with respect to groups/corporate entities, not individuals directly. 9.6 is one of Piper's main arguments for individual election and against the idea of corporate election. He argues that 9.6 proves there to be an election of individuals within Israel.[108] Paul is concerned that some individual Israelites are accursed and cut off from Christ. But I would counter that according to Piper's own unusual translation, this phrase is termed in corporate language. How else should we understand the corporate term πάντες? Piper himself unwittingly shows its force when he explains 9.6b as meaning 'πάντες οἱ ἐξ 'Ισραήλ are not the *group* to whom salvation was assured by God's word'.[109] On the other hand, if we are right and Piper's translation of 9.6b should be rejected, there is still no compelling reason to think that Paul's argument concerns individual election. For the Old Testament concept of corporate election encompassed the inclusion and exclusion of individuals *vis-à-vis* the elect people. Moreover negation of πάντες gives no indication of whether its referents are conceived of as individuals or as a group. Besides, even if conceived of as individuals, there is no indication that election is individual; what Paul indicates is that they are not among the elect people. Indeed, Paul goes on to speak of classes of people, viz., children of the flesh, children of God, and children of the promise (9.8). Even the individuals Paul speaks of in his unfolding argument are representatives of peoples and treated as types.

What I am suggesting is that Paul here views the elect primarily as a corporate entity. This does not mean that individuals are not in view at all. Rather, it means that the group is the object of election and that individuals are in view only by virtue of their connection to the group. It is a question of which is primary, the group or the individual. Is the group elect as a corporate entity, and individuals elected by their inclusion in that group, or is the individual elect, and the group elected as a group of elect individuals (i.e. only because it is an association of

107. Cf. Räisänen, 'Römer 9–11', 2907; Wiles, *Prayers*, 256.
108. Piper, *Justification*, 65–67.
109. Piper, *Justification*, 66; emphasis changed.

elect individuals)? The answer to this question is found in the socio-historical context of first-century Judaism and the New Testament. For the first-century Jew, the corporate view was clearly dominant.[110] This was also the orientation of the Old Testament, from which Paul is developing his theology and argument. Piper's own question is telling: 'How else could Paul have argued from the OT for the principle of God's freedom in election, since the eternal salvation of the individual as Paul teaches it is almost never the subject of discussion in the OT?'[111] This only shows how unlikely it is that the concept of individual election unto salvation would even occur to Paul. Of course, it is possible that he departed from the Old Testament conception. But the burden of proof should lie upon those who claim that he did.

Again, it is important to understand that such a corporate view of election takes sufficient account of the individual. There need not be an exclusive dichotomy holding that either the group or the individual is elect. Schreiner's assertion that 'groups are always composed of individuals, and one cannot have the former without including the latter'[112] would be simplistic and miss the point if applied to the present argument for the primacy of corporate election. The statement is a truism which ignores the fundamental question of how the corporate and individual aspects relate. The answer we have suggested is that Paul continues the Old Testament understanding of corporate election found in the scriptural texts he is interpreting and applying, which regards the group as the object of election and the individual to be elect only by inclusion in the elect people. In Romans 9 Paul speaks of an election which involves salvation. So an individual is elected unto salvation only by connection to the corporate people so elected. His concern is not with who is elected to be in the elect people – election as a concept simply does not apply to

110.   Cf. the discussion of individual and corporate perspectives in ch. 2 above. On the concept of corporate election with additional sources, see Abasciano, 'Election'; idem, 'Paul's Use', 314 n. 129. On the corporate perception of reality in the ancient world, see e.g., B.J. Malina, *The New Testament World* (Atlanta: John Knox, 1981), 51–70; Kee, *Knowing*, 1–6; cf. Burnett, *Paul*; Son, *Corporate*.

111.   Piper, *Justification*, 64.

112.   Schreiner, *Romans*, 498. Would Schreiner then maintain that there is no difference between the OT and NT conceptions of election, since this point argues for election of the individual as an individual as a necessary corollary of corporate election? Schreiner and others who argue for individual election unto salvation implicitly admit that corporate election does not necessitate individual election as traditionally conceived when they assert that the election of ethnic Israel did not ensure salvation for every ethnic Israelite.

entrance into the elect people – but with the elect people and who they are, as well as 'the character and mode' of their election.[113]

The same can be said of Schreiner's point that selection of a remnant out of Israel implies the selection of individuals.[114] While this is of course true in the sense that what happens to a group affects the individuals of that group, it tells us nothing about how they are viewed, whether as individuals or as a group. The very use of the collective term 'remnant' suggests the corporate view. Therefore, the 'individual decision' of ch. 10 does not demand a concept of individual election as traditionally conceived. Chapter 10 reveals how one joins the elect people – faith. Schreiner consistently confuses the distinction between election unto salvation and election to be among the elect people.[115] Paul speaks of the former with respect to corporate entities, but does not use such language of individuals. As we have said, individuals are elect only by virtue of membership in the elect people, a membership which is effected by faith. Indeed, as one progresses through Romans 9 it can be seen that the basic distinction is between two classes of people, believers (i.e. the elect/called) and unbelievers. All of Romans 9–11 concerns distinctions between classes of people, whether believers/unbelievers, Jews/Gentiles, or groups from within Israel and the Gentiles.

Thus we can see how the corporate election of two peoples in Rom. 9.12, 13 fits with 9.6b, and we avoid the pitfall of taking Paul's extreme grief in 9.1–5 lightly.[116] We can admit what is obvious – Paul's grief comes from 'the pressing problem of eternally condemned Israelites in Rom. 9.3'.[117] Indeed, the corporate perspective we are espousing inten-

---

113.   Dunn, *Romans*, 540, though he wrongly separates the character and mode of election from the fact of election (cf. H. Räisänen, 'Romans 9–11 and the "History of Early Christian Religion"', in T. Fornberg and D. Hellholm (eds.), *Texts and Contexts: Biblical Texts in Their Textual and Situational Contexts: Essays in Honor of Lars Hartman* [Oslo: Scandanavian University Press, 1995], 743–65 [750 n. 54]). 9.6b clearly grounds 9.6a with the identity of the true Israel.

114.   Schreiner, *Romans*, 498.

115.   The same is true of Moo, *Romans*; idem, 'Theology', 254–58, who concedes that Paul's Scriptures and Jewish heritage taught him only of a corporate election, but goes on to argue that the rejection of the gospel by the vast majority of the Jewish people combined with the influx of Gentiles as individuals into the Church led Paul to individualize election. But this is gratuitous reasoning; see Abasciano, 'Paul's Use', 316 n. 135; idem, 'Election'.

116.   Cf. Piper, *Justification*, 58.

117.   Piper, *Justification*, 58.

sifies our perception of Paul's grief, for it helps us to observe that Paul seems to have considered Israel as a whole to have rejected Christ.[118] This does not mean that every Jew had rejected Christ; Paul himself is proof of that (11.1). Yet the corporate failure of Israel to receive God's Messiah is evident from Paul's use of the term Ἰσραήλ throughout chapters 9–11. This explains why Paul's grief is so great. And it points up Paul's corporate perspective once again.

Paul has made the point that not all who are from ethnic Israel are part of the true, spiritual Israel, which is heir to the covenant promises of God. Therefore, God has remained true to his word. The covenant people to whom he had made promises are receiving the fulfillment of those promises.

4.7.b. *The Naming of Abraham's Covenant Seed: The Children of the Promise (Romans 9.7–8/Genesis 21.12)*

Paul confirms our general understanding of 9.6b by his interpretive restatement of the principle in v. 7a: 'nor is it that all his children are the seed of Abraham'. Most translations and commentators translate τέκνα rather than σπέρμα as the more restrictive term while taking ὅτι in a causal sense: 'nor because they are the seed of Abraham are all his children'.[119] Byrne argues most persuasively for this reckoning, asserting that the former interpretation destroys the parallelism with 9.6b, which places the more inclusive term (πάντες οἱ ἐξ Ἰσραήλ) first followed by the more exclusive term (Ἰσραήλ).[120] But there is no reason to preserve this alleged parallelism, for 6b and 7a form a chiasm:

(A1) πάντες οἱ ἐξ Ἰσραήλ (inclusive)

(B1) Ἰσραήλ (exclusive)

(B2) σπέρμα Ἀβραάμ (exclusive)

(A2) πάντες τέκνα (inclusive)

---

118. Cf. Räisänen, 'Römer 9–11', 2900, who criticizes Piper on this point.

119. So most translations; Byrne, *Romans*, 293; Fitzmyer, *Romans*, 560. The meaning of ὅτι cannot be decided on the basis of grammar. But the use of Οὐχ οἷον δὲ ὅτι in 9.6 suggests that οὐδ' ὅτι in 9.7 may be an echo of the former phrase. It is also worth noting that ὅτι always means 'that' in its four other occurrences in the NT where it immediately precedes εἰσίν (Mt. 16.28; Mk 9.1; Lk. 18.9; 1 Cor. 3.20).

120. Byrne, *Romans*, 293; cf. idem, *Sons*, 130 n. 201, where he calls attention to the parallelism with 9.8 as well. But a chiastic relationship can be discerned between 9.7a and 9.8a along the same lines as those outlined below between 9.6b and 9.7a. Perhaps the lesson to be learned here is that structure is far from determinative in this matter.

This gives the sense of σπέρμα 'Αβραάμ to the second 'Ισραήλ of 9.6b. The Old Testament citations that Paul is about to bring to bear on his argument confirm that he is referring to the covenant seed of Abraham.

Byrne also argues that τέκνα in v. 7 refers to children of God as it does in the parallel v. 8, which explains the scriptural citations of 7b. But σπέρμα is the restrictive term in 7b and 8, while τέκνα appears as a more general term needing qualification to indicate a negative (τὰ τέκνα τῆς σαρκός) or positive (τὰ τέκνα τῆς ἐπαγγελίας) connotation.[121] Lodge points to Paul's use of σπέρμα as an inclusive term in Rom. 4.13–18 as an argument against an inclusive sense here.[122] But this objection does not fully understand Paul's argument in Romans 4, where he argues 'for a redefinition of the true descendants of Abraham, one that both restricts the referent of 'seed' to those in Christ and at the same time widens the referent by including Gentile Christians'.[123] Therefore, Romans 4 actually helps to establish the meaning of σπέρμα 'Αβραάμ here in 9.7 as those who believe in Jesus Christ, whether Jew or Gentile (cf. Gal. 3.16, 19, 29). Thus, the immediate context of 9.7, the broader epistolary context, Galatians 3, and the impending Old Testament quotations all suggest that Paul is speaking of σπέρμα as the true covenant descendants of Abraham, who are heirs to his promises.[124]

In any case, Paul's point in both 9.6b and 9.7a is that the covenant descendants of Abraham who are heir to the covenant promises are not identified by physical descent. Paul does not say at this point what does identify the seed of Abraham who are children of God. But Paul has already made that clear in the epistle. The seed of Abraham are identified not by ethnicity, but by faith (Romans 2–4). We cannot cut ourselves off from the preceding argument as if Romans 9–11 is argued in a vacuum and not part of an unfolding argument. Neither can we assume that Gentiles are absent from the argument until much later in the chapter (9.24ff.) as is commonly asserted. But because of the context of the epistle, we can assume that Gentiles are part of the argument from

---

121. Cf. Dunn, *Romans*, 540, who supports σπέρμα as predicate, as do Barrett, *Romans*, 180–81; Moo, *Romans*, 575; Schreiner, *Romans*, 494–95, etc.

122. Lodge, *Romans 9–11*, 54, 58.

123. J.R. Wagner, ' "Who Has Believed Our Message?": Paul and Isaiah "in Concert" in the Letter to the Romans' (Ph.D. Thesis, Duke University, 1999), 54 n. 22.

124. Paul can use the term σπέρμα in a more physical sense as in Rom. 1.3; 9.29; 11.1; 2 Cor. 11.22. This reflects the usage of the OT texts Paul interprets. σπέρμα refers to the covenant seed of Abraham in LXX Gen 21.12, and his merely physical seed in 21.13.

the beginning of ch. 9. The fact that 9.1–5 is a response to the exalted and celebratory reflections of ch. 8 shows this to be true. Paul's lament for his fellow Israelites is elicited by their failure as a whole to obtain the fulfillment of the salvific covenantal promises of God, which are nevertheless being realized in the Christian Church made up of Jews and Gentiles. We will not need to wait long, however, for Paul's explanation of what identifies the σπέρμα 'Αβραάμ. That explanation begins with the following quotations from Genesis and Paul's more general explanation of how God has remained faithful to his promises.

We now come to Paul's first Old Testament quotation: 'but in Isaac seed will be called for you' (9.7b; Gen. 21.12). The fact that Paul introduces this quotation only with ἀλλ', substituting it for the natural grammatical completion of the sentence, shows that he assumes his audience is familiar with Scripture and will recognize it as a scriptural citation.[125] Moreover, Paul is clearly pointing back to the broad Old Testament context, for without knowledge of the Abraham-Isaac story the import of the quotation is lost. Indeed, as John Piper has noted, 'Most commentators agree that the OT quotations in Rom. 9.6–13 assume an acquaintance with the whole story of which they are a part and that without this knowledge the isolated quotations would be virtually unintelligible as part of the argument.'[126] The intimate connection of Gen. 21.12 to Gen. 18.10, 14 within the Genesis narrative itself confirms that Paul is pointing to the broad context of his quotations.

On the simplest rhetorical level, Paul uses Gen. 21.12 as the positive expression of the principle that not all of Abraham's physical children are his seed (9.7a), which is itself an interpretive expansion upon the principle that not all who are from Israel are Israel (9.6b). Thus, Gen. 21.12, along with 9.6b–7a, serves as a ground for Paul's programmatic statement in 9.6a that the word of God has not failed. As the positive statement of the general principle expressed in 9.6b–7a, emphasized by the strong adversative ἀλλ', the weight of Paul's argument comes to rest on Gen. 21.12. It may be regarded as the main ground for 9.6a. How Gen. 21.12 can mean that God's word has not failed is revealed by 9.8 which explains the quotation – 'That is, it is not the children of the

125. Cf. Gal. 3.11–12; Cranfield, *Romans*, 474; and more generally, Ellis, 'Interpretation', 697. It is inaccurate to say that Paul indicates this citation by syntactical dislocation as would Stanley, *Paul*, 56–57; Wagner, *Heralds*, 49 n. 17. Rather, the syntactical dissonance created by Paul's citation results from his assumption that his audience will recognize the quotation as such.

126. Piper, *Justification*, 60 n. 27.

flesh who are children of God, but the children of the promise are regarded as seed.' Since Gen. 21.12 positively sums up the negative assertions of 9.6b–7a, we can also say that 9.8 explains all of 9.6b–7. This is evident from the parallel structure of the two sections.[127] 9.6–7 states two negative assertions followed by a contrasting positive statement. 9.8 makes a negative assertion in the peculiar fashion of the two negative statements in 9.6–7,[128] placing the negative at the beginning of the sentence, followed by a contrasting positive statement. Consequently, Paul's summation of his defense of God's faithfulness to this point is that only the children of the promise are regarded as seed. We can gain greater insight into this statement as well as Paul's argument generally by attending to his use of Gen. 21.12.

It is striking that the original context of Gen. 21.12 emphasizes both the reliability/fulfillment of God's word of promise, and the rejection of Ishmael,[129] Abraham's physical seed/son. It is so striking because these are among Paul's main themes – the faithfulness of God's word and the rejection of ethnic Israel. The quotation is part of God's assurance to Abraham meant to encourage him to expel Ishmael. It is actually a word of comfort prompted by Abraham's great grief at the thought of expelling his own son, the reason given for the divine directive not to be distressed. Paul now quotes it in response to his own great grief at the apparent rejection of ethnic Israel. This suggests that Paul's argument in 9.6ff. is meant to soothe the grief of his lament in 9.1–5 which introduces the argument. The main word of comfort is that Isaac is the one through whom Abraham's covenant seed will be named. This itself is related to God's central promise of seed to Abraham most fully recorded in Gen. 17.19–20 and 18.10, 14. To cast Ishmael out could potentially threaten God's promise to Abraham since he was his seed in a physical sense. But God reminds Abraham that Isaac is the heir and covenant identifier. So this word of comfort and encouragement is one which affirms the reliability of God's promise.

The significance of the intertextual comfort motif is not to be underestimated. It connects Paul's answer (Gen. 21.12) to the problem of the apparent failure of God's promises in the rejection of ethnic Israel in an

---

127. See Piper, *Justification*, 67, for a detailed demonstration of this parallelism. Cf. Brandenburger, 'Schriftauslegung', 10; Lübking, *Paulus*, 62–63; Schmitt, *Gottesgerechtigkeit*, 77–78.

128. Cf. Piper, *Justification*, 67.

129. Cf. B.D. Chilton, 'Romans 9–11 as Scriptural Interpretation and Dialogue with Judaism', *Ex Auditu* 4 (1988), 27–37 (28).

even more direct way than is usually recognized, rendering the two inseparable. Therefore, we cannot hold that Paul ultimately answers the problem by asserting that all of ethnic Israel will eventually be saved without robbing Gen. 21.12 of its force. That would essentially nullify this portion of Paul's argument. But the intertextual resonance created by Paul's quotation of Gen. 21.12 calls for embracing the rejection of Israel. In a sense, Paul and his readers are called to expel Israel as an ethnic people from its place in their minds and hearts as the elect covenant people and heir.

There is another reason that God gives to ease Abraham's distress – the promise of a measure of blessing to the nonetheless rejected Ishmael (Gen. 21.13).[130] This promise epitomizes Paul's consistent approach of acknowledging privilege and blessing to the Jews while maintaining that their ancestry does not guarantee them the *covenant* blessing.[131] It also appears to have influenced Paul's understanding of the role of ethnic Israel in salvation history, anticipating the argument in Romans 9–11 that Israel as an ethnic entity is rejected from the covenant, but still experiences the blessing of God to an extent, and has an important role in God's plan. Just as Isaac, the child of promise, was heir to the covenant promises, and Ishmael, Abraham's physical offspring, was rejected from the covenant yet granted temporal blessing, so those who believe in Christ are heirs to the eschatological Abrahamic covenantal blessings, while Jews qua ethnic Israel are rejected from those blessings but still granted special advantage and privilege.

Ironically, the fulfillment of the Abrahamic covenant and promise means the rejection of Abraham's physical descendants in keeping with the distinguishing nature of God's word to him. Just as with Abraham and Ishmael, the rejection of ethnic Israel is necessary for God to fulfill his promise. But this brings extreme grief and calls forth the promise of a measure of blessing for the rejected. Surprisingly, as with Abraham

---

130. Cranfield, *Romans*, 475, recognizes that the Genesis narrative affirms God's blessing upon Ishmael, but does not develop the point except to say that it indicates that Ishamel is not excluded from God's mercy. Cosgrove, *Elusive*, 71, develops the point more substantially and perceptively (cf. Schreiner, *Romans*, 497 n. 16). Berkley, *Broken*, 163–70, develops the point still more substantially. By all but denying any real significance to God's blessing upon Ishmael for Paul's argument, Schreiner, 497, and Moo, *Romans*, 576, ignore the clear thematic correspondence between the two contexts and the importance of the whole story which is so obviously invoked by the quotation of Gen. 21.12 and 18.10, 14.

131. See Rom. 1.16; 3.1–2; cf. Acts 13.46; 18.6; 19.8–9; 26.23–28.

and Ishmael, the promise, which implies Israel's rejection, also implies the further demonstration of God's faithfulness to them, as Paul eventually reveals that the election of the Gentiles is God's means of provoking Jews to faith in Christ and consequent membership in the true Israel (11.11ff.). This leads us to yet another ironic point deriving from the Genesis narrative – that Ishmael, and now Israel, can eventually be included in the Abrahamic covenant because it had the ultimate purpose of bringing its blessing to all nations.[132]

Timothy Berkley has presented a thoughtful assessment of Paul's handling of Ishmael in Romans 9 which can partially complement what we have already said.[133] He asserts:

> In Paul's exegesis Ishmael represents the first in a line of displaced first-born children who make up a 'second line' of inheritance estranged from the covenant. They are estranged until Paul weaves his reference texts together to show how the second line regains status as children of God/children of Abraham in Romans 9. Paul does not include Ishmael in the promise in so many words. But he does include gentiles, for whom Ishmael serves as the first representative, shown by the fact that the themes Paul develops in Romans 9 are embedded in Ishmael's story.[134]

Berkley is to be commended for seeing some of the potential importance of Ishmael for Paul's exegesis. But his understanding of Ishmael's importance is somewhat flawed. His view falters on a misunderstanding of Genesis. Ishmael was not specifically re-included in the promise to Abraham. Ishmael had special status before God and special blessing from him because he was Abraham's physical seed, but he was excluded from the Abrahamic covenant (Gen. 17.18–21; 21.10ff.).[135] So in Romans 9, he stands more for those who are rejected by God covenantally, but still experience a measure of blessing. He is the pattern for non-believing Israel.

But, it is true that Jewish tradition associated Ishmael and Esau with the Gentiles,[136] and Paul probably did so here in a secondary sense.

132. Cosgrove, *Elusive*, 71, has also seen this point.
133. See Berkley, *Broken*, 163–70.
134. Berkley, *Broken*, 169.
135. Cf. Schreiner, *Romans*, 497, and Moo, *Romans*, 576, who make similar points.
136. Genesis 37; Ps. 83.7 (Eng. 83.6); *Jub.* 15.30–32; 16.16–18; cf. *Ned* 31a. S. Lyonnet, 'Le rôle d'Israël dans l'histoire du salut selon Rom. 9–11', in S. Lyonnet, *Etudes sur l'Epître aux Romains* (AnBib, 120; Rome: Editrice Pontifico Instituto Biblico, 1989), 264–73 (266), points out that Esau and his descendants became the type of the enemies of Israel, citing Amos 1.11; Obadiah; Ps. 137.7.

Even in that sense, Ishmael, in his association with the Gentiles in Genesis itself, theoretically gets back into God's covenantal blessing because the Abrahamic promise included blessing upon Gentiles. But for Paul, ironically, this is how unbelieving Israel gets back in. So Berkley has seen a valid aspect of the significance of Ishmael for Paul, but it is a secondary significance. His treatment suffers from lack of serious exegesis of Genesis 17, 21, and Romans 9.[137] But his analysis helps show the polyvalent nature of Paul's symbols/types/examples. Ishmael's story is complex enough to make him a type of anyone who is excluded from the covenant, whether Jew or Gentile. But he most closely typifies the physical descendant of Abraham who is excluded. That is the main course Paul follows in Romans 9. Nevertheless, just as for Paul the rejected Jew can be identified with the Gentile due to their common plight of separation from God (9.24–26; cf. Rom. 2–4), so Ishmael can subtly point toward the inclusion of the Gentiles even while proclaiming the inclusion of Jews. That is one more factor that makes the Abraham narrative of Genesis ideal for Paul's theological treatment of God's faithfulness *vis-à-vis* Israel, the Church, Jews, and Gentiles.

As we have already said, Rom. 9.8 gives Paul's explanation of Gen. 21.12, and hence of his whole argument thus far in support of the assertion of 9.6a. Therefore, it is crucial to understand the precise meaning of this verse. The first question of interpretation to address regards the meaning of τὰ τέκνα τῆς σαρκός. This is a relatively easy identification due to the use of the phrase κατὰ σάρκα in 9.3, 5 to indicate physical descent or relationship.[138] The meaning of τέκνα τοῦ θεοῦ is also simply determined. It is almost self-evident that the phrase refers to those who belong to God and are the recipients of all of his saving blessings. For Paul, that means those who believe in Christ. He develops the concept quite explicitly in ch. 8. There he emphasizes that children of God are those who have received the eschatological blessing of the Spirit and who are heirs together with Christ of the glory of

---

137. For further critique, see Abasciano, 'Paul's Use', 324 n. 157.

138. Cf. the use of τὴν σάρκα in 11.14 to indicate kinsmen/ethnic relatives. κατὰ σάρκα also refers to physical descent in 1.3 and 4.1. Its repeated use in ch. 8 is more complex and theological, but not completely unrelated to ethnic realities. It is interesting to note that σάρξ is used heavily in LXX Genesis 17 (see vv. 11, 14, 24–25) of the physical flesh in which circumcision was performed, a passage which is closely related to the passage Paul quotes from. The overtones emanating from Genesis 17 mediated to Romans 9 through its close relationship to Genesis 18 and 21 help attach a connotation of Law-keeping as well as ethnicity to σάρξ in this latter context.

God.[139] This is directly related to what we have seen in Gen. 21.12 where the issue is inheritance of the covenant blessing, yet another line of evidence that, for Paul, the Abrahamic covenant promises are eschatological and salvific.

A more difficult question is the meaning of τὰ τέκνα τῆς ἐπαγγελίας. Perhaps the safest starting point in ascertaining the designation's meaning is to compare it to the contrasting concept, τὰ τέκνα τῆς σαρκός. We have just seen that this latter designation means 'physical children', a genitive of description. If we apply this to the former phrase the meaning is 'children characterized by promise'.[140] While this is probably correct, the meaning still remains vague, and there are other types of genitives that are compatible with this basic sense that will yield greater clarity. So I would like to suggest that this is a genitive of description bearing several nuances which can be gleaned from two passages in Galatians where Paul deals with similar material, and of course, from the broader context of Romans and the intertext of Genesis.

In Gal. 3.26–29,[141] Paul speaks to a predominantly Gentile congregation, telling them, 'for you are all sons of God [υἱοὶ θεοῦ] through faith in Christ Jesus' (v. 26) and that 'if you are of Christ, then you are seed of Abraham [τοῦ Ἀβραὰμ σπέρμα], heirs according to promise' (v. 29). Here we have the collocation of the concepts of sonship (= τέκνα

---

139. The basic phrase τέκνα/τέκνων θεοῦ is found elsewhere in Paul only in Rom. 8.16, 21 and Phil. 2.15. As implied above, the Romans 8 context is determinative for Paul's usage here. But the Philippians passage is also noteworthy, for there Paul alludes to Deut. 32.5, which is part of the Song of Moses, which Paul later quotes (Rom. 10.19) and has been identified by some as particularly influential on his argument throughout chs. 9–11 (e.g., Bell, *Provoked*). Intriguingly, Deut. 32.5 declares that the people of Israel are not God's children because of their sinfulness in the context of a declaration of God's faithfulness and justice (32.4). In Phil. 2.15, Paul inverts this passage by applying the opposite assertion to his (predominantly Gentile) Philippian church; see G.D. Fee, *Paul's Letter to the Philippians* (NICNT; Grand Rapids: Eerdmans, 1995), 245.

140. Moo, *Romans*, 576 n 32, words the descriptive genitival option this way, though he opts for a genitive of possession for both phrases. There is very little difference between the two. For an extended treatment of the concept of promise in Rom. 9.8 against the OT background, see Luz, *Geschichtsverständnis*, 66–70.

141. Piper, *Justification*, 68–70, draws attention to this passage in a helpful discussion of the meaning of τὰ τέκνα τῆς ἐπαγγελίας in which he also highlights Gal. 4.21–31 and Rom. 2.25–29. Although his discussion is insightful, he draws some unwarranted conclusions which appear to be born from his particular theological concern to argue for individual, unconditional election.

τοῦ θεοῦ), the seed of Abraham, heirship, and promise. Being children of God is through faith in Christ, which is equivalent to being seed of Abraham, in turn equivalent to being heirs according to promise. This suggests that τὰ τέκνα τῆς ἐπαγγελίας means those who are the seed of Abraham and heirs according to promise through faith in Christ.

Gal. 4.21–31 treats the same Old Testament context dealing with Isaac and Ishmael as Rom. 9.7! In 4.23, being born according to the flesh (κατὰ σάρκα) is contrasted with being born through promise (δι' ἐπαγ-γελίας). Then, in 4.28 we encounter the same basic phrase as in Rom. 9.8, its only other occurrence in the New Testament; Paul writes to the Galatians, ὑμεῖς δέ, ἀδελφοί, κατὰ ᾽Ισαὰκ ἐπαγγελίας τέκνα ἐστέ. Now the following verse contrasts being born according to the flesh with being born according to the Spirit (κατὰ πνεῦμα), implying that being children of promise means to be born through or according to the Spirit.[142] In the context of Galatians, to be born according to the Spirit especially means to have received the promised Spirit by exercising faith in Christ. Children of promise are those who believe in Christ and are conse-quently incorporated into Christ, made children of God and therefore heirs, and thus have received the Spirit of Christ, the Spirit of adoption and heirship (Gal. 3.1–14; 4.4–7).

When we return to Romans, we find that ch. 4 emphasizes that those who believe in Christ become the promised seed of Abraham and heirs. Romans 8 also emphasizes the Spirit, sonship, and heirship. Possession of the Spirit of God/Christ indicates that one belongs to Christ (8.9), and the Spirit is the spirit of adoption, meaning heirship also. The argu-ment of Romans to this point gives every indication that those who have the Spirit and who are children and heirs are those who have believed in Christ. Thus all the evidence points to understanding τὰ τέκνα τῆς ἐπαγ-γελίας as those who have believed in Christ and so received the Spirit of adoption and heirship. They are children of God who have been born through (believing) promise and by (God's effecting of his) promise, promised children who are also heirs to promise. In sum, they are children characterized by promise in every way.

The idea of children born both through faith in God's promise and by God bringing his promise to pass is supported by the Genesis context, which Paul will go on to quote from again as a ground for the assertion of 9.8. There God promises Isaac's birth, and then shows forth his power by sovereignly bringing it about over against Sarah's doubt of his word

142. Piper, *Justification*, 69.

(cf. Gen. 18.14). Abraham is also presented as believing God's promise of a son by Sarah. At least that is how Paul understood it in Romans 4.19–22, where he interestingly considers this to be justifying faith in fulfillment of Gen. 15.6.[143] He also regarded faith as the means through which Abraham would obtain fulfillment of the promise of innumerable descendants (4.18; cf. Gen. 15.5; 17.4–5). Thus Isaac was a child/seed characterized by promise, promised to Abraham, and born both through Abraham's faith in God's promise and by the means of God's sovereign power.

The mention of Romans 4 leads us to consider the use of the verb λογίζομαι in 9.8, since it is used extensively (11x) in the former location. There it refers to God's reckoning of those who believe in Christ to be righteous, and thus heirs of the promise to Abraham, equivalent to the seed of Abraham.[144] Those who are merely ethnic descendants of Abraham (roughly equal to οἱ ἐκ νόμου) are not heirs, but those who are of the faith of Abraham (τῷ ἐκ πίστεως ᾿Αβραάμ) are. While λογίζεται in 9.8 may emphasize God's sovereign freedom in election as commonly suggested,[145] it also reveals that God's call in Paul's argument refers to a designation or naming, i.e., a divine reckoning of election. Stemming from Romans 4, the resonant connotation of the word in collocation with seed and promise is to reckon, regard, or identify those who believe in Christ as the true seed of Abraham, who are heir to God's promise to him. Gen. 21.12 makes it clear that the seed referred to is the *covenant* seed of Abraham.[146]

The verb κληθήσεται in Paul's quotation of LXX Gen. 21.12 clearly has the meaning 'to name/recognize/identify/designate'. It translates the Hebrew verb קרא which has the same meaning. The intent of Gen. 21.12 in both the MT and the LXX is to indicate that Abraham's covenant descendants would be identified by descent from Isaac. There is little

143. Romans 4 is especially relevant to 9.8, which recalls the former chapter through the repetition of key vocabulary – ἐπαγγελία, λογίζεται, and σπέρμα (Dunn, *Romans*, 541).

144. Τῷ σπέρματι in v. 13 = κληρονόμοι in v. 14. This use of λογίζομαι supports the position of Wright, *Climax*, 148, 203, 214, and others that the language of justification in Paul refers to covenant membership.

145. See e.g., Cranfield, *Romans*, 476.

146. Wright's (*Climax*; idem, 'Romans and the Theology of Paul', in Hay and Johnson (eds.), *Pauline*, 30–67) depiction of Paul as a covenant theologian is right on target, and finds corroboration from our investigation. Cf. Hays' ('Covenant', 84) call for such exegetical corroboration of Wright's approach.

doubt that this is the meaning of the term in Genesis. But is this its meaning in Romans 9?

Most notably, Cranfield has argued for this understanding.[147] But the editors of BDAG have suggested that in Rom. 9.7 the sense of the verb approaches that of 'to be' and translates, 'in (through) Isaac you are to have your descendants'.[148] However, this ignores the LXX attempt to translate קרא and the depth of Paul's engagement with the Genesis narrative. Moreover, the BDAG editors actually make a point of emphasis here, and do not deny the naming sense to the verb.[149] 'Very oft. the emphasis is to be placed less on the fact that the name is such and such, than on the fact that the bearer of the name actually is what the name says about him.'[150] But it must be remembered that the depiction of existential state derives from the name/naming and cannot be separated from it. BDAG leaves determination of the proper emphasis in translation to the subjective feeling of the interpreter. But we have two objective factors which help fix the sense of 'name/identify'.

The first is the Old Testament background already discussed. There the verb clearly means 'to name', just as it does in Paul's quotations from Hos. 2.25 and 2.1 (Heb./LXX) in 9.25–26. It is true that both the Hebrew and LXX Greek can bear a fuller meaning in which the name expresses character or existence; that is the case here. But as implied above, this is a fuller use of the term rather than an alternative, and translating more weakly by 'to be' obscures the richness of the term and the derivation of the contemplated character of the resulting state of existence. Second, Rom. 9.8, which interprets 9.7b/Gen. 21.12, uses the term λογίζομαι ('to reckon/regard') in place of καλέω. Therefore, we have solid contextual evidence that Paul took 9.7's κληθήσεται in the sense 'be named/regarded'.

Some commentators would retain the sense of call as a creative summons of God to become part of his people.[151] Schreiner points to Rom. 4.17 where καλέω appears to mean 'call/summon into existence'.[152] But upon closer examination, it is rather the naming sense which

147. Cranfield, *Romans*, 474. Cf. Dunn, *Romans*, 540–41; Zeller, *Juden*, 119 n. 155.

148. BDAG, 503; italics removed.

149. Moo, *Romans*, 575, appears to miss this point.

150. BDAG, 503.

151. Moo, *Romans*, 575–76; Schreiner, *Romans*, 495–96; cf. Dunn, *Romans*, 540–41; Byrne, *Sons*, 131ff.

152. Schreiner, *Romans*, 495–96.

stands behind the verb in this instance. The phrase in question literally reads: 'before whom he believed, God who gives life to the dead and calls the things not existing as existing' (κατέναντι οὗ ἐπίστευσεν θεοῦ τοῦ ζωοποιοῦντος τοὺς νεκροὺς καὶ καλοῦντος τὰ μὴ ὄντα ὡς ὄντα). Rather than the idea of God summoning things into existence *per se*, the thought is of a designation which effects the new existence, as at the original creation. The ὡς and participle support such an interpretation,[153] as does the fact that a summoning sense requires us to imagine the divine word as addressed to things which do not exist.[154] Even if a summoning sense be maintained, the Old Testament background and the immediate context are of even greater weight for determining the meaning of καλέω in 9.7 than is the possible echo of 4.17. But if we are correct, then the echo of 4.17 becomes even more significant, for in the context of Paul's argument there, the call of God which creates refers not only to the promised birth of Isaac,[155] but even more directly to Abraham's seed/heirs who will inherit his divine promise, both Jew and Gentile, 4.17 supporting 4.16. The designating call of God establishes its multi-ethnic objects as his (Abrahamic) covenant people.

This naming sense has considerable import for understanding Paul's argument in Romans 9.[156] A problem with many readings of Romans 9 is that the crucial concept of calling is understood as a creative summons rather than a creative naming. When we understand that a creative naming is at issue, we can see more clearly that Paul's argument does

153.   Cranfield, *Romans*, 244, admits the difficulty of ὡς for the common translation, but suggests it expresses consequence, a rare meaning in the NT and an awkward fit here. But ὡς fits comfortably with καλέω in its common function of introducing a characteristic quality of a thing: 'calling the things not existing as/to be existing' (see BDAG, 1104–05; *UBSGNT* dictionary).

154.   This is not impossible, just less likely than a meaning which does not require such an awkward metaphor. Philo's phraseology in *Spec. Leg.* 4.187 (τὰ γὰρ μὴ ὄντα ἐκάλεσεν εἰς τὸ εἶναι) could be adduced in support of this idea. But notice that his construction lacks ὡς and a participle. The construction, εἰς τό + infinitive is best seen as denoting result here so that the phrase refers to God's declaration (not summons) which results in existence.

155.   Schreiner, *Romans*, 495.

156.   J.-N. Aletti, *Israël et la loi dans la lettre aux romains* (LD, 173; Paris: Cerf, 1998), 173 n. 2, considers the divine call concept to be the thread which ties the different arguments of Romans 9 together, and thus more important to the argument than the concept of election. Cf. Cerfaux, 'privilège', 11, who finds that καλεῖν can indicate election, though rarely.

concern who is truly elect of God, i.e., who bears the name/status of God's covenant people who are heir to the covenant promises.[157] So when Paul takes up God's justice in how he has fulfilled his promises, he is defending God's right to designate the Church as his covenant people, based not on ethnicity but on faith (hence, 9.12, οὐκ ἐξ ἔργων ἀλλ' ἐκ τοῦ καλοῦντος), rather than God's right to choose some to summon to become part of his people. The latter lends to a Calvinistic predestinarian emphasis in the passage, while the former finds such an emphasis foreign to the text.[158] This conception sees that corporate election and heirship are at issue, not individual salvation *per se*, though the former directly impinges on the latter; the individual's salvation depends on whether or not he is part of the elect people. For Paul, calling and election are closely related. Calling is the application and appellation of election, the act of designating a group as God's elect people. This should inform our understanding of calling in 9.12 and finds confirmation near the end of the chapter in the Hosea quotations which bear the same naming sense (9.24–26).

Excursus: The Implications of Calling in Genesis 21.12 and Romans 9 for Understanding the Concept in the Rest of the New Testament

The naming sense of the call concept evident in Gen. 21.12 and Romans 9 is suggestive for our understanding of the idea in the rest of the New Testament. The concept has two basic senses in the New Testament, exemplified by the two basic senses of the key term, the verb καλέω: (1) to name/identify/designate; (2) to invite/summon.[159] It is typically

---

157.   Kee's (*Knowing*, 5, 63, 70–102) conclusion (following Segal and Neusner) that community identity was the central issue between early Christianity and Judaism in the first century strengthens our conclusions concerning the nature of calling and the concern of Paul's argument in Romans 9–11. See also Walters, *Ethnic Issues*, 20.

158.   Contrast Müller's (*Gerechtigkeit*, 78–79) treatment of καλεῖν as a term of predestination in Romans 9–11, referring to a call which creates faith in the individual. Berger, 'Abraham', 83, supports our understanding of Paul's argument as having to do with defending God's right to elect based on faith. He rightly argues that Paul's use of Abraham in Romans 9 does not differ at its core from his usage of Abraham in Romans 4.

159.   As my use of multiple terms shows, there are various nuances within these two basic meanings. But they all fit under the basic rubrics of naming or summoning, and we will use these broad designations for the sake of simplicity.

assumed that the figurative/theological concept of calling developed from the summoning sense of the terminology.[160] The Christian calling *vis-à-vis* salvation or service is generally understood to be a divine summons or invitation to that salvation or service, a call which many take to be effectual or creative. But, since Paul regards God's call as a naming in Romans 9, it behooves us to reassess the figurative concept of calling in the Pauline corpus and the rest of the New Testament. I would submit that the figurative Christian calling did not develop from the summoning denotation, but from the naming sense, and refers to God's designation of the Christian community as the elect people of God, his beloved children, who, as members of his family, bear the name of God and his Christ.[161] The calling of the individual Christian would refer to her coming to share in the name and attendant blessings of the eschatological messianic community upon entrance into the community at conversion. In terms of speech-act theory, such naming is performative language which transforms the status of its objects as well as their objective and existential reality.[162] More specifically, naming is a perlocutionary act which may be identified as a verdictive or declarative utterance, an ontological and institutional action of God which effects a new state of existence and brings about a divinely actuated 'world-to-word-fit'.

The verb καλέω occurs 148 times in the New Testament, the noun κλῆσις, 11 times, and the adjective κλητός, 10 times. The naming sense occurs far more often in the use of the verb than does the summoning sense. I have identified 78 indisputable cases of the former,[163]

---

160.   See e.g., BDAG, 503 (4). Among the standard dictionary articles, J. Eckert, 'καλέω, κλῆσις, κλητός', *EDNT*, 2.240–44 (241), is notable for showing awareness of the naming sense of calling in relation to salvation, though he does not explore the ramifications of the observation. For what may be the most extensive treatment of Paul's concept of calling, see now S.J. Chester, *Conversion at Corinth: Perspectives on Conversion in Paul's Theology and the Corinthian Church* (SNTW; London: T&T Clark, 2003).

161.   W.W. Klein, 'Paul's Use of *KALEIN*: A Proposal', *JETS* 27/1 (March 1984), 53–64, has argued this same basic point with respect to Paul's thought alone in a provocative article which has not received enough attention, and less technically in his *The New Chosen People: A Corporate View of Election* (Grand Rapids: Zondervan, 1990), 199–209.

162.   On speech-act theory in biblical interpretation, see Thiselton, *Hermeneutics*, 16–19, 282–312, 361–67; Vanhoozer, *Meaning*.

163.   Mt. 1.21, 23, 25; 2.23; 5.9, 19 (2x); 21.13; 22.43, 45; 23.7, 8, 9, 10; 27.8; Lk. 1.13, 31, 32, 35, 36, 59, 60, 61, 62, 76; 2.4, 21 (2x), 23; 6.15, 46; 7.11; 8.2; 9.10; 10.39; 15.19, 21; 19.2, 29; 20.44; 21.37; 22.3; 22.25; 23.33; Jn 1.42; Acts 1.12, 19, 23; 3.11;

34 instances of the latter,[164] and 36 cases which are usually considered instances of divine summoning, but are uncertain in light of the present argument.[165] It is my contention that all or almost all[166] of these are instances of the naming of Christians, whether this take the form of explicit identification (as in the undisputed 1 Jn 3.1) or appointment (e.g., Heb. 5.4) or some other nuance. The same holds true for every occurrence of κλῆσις and κλητός with the sole exception of Mt. 22.14, where κλητός clearly means 'invited'.[167]

When we posit the naming sense of call for the passages traditionally understood as a summons, we find that it makes even better sense. So in Rom. 1.1 and 1 Cor. 1.1 Paul is a called/designated apostle and his Roman readers are named/designated Christians among the Gentiles (Rom. 1.6), that is, they are designated/identified as Christ's; they are named/identified his holy ones (Rom. 1.7; cf. 1 Cor. 1.2). For the Corinthians to consider their calling was for them to consider the time of their conversion (1 Cor. 1.26), when they were designated children of God or saints. They were to remain in the life situation they were in when they were called, that is, became Christians/were designated as God's

---

4.18; 7.58; 8.10; 9.11; 10.1; 13.1; 14.12; 15.22; 15.37; 27.8, 14, 16; 28.1; Rom. 9.7, 25, 26; 1 Cor. 15.9; Heb. 2.11; 3.13; 11.18; Jas 2.23; 1 Pet. 3.6; 1 Jn 3.1; Rev. 1.9; 11.8; 12.9; 16.16; 19.11, 13.

164.   Mt. 2.7, 15; 4.21; 9.13; 20.8; 22.3 (2x), 4, 8, 9; 25.14; Mk 1.20; 2.17; 3.31; 11.17; Lk. 5.32; 7.39; 14.7, 8 (2x), 9, 10 (2x), 12, 13, 16, 17, 24; 19.13; Jn 2.2; Acts 24.2; 1 Cor. 10.27; Heb. 11.8; Rev. 19.9.

165.   Rom. 4.17; 8.30 (2x); 9.12, 24; 1 Cor. 1.9; 7.15, 17, 18 (2x), 20, 21, 22, 24; Gal. 1.6, 15; 5.8, 13; Eph. 4.1, 4; Col. 3.15; 1 Thess. 2.12; 4.7; 5.24; 2 Thess. 2.14; 1 Tim. 6.12; 2 Tim. 1.9; Heb. 5.4; 9.15; 1 Pet. 1.15; 2.9, 21; 3.9; 5.10; 2 Pet. 1.3. It should be noted that the following discussion is limited mostly, but not exclusively, to these disputed cases, precisely because they are disputed.

166.   The fact that we are dealing with what is widely recognized as technical terminology (see e.g., K.L. Schmidt, 'καλέω, κλῆσις, κλητός', *TDNT*, 3.487–96 [489]) pushes for a relatively uniform meaning throughout the figurative use of the terms.

167.   Mt. 22.14 has puzzled some scholars who assume that it refers to an effectual summons, but recognizing that the term means 'invited' in accordance with the cognate verb in the rest of the passage removes the difficulty. 1 Cor. 7.20 is also an exception of sorts, where κλῆσις might mean something like 'situation in life' (cf. BDAG, 549). But even if so, the question still remains whether this meaning derives from naming or summoning. I would argue that it relies on naming, an appointment to a life situation rather than a summons to it. κλῆσις appears in Rom. 11.29; 1 Cor. 1.26; 7.20; Eph. 1.18; 4.1, 4; Phil. 3.14; 2 Thess. 1.11; 2 Tim. 1.9; Heb. 3.1; 2 Pet. 1.10; and κλητός in Mt. 22.14; Rom. 1.1, 6, 7; 8.28; 1 Cor. 1.1, 2, 24; Jude 1; Rev. 17.14.

own (1 Cor. 7.15–24). And the addressees of 1 Peter were called/designated (children) by the Holy Father God, and therefore were to be holy as he (1 Pet. 1.14–17). While we could multiply examples, these should suffice to make the point.

Intriguingly, name/naming language and familial themes often occur in connection with the call concept. Paul's identity as a called apostle, received through Jesus Christ, the *Son* of God, had its ultimate purpose in bringing glory to the *name* (τοῦ ὀνόματος) of Jesus Christ (Rom. 1.1–5), as did the called status of Paul's Roman addressees (1.5–6), to whom Paul conveyed grace and peace from God the *Father* (1.7). God's call creates the promised *descendants/family* of Abraham, who is the *father* of all who believe (Rom. 4.16–17). Those who are called according to God's purpose are those who have been predestined to conformity to the image of his *Son*, and who are his *brothers* (Rom. 8.28–29). Israel is beloved for the sake of the *fathers* (τοὺς πατέρας), 'for the gifts and the calling of God are irrevocable' (Rom. 11.28–29). The called saints of Corinth call upon the *name* of the Lord Jesus Christ. Those who were called for the purpose of fellowship with the *Son* of God, are exhorted as *brothers* by his *name* (1 Cor. 1.9–10). And the Corinthians are exhorted as *brothers* to consider their calling. The author of Ephesians grounds his exhortation to walk in a manner worthy of the calling with which his readers were called (4.1) with his prayer and doxology addressed to 'the *Father* from whom the whole *family* [πατριά] in heaven and on earth is *named* [ὀνομάζεται]' (Eph. 3.14–15),[168] a calling which is connected to the one God and *Father* (4.4, 6). The Colossians, who were called in (the) one body (of Christ; 3.15), were to do everything in the *name* of the Lord Jesus, giving thanks to God the *Father* through him (3.17). Paul encouraged the Thessalonians as a *father* would his own *children* to walk worthy of the God who called them (1 Thess. 2.11–12). Perhaps the most striking example comes in 2 Thess. 2.11–12, where being worthy of their calling is part of what will result in the *name* of the Lord Jesus being glorified in the Thessalonian believers, and their being glorified in him. Here worthiness of the calling is directly related to bringing glory to the name of the Lord Jesus, most likely because

---

168.   Most translations translate πᾶσα πατριά as 'every family' in accordance with normal Greek grammar, but the construction is best understood as 'a Hebraism which has affected Koine usage' (see A.T. Lincoln, *Ephesians* [WBC, 42; Dallas: Word, 1990], 156, on the construction in Eph. 2.21, though he does not see such influence in 3.15) in light of the prior content of the epistle which emphasizes the unity of Jews and Gentiles in Christ who have been raised up with Christ into the heavenlies (2:6).

that is the name they bear. Their worthy conduct brings honor to the family name. They are *brothers* who were called with a view toward gaining the glory of the Lord Jesus Christ and upon whose behalf God the *Father* was invoked to give them comfort and strength (2 Thess. 4.14–17). The author of Hebrews considered Christians to be the *seed* of Abraham, *brothers* of Jesus, and holy *brothers* who partake of a heavenly calling (Heb. 2.16–3.1). Indeed, 'both the one who sanctifies and those who are sanctified are all from one; for which reason he is not ashamed to *call* them *brothers*, saying, 'I will proclaim your *name* to my *brothers* . . . '(Heb. 2.11–12). 1 Pet. 3.8–9 encourages the type of *brotherly* love (φιλάδελφοι) which returns a blessing for a curse as the purpose of the Christian calling, with a greater purpose of inheriting a blessing. And Jude 1 regards those who are the called as beloved in God the *Father*. Familial language in connection to calling may also be found in Eph. 1.17–18 (the *Father* of glory), Phil. 3.13–14 (brothers), and 1 Thess. 4.5–6 (brother).

Why all this appellative and familial language in contexts which speak of calling? I would suggest that mention of the name of Jesus Christ as a name appears as much as it does because those who have been called, those who belong to Christ, have been called by his name as his own people, so that they bear his name and have become his family; being in him who is the Son of God, they have become God's children as well, brothers and sisters of Jesus and one another. As bearers of the divine name, their behavior will bring honor or disgrace to the family name.[169] Therefore, exhortations to holy and righteous living which are often the purpose of calling might appeal to the family name/namer, and familial address is often used as an implicit appeal to the familial relationship effected by the naming of the messianic community.

The fact that the theological concept of calling almost always describes Christians and often relates to Christian conversion or existence also argues strongly for the naming sense in such cases. This does not make the summoning sense impossible, but it does render it less likely than naming. For use of the concept as a designation for Christians and their life adheres more closely to a corresponding sense of designation than to one of summons. Moreover, the summoning sense requires an additional conceptual step to arrive at the intended meaning; it requires adding the idea of response to the call so that call

---

169. On the importance and significance of, and connections between, honor, family, and name in the socio-cultural milieu of the first-century Mediterranean world, see Malina, *World*, 28–62.

means something like 'the summons you heard and responded to', and calling, 'the summons which you responded to', and called, 'having responded to the divine summons'. This seems less likely than an explanation which does not necessitate an additional idea, but simply refers to the effective act of naming.[170]

One might object to this understanding of calling because the concept is often presented in relation to a goal (e.g. 2 Thess. 2.14; 1 Tim. 6.12) or to present privilege or responsibility (e.g. Col. 3.15; 1 Cor. 7.15; Gal. 5.13), which makes good sense as a summons *to/toward* the goal, privilege or responsibility. However, these passages make just as good sense, even better in light of the evidence we have reviewed, when they are understood as speaking of the purpose or goal of the naming. It is not a summons to or toward something, but an appointment to[171] or a naming for/with a view toward some responsibility or blessing. The prepositions used in such cases can bear any of these meanings.[172] In some cases, it is clear that purpose is in view, as for example, when the construction εἰς τοῦτο is used (1 Pet. 2.21; 3.9).[173]

A more substantial objection may be made on the basis of three passages in which the preposition εἰς looks like it means 'into', either because of a possible spatial metaphor (in two cases, 1 Pet. 2.9 and 1 Thess. 2.12) or because of the language of relationship which suggests the idea of entrance (1 Cor. 1.9). 1 Pet. 2.9 is the most forceful of these because it describes calling as out of (ἐκ) darkness, an obvious spatial metaphor, and εἰς God's marvelous light. But even here, the meaning of εἰς is more probably 'for/with a view toward'. The idea would be that God has named believers so that they are taken out of the darkness of sin and separation from God for the purpose of experiencing the light of his eternal glory (cf. 1 Pet. 5.10, ὁ καλέσας ὑμᾶς εἰς τὴν αἰώνιον αὐτοῦ δόξαν ἐν Χριστῷ). This interpretation is supported by two considerations. First, in two of the five references to calling in 1 Peter, purpose

---

170. Cf. Klein, '*KALEIN*', 57.

171. Cf. 1 Chron. 23.14 LXX where καλέω εἰς means something like 'designate to/name among'; Dan. 4.30 LXX: 'appointed to/for the purpose of'. Cf. also the use of εἰς with the verb of appointment, τάσσω, to mean 'appoint to [eternal life]' in Acts 13.48; 'designate/set/devote to' in 1 Cor. 16.15; 'set/direct to' in Hag. 1.5 LXX.

172. The usual preposition in such cases is εἰς. Among the controverted references I have identified, εἰς is used in 1 Cor. 1.9; Col. 3.15; 1 Thess. 2.12; 2 Thess. 2.14; 1 Tim. 6.12; 1 Pet. 2.9, 21; 3.9; 5.10; ἐν in 1 Cor. 7.15, 18, 22; Gal. 1.6; Eph. 4.4; Col. 3.15; ὡς in 1 Cor. 7.17; διά in Gal. 1.15; ἐπί in Gal. 5.13; 1 Thess. 4.7; and ὑπό in Heb. 5.4.

173. For εἰς τοῦτο as denoting purpose, see BDAG, 290 (4f).

is the certain meaning of attendant responsibility and blessing (2.21; 3.9), while one is not accompanied by a relevant prepositional phrase (1.15), and the other is uncertain as to whether it is a summons or naming to eternal glory (5.10). This slightly favors the idea that the author of 1 Peter would have viewed the positive side of calling in relation to its purpose rather than in relation to a sphere of destination. Secondly, the author continues his sentence with a clear allusion to Hos. 2.1 (Heb./LXX; cf. 2.25), in which καλέω clearly has a naming sense.

1 Thess. 2.12 might also contain a spatial metaphor in the reference to kingdom (βασιλείαν). But the kingdom of God is not primarily a spatial reality in the New Testament, and even if so, it would still make just as good sense for God to call with a view toward that kingdom as to call to it, especially as the call is also for his glory. Moreover, as argued above, the familial language surrounding the passage points toward our view. The situation is much the same with 1 Cor. 1.9, which states that the Corinthians were called εἰς fellowship of God's Son, Jesus Christ. It makes just as good sense to understand fellowship as the purpose of the calling as it does to take it as a reality entered into, especially since the former also implies the latter and Paul immediately goes on to exhort by the *name* of the Lord Jesus Christ.

Yet another objection might proceed from the fact that calling takes place through (διά) the gospel (2 Thess. 2.14). Must this not mean that the Thessalonians were called through the gospel summons? No, not at all. Rather it probably refers to the bestowal of the Christian name/identity upon placing their faith in the gospel message,[174] as the reference to election by faith in the truth immediately preceding suggests.

All of this drives us to call for a reappraisal of the call concept in the New Testament which recognizes that it has to do with naming rather than summoning. If this view be accepted, then the traditional notion of effectual calling would be eliminated, for it is based on the idea of a *summoning* which effectively creates the response of faith and obedience to the call. While this is not the only possible interpretation of a summoning call – it could simply be used of Christians to emphasize God's grace in inviting sinful people into his kingdom and glory – the question becomes moot when the summoning background is abandoned. The Christian call is effectual. But it does not create a response; rather it is

174. Cf. Klein, '*KALEIN*', 64.

itself a response to the faith of believers which effectually identifies them as members of the Christian covenant community, bearers of the name of God their Father and of Christ their brother.

4.7.c. *The Word of Promise: Genesis 18.10, 14 (Romans 9.9)*

Rom. 9.9 now provides the ground for the important clarification of 9.8 by showing that Isaac, the typical covenant descendant through whom the covenant descendants would be named, was indeed a child of promise. Thus bolstered, Paul's interpretation of Gen. 21.12 that only those who believe are regarded as the seed of Abraham supports God's faithfulness asserted in 9.6a, for the promise was made only to the covenant seed. The frequent observation that the predicate ἐπαγγελίας is thrust forward to the beginning of the sentence for emphasis makes Paul's stress on promise and its concomitant, faith, unmistakable. That 9.9 stands in causal relationship to 9.7–8 evidences the fact that Paul is interacting with the whole story of the Abraham narrative.

The conflation of Gen. 18.10, 14 constitutes Paul's second quotation from the Old Testament in Romans 9. Again, he does not explicitly signal the quotation but assumes that his audience will recognize it. It is directly related to the first quotation of Gen. 21.12, which originally came in the context of a fulfillment of the promise recorded in 18.10, 14. Paul makes similar use of the Genesis 18 promise as does the text of Genesis. As we have seen, the promise's fulfillment brought about the expulsion of Isaac and the ensuing divine assurance quoted by Paul. In 9.9 he similarly grounds 21.12 with 18.10, 14. Taken together, the two passages show that more than physical ancestry was at issue in Genesis since Isaac and Ishmael were both physical descendants of Abraham. The difference between them was that Isaac was born through faith in God's promise and by his miraculous intervention.

It is remarkable how well suited Gen. 18.10, 14 is to the point Paul is making, for the reliability of God's word is of paramount importance in the context of those verses. Moreover, Gen. 18.10, 14 encapsulate the height of the theme's expression in the narrative. So in its original context, the (now conflated) quotation argues for the very same point Paul is seeking to defend – the faithfulness of God's word. Gen. 18.14 points to God's omnipotence as the basis for his faithfulness. This strong affirmation of God's omnipotence echoes throughout Romans 9 and is surely reflected in the emphasis on God's sovereignty embedded in the chapter.

What is just as remarkable is that this adamant Old Testament declaration of God's faithfulness which Paul quotes is directly linked to what Paul would have considered the first and paradigmatic Old Testament theodicy – the dialogue between Abraham and YHWH over the fate of Sodom. This dialogue has several characteristics which make it important for understanding Romans 9, including its justification of God in the context of the dependability of his word, a concern for God's mercy, and a concern for the salvation of what are essentially Gentiles.

The Genesis narrative in 18.16ff. portrays Abraham as a prophet who is allowed into the mystery of the divine counsel concerning YHWH's intentions toward a people. It is in this prophetic aura that Abraham enters into intercession on behalf of the people of Sodom and Gomorrah, risking his own life. By invoking this context, Paul dresses himself in the cloak of Old Testament prophetic intercessory language, portraying himself as a prophet with privileged access to the divine counsel and privy to God's secret intentions. This metalepsis serves the rhetorical function of presenting Paul to his audience as a trustworthy interpreter of Scripture, and more than that, as himself a prophet who stands in the biblical tradition of speaking the very word of God. It is not that Paul's audience would understand him to be claiming such a status directly. But the rhetorical effect of the echo subtly casts Paul in this light, perhaps unconsciously raising the scripturally astute hearer's perception of the Apostle. Paul subtly communicates that he has prophetically ascertained the Lord's will toward Israel.

This observation confirms the estimation of others that Paul takes a prophetic stance in Romans 9–11.[175] It also sheds more light on Rom. 9.3 where Paul contemplates intercession for Israel in which he would be willing to be accursed for the sake of his kinsmen. While we have already seen that Paul probably alludes to the *locus classicus* in the Old Testament of self-sacrificial intercessory prayer (Exodus 32) in 9.3, there is no reason to choose between Genesis 18 and Exodus 32, since Paul alludes to both contexts and would have considered the two to be related, recorded by the same hand. Given the fact that the Genesis texts seem to occupy a more primary place in Paul's argument, it may be that Genesis 18 helped lead him to Exodus 32. In any case, it is significant that he alludes to both, for the former describes Abraham's intercession on behalf of Gentiles, and the latter Moses' (another prophetic figure) intercession on behalf of Israel. This is another indication that Paul is concerned not only with Israel at this point, but with both Jews and

175. See note 53 in ch. 2 above, and further references in Abasciano, 'Pauls Use', 341 n. 203.

Gentiles.[176] The irony is, as we have observed in the figure of Ishmael, that Israel is now thrown in with the Gentiles because of their rejection of Christ. Paul can now plead for God's justice and mercy towards them as Abraham did for Sodom. His allusion to the Genesis 18 context helps signal their new position.[177]

This leads us to a consideration of the fact that Gen. 18.16ff. draws attention to the blessing of the Gentiles in Abraham; all the nations of the earth will be blessed in him. Gen. 18.18 presents this motif as a reason for why YHWH will disclose his mind to Abraham. It is also the reason why he reveals the mystery of Israel to Paul, the apostle to the Gentiles (11.13). Paul appears to view himself as a means of God fulfilling this great Abrahamic promise as he seeks to bring the Gentiles to the obedience of faith (1.5). What is more, just as Abraham's divinely initiated intercession on behalf of Sodom was a proleptic fulfillment of God's promise to bless all the nations in him, so Paul's justification of God, revelation of the mystery of his will, and intercession on behalf of Israel in Romans 9–11 work toward the fulfillment of this same promise.

In our exegesis of Genesis 18 we found that the fulfillment of God's promise to make Abraham a great nation and to bless all the nations in him was the ultimate ground of his decision to demonstrate his justice through dialogue with Abraham. God's righteousness depends on his blessing all the nations in Abraham, for that is what he promised him (Gen. 12.3). Paul's transumption argues that far from being a failure of God's word or an injustice perpetrated by him, the bestowal of the blessing of Abraham upon Gentiles, which necessitates the rejection of Israel qua ethnic Israel, is necessary for God to be true to his word. God would be unrighteous otherwise. His word would indeed fall to the ground in that case. Paul saw that in order for God to fulfill his word and bless the Gentiles in Abraham he must separate ethnicity from covenant membership.[178] The great nation descended from Abraham would lose

---

176.   Contra Kuss, *Römerbrief*, 699; M. Rese, 'Israel und Kirche in Römer 9', *NTS* 34 (1988), 208–17 (212–13). Chae, *Paul*, 215ff. (see esp. 224), argues from a different but complementary perspective that Paul's argument concerns Gentiles as well as Jews from the beginning of Romans 9.

177.   Cf. Paul's quotation in 9.29 from Isa., 1.9 which refers to Sodom and Gomorrah.

178.   This insight bridges the gap between the differing approaches to the theology of Romans (which, according to Hays, 'Covenant', 71, center on the importance of covenant) of L.E. Keck, 'What Makes Romans Tick?', in Hay and Johnson

its ethnic orientation so tied up with the Law. Paul probably understood the connection between the two promises contained in Gen. 18.18 (great nation and Gentile blessing), themselves representative of all the Abrahamic promises, to be that through the great nation descended from Abraham would come the means of blessing the Gentiles – Christ, who would himself sum up the true Israel in himself, and constitute that new Israel of Jews and Gentiles who believe in him. As Philo found in Ishmael a figure of the elementary and necessary giving way to the full and complete,[179] so Paul views the necessary and truly chosen physical Israel to have given way to the fulfillment of the Church; the great nation has finally reached the height of its greatness in Christ, having shed its ethnic trappings for the righteousness of faith. This turn of events does not empty Jewish ethnic identity of some advantage; there remains a special though not superior place for the Jew.

There is a circularity to God's reasoning in Gen. 18.17–19. God chose Abraham because he would inherit God's promises, and God chose him in order to accomplish what he promised him. The significance of this circularity for Paul derives in part from the content of those promises, culminating in the blessing of the nations in Abraham. God's ultimate purpose was to establish a worldwide family through Abraham and the mighty nation descended from him. Indeed, this is the ultimate purpose of Abraham's election. From the very first utterance of God's promise to Abraham (Gen. 12.1–3), the blessing of the Gentiles appears as the climactic end of the promise. The fact that the context Paul quotes from connects election with this theme argues strongly that Paul does too in Romans 9, especially since this theme figures prominently in the epistle as a whole and fits in with a related principal theme of unity between Jew and Gentile in the Church. Rather than dealing only with Israel at this point in the argument, Paul is dealing with the relationship between Jew and Gentile, raised by the rejection of ethnic Israel and the

(eds.), *Pauline*, 3–29, and Wright, 'Theology'. For Keck's marginalization of covenant is based on what he takes to be 'Paul's fundamental concern for the salvation of all humanity' (Hays, 'Covenant', 71; emphasis removed; cf. Keck, 24). Our investigation has found that it is precisely the salvation of all humanity that Paul found to be the goal of the covenant (a point already made in Wright's essay); it was God's means of accomplishing universal salvation. This point ultimately vindicates Wright's conception of covenant as central to Paul's argument despite Dunn's ('Covenant') recent shift to denying covenant as a central category for Paul's theology.

179. Philo, *Sobr.* 8ff.; *Cher.* 3–10; cf. *Poster. C.* 130–31.

accompanying election of the Church. More precisely, he is defending God's faithfulness to his promises to Israel *vis-à-vis* his right to designate only those who believe in Christ as heirs to those promises regardless of ethnicity.

The justification of God is a most striking aspect of Gen. 18.16–19.38 in light of Paul's argument in Romans 9–11. In both passages the defense of God's justice arises out of his contemplated judgment on a people, and moves beyond an assertion of his justice to an affirmation of his mercy. Paul's emphasis on mercy in his argument may well find its first impulse in Genesis 18–19. Moreover, just as Genesis 18–19 moves from a defense of God's faithfulness to his word to a defense of his justice/righteousness, so Paul moves in his argument. It is likely that the logical connections between the two themes evident in the Old Testament context obtain in the New.

For one, the justice of God serves as a ground for the dependability of his word. Paul's audience can know that the God who is the Judge of all the earth (Gen. 18.25; cf. Rom. 3.6) only does that which is right. That means he would never go back on his word. It is unthinkable. Therefore, God's word has not fallen despite any appearance to the contrary. Secondly, God's word cannot fail because he is omnipotent. Nothing is too difficult for him (Gen. 18.14; cf. Rom. 9.19ff.; 11.33–36), so nothing can stand in his way of fulfilling his promises. Thirdly, the righteousness of God consists in the fulfillment of his promise. In both Genesis 18 and Romans 9 his promise especially comprises the inclusion of the Gentiles in the blessing of Abraham. This is in fact, the purpose of election – the righteousness/glory of God through the fulfillment of his promise in the blessing of all the nations of the world.

Abraham's entreaty in Gen. 18.22–33 is designed precisely to show that God is just and will not slay the righteous with the wicked, that he does not treat the righteous and wicked alike, and that he does not disregard the moral state of people. This suggests that Paul is not thinking in Romans 9 of double predestination or unconditional election which determines individual destiny without regard for the moral state of people. The Lord's dialogue with Abraham helps to define what Paul understood by God's righteousness. God's rescue of the one righteous man/family in Sodom provides further testimony of God's concern for justice. It must be admitted that this passage does reveal a concern over individual destiny, and that Paul seems to carry this concern into Romans 9 to a degree. But it must also be remembered that just as the emphasis of Genesis 18–19 is on groups (the righteous, the wicked, etc.), so it is with Paul. His emphasis is on groups/peoples. He does give some attention to individuals and is concerned to show that God's justice extends even to his treatment of individuals, yet not as individuals *per se*, but as members of a group. The Genesis 18 justification of God stands behind Paul's theodicy in Romans 9 echoing Abraham's eloquent plea –

> Far be it from you to do such a thing, to slay the righteous with the wicked so that the righteous become like the wicked! Far be it from you! Shall the judge of all the earth not do justice? (Gen. 18.25)

It alerts us that Paul will address this theme shortly, and that these quotations anticipate the development of Paul's argument in its attention to theodicy, God's justice, human freedom/responsibility, and the calling of the Gentiles.

4.8 *Summary/Conclusion*

Structurally, Gen. 21.12 functions as the primary text of the sustained scriptural argument of Rom. 9.6–29, similar to the later rabbinic proem midrash form; Gen. 18.10, 14 functions as the secondary text.[180] This structure gives a discrete form to the section 9.6–29 and makes Genesis 18–21 the centerpiece of Paul's argument. Given Gen. 18.10, 14's supporting role, Gen. 21.12 stands out as the main ground for Paul's assertion of God's faithfulness in 9.6a, a divine word of comfort addressed to his profound grief over his kinsmen. The rest of ch. 9 up until v. 29 arises out of this main concern to identify the true heir of the covenant promise and serves to support further Paul's interpretation and use of Gen. 21.12 with a view toward supporting the programmatic assertion of 9.6a that the word of God has not failed. Thus, Rom. 9.6–29 may legitimately be called a midrash on Gen. 21.12 directed toward the faithfulness of God's word in the face of the rejection of ethnic Israel and calling of the Church *vis-à-vis* the Abrahamic covenant and the fulfillment of its promises.[181]

Our investigation has discovered that Genesis 21 and 18–19 are far more significant for Paul's argument in Romans 9–11 than has been

---

180. See ch. 2 above.

181. Although the term 'midrash' is problematic (see Hays, *Echoes*, 1–14, 161; Moo, 550 n. 9, 569–70 n. 6), it is surely warranted in cases of clear extended biblical interpretation which draw in a number of OT texts in connection with a primary text or theme, as observable here and in the rabbinic midrashim.

previously recognized. Through them, Paul draws his audience into the Scriptures of Israel and casts their eschatological present into the biblical story of Abraham, Isaac, and Ishmael. Provoked to overwhelming grief at the accursed state of Israel and faced with a challenge to the faithfulness of God's word, Paul has gone to the Scriptures and found there the pattern for his own response and the content of his own teaching. Indeed, the broad contours of Paul's argument in Romans 9–11 are anticipated by the story of Abraham in Genesis 18–21.

Faced with exceeding grief over the rejection of ethnic Israel from inheritance of the covenant blessings, Paul finds a divine word of comfort directed to Abraham over the expulsion of his physical child from the covenantal household which assures him that the covenant descendants will be determined through the child of promise, the rejection of the merely physical seed being necessary for the covenant and promise to be fulfilled. This same word of comfort is tied to the promise of special blessing and care for the nonetheless rejected physical offspring, who may also eventually find even covenantal blessing as part of the nations of the world. Faced with an accompanying charge against God's faithfulness to his word to Israel if Paul's gospel of covenant fulfillment for all who believe in Christ regardless of ethnicity be true, Paul finds an Old Testament context which argues explicitly though narratively for the faithfulness of God's covenant word over against a challenge to his faithfulness with a view toward the inclusion of all the nations in the covenant blessing of Abraham. Donning the mantle of a prophet, Paul intimates that God's glorious justice and mercy are conditioned upon the moral state of people and find expression in the fulfillment of his covenant promise to bless all the nations in Abraham. Just as it has been claimed that Deuteronomy 32 contains Romans *in nuce*,[182] and we have been able to claim in the previous chapter that Exodus 32–34 contains Romans 9–11 *in nuce*, we may now also say that Genesis 18–21 contains Romans 9–11 *in nuce* as well. Paul has used the Old Testament context as a virtual literary prototype upon which to build and pattern his argument.

We have found that many of the themes Paul deals with in Romans 9 are also present in ancient Jewish interpretive traditions surrounding Genesis 18 and 21. The former raised for ancient interpreters the issues of theodicy, the dependability of God's word to Israel, God's mercy, universalism and concern for the salvation of the Gentiles, God's

---

182. Hays, *Echoes*, 163–64.

sovereignty and foreknowledge, human free will, and faith. The latter chapter engaged ancient interpreters in the issues of the Abrahamic promises, the symbolic role of Ishmael as representative of the descendants of Abraham excluded from the covenant yet retaining a measure of blessing, corporate representation, identification of Isaac's seed based on a principle other than ethnicity, election and its basis, definition of the true Israel, determinism, ability to relate to God, faith, incomplete/complete stages in God's plan, the faithfulness of God's word, and the Gentiles. While in most cases Paul was not saying the same things about these issues as his fellow ancients, these interpretive traditions must have had some influence on him. He could not completely escape the effect of his socio-cultural milieu. Yet our investigation has not discovered any instances of clear dependence by Paul. Rather, he appears to have developed his stance mainly from a fresh encounter with Scripture in light of his experience of Christ and his Church. He has combined relatively straightforward biblical interpretation – which abstracts principles from the Old Testament text based on analogy, and in which he has identified certain legitimate emphases of the text such as the fact that more than physical descent was at issue in determining Abraham's covenant seed and the stress on promise and God's faithfulness to his word – with a typological exegesis which sees the eschatological events of redemptive history presently taking place to be prefigured in the story of Abraham, Isaac, and Ishmael.

To state Paul's argument in Rom. 9.6–9 plainly: despite the fact that ethnic Israel has been rejected and the word of God spoken to Israel has been fulfilled in the Church made up of Jews and Gentiles, the word of God has not failed, because the physical seed of Abraham is not the true Israel, heir to the covenant promises, but the true Israel is the community of those who have believed in Christ whether Jew or Gentile. Paul's basic argument in support of his contention is summed up most succinctly by Gen. 21.12, pregnant as it is with intertextual significance – 'In Isaac seed will be called for you.'

Chapter 5

THE SIGNIFICANCE OF PAUL'S USE OF THE OLD
TESTAMENT IN ROMANS 9.1–9 FOR THE EXEGESIS
AND THEOLOGY OF ROMANS AND PAULINE
INTERTEXTUALITY

5.1. *The Exegesis and Theology of Romans 9–11 and the Epistle as a Whole*

5.1.a. *Broad Exegetical Insights*

Paul's interpretive activity in Rom. 9.1–9 reveals that the issue of who are the true people of God is central to chs. 9–11. It is, in fact, hardly separable from the generally agreed upon main theme of Rom. 9–11 – the faithfulness of God to his word to Israel. Indeed, this major theme of divine faithfulness arises only because the issue of who are the true people of God has been raised by Paul's argument in Romans 1–8, which has placed Jews and Gentiles on the same footing, asserted God's impartiality, insisted that justification and salvation come only through faith in Christ, and applied the name and language of election and its blessings to the multiracial Church of Christ. Paul's identification of the Church of Jews and Gentiles as the covenant people of God inescapably raises the question of Israel and God's faithfulness to her. This question of the identity of the true Israel then comes to dominate Paul's argument in ch. 9, and to some extent chs. 10–11 also, as he defends God's faithfulness to his promises to Israel despite his rejection of her and his election of the Church. Indeed, his defense of God's faithfulness in ch. 9 takes the form of a defense of God's right/freedom to elect whom he chooses as his people.

The Old Testament background behind the beginning of Paul's argument in Romans 9–11 (i.e., 9.1–9) helps us to detect the direction of his argument by its concern for this very issue – who are the covenant people and on what basis are they so reckoned. The answers it provides through

Paul's own prophetic-apocalyptic-Jewish-Christian perspective are that God's covenant people are none other than the Church of Jews and Gentiles, the eschatological messianic community identified by God's call in his free mercy on the basis of promise and faith. Paul's allusions reveal that his calling language speaks of the naming/identification/recognition of God's covenant people. Even near the end of the chapter Paul is still speaking of calling (9.25–26), where it is crystal clear that he speaks of the naming of God's people as his sons.

This understanding of the thrust of Romans 9 helps us to discern the function of chs. 10–11 more fully. We have argued in ch. 2 that 9.30–11.32 supports the main thesis statement of 9.6a by showing the guilt of Israel (esp. 9.30–10.21) and the faithfulness of God to his promises to her (9.30–11.32). God was faithful to fulfill his promises in the gospel and is not to be blamed because ethnic Israel rejects the realization of those promises, which have been offered to them freely in Christ. But now we may also say that Romans 10–11 also supports the point represented negatively by 9.6b, and positively by Paul's citation of Gen. 21.12 in Rom. 9.7 and its clarifying interpretation in 9.8. Romans 10–11's support of 9.6a and 9.6b/9.7/9.8 respectively should be regarded as complementary. The support for 9.6b is to be found in its discussion of the basis of inclusion in the true Israel – faith in Jesus Christ, and God's grace and mercy. Romans 10 especially further reveals the identity of the true Israel, and even more explicitly, the basis for participation in her. Additionally, we can also now appreciate more sharply that this same issue of the identity of the covenant people and the criteria for covenant membership looms in the background of the previous chapters (Romans 1–8). Romans 2 and 4 are especially put into sharper relief.

Our intertextual exegesis has repeatedly emphasized the importance of covenant for Paul's argument. The whole of Romans 9–11 must be seen in a covenantal context. Paul is defending God's covenant faithfulness to his covenant word *vis-à-vis* his covenant promises. The covenantal significance of Paul's argument has, of course, been noticed before.[1] But it is a matter of controversy, and Hays has called for attention to this very issue in order to move scholarship forward in its understanding of Paul's theology, especially in Romans.[2] Indeed, Hays suggests 'that the study of Paul's exegesis of scripture might offer us the only viable way to adjudicate the question of the role played by "covenant" in Pauline

---

1. See especially, Wright, *Climax*, 231–57; idem, 'Theology', 56–62.
2. See notes 146 and 178 in ch. 4 above.

theology'.[3] Therefore, this investigation is especially suited to contribute to addressing this crucial question before Pauline scholarship. Our analysis bears out the covenantal approach, contributing to the corroboration of the perspective represented by Wright.

Relatedly, our investigation has found Paul to have a fundamental corporate perspective in Romans 9–11. This carries forward the orientation of the texts he is interpreting in all their covenantal richness. The corporate and covenantal thrust of Paul's argument ties into two complementary factors we have found in both the Old Testament background and the text of Romans 9–11. For one, Paul's argument concerns both Jews and Gentiles from the very beginning. It is the enjoyment of the blessings of the covenant by a predominantly Gentile church that forms the contrasting backdrop to the Jews' rejection of those same blessings, the former exacerbating the latter to no small degree. And that raises the other factor related to a corporate covenantal perspective, viz., that Paul considers ethnic Israel to be anathema, i.e., rejected from the covenant and its elect status, and under its fatal divine curse.

5.1.b. *Theological Insights*

The intertextual calling motif, the corporate-covenantal character of Paul's argument, and a number of exegetical conclusions I have drawn in the course of this investigation have decidedly theological ramifications. We have observed a dynamic interaction between God's sovereignty and human will and action in the Old Testament texts that has been suggestive for understanding Paul's rhetoric. Paul regarded God as both omnipotent (cf. Gen. 18.14) and just, one who would never treat the wicked and the righteous indiscriminately. He held a conception of the divine sovereignty that found God to maintain ultimate control while limiting his own determinations to some extent so that he might respond to the free will of his creatures and grant them important roles in the outworking of his cosmic plan of salvation.

Paul speaks not of unconditional eternal decrees regarding individual election and salvation, but of the corporate election and naming of God's people. For Paul, the divine call is not a gospel summons that irresistibly creates a response of faith and obedience; rather it is a naming of those who are in Christ through faith as his covenant people. Applied individually, Christian calling relates to conversion, when one comes to share in the name and attendant blessings of the eschatological messianic community, 'as well as continuing divine acknowledgment of sonship/

---

3. Hays, 'Covenant', 86.

covenant membership.' To be sure, election and its appellation (i.e., calling) have to do with eschatological salvation, which necessarily affects individuals. But both of these divine actions apply first and foremost to the people of God as a group, and then to individuals as members of the elect people.[4] Therefore, election and calling are conditional upon faith in Jesus Christ. In traditional theological terminology, Paul's use of the Old Testament in Rom. 9.1–9 argues for an Arminian rather than a Calvinistic interpretation of Romans 9, albeit on untraditional grounds.

Beyond this, the picture of God that emerges is one of the utmost moral goodness and beauty. In addition to being completely just, he is absolutely faithful and thoroughly merciful. He also appears to be triune. Jesus Christ is the glory/personal presence of God which bestows the divine election and may be called God. By the same token, the Holy Spirit is also the glory/personal presence of God that conveys election. On the eschatological front, where both Christ and the Spirit also belong, we have seen that Paul considered the Abrahamic promises of the Old Testament to be eschatological in nature. They have now been brought to inaugurated fulfillment in Christ and belong ideally to ethnic Israel and believing Gentiles but practically only to the eschatological people of God, which is the Church of Jesus Christ.

Paul is best taken as a covenant theologian, which means that the theological concept of covenant is foundational to his theology, coloring and directing much of his thought. Indeed, the covenantal contours of Paul's theology actually bring together the forensic and participationist aspects of his thought.[5] For participation in Christ is by faith and equivalent to participation in the covenant while justification by faith results in God's declaration/calling of the covenant status of those who believe in Christ.[6] Paul conceived of the gospel and the events of

4. To be more theologically precise, election and calling apply first and foremost to Christ, the elect Son of God and corporate representative of the covenant people, and then to the people united to him in the New Covenant by faith, the individual members of which enjoy the blessings of the covenant.

5. Cf. Wright, *Climax*, 213–14; M.A. Seifrid, 'Righteousness Language in the Hebrew Scriptures and Early Judaism', in Carson, O'Brien, and Seifrid (eds.), *Justification*, 1.415–42 (424).

6. Therefore, Sanders' (*Paul*, 513–14) opposition to covenant as fundamental to Paul's thought based on its supposed inadequacy for accounting for his participationist soteriology is invalid; see further Abasciano, 'Pauls Use', 356 n. 17. Perhaps it is worth noting here that even Paul's concept of imputation is grounded in covenant theology; imputation is a covenantal practice of regarding and treating others based on their covenant membership/identification with the covenant representative.

salvation-history wrought in Christ as the outworking of the covenant between God and Israel described in the Scriptures. This reading of Paul is crucial to understanding him on his own terms, for he claims that his gospel is the fulfillment of the Scriptures of Israel (e.g., Rom. 1.1–5; 3.21–22, 31).

Romans and the gospel it presents stand or fall with Paul's interpretation of Scripture. But how could his interpretation of the Scriptures stand if he were to dispense with the covenant so central to them while plundering promise after promise from that covenant? Consequently, we may say that Romans and Paul's gospel stand or fall with his interpretation of the covenant. We can sum up some of the practical implications of Paul's covenant theology by the words continuity and fulfillment – in relation to the Old Covenant, Scripture, the Law, Judaism, Israel, between Israel and the Church, etc. Although there are undeniable elements of discontinuity and the nature of the continuity Paul envisages may be varied, complex, and oftentimes surprising, it all centers on Christ and his fulfillment of the covenant purposes of God.

Paul's identity as a covenant theologian raises the hotly debated issue of the so-called New Perspective on Paul with its postulate of covenantal nomism as the pervasive pattern of religion in first-century Judaism.[7] This investigation certainly gives some support to the New Perspective with our findings of significant continuity between Paul and Judaism, his positive view of the Law, his attack on a notion of salvific Jewish national privilege, etc. We have seen reason to believe that while the vocabulary of God's righteousness is rich and multifaceted, to a significant degree it should be understood covenantally as God's faithfulness to fulfill his promises. Likewise, the vocabulary of human righteousness should be understood as including the notion of covenant membership.[8]

---

7. For the standard description of this pattern, see Sanders, *Paul*, 422. On the mounting opposition to the New Perspective, see note 56 in ch. 2 above.

8. For a helpful description of the recent weight of scholarly opinion concerning righteousness language as relational rather than merely forensic in the OT, first-century Judaism, and Paul, see Burnett, *Paul*, 117–31. But contra Burnett, 127, it is going too far to suggest that ethics was not part of the fundamental essence of righteousness; see Abasciano 'Paul's Use', 356 n. 15. Seifrid, 'Righteousness', 422–27, correctly challenges too sharp a distinction between status and behavior, but his attempt to separate covenant from righteousness seems misguided and subject to the criticism that it is shortsighted to demand the presence of the word 'covenant' for the concept to be present; cf. S.E. Porter, 'The Concept of Covenant in Paul', in S.E. Porter and J.C.R. de Roo (eds.), *The Concept of the Covenant in the Second Temple Period* (JSJSup, 71; Leiden: Brill, 2003), 269–85 (282–85).

However, in relation to the pattern of religion in first-century Judaism or Paul our study provides only limited support for the New Perspective since we treat only a limited number of texts. To see, for example, that Paul attacks Jewish ethnocentrism in Rom. 9.1–9 is not to deny that he attacks a traditional notion of works-righteousness elsewhere in his writings. In my view, the New Perspective has contributed many valuable insights into Paul's theology, but does not exhaust his view.[9]

5.1.c. Some Specific Exegetical Insights Elsewhere in Romans 9–11
The insights we have gained through the present study carry implications for virtually every verse in the rest of Romans 9–11. As the introductory and early stages of Paul's argument, Rom. 9.1–9 set an orientation with which to approach the larger passage. Having set forth some of the more important broader emphases established by Rom. 9.1–9, understood intertextually, we should note a few of the places in the rest of chs. 9–11 where our findings most directly impinge on exegesis.

To begin with, we have seen that the background of Rom. 9.9/Gen. 18.10, 14 identifies the ultimate purpose of Abraham's covenantal election to be the fulfillment of the Lord's promise to Abraham. In the context of Genesis, God's promise is to culminate in the blessing of all the nations of the world in Abraham. This is the purpose of Abraham's election according to Gen. 18.17–19. All of this in turn suggests that the debated phrase ἡ κατ᾽ ἐκλογὴν πρόθεσις τοῦ θεοῦ in Rom. 9.11 refers to the same purpose of election,[10] found as it is in the Abraham cycle of Genesis to which Paul continues to allude in Rom. 9.10–13 (cf. Rom. 4 and its concern for inheritance of the Abrahamic promises). Thus, Paul's use of the Old Testament again steers us away from an individualistic predestinarian reading of Romans 9 and helps us to see that Paul maintains focus upon God's right to identify whom he will as his covenant people. More specifically, he maintains focus upon God's plan of including Gentiles in

---

9. See further Abasciano, 'Paul's Use', 353–56.
10. It is beyond the scope of the present discussion to analyze this phrase and the various options for its interpretation in detail. For some of the main options, see Moo, *Romans*, 581 n. 53. For a thorough view of the grammatical options of the general construction, see BDAG, 511–13, esp. B7. Suffice it to say here that most options are compatible with the interpretation we are suggesting, as are the views of most interpreters. Perhaps the most likely meaning of the phrase is also the one that commands the most scholarly support in one way or another, effectively taking it to reveal election as the manner in which the divine purpose operates.

the covenant and the necessary consequence of excluding unbelieving Jews, since faith is the means by which the whole world, Jews and Gentiles, can participate in the covenant and its blessings. This perspective is confirmed by the fact that 9.10–13 actually supports 9.8, furnishing further substantiation for the contention that it is the children of the promise (rather than the children of the flesh), who believe in Christ and have the Spirit, that are regarded as children of God and covenant seed.

A superficial reading of 9.10–13 might suggest that Paul speaks of individual election because he uses individuals as examples. But as we have seen, he has already used Abraham and Isaac in 9.7–9 in relation to corporate election, and, as is commonly pointed out, the Old Testament passages Paul quotes in 9.12–13 refer primarily to the peoples represented by these individuals.[11] Hence, Paul's consideration of the divine decision about Jacob and Esau before they were born applies to the character of Israel's corporate election and is employed to argue that the fulfillment of God's purpose/promises to bless the world rests not on human works but on his sovereign freedom to designate whom he will as his covenant people on whatever basis he chooses. Individuals figure into the picture by consequence of their participation or lack thereof in the corporate covenant on the terms God lays down. Our conclusions about Paul's intertextually based concept of calling in 9.6–9 lend further support to this reading of 9.10–13 in primarily corporate terms since it has emerged as a primarily corporate concept that applies to individuals based on their relationship to the covenant community and its representative. Indeed, Paul's intertextual use of the concept supports the claim, based on the deduction that the works/calling contrast of 9.12 is equivalent to the familiar Pauline works/faith contrast used earlier in Romans, that its reappearance in 9.12 implies faith as the condition of election in the New Covenant.[12] For the divine call is pronounced over those who believe (Rom. 4.17; 9.7–8, 24–26, 30–33).

Similarly, Rom. 9.15's citation of Exod. 33.19 cannot be interpreted as some sort of statement of God's righteousness in unconditionally

11.   Gen. 25.23; Mal. 1.2–3; see e.g., Cranfield, *Romans*, 479; Bruce, *Romans*, 193. Those who do not think Paul carries forward the corporate perspective of the OT texts include Moo, *Romans*, 584–86; Piper, *Justification*, esp. 56–72.

12.   Moo, *Romans*, 583 n. 60, lists several representatives of this view; see also Barrett, *Romans*, 182–83, for the claim that the two contrasts are equivalent. On the objection that the same circumstances which preclude election and rejection on the basis of anything the twins had done must also preclude faith as a condition of election, see Abasciano, 'Paul's Use', 358–59 n. 20.

electing individuals to salvation or damnation as was common in the past and as is still advocated by a handful of influential commentators. This verse requires a detailed exegesis founded upon the analysis of its Old Testament background which we have provided in chapter three that goes beyond the scope of our present purposes. Here we can only make a few suggestive observations. First, Paul's use of the Old Testament in Rom. 9.1–9 urges us to take 9.15 as a statement of God's merciful character and freedom to determine the basis on which he bestows his mercy, and therefore, who will receive it. Moreover, his mercy in this intertextual context again has to do with covenant and election. In Exodus, God speaks in relation to the question of whether he will again acknowledge Israel as his covenant people. Thus, Paul is again defending God's right to choose whom he will as his covenant people generally and his righteousness in electing the Church specifically. As for the concept of the hardening of Israel to which Rom. 9.15 is directly connected, our examination of Paul's use of Exodus 32–34 would suggest both a divine judicial hardening rather than a divine prevenient decree and a stress on Israel's own character and guilt.

As for the vexing question of the meaning of τέλος in Romans 10.4, our observations concerning the covenantal orientation of Paul's argument and its focus on the fulfillment of the Abrahamic promises, which are to be understood as previously developed in the Mosaic covenant and its Law, support a primary teleological meaning. This is not to say that the idea of termination is not present at all. It probably is, but as a result of the Law's fulfillment in Christ. Thus, both goal and termination are in view in Rom. 10.4,[13] but our intertextual exegesis of 9.1–9 suggests that goal is the more primary meaning.[14]

Finally, we must comment on the supreme interpretive debate of Romans 9–11, located in 11.26. Our investigation has found Paul granting the name and blessings of the true Israel to the Church. Significantly, he states this negatively as a principle in 9.6b, which is directly connected to the programmatic statement of Romans 9–11, viz., 9.6a. Indeed, 9.6b is itself programmatic, standing over 9.7–11.32 in some measure, as we

---

13.   See esp. Moo's (*Romans*, 641) commonsense comments combining the two basic senses of τέλος.

14.   Two recent intertextual investigations have also affirmed a double meaning of goal and termination with a primary emphasis on the former: Wagner, *Heralds*, 152ff.; Mohrmann, 'Collisions', 237–40 (who also intriguingly asserts [239] that Rom. 10.4 echoes 9.4–5, giving greater weight to the present argument); cf. Shum, *Paul's Use*, 220 n. 128; Berkley, *Broken*, 194.

mentioned earlier in this chapter. Therefore, while the interpretation of 11.26, which involves numerous questions,[15] is far beyond the scope of this study, we can dispel a very frequent objection to an ecclesiological understanding of Israel in the verse, namely, that it is thoroughly implausible that Paul would shift the meaning of Israel from one verse (11.25) to the next (11.26) or that he would use the term 'Ἰσραήλ differently in 11.26 than in the rest of chs. 9–11.[16] For one cannot reasonably argue this in relation to a unified argument like Romans 9–11 in which Paul begins with a programmatic assertion essentially redefining Israel as the Church and then goes on to spend much of his argument developing this redefinition in one way or another. Indeed, the polyvalence of the term in Romans is well known.[17] The objection is particularly weak when one considers that Paul's programmatic assertion concerning the identity of the true Israel uses two different definitions of Israel in one half of a verse! Therefore, I would submit that my intertextual exegesis of Rom. 9.1–9 supports an ecclesiological interpretation of Romans 11.26 along the lines argued by Wright.[18] This also argues for the consistency of Paul's argument.

5.1.d. *Exegetical Insights into the Epistle as a Whole*

Our findings in relation to Rom. 9.1–9 also help to clarify Paul's argument in the epistle as a whole. They serve to confirm the recent approach of Pauline scholarship in Romans that interprets the letter primarily via corporate and covenantal concerns,[19] concerns that we have identified as the main thrust of Rom. 9.1–9. Thus, it is not only true of Romans 9, but also for the epistle as a whole that we find among Paul's main concerns the identity of the covenant people of God, the faithfulness of God to his covenant promises, and the relationship between Jews and Gentiles in the divine purposes. Indeed, the fact that the main concerns of Rom. 9.1–9 identified by our investigation coincide with the

---

15. For recent treatments of Rom. 11.26 that are especially attuned to Paul's use of the OT, see Wagner, *Heralds*, 276–98 (see 277 n. 190, for recent literature on this passage in general); Shum, *Paul's Use*, 235–45; Wilk, *Jesajabuches*, 64–73.

16. See e.g., Cranfield, *Romans*, 576; Moo, *Romans*, 721.

17. See e.g., Cosgrove, *Elusive*; Luz, *Geschichtsverständnis*, 269–70.

18. See Wright, *Climax*, 246–51; idem, 'Theology', 59–62.

19. For a documented description and critical assessment of this current consensus, see Burnett, *Paul*, 91–114, who approves of this consensus in general, but rightly seeks to redress an overemphasis on collective to the exclusion of individual concerns. For critique of Burnett, see Abasciano, 'Paul's Use', 109 n. 214, 361 n. 28.

conclusions of the majority of recent scholarship regarding the main concerns of Romans further supports our position and the increasingly popular view that Romans 9–11 is indeed the climax of the theological argument of Romans (chs. 1–11).

It is this theological climax that has demonstrated to us so clearly that Paul's opening statement on the gospel of Jesus Christ as the fulfillment of the promises of the Scriptures (1.1–4) is not merely a nod at tradition, but a foundational part of his gospel and its explication in Romans. Our intertextual investigation of Rom. 9.1–9 would suggest that understanding Paul's use of the Old Testament is of paramount importance for fully understanding this grand epistle. Indeed, I would suggest that attention to Paul's use of the Old Testament may well be the most important avenue for understanding his epistles in general at this juncture in the history of Pauline scholarship.

5.2. *Paul's Use of the Old Testament*

The three allusions we have investigated can only go so far for generalizing about Paul's use of the Old Testament. But general practices are observed from a collection of individual instances. Therefore, while recognizing the limited nature of the data we have to work with, it is nonetheless valuable to reflect on the implications that this study might have for Paul's use of the Old Testament in general with sensitivity to the history of research in this area. Each analysis of individual instances of Pauline intertextuality in New Testament scholarship contributes to the growing body of literature on Paul's use of Scripture in specific texts. Together these individual investigations will offer an account of Paul's interpretive activity. Moreover, practices we observe here receive confirmation as general tendencies when observed by others in other texts and simultaneously contribute to the confirmation of their conclusions regarding Paul's use of the Old Testament.

5.2.a. *Textual Issues*
We have found that in his citations from Genesis, Paul has used the LXX. The allusion to Exod. 32.32 in Rom. 9.3 has no verbal correspondence with the intertext. But we may note that Paul's quotation from the same general context (Exod. 33.19/Rom. 9.15) is an exact quotation of the LXX. So our investigation supports the standard view that Paul's quotations of Scripture rely on the Septuagint.

However, Paul's conflated quotation of Gen. 18.10, 14 in Rom. 9.9 presents a unique wording in its use of ἐλεύσομαι in place of ἐπαναστρέφων ἥξω of Gen. 18.10 LXX and/or ἀναστρέψω of Gen. 18.14 LXX, both of which render Hebrew שׁוב. This raises the possibility that Paul used a Greek manuscript that is no longer extant or made his own translation from Hebrew. Unfortunately, the data is inconclusive in this case since Paul could have reasonably changed either of the Septuagint renderings without substantially altering the sense of the quotation while simultaneously sounding the eschatological chord he obviously wanted to strike. Of the possible options it appears that Paul adapted the ἥξω of Gen. 18.10 LXX, since ἔρχομαι and ἥξω are reasonably close in meaning. Therefore, this investigation again supports the consensus that Paul generally relied on the LXX for his scriptural quotations, but it in no way argues against the possibility that he sometimes made use of Hebrew.

Wagner has recently classified the conflation of texts as an interpretive strategy employed by Paul in his citation of Isaiah in Romans 9–11.[20] While he finds that the conflation of texts is sometimes unintentional, he also finds that it is often filled with interpretive significance arising from Paul's understanding of the biblical text. We have found this to be the case with Paul's conflation of Gen. 18.10, 14, where he combines pieces of the pivotal moments of the narrative, evoking a scriptural pattern that mirrors the situation he is addressing and supporting his point of the faithfulness of God with exquisite artistry. Thus, Paul communicates his understanding of the biblical text and its relationship to the present stage of redemptive history by intentional conflation.

At the same time, the allusion to Exod. 32.32 in Rom. 9.3 shows how revealing research into Paul's allusions (as opposed to his quotations) can be, confirming our methodology in its appreciation of allusion on a par with quotation. Indeed, for research purposes, attention to allusions may be even more necessary given the traditional emphasis upon quotation over allusion.

5.2.b. *Paul's Hermeneutic*
We have found Paul's interpretive practices to be at home in a first-century Jewish context. He addresses many of the same issues that his contemporaries did in the biblical texts he alludes to. And in some cases

---

20.   Wagner, *Heralds*, 346–51. Cf. Ellis, *Paul's Use*, 49–51.

he even appears to follow prior interpretive tradition. But for the most part, Paul breaks new ground in his bold and brilliant interpretive activity. This is no doubt due largely to Paul's own genius and religious experience. But these have been directed by Paul's interpretive presuppositions, apparently shared with the other New Testament authors.[21]

We have seen a concept of corporate solidarity at work in Paul's approach to Scripture. This is true in his allusion to Exod. 32.32, through which he identifies profoundly with the Jewish people and contemplates appeal to the faithful remnant as embodied in himself. It is even more so with Paul's quotation of Gen. 21.12 in Rom. 9.7, in which we are told that Abraham's seed would be identified by relationship to Isaac. Paul understands this to be equivalent to the identification of Abraham's seed by relationship to Jesus Christ, the true seed of Abraham (cf. Galatians 3) and corporate representative of the covenant people. Paul's intertexual activity reveals that the concept of corporate solidarity was especially (though not necessarily exclusively) a covenantal matter.

The emphasis that we have observed in Paul's use of the Old Testament on matters of covenant and election supports Hays' controversial assertion that Paul's hermeneutic was ecclesiocentric rather than Christocentric.[22] But we must beware of getting sidetracked by mere terminology here. The point of labeling Paul's hermeneutic as ecclesiocentric is to acknowledge that he most often uses Scripture 'to argue for a particular vision of the church'[23] or to make application to the life of the Church. This is not to deny that he engages in theocentric or Christocentric interpretation at times, but to identify the typical focus of his interpretive activity. Hays is right to point out that: (1) even though Paul's hermeneutic is theocentric, his focus is not (typically) on God's activity in itself but on God's activity as directed toward his people;[24]

21. See note 46 in ch. 1 above.

22. See Hays, *Echoes*, ch. 3. But the basic point was observed long before Hays' work sparked such controversy by Ellis, *Paul's Use*, 115; cf. Smith, 'Pauline', 275. For critiques of Hays' position, see Sanders, 'Paul', 53–54; J.C. Beker, 'Echoes and Intertextuality: On the Role of Scripture in Paul's Theology', in Evans and Sanders (eds.), *Paul*, 64–69 (68–69). For Hays' compelling response, see Hays, 'Rebound', 77–78 and 93ff. respectively.

23. Hays, *Echoes*, xiii.

24. Hays, 'Rebound', 77–78. It would be more accurate to categorize Paul's theology as theocentric rather than his hermeneutic. But at a deeper level, everything is unquestionably theocentric/Christocentric for Paul since the glory of God is the ultimate reality and goal of all things for him. But there has got to be a way to indicate that Paul most often uses Scripture primarily in relation to the Church.

and (2) Christological interpretation is the substructure upon which ecclesiocentric interpretation is based.[25] But all of this is to be expected given the contingent character of Paul's letters, which were written to address the situations of churches. Nevertheless, Paul's ecclesiocentric hermeneutic testifies to the fundamental community orientation of the apostle's gospel as an expression of his theology.

Perhaps the most fundamental Pauline interpretive strategy that we have observed is typology. In each allusion we have studied, Paul has consistently operated on a typological approach to Scripture. He has found the contemporary events of the present eschatological moment prefigured in the salvation history of Israel. It is through the events of *Heilsgeschichte* that he understands the present events of the eschatological age inaugurated in Christ. They are the lens through which he interprets them, even as God's eschatological works in Christ fashion his perception of redemptive history. Thus, the content of the Old Testament contexts Paul alludes to suggests to him what God is doing now, and what his own response and that of his readers should be.

It has long been recognized that typology is a central feature of Paul's scriptural interpretation.[26] What has escaped the notice of Pauline scholars, however, is the utter depth of Paul's typological approach to the Old Testament. We have seen in his allusions to Exodus and Genesis that his entire personal response to the circumstances surrounding him was conditioned by what he found in Scripture. Even his emotional reaction was largely determined by the Scriptures through which he interpreted his times. Paul truly lived and breathed Scripture, and to a

---

25. Hays, *Echoes*, 120–21; idem, 'Rebound', 93–94. This point is tied to the concepts we have observed of covenantal/corporate solidarity and Christ's covenantal/corporate representation of his people.

26. See J.W. Aageson, 'Typology, Correspondence, and the Application of Scripture in Romans 9–11', *JSNT* 31 (1987), 51–72, for a rare objection to typology as a feature of Paul's scriptural interpretation; cf. Sanders, 'Paul', 54. Hays, *Echoes*, 161, admits to the centrality of typology in Paul's interpretation of Scripture, but contests that it is itself a method of interpretation (cf. Ellis, 'How', 210–11; D.L. Baker, 'Typology and the Christian Use of the Old Testament', in Beale [ed.], *Right Doctrine*, 313–30 [324, 328–29], and the opposing comments of Beale, 'Right Doctrine', 401–402) and argues that it is unconcerned with history. Aageson also thinks Paul was not concerned with history, rejecting the concept of typology in favor of what he terms 'correspondence'. Against Aageson and the similar view of Luz, *Geschichtsverständnis*, 30–33, and in favor of the importance of history for Paul's use of the OT, see Smith, 'Pauline', 279. The majority of scholars are surely correct to recognize in typology a historical character; see Baker, 324–25.

degree that has seldom been fathomed despite the common appreciation of its supreme importance to him.

Related to Paul's typological interpretation but distinct from it is his analogical approach. This may be seen especially in his treatment of Genesis 18–21. There we find Paul extracting a principle of how God works in salvation history and applying it to the contemporary situation. Just as promise rather than physical descent was the basis of the Lord's covenantal election in the case of Abraham/Isaac/Ishmael, so it is in the present phase of redemptive history. This is another way of saying that faith rather than ethnicity is the basis of election in the New Covenant age. It is a principle by which the faithful God acts. But it is more than that. In this case it is an analogical principle that plays into a typological configuration. That is, as this specific principle is actualized in the present eschatological age it produces a pattern that significantly reproduces former personages and events so that the former may be regarded as pointing forward to the latter in the divine intention *vis-à-vis* their recording in the text of holy Scripture.

Another aspect of Paul's interpretation of Scripture related to typology and also widely recognized by scholars that we have seen in Paul's use of the Old Testament in Rom. 9.1–9 is his eschatological perspective.[27] Simply put, Paul finds each of the passages to which he alludes to have special significance for the present age of salvation history when the purposes and promises of God have come to inaugurated fulfillment in Christ. This is tied to another widely recognized aspect of typology and Paul's interpretive practice – escalation. So the apostasy, punishment, and restoration of Israel in relation to the golden calf adumbrates the same pattern *vis-à-vis* Israel's rejection of the Christ, bearer and mediator of the eschatological fulfillment of the promises of God. The New Covenant formed in these latter days is the great hope of Israel, the promised restoration of the holy writings and the Deuteronomic tradition. Similarly, both the rejection of contemporary Israel seen in the rejection of Ishmael recorded in Genesis and the promise to Abraham take on an obvious heightened significance in the critical time of fulfillment. Each of these situations is fuller when contemplated on this side of the cross and carries a more urgent message to those who encounter it.

Yet another aspect of Paul's scriptural interpretation evident from this investigation is his attention to the narratives contained in the

27. Ellis, 'How', 207, also observes an eschatological perspective in Paul's use of the OT in Rom. 9.7–9.

passages he alludes to. Thus, this study has provided some corroboration for Stockhausen's suggestion that one of Paul's fundamental principles of Old Testament exegesis is that he

> takes as the basis for his interpretative task the Torah; that is to say, narrative texts from the Pentateuch are usually (perhaps always) at the core of his arguments. In interpreting selected Pentateuchal narratives, he is usually (perhaps always) extremely concerned with the stories themselves – that is, with plot-line, character, narrative event and especially the inexplicable, unusual or unmotivated character or action.[28]

It is striking that Stockhausen articulated this principle on the basis of 2 Corinthians 3–4 and Galatians 3–4 apart from Romans 9. Whether or not she has isolated a consistent principle of Pauline exegesis, her findings together with ours surely demonstrate at least a Pauline tendency. When we consider that a number of scholars now regard Paul's hermeneutic to be based on a narrative framework of interpretation,[29] we can conclude that his concern for the larger story of the narratives he alludes to is indeed a general principle of Pauline exegesis and that his foundational use of Pentateuchal narratives is at least a Pauline inclination.

We have further been able to confirm a pattern of Pauline interpretive activity that has been observed by Richard Hays in other texts – Paul's Old Testament allusions frequently anticipate the next or otherwise later stage of his argument.[30] As Hays describes it, 'an unvoiced element of the explicitly cited text subliminally generates the next movement of discourse'.[31] This is evident in a number of themes evoked by Paul's allusion to Exod. 32.32 in Rom. 9.3 and further developed in the rest of Romans 9–11, including the theme of God's faithfulness to his promises which is then taken up in Rom. 9.6ff. It is also evident in a number of themes evoked by Paul's citations from Genesis 18–21 in Rom. 9.7, 9 that are subsequently developed in the rest of Romans 9–11, including the theme of theodicy and the justice of God taken up in the next major segment of the argument (9.14ff.). This pattern of Paul's scriptural usage substantiates our view of the contextual character of his *Schriftgebrauch* to be argued below. Indeed, all that we have seen in Paul's hermeneutic activity holds more significance than merely identifying a feature of his rhetorical strategy or underscoring the growing

28. Stockhausen, 'Principles', 144.
29. See Abasciano, 'Paul's Use', 368 n. 43.
30. See Hays, *Echoes*, 51–52, 66ff., 70, 158.
31. Hays, *Echoes*, 70.

appreciation of narrative in his interpretation of Scripture. It supports the contention that Paul does not tend to use the Old Testament out of context and/or atomistically and confirms our method of investigating Paul's allusions as possible pointers to their original broader contexts.

5.2.c. *Intertextual Quotation/Allusion,*[32] *the Legitimacy of Paul's Hermeneutic, and Pauline Scholarship*

With each of the allusions we have examined, we have found that Paul argues on the basis of the broader context of the Old Testament text alluded to. He appears to pay close attention to the contexts of his Old Testament allusions and to develop his argument based on their content. Without fail, he draws upon these texts for main themes contained in the broader contexts which were relevant to his argument.[33] A good example of this, common to each allusion analyzed, is the theme of God's faithfulness to his word, the main theme of Rom. 9.1–9 and of all of Romans 9–11.

This is not to say that Paul operates as a modern historical biblical critic. He had no interest in rigidly isolating what the Old Testament text meant in its original historical and literary setting from what it meant in his own time, for his own life and ministry, and for his readers. Yet it is not that he could not distinguish between these differing contexts. Rather, he would find no need to.

The question of Paul's contextual/non-contextual use of the Old Testament depends on our definition of contextual interpretation.[34] If we mean interpretation that speaks only of a passage's strict original intention, then we must say that Paul's use of the Old Testament in Rom. 9.1–9 is non-contextual. But that is surely a shortsighted and far too restrictive definition that is inappropriate for assessing Paul's or anyone else's use of the Old Testament. What we have found is that Paul does use the Old Testament passages he alludes to in Rom. 9.1–9 in accordance with their original intentions and that he appears to have reflected carefully and thoughtfully on these Old Testament texts in their

32. Practically, intertextual quotation/allusion refers to allusions as pointers to their broad original contexts.

33. Paul's regard for context supports Ellis' (*Paul's Use*, 50) accurate description of Paul's use of hook-words as subordinate to thematic concerns for linking passages; cf. Wagner, *Heralds*, 347 n. 17. Though advocating the opposite view, Berkley, *Broken*, 57, rightly insists that Paul's use of hook-words is not merely unconscious.

34. For a discussion of the notion of context in relation to study of the use of Scripture in ancient Judaism/Christianity, see Shum, *Paul's Use*, 17–21.

contexts.[35] As Beale has observed, 'One reason why many see the New Testament typically interpreting the Old Testament non-contextually is often because the New Testament applies the Old Testament to new situations, problems, and people which were not in the minds of the Old Testament authors.'[36] Many scholars mistakenly contest the contextuality of Paul's interpretation of the Old Testament when the underlying issue is often rather one of application. That is, as we have seen in this investigation, and as many scholars have come to conclude,[37] Paul frequently argues in concert with themes, structures, and details deriving from the wider original contexts of his citations and allusions. This can scarcely be considered anything else but contextual interpretation. But in his application of Scripture to the present, Paul (usually) obviously and necessarily advances a meaning that differs from the exact original intention of his intertext. So the real question becomes one of Paul's presuppositions by which he interprets/applies the Old Testament.

Rom. 9.6–9 happens to provide us with an example of Paul arguing explicitly and scripturally for one of his hermeneutical presuppositions – that the Church of Christ is the true Israel who is the heir of the promises of God.[38] This conviction is itself founded upon scriptural interpretation that can be scrutinized. Such scrutiny need not detain us here since it is well beyond the scope of the present discussion. More to the point is Beale's significant observation that many allegations of Paul's misuse of the Old Testament involve 'passages where what was intended for Israel (or leaders or righteous individuals in Israel) in the Old Testament is now applied often by a typological method to either Christ or the church'.[39] Once we recognize this presupposition in Paul's approach to Scripture, then we should not be surprised to find him applying Old Testament passages regarding Israel to Gentile Christians or to the administration of the New Covenant.

---

35. Some of my language here reflects that of Silva, 'Old Testament', 639. To say that Paul uses OT texts in accordance with their original intentions at least means that his application of them is a logical extension or development of those intentions.

36. Beale, 'Right Doctrine', 395.

37. See e.g., a number of the scholars included in Beale (ed.), *Right Doctrine* or referred to by Beale, 'Right Doctrine'; Wagner, *Heralds*, and those he lists (11 n. 40).

38. Cf. Ellis, *Paul's Use*, 122. Ellis claims that this presupposition underlies the whole argument of Rom. 9–11, 'and indeed the whole of Paul's OT exegesis'.

39. Beale, 'Right Doctrine', 395.

The case is much the same with other presuppositions that formed part of Paul's interpretive framework.[40]

While it is certainly an appropriate question for New Testament scholarship, it is beyond the concern of pure exegesis to evaluate the legitimacy of Paul's scriptural interpretation or hermeneutical presuppositions. The goal of Pauline exegesis is to determine his original intention in what he has written. Once we have regard for his hermeneutical presuppositions and realize that he respects the contexts and intentions of his Old Testament allusions, then much of his biblical interpretation becomes comprehensible and we can see that it proceeds along predictable lines in relation to the content of the broad Old Testament contexts to which he refers.[41]

I mention the distinct concerns of exegesis and evaluation of the legitimacy of Paul's use of Scripture for two reasons. First, to point out that the exegetical focus of this investigation precludes appraisal of the validity of the interpretive framework that underlies Paul's use of the Old Testament. Second, to urge thorough investigation of the original contexts of Paul's allusions on the working assumption that they are pointers to these broad contexts. For there is a danger of ignoring what may be the most important background for interpreting a host of Pauline texts due to an unjustified assumption of its irrelevancy to Paul, an assumption that has plagued Pauline scholarship for far too long.[42] Regardless of whether one approves of Paul's first-century Jewish-Christian hermeneutical presuppositions, there is a great treasure trove of exegetical insights to be mined from the original contexts of his allusions to the Old Testament that he loved so much.

This study has shown that in Rom. 9.1–9 at least, Paul's Old Testament allusions function as pointers to their broad original contexts. This is born out even by the way Paul quotes and alludes to the Old Testament. For in no case does he clearly and explicitly indicate that

40. Concerning such presuppositions, see again note 46 in ch. 1 above.

41. Contra Hays, *Echoes*, 160–61, who contends that Paul had no exegetical procedures, and in support of Stockhausen, 'Principles', and her student Berkley, *Broken*, esp. 50–52, 203–204. Moyise, 'Intertextuality', 32–33, takes issue with Beale for the type of approach I am advocating. But Beale, 'Questions', 167–72, responds to Moyise on this point compellingly and at length. In support of Beale, see Abasciano, 'Paul's Use', 372 n. 55.

42. Though this assumption has been steadily receding for over a decade. Nevertheless, as Wagner, *Heralds*, 11 n. 40, observes, it continues unabated in many quarters.

he refers to Scripture. Rather, he assumes his audience is familiar with the Scriptures to which he alludes and will recognize his intertextual activity. Together with the mass of growing literature on Paul's use of the Old Testament effectively sharing the same conclusion for Paul generally, this study has demonstrated the value of carefully investigating the original contexts of Paul's allusions. Indeed, I would suggest that assuming Paul's allusions to be pointers to their original contexts will help give interpreters eyes to see what Paul saw and make for a more empathetic, and therefore accurate, reading of his epistles. It will also aid us in identifying more accurately those places where Paul may not be pointing to the Old Testament.

One could argue that such a method could lead to all sorts of ingenious suggestions that are nevertheless far from Paul's intention and thus hinder the cause of exegesis. Maybe so. But there is risk in any imaginative enterprise that moves the state of scholarship forward. There will undoubtedly be a mixture of more and less convincing intertextual readings of Paul. But let there be no mistake about it, it is indeed creative and imaginative exegesis that is necessary truly to understand a man of such genius and of such different time, culture, and conviction.

It may well be that the most significant contribution of the present investigation lies in its exegesis of the specific text under consideration (Rom. 9.1–9) based upon an analysis of Paul's use of the Old Testament in its socio-historical milieu. The time of unfounded assumptions and rash statements about Paul's disregard of the original contexts of his Old Testament allusions is past. It is now time for standard exegetical procedure to include substantial attention to intertextuality and for the current stream of intertextual research to continue unabated. Indeed, it remains for a study of the sort we have conducted to be done in the rest of Romans 9,[43] and then beyond that, for Romans 9–11 as a whole and the Pauline corpus. While a number of studies have been done on this or that theme in relation to Old Testament background or on a certain Old

---

43. I am particularly eager to explore the implications of the groundwork already laid in ch. 3 above for an intertextual analysis of Rom. 9.15, and even more so the OT background behind Paul's potter/clay metaphor in 9.19–21. Interpreters have missed the richness of Paul's allusions to potter/clay passages such as Isa. 29.16; 45.9; 64.8, and Jeremiah 18. Although the theme of repentance has been spotted in some of these texts, it has not received the attention it deserves. Moreover, the fact that Isa. 45.9 has to do with Israel's rebellion against the Lord's use of a Gentile (Cyrus) has gone undetected. And above all, scholars have missed just how closely the context of Jeremiah 18 fits Paul's argument in 9.19–21.

Testament book in Paul's argument in Romans 9–11, there have been relatively few, if any, to move simply and straightforwardly through the text in an intertextual exegesis which is governed by attention to Paul's use of Scripture as well as an appreciation of the history of its interpretation in Judaism and Christianity prior to and roughly contemporaneous with Paul. It is our conviction that such study will confirm our view of the contextual character of his *Schriftgebrauch* and the profound influence of Scripture upon his theology and proclamation in general and his argument in Romans 9–11 in particular.

Indeed, we have found that the famous judgment of Barnabas Lindars with respect to the role of the Old Testament in New Testament theology is wide of the mark in relation to Paul: 'The place of the Old Testament in the formation of New Testament theology is that of a servant, ready to run to the aid of the gospel whenever it is required, bolstering up arguments, and filling out meaning through evocative allusions, but never acting as the master or leading the way, nor even guiding the process of thought behind the scenes.'[44] Quite to the contrary, we have found that the Old Testament is both master and servant in Paul's theology and argumentation – much like Paul's Lord! Paul interprets the Old Testament through the lens of Christ and the gospel even as he interprets Christ and the gospel through the lens of the Old Testament. Very often the gospel provides the presuppositions by which to interpret the Old Testament, and in addition to argumentative proof or illustration, the Old Testament provides much of the content and direction of Paul's teaching within the metanarrative of the gospel and redemptive history.

---

44. B. Lindars, 'The Place of the Old Testament in the Formation of New Testament Theology: Prolegomena', in Beale (ed.), *Right Doctrine*, 137–45 (145).

BIBLIOGRAPHY

Aageson, J.W., 'Paul's Use of Scripture: A Comparative Study of Biblical Interpretation in Early Palestinian Judaism and the New Testament with Special Reference to Romans 9–11' (unpublished D.Phil. thesis; University of Oxford, 1984).

—'Scripture and Structure in the Development of the Argument in Romans 9–11', *CBQ* 48 (1986), 265–89.

—'Typology, Correspondence, and the Application of Scripture in Romans 9–11', *JSNT* 31 (1987), 51–72.

—*Written Also for Our Sake: Paul and the Art of Biblical Interpretation* (Louisville: Westminster/John Knox, 1993).

Abasciano, B.J., 'Corporate Election in Romans 9: A Reply to Thomas Schreiner', forthcoming in *JETS*.

—'Paul's Use of the Old Testament in Romans 9.1–9: An Intertextual and Theological Exegesis' (Ph.D. thesis; University of Aberdeen, 2004).

Achtemeier, P.J., '*Omni Verbum Sonat:* The New Testament and the Oral Environment of Late Western Antiquity', *JBL* 109 (1990), 3–27.

—*Romans* (IBC; Atlanta: John Knox, 1985).

Aletti, J.-N., *Israël et la loi dans la lettre aux romains* (LD, 173; Paris: Cerf, 1998).

—'L'argumentation paulinienne en Rm 9', *Bib* 68 (1987), 41–56.

Aust, H., and D. Müller, 'ἀνάθεμα', *NIDNTT*, 1.413–15.

Badenas, R., *Christ the End of the Law: Romans 10.4 in Pauline Perspective* (JSNTSup, 10; Sheffield: *JSOT*, 1985).

Baker, D.L., 'Typology and the Christian Use of the Old Testament', in Beale (ed.), *Right Doctrine*, 313–30.

Balentine, S.E., 'Prayers for Justice in the OT: Theodicy and Theology', *CBQ* 51 (1989), 597–616.

Balz, H., 'λατρεύω, λατρεία', *EDNT*, 2.344–45.

Barrett, C.K., *A Commentary on the Epistle to the Romans* (HNTC; New York: Harper & Row, 1957).

—'Romans 9.30–10.21: Fall and Responsibility of Israel', in Lorenzi (ed.), *Israelfrage*, 99–121.

Barth, M., *The People of God* (JSNTSup, 5; Sheffield: *JSOT*, 1983).

Bartlett, D.L., *Romans* (Westminster Bible Companion; Louisville, Kentucky: Westminster/John Knox, 1995).

Bartsch, H.W., 'Röm. 9, 5 und Clem. 32, 4: Eine notwendige Konjektur im Römerbrief', *TZ* 21 (1965), 401–409.

Beale, G.K., 'Did Jesus and His Followers Preach the Right Doctrine from the Wrong Texts?', in Beale (ed.), *Right Doctrine*, 387–404.

—'Questions of Authorial Intent, Epistemology, and Presuppositions and Their Bearing on the Study of the Old Testament in the New: A Rejoinder to Steve Moyise', *IBS* 21 (Nov. 1999), 151–80.

Beale, G.K., Review of J. Piper, *The Justification of God: An Exegetical and Theological Study of Romans 9:1–23*, *WTJ* 46 (1984), 190–97.

—*The Book of Revelation* (NIGTC; Grand Rapids: Eerdmans, 1999).

—'The Old Testament Background of Reconciliation in 2 Corinthians 5–7 and Its Bearing on the Literary Problem of 2 Corinthians 6:14–7:1', in Beale (ed.), *Right Doctrine*, 217–47.

Beale, G.K. (ed.), *The Right Doctrine from the Wrong Texts? Essays on the Use of the Old Testament in the New* (Grand Rapids: Baker, 1994).

Beker, J.C., 'Echoes and Intertextuality: On the Role of Scripture in Paul's Theology', in Evans and Sanders (eds.), *Paul*, 64–69.

Bell, R.H., *Provoked to Jealousy: The Origin and Purpose of the Jealousy Motif in Romans 9–11* (WUNT, 2.63; Tübingen: Mohr Siebeck, 1994).

Belleville, L.L., 'Moses', *DPL*, 620–21.

— *Reflections of Glory: Paul's Polemical Use of the Moses-Doxa Tradition in 2 Corinthians 3.1–18* (JSNTSup, 52; Sheffield: Sheffield Academic Press, 1991).

Ben Zvi, E., 'The Dialogue between Abraham and YHWH in Gen 18:23–32: A Historical-Critical Analysis', *JSOT* 53 (1992), 27–46.

Berger, K., 'Abraham in den paulinischen Hauptbriefen', *MTZ* 17 (1966), 47–89.

Berkley, T.W., *From a Broken Covenant to Circumcision of the Heart: Pauline Intertextual Exegesis in Romans 2:17–29* (SBLDS, 175; Atlanta: SBL, 2000).

Birnbaum, E., *The Place of Judaism in Philo's Thought: Israel, Jews, and Proselytes* (BJS, 290; Studia Philonica Monographs, 2; Atlanta: Scholars Press, 1996).

Black, M., *Romans* (NCB; London: Marshall, Morgan, and Scott, 1973).

Blenkinsopp, J., 'The Judge of All the Earth: Theodicy in the Midrash on Gen 18:22–33', *JJS* 41 (1990), 1–12.

Borgen, P., *Philo of Alexandria: An Exegete for His Time* (NovTSup, 86; Leiden: Brill, 1997).

Bornkamm, G., 'The Letter to the Romans as Paul's Last Will and Testament', in Donfried (ed.), *Romans*, 16–28.

Brandenburger, E., 'Paulinische Schriftauslegung in der Kontroverse um das Verheissungswort Gottes (Röm 9)', *ZTK* 82 (1985), 1–47.

Bratsiotis, P., 'Eine exegetische Notiz zu Röm. IX.3 and X.1', *NovT* (1962), 299–300.

Brotzman, E.R., *Old Testament Textual Criticism: A Practical Introduction* (Grand Rapids: Baker, 1994).

Bruce, F.F., *The Epistle of Paul to the Romans* (TNTC, 6; Grand Rapids: Eerdmans, 1963).

Brueggemann, W., *Genesis* (IBC; Atlanta: John Knox, 1982).

Burkes, S., *God, Self, and Death: The Shape of Religious Transformation in the Second Temple Period* (JSJSup, 79; Leiden: Brill, 2003).

Burnett, G.W., *Paul and the Salvation of the Individual* (Biblical Interpretation Series, 57; Leiden: Brill, 2001).

Byrne, B., *Romans* (Sacra pagina, 6; Collegeville, MN: Liturgical Press, 1996).

—*'Sons of God' – 'Seed of Abraham': A Study of the Idea of Sonship of God of All Christians in Paul against the Jewish Background* (AnBib, 83; Rome: Pontifical Biblical Institute, 1979).

Calvert, N.L., 'Abraham', *DPL*, 1–9.

Campbell, W.S., 'The Freedom and Faithfulness of God in Relation to Israel', in
    W.S. Campbell, *Paul's Gospel in an Intercultural Context: Jew and Gentile in the Letter to
    the Romans* (SIHC, 69; New York: Peter Lang, 1992), 43–59.
Caragounis, C.C., 'From Obscurity to Prominence: The Development of the Roman Church
    between Romans and *1 Clement*', in Donfried and Richardson (eds.), *Judaism*, 245–79.
Carson, D.A., *The Gospel According to John* (Grand Rapids: Eerdmans, 1991).
Carson, D.A., P.T. O'Brien, and M. Seifrid (eds.), *Justification and Variegated Nomism*
    (WUNT, 2.140, 181; 2 vols.; Grand Rapids: Baker, 2001–2004).
Cerfaux, L., 'Le privilège d'Israël selon Saint Paul', *ETL* 17 (1940), 5–26.
Chae, D.J.-S., *Paul as Apostle to the Gentiles: His Apostolic Self-Awareness and Its Influence on
    the Soteriological Argument in Romans* (Paternoster Biblical and Theological
    Monographs; Carlisle, U.K.: Paternoster Press, 1997).
Charles, R.H., *The Assumption of Moses* (London: Adam and Charles Black, 1897).
—*The Book of Enoch* (Oxford: Clarendon, 1893).
Charlesworth, J.H. (ed.), *The Old Testament Pseudepigrapha* (2 vols.; New York: Doubleday,
    1983–85).
—*The Pseudepigrapha and Modern Research* (SBLSCS, 7; Missoula, MT: Scholars Press, 1976).
Chester, S.J., *Conversion at Corinth: Perspectives on Conversion in Paul's Theology and the
    Corinthian Church* (SNTW; London: T&T Clark, 2003).
Childs, B.S., *The Book of Exodus: A Critical, Theological Commentary* (OTL; Philadelphia:
    Westminster, 1974).
Chilton, B.D., 'Romans 9–11 as Scriptural Interpretation and Dialogue with Judaism',
    Ex Auditu 4 (1988), 27–37.
Ciampa, R.E., *The Presence and Function of Scripture in Galatians 1 and 2* (WUNT, 2.102;
    Tübingen: Mohr Siebeck, 1998).
Clayton, J., and E. Rothstein, 'Figures in the Corpus: Theories of Influence and
    Intertextuality', in Clayton and Rothstein (eds.), *Influence and Intertextuality*, 3–36.
Clayton, J., and E. Rothstein (eds.), *Influence and Intertextuality in Literary History* (Madison:
    University of Wisconsin Press, 1991).
Coats, G.W., *Genesis with an Introduction to Narrative Literature* (FOTL, 1; Grand Rapids:
    Eerdmans, 1983).
—'The King's Loyal Opposition: Obedience and Authority in Exodus 32–34', in G.W. Coats
    and B.O. Long (eds.), *Canon and Authority: Essays in Old Testament Religion and
    Theology* (Philadelphia: Fortress, 1977), 91–109.
Cole, R.A., *Exodus: An Introduction and Commentary* (TOTC, 2; Downers Grove: InterVarsity
    Press, 1973).
Cosgrove, C.H., *Elusive Israel: The Puzzle of Election in Romans* (Louisville: Westminster/John
    Knox, 1997).
Cottrell, J., *Romans*, II (The College Press NIV Commentary; Joplin, Missouri: College Press,
    1998).
Cranfield, C.E.B., *A Critical and Exegetical Commentary on the Epistle to the Romans* (ICC;
    2 vols.; Edinburgh: T&T Clark, 1975–79).
Cranford, M., 'Election and Ethnicity: Paul's View of Israel in Romans 9.1–13', *JSNT* 50
    (1993), 27–41.
Dahl, N.A., 'The Future of Israel', in Dahl, *Studies*, 137–58.
—'The Missionary Theology in the Epistle to the Romans', in Dahl, *Studies*, 70–94.
— *Studies in Paul* (Minneapolis: Augsburg, 1977).
Das, A.A., *Paul, the Law, and the Covenant* (Peabody, MA: Hendrickson, 2001).

Davenport, G.L., *The Eschatology of the Book of Jubilees* (Leiden: Brill, 1971).

Davies, G.H., *Exodus: Introduction and Commentary* (London: SCM, 1967).

Davis, W.H., 'Anathema – Romans 9:3', *RevExp* 31 (1934), 205–207.

Dodd, C.H., *According to the Scriptures: The Sub-structure of New Testament Theology*, (London: Nisbet, 1952).

—*The Epistle of Paul to the Romans* (MNTC; New York: Harper and Bros., 1932).

Donfried, K.P. (ed.), *The Romans Debate* (Peabody, MA: Hendrickson, rev. edn., 1991).

Donfried, K.P., and P. Richardson (eds.), *Judaism and Christianity in First-Century Rome* (Grand Rapids: Eerdmans, 1998).

Dreyfus, F., 'Le passé et le présent d'Israël (Rom 9, 1–5; 11, 1–24)', in Lorenzi (ed.), *Israelfrage*, 140–51.

Driver, S.R., *The Book of Exodus* (Cambridge: Cambridge University Press, 1911).

—*The Book of Genesis* (Westminster Commentaries; London: Methuen & Co., 11th edn., 1920).

Dunn, J.D.G., 'Did Paul Have a Covenant Theology? Reflections on Romans 9.4 and 11.27', in S.E. Porter and J.C.R. de Roo (eds.), *The Concept of the Covenant in the Second Temple Period* (JSJSup, 71; Leiden: Brill, 2003), 287–307.

—*Romans* (WBC, 38; 2 vols.; Dallas: Word, 1988).

Durham, J.I., *Exodus* (WBC, 3; Waco: Word, 1987).

Eckert, J., 'καλέω, κλῆσις, κλητός', *EDNT*, 2.240–44.

Ellis, E.E., 'Biblical Interpretation in the New Testament Church', in Mulder (ed.), *Mikra*, 691–725.

—'How the New Testament Uses the Old', in I.H. Marshall (ed.), *New Testament Interpretation: Essays on Principles and Methods* (Grand Rapids: Eerdmans, 1977), 199–219.

—*Paul's Use of the Old Testament* (Grand Rapids: Baker, 1957).

—*Prophecy and Hermeneutic in Early Christianity* (WUNT, 2.18; Tübingen: Mohr Siebeck, 1978).

Ellison, H.L., *The Mystery of Israel: An Exposition of Romans 9–11* (Exeter: Paternoster, 3rd edn., rev. and enl., 1976).

Endres, J.C., *Biblical Interpretation in the Book of Jubilees* (CBQMS, 18; Washington, DC: CBAA, 1987).

Enns, P., *Exodus* (NIVAC; Grand Rapids: Zondervan, 2000).

Epp, E.J., 'Jewish-Gentile Continuity in Paul: Torah and/or Faith (Romans 9:1–5)', in G.W.E. Nickelsburg and G.W. MacRae (eds.), *Christians Among Jews and Gentiles: Essays in Honor of Krister Stendahl on His Sixty-fifth Birthday* (Philadelphia: Fortress, 1986), 80–90.

Evans, C.A., 'Listening For Echoes of Interpreted Scripture', in Evans and Sanders (eds.), *Paul*, 47–51.

—'Paul and the Hermeneutics of "True Prophecy": A Study of Rom 9–11', *Bib* 65 (1984), 560–70.

Evans, C.A., and J.A. Sanders (eds.), *Early Christian Interpretation of the Scriptures of Israel: Investigations and Proposals* (JSNTSup, 148; SSEJC, 5; Sheffield: Sheffield Academic Press, 1997).

—*Paul and the Scriptures of Israel* (JSNTSup 83; SSEJC 1; Sheffield: *JSOT*, 1993).

Fee, G., *New Testament Exegesis: A Handbook for Students and Pastors* (Louisville: Westminster/John Knox, rev. edn., 1993).

—*Paul's Letter to the Philippians* (NICNT; Grand Rapids: Eerdmans, 1995).

—*The First Epistle to the Corinthians* (NICNT; Grand Rapids: Eerdmans, 1987).

Feldman, L.H., 'Prolegomenon', in James, *Philo* (The Library of Biblical Studies; New York: KTAV, 1971), vii–CLXIX.

Fitzmyer, J.A., *Romans: A New Translation with Introduction and Commentary* (AB, 33; New York: Doubleday, 1993).

Forster, R.T., and V.P. Marston, *God's Strategy in Human History: God's Sovereignty and Human Responsibility* (Crowborough, East Sussex: Highland, 1973).

France, R.T., 'The Formula-Quotations of Matthew 2 and the Problem of Communication', in Beale (ed.), *Right Doctrine*, 114–34.

Freedman, D.N., 'The Name of the God of Moses', *JBL* 79 (1960), 151–56.

Fretheim, T.E., *Exodus* (IBC; Louisville: John Knox, 1991).

Friedman, S.S., 'Weavings: Intertextuality and the (Re)Birth of the Author', in Clayton and Rothstein (eds.), *Influence and Intertextuality*, 146–80.

Gábris, K., 'Das Gewissen – normiert durch den Heiligen Geist: Bibelarbeit über Röm. 9,1–5', *Communio viatorum* 27 (1984), 19–32.

Gaster, T.H., *The Dead Sea Scriptures with Introduction and Notes* (New York: Anchor/Doubleday, 3rd edn., rev. and enl., 1976).

Gaston, L., 'Israel's Enemies in Pauline Theology', in L. Gaston, *Paul and the Torah* (Vancouver: University of British Columbia Press, 1987), 80–99.

Getty, M.A., 'Paul and the Salvation of Israel: A Perspective on Romans 9–11', *CBQ* 50 (1988), 456–69.

Ginzberg, L., *The Legends of the Jews* (7 vols.; Philadelphia: Jewish Publication Society, 1909–38).

Godet, F., *Commentary on St. Paul's Epistle to the Romans*, II (Edinburgh: T&T Clark, 1892).

Gorday, P., *Principles of Patristic Exegesis: Romans 9–11 in Origen, John Chrysostom, and Augustine* (New York; Toronto: Mellen, 1983).

Gowan, D.E., *Theology in Exodus: Biblical Theology in the Form of a Commentary* (Louisville: Westminster/John Knox, 1994).

Green, W.S., 'Doing the Text's Work for It: Richard Hays on Paul's Use of Scripture', in Evans and Sanders (eds.), *Paul*, 58–63.

Grossfeld, B., *The Targum Onqelos to Exodus: Translated with Apparatus and Notes* (TAB, 7; Wilmington, DE: Michael Glazier, 1988).

—*The Targum Onqelos to Genesis: Translated with a Critical Introduction, Apparatus and Notes* (TAB, 6; Wilmington, DE: Michael Glazier, 1988).

Guerra, A.J., *Romans and the Apologetic Tradition: The Purpose, Genre and Audience of Paul's Letter* (SNTSMS, 81; Cambridge: Cambridge University Press, 1995).

Gundry Volf, J.M., *Paul and Perseverance: Staying In and Falling Away* (WUNT, 2.37; Tübingen: Mohr Siebeck, 1990).

Güttgemanns, E., 'Heilsgeschichte bei Paulus oder Dynamik des Evangeliums: Zur strukturellen Relevanz von Röm 9–11 für die Theologie des Römerbriefes', in E. Güttgemanns, *Studia Linguistica Neotestamentica* (Munich: Kaiser, 1971), 34–58.

Haacker, K., *Der Briefe des Paulus an die Römer* (THKNT, 6; Leipzig: Evangelische Verlagsanstalt, 1999).

—'Die Geschichtstheologie von Röm 9–11 im Lichte philonischer Schriftauslegung', *NTS* 43 (1997), 209–22.

Hafemann, S.J., 'Corinthians, Letters to the', *DPL*, 164–79.

—'Paul and His Interpreters', *DPL*, 666–79.

—*Paul, Moses, and the History of Israel: The Letter/Spirit Contrast and the Argument from Scripture in 2 Corinthians 3* (Peabody, MA: Hendrickson, 1995).

Hamilton, V.P., *The Book of Genesis: Chapters 18–50* (NICOT; Grand Rapids: Eerdmans, 1995).

Hanson, A.T., 'The Oracle in Romans XI.4', *NTS* 19 (1973), 300–302.

Harrington, D.J., 'Pseudo-Philo: A New Translation and Introduction', in Charlesworth (ed.), *Pseudepigrapha*, 2.297–377.

Harris, M.J., '*hyper*', *NIDNTT*, 3.1196–97.

Harvey, G., *The True Israel: Uses of the Names Jew, Hebrew and Israel in Ancient Jewish and Early Christian Literature* (AGJU, 35; Leiden: Brill, 1996).

Harvey, J.D., *Listening to the Text: Oral Patterning in Paul's Letters* (Grand Rapids: Baker, 1998).

Hatina, T.R., 'Exile', *DNTB*, 348–51.

—'Intertextuality and Historical Criticism in New Testament Studies: Is There a Relationship?', *BibInt* 7, 1 (1999), 28–43.

Hauge, M.R., *The Descent from the Mountain: Narrative Patterns in Exodus 19–40* (JSOTSup, 323; Sheffield: Sheffield Academic Press, 2001).

Hay, D.M., and E.E. Johnson (eds.), *Pauline Theology III: Romans* (Minneapolis: Fortress, 1995).

Haynes, S.R., 'Recovering the Real Paul: Theology and Exegesis in Romans 9–11', *Ex Auditu* 4 (1988), 70–84.

Hays, R.B., 'Adam, Israel, Christ – The Question of Covenant in the Theology of Romans: A Response to Leander E. Keck and N. T. Wright', in Hay and Johnson (eds.), *Pauline*, 68–86.

—'Crucified with Christ' in D.J. Lull (ed.), *Society of Biblical Literature 1988 Seminar Papers* (Atlanta: Scholars Press, 1988), 318–35.

—*Echoes of Scripture in the Letters of Paul* (New Haven & London: Yale University Press, 1989).

—'On the Rebound: A Response to Critiques of *Echoes of Scripture in the Letters of Paul*', in Evans and Sanders (eds.), *Paul*, 70–96.

Hays, R.B., and J.B. Green, 'The Use of the Old Testament by New Testament Writers', in J.B. Green (ed.), *Hearing the New Testament: Strategies for Interpretation* (Grand Rapids: Paternoster Press/Carlisle, 1995), 222–38.

Hebel, U.J., *Intertextuality, Allusion, and Quotation: An International Bibliography of Critical Studies* (Bibliographies and Indexes in World Literature, 18; New York & London: Greenwood, 1989).

Hillert, S., *Limited and Universal Salvation: A Text-Oriented and Hermeneutical Study of Two Perspectives in Paul* (*ConNT*, 31; Stockholm: Almqvist & Wiksell International, 1999).

Hirsch, E.D., Jr., *Validity in Interpretation* (New Haven: Yale University Press, 1967).

Hofius, O., 'Das Evangelium und Israel: Erwägungen zu Römer 9–11', *ZTK* 83 (1986), 297–324.

Hollander, J., *The Figure of Echo: A Mode of Allusion in Milton and After* (Berkeley: University of California Press, 1981).

Houtman, C., *Exodus Volume 3: Chapters 20–40* (Historical Commentary on the Old Testament; Leuven: Peeters, 2000).

Hübner, H., *Gottes Ich und Israel: Zum Schriftgebrauch des Paulus in Römer 9–11* (Göttingen: Vandenhoeck & Ruprecht, 1984).

Hugenberger, G.P., *Marriage as a Covenant: A Study of Biblical Law and Ethics Governing Marriage Developed from the Perspective of Malachi* (VTSup, 52; Leiden: Brill, 1994).

Isaac, E., '1 (Ethiopic Apocalypse of) Enoch: A New Translation and Introduction', in Charlesworth (ed.), *Pseudepigrapha*, 1.5–89.

Jacobson, H., *A Commentary on Pseudo-Philo's Liber Antiquitatum Biblicarum with Latin Text and English Translation* (2 vols.; Leiden: Brill, 1996).

James, M.R., *The Biblical Antiquities of Philo* (The Library of Biblical Studies; New York: KTAV, 1971).

Johnson, E.E., *The Function of Apocalyptic and Wisdom Traditions in Romans 9–11* (SBLDS, 109; Atlanta: Scholars Press, 1989).

Johnson, L.T., *Reading Romans* (New York: Crossword, 1997).

Käsemann, E., *Commentary on Romans* (trans. G.W. Bromiley; Grand Rapids: Eerdmans, 1980).

Keck, L.E., 'What Makes Romans Tick?', in Hay and Johnson (eds.), *Pauline*, 3–29.

Kee, H.C., *Knowing the Truth: A Sociological Approach to New Testament Interpretation* (Minneapolis: Fortress, 1989).

Keesmaat, S.C., *Paul and His Story: (Re)interpreting the Exodus Tradition* (JSNTSup, 181; Sheffield: Sheffield Academic Press, 1999).

Kim, J.D., *God, Israel, and the Gentiles: Rhetoric and Situation in Romans 9–11* (SBLDS, 176; Atlanta: SBL, 2000).

Kim, S., *Paul and the New Perspective: Second Thoughts on the Origin of Paul's Gospel* (Grand Rapids: Eerdmans, 2002).

—*The Origin of Paul's Gospel* (WUNT, 2.4; Tübingen: Mohr Siebeck, 2nd edn., rev. and enl., 1984).

Klappert, B., 'Traktat für Israel (Römer 9–11)', in M. Stöhr (ed.), *Jüdische Existenz und die Erneuerung der christlichen Theologie* (Munich: Kaiser, 1981), 58–137.

Klein, W.W., 'Paul's Use of *KALEIN*: A Proposal', *JETS* 27/1 (March 1984), 53–64.

—*The New Chosen People: A Corporate View of Election* (Grand Rapids: Zondervan, 1990).

Kline, M.G., *The Structure of Biblical Authority* (Grand Rapids: Eerdmans, 2nd edn., 1975).

Klumbies, P.-G., 'Israels Vorzüge und das Evangelium von der Gottesgerechtigkeit in Römer 9–11', *WD* 18 (1985), 135–57.

Knibb, M.A., 'Martyrdom and Ascension of Isaiah: A New Translation and Introduction', in Charlesworth (ed.), *Pseudepigrapha*, 2.143–76.

Knight, J., *Disciples of the Beloved One: The Christology, Social Setting and Theological Context of the Ascension of Isaiah* (JSPSup, 18; Sheffield: Sheffield Academic Press, 1996).

—*The Ascension of Isaiah* (Sheffield: Sheffield Academic Press, 1995).

Knowles, M., *Jeremiah in Matthew's Gospel: The Rejected Prophet Motif in Matthaean Redaction* (JSNTSup, 68; Sheffield: *JSOT*, 1993).

Koch, D.-A., *Die Schrift als Zeuge des Evangeliums: Untersuchungen zur Verwendung und zum Verständnis der Schrift bei Paulus* (BHT, 69; Tübingen: Mohr Siebeck, 1986).

Kotansky, R.D., 'A Note on Romans 9:6: *Ho Logos Tou Theou* as the Proclamation of the Gospel', *Studia Biblica et Theologica* 7 (1977), 24–30.

Kraus, W., *Das Volk Gottes: Zur Grundlegung der Ekklesiologie bei Paulus* (Tübingen: Mohr Siebeck, 1996).

Kugel, J.L., *Traditions of the Bible: A Guide to the Bible as It Was at the Start of the Common Era* (Cambridge, MA; London: Harvard University Press, 1998).

Kuhli, H., 'Ἰσραηλίτης', *EDNT*, 2.204–205.

Kümmel, W.G., *Introduction to the New Testament* (Nashville: Abingdon, rev. edn., 1975).

Kuss, O., *Der Römerbrief*, III, (Regensburg: Pustet, 1978).

—'Zu Römer 9,5', in J. Friedrich, W. Pöhlmann, and P. Stuhlmacher (eds.), *Rechtfertigung: Festschrift für Ernst Käsemann zum 70. Geburstag* (Tübingen: Mohr Siebeck; Göttingen: Vandenhoeck & Ruprecht, 1976), 291–303.

Lane, W.L., 'Social Perspectives on Roman Christianity during the Formative Years from Nero to Nerva: Romans, Hebrews, 1 Clement', in Donfried and Richardson (eds.), *Judaism*, 196–244.

Lindars, B., 'The Place of the Old Testament in the Formation of New Testament Theology: Prolegomena', in Beale (ed.), *Right Doctrine*, 137–45.

Lincoln, A.T., *Ephesians* (WBC, 42; Dallas: Word, 1990).

Lodge, J.G., *Romans 9–11: A Reader-Response Analysis* (ISFCJ, 6; Atlanta: Scholars Press, 1996).

Longenecker, B.W., *Eschatology and the Covenant: A Comparison of 4 Ezra and Romans 1–11* (JSNTSup, 57; Sheffield: *JSOT*, 1991).

Longenecker, R., *Biblical Exegesis in the Apostolic Period* (Grand Rapids: Eerdmans, 1975).

—'Prolegomena to Paul's Use of Scripture in Romans', *BBR* 7 (1997), 145–68.

Lorenzi, L. de (ed.), *Die Israelfrage nach Röm 9–11* (Monographische Reihe von <Benedictina>> Biblisch-ökumenische Abteilung, 3; Rome: Abtei von St Paul vor den Mauern, 1977).

Lorimer, W.L., 'Romans ix. 3–5', *ExpTim* 35 (1923–24), 42–43.

Lübking, H.-M., *Paulus und Israel im Römerbrief: Eine Untersuchung zu Römer 9–11* (Frankfurt: Lang, 1986).

Lundbom, J.R., 'God's Use of the *Idem per Idem* to Terminate Debate', *HTR* 71 (1978), 193–201.

Lung-kwong, L., *Paul's Purpose in Writing Romans: The Upbuilding of a Jewish and Gentile Christian Community in Rome* (Jian Dao Dissertation Series 6; Bible and Literature 4; Hong Kong: Alliance Bible Seminary, 1998).

Luz, U., *Das Geschichtsverständnis des Paulus* (BevT, 49. Munich: Kaiser, 1968).

Lyonnet, S., 'Le rôle d'Israël dans l'histoire du salut selon Rom 9–11', in S. Lyonnet, *Etudes sur l'Epître aux Romains* (AnBib, 120; Rome: Editrice Pontificio Instituto Biblico, 1989), 264–73.

Maher, M., *Targum Pseudo-Jonathan: Genesis. Translated, with Introduction and Notes* (Collegeville, MN: The Liturgical Press, 1992).

Maier, G., *Mensch und freier Wille nach den jüdischen Religionspartien zwischen Ben Sira und Paulus* (WUNT, 12; Tübingen: Mohr Siebeck, 1971).

Malina, B.J., *The New Testament World* (Atlanta: John Knox, 1981).

Marshall, I.H., 'An Assessment of Recent Developments', in Beale (ed.), *Right Doctrine*, 195–216.

—*The Acts of the Apostles: An Introduction and Commentary* (TNTC, 5; Grand Rapids: Eerdmans, 1980).

Martin, R.P., *2 Corinthians* (WBC, 40; Milton Keynes, England: Word, 1986).

Mayer, B., *Unter Gottes Heilsratschluss: Prädestinationsaussagen bei Paulus* (Würzburg: Echter, 1974).

McNamara, M., and R. Hayward, *Targum Neofiti 1: Exodus* (TAB, 2; Collegeville, MN: Liturgical Press, 1994).

Metzger, B.M., *A Textual Commentary on the Greek New Testament* (Stuttgart: UBS, 2nd edn., 1994).

—'The Fourth Book of Ezra: A New Translation and Introduction', in Charlesworth (ed.), *Pseudepigrapha*, 1.517–59.

—'The Punctuation of Rom. 9:5', in B. Lindars and S.S. Smalley (eds.), *Christ and Spirit in the New Testament* (Festschrift C.F.D. Moule; Cambridge: Cambridge University Press, 1973), 95–112.

Michel, O., 'Opferbereitschaft für Israel', in W. Schmauch (ed.), *In Memoriam Ernst Lohmeyer* (Stuttgart: Evangelisches Verlagswerk, 1951), 94–100.

Miller, J.C., *The Obedience of Faith, the Eschatological People of God, and the Purpose of Romans* (SBLDS, 177; Atlanta: SBL, 2000).

Moberly, R.W.L., *At the Mountain of God: Story and Theology in Exodus 32–34* (JSOTSup, 22; Sheffield: *JSOT*, 1983).

Mohrmann, D.C., 'Semantic Collisions at the Intertextual Crossroads : A Diachronic and Synchronic Study of Romans 9:30–10:13' (unpublished Ph.D. thesis; University of Durham, 2001).

Moo, D.J., *The Epistle to the Romans* (NICNT; Grand Rapids: Eerdmans, 1996).

—'The Theology of Romans 9–11: A Response to E. Elizabeth Johnson', in Hay and Johnson (eds.), *Pauline*, 240–58.

Moore, S.D., *Poststructuralism and the New Testament: Derrida and Foucault at the Foot of the Cross* (Minneapolis: Fortress, 1994).

Morison, J., *Exposition of the Ninth Chapter of the Epistle to the Romans: A New Edition, Re-written, to which is Added an Exposition of the Tenth Chapter* (London: Hodder & Stoughton, 1888).

Morris, L., *The Epistle to the Romans* (Grand Rapids: Eerdmans, 1988).

Moyise, S., 'Intertextuality and the Study of the Old Testament in the New Testament', in S. Moyise (ed.), *The Old Testament in the New Testament: Essays in Honour of J. L. North* (JSNTSup, 189; Sheffield: Sheffield Academic Press, 2000), 14–41.

—'The Old Testament in the New: A Reply to Greg Beale', *IBS* 21 (May, 1999), 54–58.

Muilenburg, J., 'The Intercession of the Covenant Mediator (Exodus 33:1a, 12–17)', in P.R. Ackroyd and B. Lindars (eds.), *Words and Meanings: Essays Presented to David Winton Thomas* (Cambridge: Cambridge University Press, 1968), 159–181.

Mulder, M.J., 'The Transmission of the Biblical Text', in Mulder (ed.), *Mikra*, 87–135.

Mulder, M.J. (ed.), *Mikra: Text, Translation, Reading, and Interpretation of the Hebrew Bible in Ancient Judaism and Early Christianity* (CRINT, 2/1; Assen: Van Gorcum; Philadelphia: Fortress, 1988).

Müller, C., *Gottes Gerechtigkeit und Gottes Volk: Eine Untersuchung zu Römer 9–11* (FRLANT, 86; Göttingen: Vandenhoeck & Ruprecht, 1964).

Munck, J., *Christ and Israel: An Interpretation of Romans 9–11* (Philadelphia: Fortress, 1967).

Murray, J., *The Epistle to the Romans* (NICNT; 2 vols. in 1; Grand Rapids: Eerdmans, 1959–65).

Nanos, M.D., *The Mystery of Romans: The Jewish Context of Paul's Letter* (Minneapolis: Fortress, 1996).

Noack, B., 'Current and Backwater in the Epistle to the Romans', *ST* 19 (1965), 155–66.

Nicole, R., 'The New Testament Use of the Old Testament', in Beale (ed.), *Right Doctrine*, 13–28.

Niehaus, J.J., *God at Sinai: Covenant and Theophany in the Bible and Ancient Near East* (SOTBT; Grand Rapids: Zondervan, 1995).

O'Neill, J.C., *Paul's Letter to the Romans* (Harmondsworth: Penguin, 1975).

Osborne, G.R., *The Hermeneutical Spiral: A Comprehensive Introduction to Biblical Interpretation* (Downers Grove: InterVarsity Press, 1991).

Österreicher, J.M., 'Israel's Misstep and Her Rise: The Dialectic of God's Saving Design in Rom 9–11', in *Studiorum Paulinorum Congressus Internationalis Catholicus 1961*, I (AnBib, 17; Rome: Pontifical Biblical Institute, 1963), 317–27.

Piper, J., *The Justification of God: An Exegetical and Theological Study of Romans 9:1–23* (Grand Rapids: Baker, 2nd edn., 1993).

Plastaras, J., *The God of Exodus: The Theology of the Exodus Narratives* (Milwaukee: Bruce, 1966).

Porter, S.E., 'The Concept of Covenant in Paul', in S.E. Porter and J.C.R. de Roo (eds.), *The Concept of the Covenant in the Second Temple Period* (JSJSup, 71; Leiden: Brill, 2003), 269–85.

—'The Use of the Old Testament in the New Testament: A Brief Comment on Method and Terminology', in Evans and Sanders (eds.), *Christian Interpretation*, 79–96.

Priest, J., 'Testament of Moses: A New Translation and Introduction', in Charlesworth (ed.), *Pseudepigrapha*, 1.919–34.

Rad, G. von, *Genesis: A Commentary* (OTL; Philadelphia: Westminster, rev. edn., 1972).

Räisänen, H., 'Romans 9–11 and the "History of Early Christian Religion"', in T. Fornberg and D. Hellholm (eds.), *Texts and Contexts: Biblical Texts in Their Textual and Situational Contexts: Essays in Honor of Lars Hartman* (Oslo: Scandanavian University Press, 1995), 743–65.

—'Römer 9–11: Analyse eines geistigen Ringens', *ANRW* 2.25.4 (1987), 2891–939.

Reichert, A., *Der Römerbrief als Gratwanderung: Eine Untersuchung zur Abfassungsproblematik* (FRLANT, 194; Göttingen: Vandenhoeck & Ruprecht, 2001).

Rese, M., 'Die Vorzüge Israels in Röm. 9,4f. und Eph. 2,12: Exegetische Anmerkungen zum Thema Kirche und Israel', *TZ* 31 (1975), 211–22.

—'Israel und Kirche in Römer 9', *NTS* 34 (1988), 208–17.

Richardson, N., *Paul's Language About God* (JSNTSup, 99; Sheffield: Sheffield Academic Press, 1994).

Roetzel, C.J., 'Διαθῆκαι in Romans 9,4', *Bib* 51 (1970), 377–90.

Rosner, B.S., *Paul, Scripture & Ethics: A Study of 1 Corinthians 5–7* (AGJU, 22; Leiden: Brill, 1994).

—Review of Christopher D. Stanley, *Paul and the Language of Scripture: Citation Technique in the Pauline Epistles and Contemporary Literature*, *EvQ* 68:4 (1996), 360–62.

Ruse, C., and M. Hopton, *The Cassell Dictionary of Literary and Language Terms* (London: Cassell, 1992).

Sand, A., 'ἐπαγγελία, κτλ', *EDNT*, 2.13–16.

Sanday, W., and A.C. Headlam, *A Critical and Exegetical Commentary on the Epistle to the Romans* (ICC; New York: Charles Scribner's Sons, 1895).

Sanders, E.P., *Paul and Palestinian Judaism: A Comparison of Patterns of Religion* (Philadelphia: Fortress, 1977).

Sanders, J.A., 'Paul and Theological History', in Evans and Sanders (eds.), *Paul*, 52–57.

Sandmel, S., 'Parallelomania', *JBL* 81 (1962), 1–13.

Schelkle, K.H., *The Epistle to the Romans: Theological Meditations* (New York: Herder and Herder, 1964).

Schlier, H., *Der Römerbrief* (HTKNT; Freiburg: Herder, 1977).

Schmidt, K.L., 'καλέω, κλῆσις, κλητός', *TDNT*, 3.487–96.

Schmithals, W., *Der Römerbrief: Ein Kommentar* (Gütersloh: Gütersloher, 1988).

Schmitt, R., *Gottesgerechtigkeit-Heilsgeschichte-Israel in der Theologie des Paulus* (Frankfurt: Lang, 1984).

Schoeps, H.J., *Paul: The Theology of the Apostle in the Light of Jewish Religious History* (London: Lutterworth, 1961).

Schreiner, T.R., 'Does Romans 9 Teach Individual Election unto Salvation? Some Exegetical and Theological Reflections', *JETS* 36/1 (March 1993), 25–40.

—*Romans* (BECNT, 6; Grand Rapids: Baker, 1998).

Scott, J.M., *Adoption as Sons of God: An Exegetical Investigation into the Background of* ΥΙΟΘΕΣΙΑ *in the Pauline Corpus* (WUNT, 2.48; Tübingen: Mohr Siebeck, 1992).

Scott, J.M., 'Restoration of Israel', *DPL*, 796–805.

Scroggs, R., 'Paul as Rhetorician: Two Homilies in Romans 1–11', in R. Hamerton-Kelly and R. Scroggs (eds.), *Jews, Greeks, and Christians: Religious Cultures in Late Antiquity* (Festschrift W.D. Davies; trans. J. Smith; SJLA, 21; Leiden: Brill, 2nd edn., 1976), 271–98.

Seifrid, M.A., 'Righteousness Language in the Hebrew Scriptures and Early Judaism', in Carson, O'Brien, and Seifrid (eds.), *Justification*, 1.415–42.

Shum, S.-L., *Paul's Use of Isaiah in Romans: A Comparative Study of Paul's Letter to the Romans and the Sybilline and Qumran Sectarian Texts* (WUNT, 2.156; Tübingen: Mohr Siebeck, 2002).

Siegert, F., *Argumentation bei Paulus: gezeigt an Röm 9–11* (WUNT, 34; Tübingen: Mohr Siebeck, 1985).

Siker, J.S., *Disinheriting the Jews: Abraham in Early Christian Controversy* (Louisville: Westminster/John Knox, 1991).

Silva, M., 'Old Testament in Paul', *DPL*, 630–42 (634).

Smith, D.M., 'The Pauline Literature', in D.A. Carson and H.G.M. Williamson (eds.), *It is Written: Scripture Citing Scripture: Essays in Honour of Barnabas Lindars* (Cambridge: Cambridge University Press, 1988), 265–91.

Smolar, L., and M. Aberbach, 'The Golden Calf Episode in Postbiblical Literature', *HUCA* 39 (1968), 91–116.

Snodgrass, K., 'The Use of the Old Testament in the New', in Beale (ed.), *Right Doctrine*, 29–51.

Son, S.-W.(A.), *Corporate Elements in Pauline Anthropology: A Study of Selected Terms, Idioms, and Concepts in the Light of Paul's Usage and Background* (Rome: Editrice Pontificio Instituto Biblico, 2001).

Soulen, R.N., *Handbook of Biblical Criticism* (Guilford/London: Lutterworth Press, 1977).

Spilsbury, P., *The Image of the Jew in Flavius Josephus' Paraphrase of the Bible* (TSAJ, 69; Tübingen: Mohr Siebeck, 1998).

Stählin, G., 'Zum Gebrauch von Beteurungsformeln im Neuen Testament', *NovT* 5 (1962), 115–43.

Stanley, C.D., *Paul and the Language of Scripture: Citation Technique in the Pauline Epistles and Contemporary Literature* (SNTSMS, 69; Cambridge: Cambridge University Press, 1992).

—' "Pearls Before Swine": Did Paul's Audiences Understand His Biblical Quotations?', *NovT* 41, 2 (1999), 124–44.

—'The Rhetoric of Quotations: An Essay on Method', in Evans and Sanders (eds.), *Christian Interpretation*, 44–58.

—'The Social Environment of "Free" Biblical Quotations in the New Testament', in Evans and Sanders (eds.), *Christian Interpretation*, 18–27.

Stegner, W.R., 'Romans 9:6–29 – A Midrash', *JSNT* 22 (1984), 37–52.

Stockhausen, C.K., '2 Corinthians 3 and the Principles of Pauline Exegesis', in Evans and Sanders (eds.), *Paul*, 143–64.

Stone, M.E., *Fourth Ezra: A Commentary on the Book of Fourth Ezra* (Hermeneia; Minneapolis: Fortress, 1990).

Strathmann, H., 'λατρεύω, λατρεία', *TDNT*, 4.58–65.

Stuart, D., *Hosea-Jonah* (WBC, 31; Waco: Word, 1987).

—*Old Testament Exegesis: A Primer for Students and Pastors* (Philadelphia: Westminster, 2nd edn., rev. and enl., 1984).

Stuhlmacher, P., *Paul's Letter to the Romans: A Commentary* (trans. S.J. Hafemann; Louisville, KY: Westminster/John Knox, 1994).

Sundberg, A.C., Jr., 'On Testimonies', in Beale (ed.), *Right Doctrine*, 182–94.

Thiselton, A.C., *New Horizons in Hermeneutics* (Grand Rapids: Zondervan, 1992).

Thompson, A.L., *Responsibility for Evil in the Theodicy of IV Ezra* (SBLDS, 29; Missoula, MT: Scholars Press, 1977).

Thompson, M., *Clothed with Christ: The Example and Teaching of Jesus in Romans 12.1–15.13* (JSNTSup, 59; Sheffield: *JSOT*, 1991).

Tiede, D.L., 'The Figure of Moses in *The Testament of Moses*', in G.W.E. Nickelsburg (ed.), *Studies on the Testament of Moses* (Septuagint and Cognate Studies, 4; Cambridge, MA: SBL, 1973), 86–92.

Tov, E., 'The Septuagint', in Mulder (ed.), *Mikra*, 161–88.

Tromp, J., *The Assumption of Moses: A Critical Edition with Commentary* (SVTP, 10; Leiden: Brill, 1993).

Vanhoozer, K.J., *Is there a Meaning in this Text? The Bible, the Reader, and the Morality of Literary Knowledge* (Grand Rapids: Zondervan, 1998).

Villiers, J.L. de, 'The Salvation of Israel according to Romans 9–11', *Neot* 15 (1981), 199–221.

Wagner, J.R., *Heralds of the Good News: Isaiah and Paul 'in Concert' in the Letter to the Romans* (NovTSup, 101; Leiden: Brill, 2002).

—' "Who Has Believed Our Message?": Paul and Isaiah "in Concert" in the Letter to the Romans' (Ph.D. Thesis; Duke University, 1999).

Walters, J.C., *Ethnic Issues in Paul's Letter to the Romans: Changing Self-Definitions in Earliest Roman Christianity* (Valley Forge, PA: Trinity Press International, 1993).

Watson, F., *Paul, Judaism and the Gentiles: A Sociological Approach* (SNTSMS, 56; Cambridge: Cambridge University Press, 1986).

—*Text and Truth: Redefining Biblical Theology* (Edinburgh: T&T Clark, 1997).

Wedderburn. A.J.M., *The Reasons for Romans* (Minneapolis: Fortress, 1991).

Wenham, G.J., *Genesis* (WBC, 1–2; 2 vols.; Dallas: Word, 1987).

Westerholm S., 'Paul and the Law in Romans 9–11', in J.D.G. Dunn (ed.), *Paul and the Mosaic Law* (WUNT, 89; Tübingen: Mohr Siebeck, 1996), 215–37.

Westermann, C., *Genesis 12–36: A Commentary* (Minneapolis: Augsburg, 1985).

Wevers, J.W., *Notes on the Greek Text of Exodus* (SBLSCS, 30; Atlanta: Scholars Press, 1990).

—*Notes on the Greek Text of Genesis* (SBLSCS, 35; Atlanta: Scholars Press, 1993).

Wiefel, W., 'The Jewish Community of Ancient Rome and the Origins of Roman Christianity' in Donfried (ed.), *Romans*, 85–101.

Wilckens, U., *Der Brief an die Römer*, II: Röm 6–11 (EKKNT, 2; Zürich: Benziger/Neukirchen: Neukirchener Verlag, 1980).

Wiles, G.P., *Paul's Intercessory Prayers: The Significance of the Intercessory Prayer Passages in the Letters of St. Paul* (Cambridge: Cambridge University Press, 1974).

Wilk, F., *Die Bedeutung des Jesajabuches für Paulus* (FRLANT, 179; Göttingen: Vandenhoeck & Ruprecht, 1998).

Willett, T.W., *Eschatology in the Theodicies of 2 Baruch and 4 Ezra* (JSPSup, 4; Sheffield: *JSOT*, 1989).

Williams, S.K., 'The "Righteousness of God" in Romans', *JBL* (1980), 241–90.

Wintermute, O.S., 'Jubilees: A New Translation and Introduction', in Charlesworth (ed.), *Pseudepigrapha*, 2.35–142.

Wolde, E. van, 'Trendy Intertextuality?', in S. Draisma (ed.), *Intertextuality in Biblical Writings: Essays in Honour of Bas van Iersel* (Kampen: J.H. Kok, 1989), 43–49.

Worgul, G.S., Jr., 'Romans 9–11 and Ecclesiology', *BTB* 7 (1977), 99–109.

Wright, N.T., 'Romans and the Theology of Paul', in Hay and Johnson (eds.), *Pauline*, 30–67.

—*The Climax of the Covenant: Christ and the Law in Pauline Theology* (Edinburgh: T&T Clark, 1992).

Yonge, C.D. (trans.), *The Works of Philo: New Updated Edition Complete and Unabridged in One Volume* (Peabody, MA: Hendrickson, 1993).

Zeller, D., *Juden und Heiden in der Mission des Paulus: Studien zum Römerbrief* (FzB, 1; Stuttgart: Katholisches Bibelwerk, 1973).

Ziesler, J., *Paul's Letter to the Romans* (TPINTC; Philadelphia: Trinity Press International, 1989).

INDEX OF REFERENCES

OLD TESTAMENT

Genesis
3	46
11.12	177
12	74
12–25	52, 107, 171
12.1–3	171, 211
12.3	51, 76, 154, 210
12.7	74
15.5	198
15.6	198
16.4	167
16.10–12	168, 171
17	154, 165, 167, 169, 195
17–21	154, 164
17.4–5	198
17.6	171
17.8	74
17.11	195
17.14	195
17.15	149
17.15–21	149–50, 168–69
17.18–21	194
17.19	165
17.19–20	192
17.20	168–69, 171
17.21	165
17.24–25	195
18	50, 107, 147–48, 151, 153–54, 156–57, 161–62, 164–65, 167, 169, 176, 181, 195, 208–10, 212–14
18–19	148, 150, 152, 154, 157, 161–62, 164, 212–13
18–20	169
18–21	213–14, 229
18.1	148–49
18.1–8	148
18.1–15	147–48, 150, 152, 154, 156
18.9	148
18.9–15	148
18.10	40, 147,149, 154–57, 163, 165, 177, 191–93, 208, 213, 221, 226
18.11	149
18.11–13	149
18.12	149
18.12–14	150
18.13–14	149
18.14	40, 147, 150, 153–57, 164–65, 177, 191–93, 198, 208, 212–13, 218, 221, 226
18.15	150, 153
18.16	209–10
18.16–21	150
18.16–33	147–48, 150, 152–54
18.16–19.29	148
18.16–19.38	212
18.17	153
18.17–19	150, 153, 211, 221
18.18	153–54, 210–11
18.18–19	153
18.19	153, 166
18.20–21	150, 162
18.21	162, 164
18.22	148
18.22–32	153, 158
18.22–33	150, 152, 212
18.23	151, 161
18.23–32	151–52
18.25	151, 212–13
18.32	162
18.33	148, 151
19	147
19.1	148

19.1–29	148, 151–52	4.13	67
19.16	152	4.14	67
19.19	152	4.22–23	122, 124
19.26	151	12.36	59
19.29	152	13.5	112
19.30–38	148, 151–52, 154	13.21	125
20	154	16.2	67
20.13	112	16.10	125
21	107, 154,169, 174–75, 181, 195, 213–14	16.23	68
		17.14–16	56
21.1	163, 165	19–31	47
21.1–2	165	19–40	60
21.1–4	166	19.5–6	172
21.1–7	165, 167, 175	19.9–25	125
21.1–21	165, 169	19.10–13	47
21.2	165	20–40	46
21.3	165–66	20.2	49
21.4	166	20.3	47
21.5	166	20.5–6	69
21.6	150, 166–67, 174	20.5–7	56
21.6–7	166, 169	20.18–21	47, 71
21.7	166	20.23	47
21.8	165, 167	21.11	50
21.8–21	165, 167	23.20–23	58
21.9	167	23.20–31	57
21.10	129, 167, 194	24	47
21.12	39, 129, 147, 160, 165, 169–72, 174–77, 189–93, 195–96, 198–99, 201, 208, 213, 227	24.4	56
		24.7	56
		24.12–18	125
21.12–13	168	25.22	85
21.13	168–69, 171, 190, 193	29.43	125
21.14	168	31.18	131
21.14–19	168–69	32	52, 56, 74, 78–79, 87, 102, 104, 109, 136–37, 140, 142–43, 161, 209
21.14–21	168		
21.15–16	168	32–34	45–47, 49, 52, 56, 61, 62, 65, 68, 70–78, 81–89, 94, 101, 103–12, 114–15, 124–26, 128–29, 131–34, 141–44, 214, 223
21.17–19	168		
21.18	171		
21.20	169		
21.20–21	168–69	32.1	48, 87
22.18	154	32.1–6	48
24.41	112	32.2–4	49
25	107	32.4	49
25.23	85, 222	32.4–5	49
26.4	154	32.6	113
27.40	112	32.7	49–50, 84, 85
28.14	154	32.7–10	49
37	172, 194	32.7–14	48–49
38.10	168	32.8	49
43.14	67	32.9	50, 71, 88
		32.10	51–52, 76
Exodus		32.11–12	50
3.14	67	32.11–13	50, 75
3.22	59	32.11–14	81

32.12	50
32.13	51, 74, 77, 89, 107, 116, 128, 135
32.14	51–53
32.15–16	53, 131
32.15–29	48, 53
32.16	85
32.17	84
32.19	76, 112, 114
32.22	71
32.23	87
32.25–29	114
32.27–29	84
32.29	53–54
32.30	53–54
32.30–35	75
32.30–33.6	48, 54, 68, 105
32.31	54
32.31–32	45, 115
32.32	45–46, 54, 55, 56, 72–74, 79, 84, 85, 87, 89, 94–96, 105, 114, 117, 128, 133, 135, 142, 144–46, 225–27, 230
32.32–33	97
32.33	57, 68
32.33–34	57, 58, 75
32.34	57
32.35	57
33.1	61, 62, 74
33.1–3	61
33.2	57
33.3	58, 65, 71, 85, 88
33.3–5	106, 114
33.4–6	59, 60, 68, 92
33.5	59, 61, 65, 71, 85, 88
33.5–6	59
33.6	59, 102
33.7	60, 84
33.7–11	48, 59, 60, 68, 71, 125
33.8	112
33.22	112
33.11	83
33.12	61–62, 85, 86
33.12–17	61–62
33.12–23	48, 61, 66
33.13	61–64, 70, 84, 85, 121, 145
33.14	61, 63
33.15–16	63–64
33.16	58, 64
33.17	63–64, 84
33.17–34.6	89
33.18	64–65
33.18–23	64
33.19	52, 61, 66–69, 72–73, 104, 222, 225
33.19–20	65

33.20	79–81, 83, 84, 89, 142
33.20–23	66
33.21–23	66
33.23	85
33.26	84
34	133
34.1	86, 131
34.1–9	48, 69
34.1–28	65
34.4	131
34.5–7	69
34.5–28	66
34.6	89, 142
34.6–7	52, 68, 69, 85
34.7	68
34.9	58, 60, 70, 88
34.10–28	48, 70, 131, 133
34.12–26	70
34.24	112
34.27	70
34.27–29	131
34.28	84, 89
34.29	72, 83
34.29–35	48, 71, 114, 125
34.30	72
34.34	111–12
34.35	72
35–40	59, 133
40.34–35	125

Leviticus
5.23	112
27.28	97

Numbers
11.10	168
11.15	73
23.18	163
35.30	91

Deuteronomy
1.31	122
7.26	97
9	77–78
9–10	77
9.5	77
9.25	67
9.27	77
13.16	97
13.18	97
14.1	122
17.6	91
19.15	91

20.17	97	*2 Chronicles*	
24.16	68	10.5	155
25.19	112		
27.3	112	*Nehemiah*	
28.58	56	9.38–10.27	56
28.61	56		
29.19–20	56	*Esther*	
29.20–21	56	4.16	67
29.21	56	4.17	72
29.27	56		
30.10	56	*Psalms*	
31.24	56	17.50	6
31.26	56	17.51	6
32	46, 143, 214	18	6
32.4	196	18.49	6
32.5	196	18.50	6
32.6	122	68.29	56
		69.28	56
Joshua		69.29	56
6.17	97	83.6	172, 194
6.18	97	83.7	172, 194
7	97	105	87, 102
7.1	97	106	87, 103
7.11	97	106.20	87, 102
7.12	97	116.2	6
7.13	97	137.7	194
22.20	97		
24.20	112	*Isaiah*	
24.27	112	1.2	122
		1.9	81, 210
Judges		1.10	81
11.8	155	2.2–4	76
21.11	97	6	103
		6.1	81
1 Samuel		6.9	88
1.24	67	6.9–10	88, 103
18.8	168	29.16	234
23.13	67	35.10	92
		40.7–8	177
2 Samuel		45.9	160, 234
5.1–3	98	45.11	160–61
11.7	168	51.11	92
15.20	67	56.6–8	76
		60.1–22	76
2 Kings		63.16	122
8.1	67	64.7	86
8.11	125	64.8	122, 234
1 Chronicles		*Jeremiah*	
2.7	97	3.19–22	122
23.14	206	18	86, 234
		18.1–10	68, 163
		18.6	86

31.9	122	*3 Maccabees*	
31.31–34	132	3.17	97
Ezekiel		*4 Maccabees*	
12.25	67	5.35	131
13.9	56	17.16	131
18	68, 163		
36.27	132	*Tobit*	
		13.3–14	76
Daniel			
4.30	206	NEW TESTAMENT	
12.1	56		
		Matthew	
Hosea		1.21	202
2	86	1.23	202
2.1	199, 207	1.25	202
2.25	199, 207	2.7	203
11.1	122	2.15	203
		2.23	202
Amos		3.7–11	75
1.11	194	3.9	180
3.2	58	4.2	89
		4.21	203
Jonah		5.9	202
4.2	163	5.19	202
		9.13	203
Micah		13.10–17	103
4.1–5	76	13.56	184
		16.28	189
Haggai		19.26	164
1.5	206	20.8	203
		21.13	202
Zechariah		22.3	203
2.8–13	76	22.4	203
10.8	67	22.8	203
14.1–21	76	22.9	203
14.11	97	22.14	203
		22.43	202
Malachi		22.45	202
1.2–3	222	23.7	202
1.6	86, 122	23.8	202
2.10	122	23.9	202
3.16	56	23.10	202
		25.14	203
APOCRYPHA		27.8	202
Judith		*Mark*	
14.2	112	1.20	203
16.19	97	2.17	203
		3.31	203
2 Maccabees		4.10–12	103
2.13	97	6.2	184
6.23	131	9.1	189
9.16	97		

10.27	164
11.17	203
Luke	
1.13	202
1.31	202
1.32	202
1.35	202
1.36	202
1.37	164
1.59	202
1.60	202
1.61	202
1.62	202
1.76	202
2.4	202
2.21	202
2.23	202
3.7–9	75
3.8	180
5.32	203
6.15	202
6.46	202
7.11	202
7.39	203
8.2	202
8.9–10	103
9.10	202
10.20	89
10.39	202
14.7	203
14.8	203
14.9	203
14.10	203
14.12	203
14.13	203
14.16	203
14.17	203
14.24	203
15.19	202
15.21	202
18.9	189
19.2	202
19.13	203
19.29	202
20.44	202
21.5	97
21.37	202
22.3	202
22.25	202
23.33	202

John	
1.11	89
1.14–18	89
1.17–18	89, 142, 145
1.42	202
2.2	203
8.37–39	180
12.37–41	103
19.22	67

Acts	
1.12	202
1.19	202
1.23	202
3.11	202
3.22	109
4.18	203
7	86, 88, 110, 145
7.37	109
7.40–41	87, 103
7.41–42	87
7.51	88, 102–03
7.51–53	88
7.58	203
8.10	203
9.3–9	109
9.11	203
10.1	203
13.1	203
13.42	156
13.46	193
13.48	206
14.12	203
15.22	203
15.37	203
18.6	193
19.8–9	193
21.20–21	92
21.28	92
22.6–11	109
23.14	97
24.2	203
26.12–18	109
26.23–28	193
26.29	95
27.8	203
27.14	203
27.16	203
27.29	95
28.1	203
28.25–27	88, 103
28.28	88

Romans	
1	102, 103
1–8	34–35, 118, 216–17
1–11	34, 134, 158, 225
1.1	203
1.1–2	182
1.1–4	225
1.1–5	204, 220
1.3	190, 195
1.3–5	7
1.5	210
1.5–6	28, 204
1.6	203
1.7	203–04
1.8	141
1.9	134
1.10–15	30
1.13	28
1.16	31, 119, 193
1.16–17	31
1.17	116
1.18–32	102–04
1.18–3.20	102
1.21	134
1.23	73, 102
1.23–24	87
1.23–32	87, 103
1.25	134
2	217
2–4	190, 195
2.9	116
2.10	31, 116
2.15	91
2.17	116
2.17–29	5, 182
2.25–29	121, 196
2.28	116
2.28–29	183
2.29	116
3.1	116, 121
3.1–2	193
3.2	121, 179
3.3–5	159
3.4	158
3.6	212
3.9	116
3.8	92
3.9	102
3.21–22	220
3.24	97
3.29	116, 142
3.31	220
4	135–37, 181–82, 190, 197–98, 201, 217
4.1	195
4.9–25	183
4.10	181
4.11	141
4.13	135, 198
4.13–18	190
4.14	135, 198
4.16	135, 141, 200
4.16–17	204
4.17	199–200, 203, 222
4.18	198
4.19–22	198
4.20	135
5.2	109
6	134
6.11	97
6.17–18	132
6.23	97
7.15	184
7.16	185
8	35, 90, 109, 112, 123, 125–27, 129, 132, 142, 191, 195–97
8.1	97
8.1–17	132
8.2	97, 132
8.4	132
8.9	126, 142, 197
8.14–16	126
8.15	123
8.16	91, 196
8.17	126
8.18	126
8.21	126, 196
8.23	123
8.28	203
8.28–29	204
8.30	126, 203
8.32	141
8.35–39	97
8.39	97
9	1–5, 10, 13, 22–23, 27, 35, 37–40, 46, 61, 77, 78–79, 81, 83–84, 86, 92, 102, 107, 122, 135–36, 152–53, 157–60, 162, 173–74, 177, 182, 185, 187–88, 191, 194–95, 199–202, 208–14, 216–17, 219, 221, 224, 230, 234
9–11	2–5, 27–45, 73–76, 80, 81, 83, 85–89, 94–95, 99, 100, 103–07, 110–20, 124–26, 129, 138, 143–46, 158, 161, 164, 174, 177–78, 180–82, 185–86, 188–90, 193–94, 196, 201, 209–10, 212–14, 216–18, 221, 223–26, 230–32, 234–35

9.1	91, 93–94, 100	9.16	38
9.1–2	90, 110	9.17	38
9.1–3	90, 118, 120, 186	9.18	38, 61
9.1–5	35–37, 45, 46, 82–83, 89–90, 94,	9.19	37, 212
	96, 104–05, 110, 116, 123, 126,	9.19–21	234
	144, 146, 159–60, 179, 181–82,	9.19–24	38
	185–86, 188, 191–92	9.19–29	38
9.1–9	1–5, 25, 27, 44, 216, 219, 221,	9.20–21	158–60
	223–25, 229, 231, 233–34	9.22	38
9.1–13	93	9.22–29	106
9.1–23	3, 67, 185	9.22–10.1	33
9.1–24	110	9.23	38, 109, 126
9.1–29	2, 36	9.24	39, 116, 160, 190, 203
9.2	90–91, 93, 94	9.24–26	83, 195, 201, 222
9.3	33, 45, 54, 72–73, 89, 93–98, 100,	9.24–29	181, 183
	101, 105, 113, 130, 139, 142–44,	9.25	38–39, 203
	146, 188, 195, 209, 225–26, 230	9.25–26	38, 199, 217
9.3–5	94, 139	9.26	39, 203
9.4	85, 89, 110, 116, 118, 120, 122,	9.27	38, 116
	124–25, 127–30, 134, 137–38, 157,	9.27–29	38, 115, 183
	180, 221	9.29	38, 81, 190, 210, 213
9.4–5	33, 93–94, 113, 115, 117–23,	9.30	37, 160
	126, 130, 141, 144, 181, 223	9.30–33	37–38, 162, 222
9.5	4, 89, 99, 102, 117, 135–36,	9.30–10.4	85
	138–42, 145, 180, 195	9.30–10.13	18
9.6	4, 32, 36, 38, 39, 99, 107, 116,	9.30–10.21	36–37, 217
	120, 130, 138, 157, 177–86, 188–92,	9.30–11.32	217
	195, 208, 213, 217, 223, 230	9.31	116
9.6–7	183, 191–92	9.33	186
9.6–9	38, 147, 170, 177, 215, 222, 232	10	37, 188
9.6–13	37–38, 137, 157, 191	10–11	216–17
9.6–29	38–40, 213	10.1	72, 95, 116, 186
9.6–33	36	10.1–21	38
9.7	38–39, 122, 129, 168, 170, 177,	10.4	89, 223
	184, 189–91, 197, 199–200, 203, 217,	10.12	116, 141
	227, 230	10.14	108
9.7–8	189, 208, 222	10.19	116, 196
9.7–9	135, 222, 229	10.21	116
9.7–11.32	223	11	36, 100, 108, 113, 116
9.8	33, 38, 177, 186, 189–92, 195–99,	11.1	116, 180, 189–90
	208, 217, 222	11.1–10	115
9.8–9	179	11.1–32	37
9.9	50, 154–55, 164, 178–79, 208, 221,	11.2	116
	226, 230	11.5	104
9.10–13	8, 172, 221–22	11.7	116
9.11	110, 179, 221	11.7–10	88, 104
9.12	39, 85, 188, 201, 203, 222	11.8	88, 103
9.12–13	222	11.11	194
9.13	38, 188	11.11–32	106
9.14	37, 230	11.13	28, 210
9.14–18	38, 104, 159	11.13–14	104
9.14–24	39	11.14	195
9.15	38, 61, 66, 73, 222–23, 225, 234	11.16–24	159

11.17–24	75, 183	10.6	113
11.23	104	10.7	73, 113
11.25	116, 224	10.27	203
11.26	116, 224	11.24	120
11.27	118, 129	10.11	113
11.28	107, 137	11.25	109, 129
11.28–29	204	12.3	97
11.29	203	15.8	109
11.30–31	104	15.9	203
11.32	107	15.10	67
11.33–36	36–37, 212	16.15	206
12–16	35	16.22	97
12.1	134		
12.17	141	*2 Corinthians*	
12.18	141	1.20	97
14	29	3	46, 73, 103, 109–12, 125, 127, 132, 142
15	35, 108	3–4	230
15.7–13	6, 135	3.1–4.6	110, 142
15.8	135	3.3–6	132
15.9	6	3.6	109–10, 129
15.9–12	6	3.7–11	110
15.15–19	28	3.7–18	4, 71, 104, 125, 129
15.18	119	3.12	111
15.22–24	30	3.12–18	111
15.23–24	30	3.13–14	111
15.25–32	35	3.14	110–11, 129
15.33	141	3.14–15	111
16	28	3.14–16	112
		3.15	127
1 Corinthians		3.15–16	112
1.1	203	3.15–18	111
1.2	203	3.16	87, 112
1.9	203, 206–07	3.17–18	112
1.9–10	204	3.18	127
1.24	203	4.1–6	112
1.26	203	4.3–4	111
3.16–17	134	4.4	109, 127, 143
3.20	189	4.6	109, 143
5–7	3	5–7	178
6.19	133	6.14–7.1	178
7.1	119	6.16	134
7.15	203, 205–06	11.22	190
7.15–24	204	11.31	91–92
7.17	203, 206	13.1	91
7.18	203, 206	13.7	95
7.20	203	13.9	95
7.21	203		
7.22	203, 206	*Galatians*	
7.24	203	1–2	2
9.1	109	1.6	203, 206
10.1	113	1.8	97
10.1–2	113	1.9	97
10.1–13	109	1.12	109

1.15	203, 206
1.16	109
1.20	91–92
3	129, 190, 227
3–4	4, 132, 135–36, 230
3.1–14	109, 197
3.7	183
3.8	154
3.9	181
3.10–20	136
3.11–12	191
3.14	183
3.15	129
3.15–17	129
3.16	190
3.17	129
3.19	190
3.26	196
3.26–29	196
3.29	183, 190, 196
4.4–7	109, 197
4.5	123
4.21–31	109, 129, 174–75, 196–97
4.23	197
4.24	129
4.27	129
4.28	197
4.29	167, 174–75
4.30	129
5.8	203
5.13	203, 205–06
6.16	113, 183

Ephesians

1.3	97
1.5	123
1.17–18	205
1.18	203
2	130
2.6	204
2.11	130
2.11–21	134
2.12	120, 129–30
2.12–21	130
2.21	204
2.21–22	134
3.14–15	204
3.15	204
4.1	203–04
4.4	203–04, 206
4.6	204
5.9	75
5.11	75

Philippians

2.6	109
2.15	196
3.3	130, 134, 183
3.13–14	205
3.14	203
4.3	73, 89

Colossians

1.15	109
1.19	109
3.15	203–06
3.17	204

1 Thessalonians

2.11–12	204
2.12	203, 206–07
2.13–16	101
4.5–6	205
4.7	203, 206
5.24	203

2 Thessalonians

1.11	203
2.11–12	204
2.14	203, 205–07
4.14–17	205

1 Timothy

2.7	91
6.12	203, 205–06
6.16	89

2 Timothy

1.3	134
1.9	203

Hebrews

2.11	203
2.11–12	205
2.16–3.1	205
3.1	203
3.13	203
5.4	203, 206
9.15	203
11	164, 177
11.7–9	177
11.8	203
11.11	164, 176
11.12	89
11.18	176–77, 203
11.19	177

James		25.1		83
2.23	203	37.2		83
5.11	89			
5.16	95	*4 Ezra*		
		6–8		160
1 Peter		6.35		158
1.14–17	204	6.35–9.25		81, 83, 159
1.15	203, 207	6.55–59		82, 83, 102, 158
2.9	203, 206	6.58–59		160
2.21	203, 206–07	7.10–16		159
3.6	203	7.19		158
3.8–9	205	7.20		158
3.9	203, 206–07	7.21–22		159
5.10	203, 206–07	7.45		158
		7.46–48		82
2 Peter		7.72–74		159
1.3	203	7.105		158
1.10	203	7.106		81, 83, 158
		7.107–10		158
1 John		7.111		158
3.1	203	7.112–15		81
		7.116–26		158
3 John		7.116–31		160
2	95	7.127–31		159
		7.130		159
Jude		7.132		160
1	203, 205	7.133		159
		8.4–14		160
Revelation		8.7		160
1.9	203	8.15–17		83, 159–60
3.5	89	8.31–32		159
11.8	203	8.36		159–60
12.9	203	8.37–38		159
13.8	89	8.41		159
16.16	203	8.56		159
17.8	89	8.56–58		159
17.14	203	8.58–60		159
19.9	203	8.63		159
19.11	203	9.7–12		159
19.13	203	9.14–16		82
20.12	89	9.21–22		159
20.15	89			
21.27	89	*Jubilees*		
		10.8		173
PSEUDEPIGRAPHA		12.22–24		171
		15.8		171
1 Enoch		15.20		171
47.3	83	15.30–32		173, 194
89.32–35	79	15.33–34		173
89.33	79	16		170
89.35	79	16.16		170, 174
		16.16–18		170, 172–73, 194
2 Enoch		16.17		173

16.18	172	*Testament of Zebulun*	
17.4	174	9.5–9	76
17.6	174		
17.17	174	QUMRAN	
LAB		4Q180	162
12	74		
12.4	74, 76	*Ages of Creation*	
12.6	74	3	162
12.7	75		
12.8	75	CD	
12.8–9	75	3.13–14	183
19.7	76		
		TARGUMS	
Martyrdom of Isaiah			
3.8–9	79, 80	*Onqelos*	
3.8–10	81, 102	Genesis	
3.10	81	21.7	175
Psalms of Solomon		*Neofiti*	
9.2	179	Genesis	
		21.7	175
Questions of Ezra		Exodus	
39	83	32.32	56
Sibylline Oracles		*Pseudo-Jonathan*	
3.17–19	83	Genesis	
3.702–23	76	21.9	175
Testament of Moses		*Song of Songs*	
1.8–9	77	1.5	75
1.12–14	78, 102		
1.13	77–78	MISHNAH	
1.14	78		
3.9	77, 114	*Sanhedrin*	
3.9–13	78	10.1	180
3.9–14	114		
3.10	77	BABYLONIAN TALMUD	
3.11	78		
4.2–6	77	*Nedarim*	
11.11	78	31a	176, 194
11.14	78		
11.17	78	TALMUD YERUSHALMI	
12.2–13	77		
12.4	78	*Nedarim*	
12.4–5	77, 78	2.10	176
12.4–12	78, 102		
12.4–13	78	MIDRASH	
12.5	78		
12.10–13	78	*Gen. R.*	
12.11	78	53.4	163
12.13	78	53.12	175–76

Exod. R.
41.6–47.9   86
44.10   51
45.1–2   86
46.4–5   86
47.9   56

PHILO

Abr.
107   161
126   157
127   161
142–43   161
167   147, 161

Cher.
3–10   174, 211

Congr.
106–109   162

Det. Pot. Ins.
123   174
124   174
160   84

Deus Imm.
109   84

Ebr.
67   84
96   84
100   84

Fug.
90   84
165   85

Gig.
54   84

Leg. All.
2.54   84
3.9–10   161
3.46   84
3.65–106   85
3.88   85
3.101   84–85
3.142   84
3.219   174
82   174

Migr. Abr.
8   84
85   85
171   85

Mut. Nom.
8   85
9   85
137   174
138   174
267   157

Poster. C.
16   85
130–31   174, 211
136   84–85
158   84
169   85

Rer. Div. Her.
20   84
24–31   84
33   84
167   85

Sobr.
8   174, 211
66   76

Spec. Leg.
2.53–55   161
2.163   76
3.125–27   83
4.187   200

Vit. Mos.
1.149   76
2.161–72   83
2.224–25   76
2.270–74   83

JOSEPHUS

Ant.
1.196–206   147
1.213–19   174

EARLY CHRISTIAN WRITINGS

Clement
32.4   117

Index of Modern Authors

Aageson, J.W. 3, 5–6, 37, 40, 183, 228
Abasciano, B.J. 1–3, 22, 25–28, 30, 32, 34, 36–37, 39–41, 49, 57–59, 68, 85, 91, 92, 105, 111, 127, 140, 167, 178, 180, 185, 187–88, 195, 209, 219–22, 224, 230, 233
Aberbach, M. 80, 86
Achtemeier, P.J. 15, 94
Ackroyd, P.R. 62
Aletti, J.-N. 38–39, 200
Aust, H. 97

Badenas, R. 35, 40
Baker, D.L. 228
Balentine, S.E. 163
Balz, H. 134
Barrett, C.K. 36, 95, 125, 128, 135, 190, 222
Barth, M. 115, 130
Bartlett, D.L. 94, 101–02
Bartsch, H.W. 117, 139, 141
Beale, G.K. 8–10, 13–15, 21, 24, 26, 41, 67, 178, 228, 232–33, 235
Beker, J.C. 227
Bell, R.H. 8, 27–28, 143, 196
Belleville, L.L. 109–10
Ben Zvi, E. 151
Berger, K. 181, 201
Berkley, T.W. 5, 10, 13, 18, 22–23, 182, 193–94, 223, 231, 233
Birnbaum, E. 183
Black, M. 29
Blenkinsopp, J. 151–52, 163
Borgen, P. 85
Bornkamm, G. 35
Brandenburger, E. 92, 94, 177, 192
Bratsiotis, P. 72
Bromiley, G.W. 45
Brotzman, E.R. 11

Bruce, F.F. 100, 128, 137, 222
Brueggemann, W. 154, 165
Burkes, S. 42
Burnett, G.W. 42, 44, 187, 220, 224
Byrne, B. 99, 115, 117, 122, 126, 178–81, 185, 189–90, 199

Calvert, N.L. 181
Campbell, W.S. 122
Caragounis, C.C. 29
Carson, D.A. 5, 41, 89, 219
Cerfaux, L. 118, 200
Chae, D.J.-S. 34, 40, 117, 120, 122, 180, 210
Charles, R.H. 56, 78
Charlesworth, J.H. 74, 77, 79–80, 83, 158, 170
Chester, S.J. 202
Childs, B.S. 48–49, 53, 58–59, 67, 72
Chilton, B.D. 192
Ciampa, R.E. 2, 22
Clayton, J. 19–20
Coats, G.W. 49–52, 63, 165, 167
Cole, R.A. 53, 55, 67
Cosgrove, C.H. 180, 193–94, 224
Cottrell, J. 34, 96, 119, 128
Cranfield, C.E.B. 32, 45, 91–93, 95–98, 101, 102, 106, 116–18, 125, 128, 131, 133, 135, 139–40, 178–80, 191, 193, 198–99, 200, 222, 224
Cranford, M. 93, 98–99, 182

Dahl, N.A. 35–36
Das, A.A. 35, 110
Davenport, G.L. 171
Davies, G.H. 46, 53, 61
Davis, W.H. 96–97
Dodd, C.H. 7–9, 21, 35

Donfried, K.P. 27, 29–30, 34–35
Draisma, S. 18
Dreyfus, F. 110, 118, 123, 126, 128, 133
Driver, S.R. 55, 67, 147, 151
Dunn, J.D.G. 25, 27–28, 32, 34–36, 38–39,
    41, 73, 90, 92–96, 98–99, 101, 115,
    117–18, 120, 122–26, 128, 131, 134, 137,
    141, 157, 177–78, 180–84, 188, 190,
    198–99, 211
Durham, J.I. 46–48, 50, 53–54, 56, 58–59,
    64

Eckert, J. 202
Ellis, E.E. 13–14, 16, 39–40, 42, 191,
    226–29, 231–32
Ellison, H.L. 94, 128
Endres, J.C. 171–72
Enns, P. 61, 64
Epp, E.J. 126, 128, 131, 133, 135
Evans, C.A. 1, 3, 11–12, 14–15, 18, 40–41,
    227

Fee, G. 21, 113, 196
Feldman, L.H. 74
Fitzmyer, J.A. 27, 29, 92, 95, 98, 102, 118,
    122, 135, 183, 185, 189
Fornberg, T. 188
Forster, R.T. 65
France, R.T. 26
Freedman, D.N. 67
Fretheim, T.E. 46, 51–53, 56, 58
Friedman, S.S. 19
Friedrich, J. 139

Gábris, K. 96, 110, 128
Gaster, T.H. 162
Gaston, L. 32, 106, 180
Getty, M.A. 32
Ginzberg, L. 86
Godet, F. 126, 139
Gorday, P. 27
Gowan, D.E. 51–53, 55, 58, 72
Green, J.B. 1, 10
Green, W.S. 18
Grossfeld, B. 85, 175
Guerra, A.J. 28
Gundry Volf, J.M. 99–101, 118
Güttgemanns, E. 178

Haacker, K. 95, 122, 139, 161, 177–78, 180
Hafemann, S.J. 4, 34, 46–51, 53, 55–56,
    58–60, 63, 65, 70–73, 75, 86–87, 109–12,
    114

Hamerton-Kelly, R. 34
Hamilton, V.P. 151, 165–66
Hanson, A.T. 106
Harrington, D.J. 74
Harris, M.J. 100
Hartman, L. 188
Harvey, G. 180
Harvey, J.D. 38
Hatina, T.R. 18–19, 87
Hauge, M.R. 60
Hay, D.M. 4, 185, 198, 210
Haynes, S.R. 34
Hays, R.B. 1–4, 6–10, 12–13, 17–26, 34, 36,
    76, 95–96, 109, 143, 182, 198, 210–11,
    213–14, 217–18, 227–28, 230, 233
Hayward, R. 56
Headlam, A.C. 27, 93, 139
Hebel, U.J. 7–8, 15–16, 19–20
Hellholm, D. 188
Hillert, S. 185
Hirsh, E.D., Jr. 21
Hofius, O. 33, 178
Hollander, J. 9, 17, 19
Hopton, M. 16
Houtman, C. 46, 48, 49, 58, 59, 63, 64
Hübner, H. 3, 39, 101, 117, 182
Hugenberger, G.P. 62

Iersel, B. van 18
Isaac, E. 79

Jacobson, H. 74–76
James, M.R. 74–75
Johnson, E.E. 5, 34, 41, 180, 185, 198, 210
Johnson, L.T. 94, 119, 141

Kaminsky, J.S. 44
Käsemann, E. 45, 98–99, 131, 140–41
Keck, L.E. 4, 210–11
Kee, H.C. 43, 187, 201
Keesmaat, S.C. 22
Kim, J.D. 180
Kim, S. 88, 110, 142
Klappert, B. 99
Klein, W.W. 202, 206–07
Kline, M.G. 41
Klumbies, P.-G. 94, 118, 181
Knibb, M.A. 80
Knight, J. 79–80
Knowles, M. 12, 22
Koch, D.-A. 8
Kotansky, R.D. 178
Kraus, W. 120, 177, 179

Kristeva, J. 7
Kugel, J.L. 157
Kuhli, H. 116
Kümmel, W.G. 28
Kuss, O. 139, 185, 210

Lane, W.L. 29
Lincoln, A.T. 204
Lindars, B. 62, 139, 235
Lodge, J.G. 119, 139, 180, 190
Lohmeyer, E. 91
Long, B.O. 49
Longenecker, B.W. 158, 183
Longenecker, R. 13–14, 29
Lorenzi, L. de 36, 110
Lorimer, W.L. 139
Lübking, H.-M. 34, 120, 192
Lull, D.J. 2
Lundbom, J.R. 67
Lung-kwong, L. 29–30, 100
Luz, U. 34, 41, 110, 116, 120, 177, 196, 224, 228
Lyonnet, S. 194

MacRae, G.W. 126
Maher, M. 175
Maier, G. 179
Malina, B.J. 187, 205
Marshall, I.H. 8, 13, 86–88
Marston, V.P. 65
Martin, R.P. 111
Mayer, B. 178
McNamara, M. 56
Metzger, B.M. 83, 139–40, 158, 160, 164
Michel, O. 91, 96–97, 100
Mihaly, E. 40
Miller, J.C. 28, 30–31
Moberly, R.W.L. 46–47, 49–54, 56, 58–61, 63–65, 67, 70, 72, 107
Mohrmann, D.C. 18, 22, 27, 88, 119, 223
Moo, D.J. 45, 92–95, 99, 102, 116–18, 123–24, 126, 128, 131, 133, 138–39, 177–79, 181, 183, 185, 188, 190, 193–94, 196, 199, 213, 221–24
Moore, S.D. 18
Morison, J. 96, 139
Morris, L. 30, 93–94, 99–100, 127–28, 133, 135
Moule, C.F.D. 139
Moyise, S. 17–18, 21, 233
Mulder, M.J. 11, 13
Muilenburg, J. 62
Müller, C. 34, 201

Müller, D. 97
Munck, J. 45, 94, 99, 100
Murray, J. 94, 127, 137

Nanos, M.D. 28, 178
Neusner, J. 201
Nickelsburg, G.W.E. 78, 126
Nicole, R. 15
Niehaus, J.J. 65
Noack, B. 34
North, J.L. 27

O'Brien, P.T. 41, 219
O'Neill, J.C. 135
Osborne, G.R. 17, 21, 25
Österreicher, J.M. 120

Piper, J. 3, 4, 64, 66–68, 70, 76, 84, 93–95, 97, 101, 115–18, 120, 123, 126–28, 131, 133, 135–38, 178–80, 183–88, 191–92, 196, 222
Plastaras, J. 53, 61
Pöhlmann, W. 139
Porter, S.E. 15–18, 22, 26, 118, 220
Priest, J. 77–78

Rad, G. von 148, 165
Räisänen, H. 29, 32, 39, 101, 110, 117, 182, 186, 188–89
Reichert, A. 34, 91–92, 94, 140, 178
Rese, M. 120, 130, 210
Richardson, N. 34, 157
Richardson, P. 29
Roetzel, C.J. 127
Roo, J.C.R. de 118, 220
Rosner, B.S. 3, 11, 22, 156
Rothstein, E. 19–20
Ruse, C. 16

Sand, A. 136
Sanday, W. 27, 93, 139
Sanders, E.P. 41–42, 219–20
Sanders, J.A. 1, 3, 11–12, 14–15, 18, 40, 227–28
Sandmel, S. 13, 22
Sarna, N.M. 64
Schelkle, K.H. 122
Schlier, H. 178
Schmauch, W. 91
Schmithals, W. 92, 94, 128, 180
Schmidt, K.L. 203
Schmitt, R. 93, 192
Schoeps, H.J. 122

Schreiner, T.R. 32, 90, 92–96, 101, 115–18, 123, 125–28, 133, 136–38, 183, 185, 187–88, 190, 193–94, 199–200
Scott, J.M. 87, 109, 116–17, 122–23, 143
Scroggs, R. 34–35, 121
Segal, A.F. 201
Seifrid, M.A. 41, 219–20
Shum, S.-L. 18, 22, 223–24, 231
Siegert, F. 73, 101, 115
Siker, J.S. 181
Silva, M. 15, 17, 232
Smalley, S.S. 139
Smith, D.M. 5, 227–28
Smolar, L. 80, 86
Snodgrass, K. 10, 13, 14, 89
Son, S.-W.(A.) 42, 187
Soulen, R.N. 21
Spilsbury, P. 183
Stählin, G. 93, 99
Stanley, C.D. 10–11, 14–16, 25–26, 155–57, 191
Stegner, W.R. 39–40, 160, 163, 175–76
Stendahl, K. 126
Stockhausen, C.K. 40, 109, 230, 233
Stöhr, M. 99
Stone, M.E. 81, 158, 160
Strathmann, H. 134
Stuart, D. 21, 41
Stuhlmacher, P. 34, 137, 139
Sundberg, A.C., Jr. 8

Thiselton, A.C. 18, 21, 202
Thomas, D.W. 62
Thompson, A.L. 153, 163
Thompson, M. 17, 22–24

Tiede, D.L. 78–79
Tov, E. 10–11
Tromp, J. 77–78

Vanhoozer, K.J. 21–22, 202
Villiers, J.L. de 92

Wagner, J.R. 2, 12, 22, 25–26, 94, 101, 181, 190–91, 223–24, 226, 231–33
Walters, J.C. 27–28, 201
Watson, F. 21, 28, 182
Wedderburn, A.J.M. 30
Wenham, G.J. 147–49, 151–52, 154, 165, 167–69
Westerholm, S. 181
Westermann, C. 167
Wevers, J.W. 54, 61, 73, 155
Wiefel, W. 27–28
Wilckens, U. 25, 32
Wiles, G.P. 45, 95, 186
Wilk, F. 177, 183, 224
Willett, T.W. 151
Williams, S.K. 178
Williamson, H.G.M. 5
Wintermute, O.S. 170–72
Wolde, E. van 18–19
Worgul, G.S. Jr. 118
Wright, N.T. 4, 30–32, 34, 98, 109, 136, 177–78, 180, 185, 198, 211, 217–19, 224

Yonge, C.D. 161

Zeller, D. 120, 199
Ziesler, J. 33–34, 76, 125, 139